PAVED WITH GOLD

PAVED WITH GOLD

THE LIFE AND TIMES OF
THE REAL DICK WHITTINGTON

Gregory Holyoake.

GREGORY HOLYOAKE

AMBERLEY

Seest thou a man diligent in business? He shall stand before kings.
Proverbs 22 v 29

For Vanessa Bond, my great friend from theatre.

First published 2023

Amberley Publishing
The Hill, Stroud
Gloucestershire, GL5 4EP

www.amberley-books.com

British Library Cataloguing in Publication Data.
A catalogue record for this book is available from the British Library.

ISBN 978 1 3981 1703 7 (hardback)
ISBN 978 1 3981 1704 4 (ebook)

1 2 3 4 5 6 7 8 9 10

Typeset in 10pt on 12pt Sabon.
Typesetting by SJmagic DESIGN SERVICES, India.
Printed in the UK.

Contents

Whittington's Benefactions

Introduction

The story of Dick Whittington retold down the centuries is a delightful mixture of fact and fiction. A penniless orphan from the countryside walks all the way to London to seek a new life. He is pitied by kindly Alderman Fitzwarren who employs him as a scullery boy. His mistress, Sara the Cook, beats and scolds him so he runs away to Highgate Hill where he is befriended by a stray cat. There the distant ringing of Bow Bells seems to recall him to the City where he will secure fame and fortune.

Dick returns just as the Alderman is loading a ship, the *Unicorn*, and he is invited to place on board his only possession – the cat – in the hope it will being him good luck. The ship is wrecked off the coast of Barbary, a land plagued with rats. Dick's cat chases away the vermin and the King of Morocco is so grateful he rewards the cat's owner with a treasure chest. Back in London, Dick receives his fortune, marries Fitzwarren's daughter, Alice, and is proclaimed Lord Mayor of London.

The legend has been presented over the centuries in various modes of entertainment: toy theatres, magic lanterns, plays, pantomimes, television and ice show extravaganzas. The diarist, Samuel Pepys, watched it as a puppet show one autumn afternoon in 1668 and was enchanted. He recorded in his Diary how he crossed over London Bridge to 'Southwarke-Fair, very dirty, and there saw the Puppet-Show of Whittington, which was pretty to see.' Curiously, the character of Whittington was regularly presented as Mr Punch with his trademark shrill voice produced by a 'squeaker' (a 'swatchel' or 'swazzle').

First mention of Richard Whittington in fiction is the play *Eastward Ho* by Ben Jonson, published in 1605, which contains a tenuous reference to him and his celebrated 'pusse'. The following year a drama by Thomas Heyward, *If You Know Not Me, You Know No Bodie*, reveals the notion Whittington owed his fortune to a cat and also demonstrates a knowledge of Dick's true origins, plus his numerous benefactions to the City of London.

Two further literary works featuring Whittington were licensed for the press around this time: a dramatic version of the fable, *The History of Richard Whittington, of his lowe byrthe and his great fortune, as it was plaid by the prynces servants* (1604/5) and a ballad, *The Vertuous Lyfe and Memorable Death of Sir Richard Whittington, mercer, sometime Lord Maiour of the honorable Citie of London* (1605). Alas, no trace of either can be found.

However, a charming ballad, *A Song of Sir Richard Whittington*, is contained in *A Crowne Garland of Goulden Roses Gathered out of England's Royal Garden* by Richard Johnson, a composer of ballads that interwove history and myth, published in 1612. Consisting of eighteen verses mixing fact with fantasy, it is regarded as the earliest surviving account of the Whittington legend. His unnamed cat features prominently and is placed aboard a ship which voyaged to 'a land farre unknowne, troubled with Rats and Mice'.

Almost identical is another ballad, *London's Glory and Whittington's Renowne: A Looking Glass for the Citizens of London*, reproduced in the Roxborough Collection of Ballads published *c*.1641. The title page of this broadside depicts an amusing woodcut of Mayor Whittington, sporting a Carolean costume and riding a palfrey through London. A later edition displays a moralising tone. An inserted first stanza exhorts the City apprentices to apply themselves to their labours since God was sure to reward their industry. This maxim Richard Whittington would surely have endorsed.

The most familiar presentation of 'Dick Whittington', however, remains the hugely popular pantomime. The colourful cast of characters number Dick (traditionally played by a female actor), Tommy the Cat, Alice, Fairy Bow Bells, Sarah the Cook (Dame), the Sultan of Morocco, Master and Mate of the *Unicorn* (a comedy double act), the doddery Alderman Fitzwarren, and the dastardly King Rat.

The first recorded 'Dick Whittington' pantomime was performed at Covent Garden Theatre on 26 December 1814. It starred Joseph Grimaldi (1778-1837) the Regency actor, acrobat, singer, dancer and the original 'Clown Joey'. Joe played Dame Cecily Suet who, at one point, flew over the heads of the audience in an air balloon.

During the Victorian period, pantomimes as family entertainments came to the fore with the arrival of Augustus Harris (1852-1896) as manager of London's premier venue at the Theatre Royal, Drury Lane, in 1879. 'Druriolanus', as he was affectionately named introduced fairy tale themes with recognisable characters in magical pantomimes that could last for an incredible five hours. His popular 'Annuals' combined singing, dancing and, above all, spectacle with elaborate parades involving hundreds of costumed actors through the auditorium, runs that began on Boxing Day and might last until the following March. And Harris was renowned for casting his 'principals' without parsimony, recruiting performers from the world of Music Hall.

When Harris presented his first 'Dick Whittington' in 1884, the combination of Harry Nicholls as Tom and Herbert Campbell as Eliza the Cook ensured success. (On that occasion Fannie Leslie played Dick.) When Harris revived this pantomime in 1894 the comic role of Idle Jack was played by Dan Leno, famous for his eccentric monologues, and he was engaged to perform in pantomimes there for the next fifteen years until his demise in 1904. Marie Lloyd, the irrepressible singer beloved by Londoners, with her protruding teeth and flaxen wig, was later engaged to perform at 'the Lane' although she did not play the title role in 'Dick Whittington' until engaged at the Crown Theatre, Peckham, at Christmas 1898.

The most prestigious presentations of 'Dick Whittington' in modern times were undoubtedly those staged at the London Palladium. Comedian Frankie Howerd starred there as Idle Jack in 1952. At the time Frankie, lacking in confidence, was making a tentative foray from radio into television and he was heartened by fulsome praise for his performance by that stern critic, Kenneth Tyson.

The subject of 'Dick Whittington' was repeated three more times before pantomime was abandoned at the Palladium in favour of lavish musicals. The title role was taken successively by Norman Wisdom (1960), Tommy Steele (1969) and Jim Davidson (1980). On all these occasions, the Palladium had broken with theatrical tradition by casting a male actor as 'Dick'.

Dick Whittington runs away from London with his spotted bundle and faithful cat and falls asleep exhausted on High Highgate Hill. (This takes its name from the ancient toll gate on the high hill across the route frequented by drovers on their way to Smithfield Market.) The lad slumbers, according to storybook, until he is awakened by the distant Bow Bells that summon him back to the City:

Turn again, Whittington,
Lord Mayor of London.
Turn again, Whittington,
You must be bold.
Turn again, Whittington,
Learn again, learn again,
Then London will bring you
Your streets paved with gold.'

Today a stone halfway up the hill commemorates our hero's supposed association with Highgate. Originally, this was the base of a wayside cross where alms were left for lepers from an adjacent Hospital. The present stone – perhaps the third on this site – dates from 1821 and it is surmounted by a granite cat which peers purposefully through the decorative railings towards the City. This later sculpture was commissioned by Donald Bisset (1910-1995) an eccentric character actor and prolific children's author, supported by his friends. It bears the legend:

Whittington Stone
Sir Richard Whittington
Thrice Lord Mayor of London
1397 Richard II
1406 Henry IV
1420 Henry V
Sheriff 1393

It can be seen that this brief inscription perpetuates several inaccuracies: Whittington was never knighted nor was he 'Lord' Mayor but four times Mayor of London. The title, 'Lord Mayor' was a later elaboration. Nevertheless, Whittington's election by the leading citizens as London's Mayor would have been the focus of jubilation on three – if not four – occasions.

What of the cat? Inexorably, Dick Whittington's name is linked with a cat which brings him his incredible fortune. Cats have roamed the streets since time immemorial and the night in the capital was their domain. 'They were guardians of London,' comments Peter Ackroyd, 'patrolling city streets down which their distant ancestors once trod on quiet paws.'

Wild or tame cats are often depicted in Medieval manuscripts, psalters and missals, where they indulge in a variety of amusing activities – hunting, fighting, playing, feeding, grooming, sleeping – and sometimes playing musical instruments. Tame cats were often treasured as household pets by wealthy citizens who doted on them, although their owners were censured for feeding them at table in an early book of 'Curtesy'.

The development of rooms within Medieval houses, dividing work areas from living quarters, encouraged the owners to shelter and domesticate their favourite animals. 'Exotic animals,' says Brigitte Risl, 'found their way into the houses of the mercantile middle class, high ecclesiastics, and nobility.' And it is in this context, she proposes, that certain animals, including cats, eventually become pets.

Generally, though, cats were never totally accepted as pets in Medieval England. Their purpose was to control rodents. Owners declined to feed them because this would weaken their natural instinct to hunt and kill pests that destroyed crops. In addition, there was too much prejudice against cats for them to command a place as an adored member of many households. They were spurned because of their symbolic associations with evil, death, witchcraft, devilry and heresy. Perhaps if their importance as predators had been completely understood, keeping a pet cat would have assisted enormously in conquering the nationwide spread of plague transferred by fleas on black rats, thus slowing the Medieval Apocalypse.

Disappointingly, then, Whittington because of his abhorrence of heresy, may never actually have owned a domestic cat. It was not until several centuries after his death that owners overcame the strong cultural and religious bigotry against keeping cats as pets in England. Indeed, it was not until the sixteenth century that they began to be accepted as a welcome addition to the family home. And it was around this period that the character of the historical Richard Whittington – London's prosperous merchant and astute Mayor – was softened by his legendary acquisition of a feline friend, the which charming association began to appear in chapbooks, poems, songs and plays.

THE REIGN OF KING EDWARD III

1

The Whittingtons of Gloucestershire

RICHARD WHITTINGTON'S eventful life – as apprentice, merchant, Mayor and benefactor of the City of London – stretched across the reigns of five later Medieval kings, Edward III, Richard II, Henry IV, Henry V and Henry VI, and his meteoric career, fabulous wealth, fame and enduring charitable works were inexorably bound up with their conflicting personalities, aims and achievements. He was born at a time of turbulence and transience when England was experiencing great political and economic change. Inevitably, his life was touched at times by the traumas of disease and the triumphs and tragedies of war, although his own concerns remained focused entirely upon peace and prosperity. His immediate family, however, was involved in three spectacular military victories – Crecy, Poitiers and Agincourt – of the Hundred Years' War.

Families of the fourteenth and fifteenth centuries actually knew little about their ancestry. They lacked access to documents, deeds or seals antedating the twelfth century; few hereditary arms stretched back even further. There was an absence of early portraits. Precise genealogical information was unavailable. The pedigrees of which people often boasted were inherited orally through the memories of elderly relatives, a method that invited imagination and speculation.[1] Although the actual date of Richard's birth remains unrecorded, it is certain that he was born around the time when that series of bloody battles, where chivalry mingled with barbarism, 'rendered England the dominant military nation in Christendom'.[2]

The Hundred Years' War

Edward III – proud, haughty, extrovert, domineering and inspirational – was the seventh Plantagenet king.[3] Eventually, he would aspire to the thrones of both England and France. He was born on 13 November 1312 at Windsor Castle and was therefore often referred to as 'Edward of Windsor'. His father, Edward II, was scorned for his repeated failures in the war with Scotland and his patronage of male favourites, Piers Gaveston[4] and Hugh Despenser the Younger.[5] Trouble brewed in 1325 when the new French King, Charles IV, demanded that Edward II perform homage for the English Duchy of Aquitaine in south-west France.[6] (This had become part of English territory within the kingdom of France when Eleanor of Aquitaine married Henry of Anjou, later Henry II, in 1152.)

Unwisely, the King-Duke remained at home but sent his teenage son in his stead, after creating him Earl of Aquitaine. Prince Edward was escorted by his bold and spirited mother, Queen Isabella, who was charged with instructions to negotiate a peace treaty with the French. Duplicitously (some would say shrewdly), Isabella[7] conspired with her lover, the exiled Roger Mortimer, to depose her husband. To ensure military support for her venture, she arranged her son's marriage to the young Philippa of Hainault.[8] An invasion of England was launched. Edward II's forces jettisoned him. The King reluctantly relinquished his throne to his son.[9] At the age of fourteen, Edward III was crowned on 1 February 1327.

Immediately, Isabella and Mortimer assumed control of the kingdom and their intention was to reduce Edward to becoming their puppet king. Mortimer, created First Earl of March, acquired vast estates and titles and became increasingly powerful. He treated King Edward with disrespect and subjected him to humiliation. There was constant conflict between the young King and his manipulative guardian. Tension escalated after his cherished consort, Philippa, gave birth to their first son, Edward, Prince of Wales, on 15 June 1330. King Edward mounted a surprise attack on Mortimer at Nottingham Castle[10] and ordered his summary execution. Spurning the required regency, Edward III, at the tender age of seventeen, commenced his highly successful, personal and absolute rule.

At the start of Edward III's reign it was realised that the number of knights who could be fielded in battle had dwindled, and so the King decided to rectify this by persuading the landed gentry of sufficient means to accept the honour of knighthood. He compelled landowners between the ages of sixteen and sixty who were deemed fit and healthy to become knights, or pay up. It was a revenue earner first exploited by Henry III. They would be expected to train regularly, to provide appropriate armour and to supply sturdy warhorses. The Crown would not lose either way since this enforcement of distraint of knighthood would provide Edward with a source of income to help fund his lust for war.

Yet there was a reluctance among members of the landed gentry to assume this high rank. The cost of the attendant ceremonies was excessive and the required wartime equipment was expensive. Further, it was the responsibility of knights to take a lead in the government of their own shires and this was a time-consuming commitment. Landowners, preferred simply to pay the imposed fines for declining the proffered honour and this swelled the coffers of the Treasury in anticipation for the King's planned military forays into France.

Gloucestershire, however, responded positively to the King's invitation and was soon able to boast a far greater number of knights than most shires in the country.[11] Named among the newly created knights was 'William de Whittington'. (Sir William had previously declined the offer of knighthood and been distrained thrice before – in 1313, 1316 and 1325 – in the previous reign.) He was commanded forthwith to represent Gloucestershire in Parliament – the first in the new King's reign – held at Lincoln in September 1327.[12] He died three years later without knowing that his son, William, would fight at Crecy, nor that his grandson, Richard, would become London's most celebrated Mayor.

His influential neighbour, Thomas de Berkeley from Coberley, was also knighted around this time because he was appointed High Sheriff of Gloucester[13] in 1330. He may also have figured in the story of Richard Whittington. Certainly, these two country gentlemen, both elevated to Knights of the Shire, would have known each other either personally, or by reputation. Not only did they share civic duties on occasions but their lands practically adjoined. Even by the middle of the 14th century, the country elite remained a relatively small band.

King Edward III, 'confident, popular and patriotic',[14] was a dedicated military commander who, through his defiance and determination, swiftly transformed his kingdom into one of the most formidable powers in Europe. After his father's disastrous defeat[15] at Bannockburn (23 June 1314), when King Robert I[16] secured independence for Scotland, marauding clans roamed unchecked throughout the north of England. King Edward sought to restore the tarnished prestige of the Crown by renewing an aggressive policy towards Scotland. Aware of a hostile alliance between the Scots and the French, he ensured his armies gained victories against the new Scottish King, David II, at Dupplin Moor in 1332 and Halidon Hill in 1333.[17] In 1337, the French King Philip VI confiscated the English-held Duchy of Aquitaine along with the county of Ponthieu in Normandy.[18]

Edward responded by laying claim to the French Crown, as the grandson of Philip IV ('Philip the Fair'), who had died in the year of Bannockburn. France, which had a population four times the size of England, was then recognised as the most powerful state in Western Christendom. Defiantly, Edward prepared for an armed invasion and crossed to Flanders. His first significant victory at the Battle of Sluys (24 June 1340) secured English naval supremacy in the English Channel and allowed him to claim the title, 'Lord of the Sea'.[19] Though in fact Sluys barely interrupted French raids on English territories and shipping. This minor conflict set the stage for what became known to historians as the Hundred Years' War (1337-1453).[20]

Crecy and Calais

Edward III's inspired leadership were perfectly demonstrated at the Battle of Crecy (26 August 1346) in his disputed Duchy of Aquitaine. The King made an excellent choice for the site of battle. He raised his standard atop a steep hill, rising above a dense forest, where there was a convenient postmill from which to direct operations. He arranged his army in three equal battalions: the Prince of Wales at the vanguard, the Earl of Northampton in the centre while he commanded the rear. It became common practice to organise the English army into three 'battles' – vanguard, middle ward and rearguard – in Medieval warfare. Artfully, Edward, concealed a score of revolutionary cannons[21], firing iron bolts or stone shot, among the four thousand longbowmen, protecting their flanks. The conflict was preceded by a brief thunderstorm.

King Philip VI commanded 30,000 men – far outnumbering the English force – yet he displayed appalling arrogance when considering his own battleplan. The French King had at his disposal the largest and best equipped army in Europe. Carelessly, he stationed his Genoese archers, whose cumbersome crossbows, hampered by their damp strings, took an inordinate time to reload, as a disorderly first line of defence. These mercenaries were soon ripped apart by firepower as they advanced uphill into the deadly ambush of Edward's combined archers and engineers. They cut their strings, indicating surrender, before fleeing the field. Next came wave after wave of experienced French cavalry who charged up the same steep hill in organised rows in an attempt to drive the English from their commanding position, but they, too, were repeatedly repulsed.

Here was a truly terrifying scene. English longbows fired repeated volleys of arrows that penetrated the colourful surcoats and polished armour of the mounted French cavalry. Chaos reigned. Trumpets blared, horses whinnied, cannons boomed. Philip had brought musical instruments to play as scare tactics, which added to the confusion.[22] Amid all this carnage, the English archers tenaciously held their formation. Initially, Edward ordered his men-at-arms to fight on foot, an unusual but not unique tactic, but he then signalled for his own battalion to mount their horses and charge downhill in a furious stampede. French knights were scattered across the wide, slippery slope and, frustrated and confused, they deserted in their thousands. Philip – certainly no coward – fought bravely, then faltered, as his horse was killed beneath him and an arrow sliced through his cheek. When night fell, the humiliated French King was led, battered and bleeding, from the battlefield. France's Oriflamme – that hallowed war banner – lay in shreds, trodden into the blood-soaked mire.

Edward's son, a tall blond figure whose soubriquet, probably based upon his characteristic dark armour, was the 'Black Prince', greatly distinguished himself at the Battle of Crecy. Commanding the vanguard, he had faced his foe 'brimful of confidence', when only nineteen years of age. At one point in this most bloody battle, a company of French knights penetrated the leading English battalion. They made a concerted effort to seize Prince Edward's personal standard and disarm him. In furious retaliation, he rushed at them, 'slashing at their horses and bringing down their riders', until, exhausted, he fell to his knees. Immediately, his bodyguard raced to his rescue among a mound of corpses. The King had declined to send help, confident in the belief that his son would that day 'win his spurs'. Picking up a fallen ostrich feather from a helmet crest, the Black Prince fell on his knees before his father and repeated his promise: 'Ich Dien' (I serve).[23]

Edward III's personal glory in this decisive victory was recognised throughout Europe.[24] His combination of modern weapons and daring tactics, employed against a superior force, was hailed as a major military achievement.[25] His strategies, developed through analysing previous battles, included the systematic deployment of lowborn archers (later to be used with devastating effect by Henry V at Agincourt) and the innovative employment of projectile weaponry – transportable and manoeuvrable – on the battlefield. Previously, cannon had been reserved for siege warfare and this would appear to be the moment when primitive artillery was introduced on the battleground. Crecy, in this sense, marked the advent of modern warfare.

Next, Edward turned his attention to Calais. This was the most strongly defended city on the French coast and the nearest port across the Channel from England. Strategically vital, Edward realised Calais was impregnable and so he decided to starve the luckless inhabitants into submission. Inevitably, this was a lengthy procedure, but Edward again proved patient and methodical. Perhaps his true plan was to tempt Philip once more onto the battlefield where he might raise his newly embroidered Oriflamme? This displayed a flaming gold sun against a blood red background and indicated that mercy would not be shown to captives. As the tedious months passed Edward received the exhilarating news that the young and inexperienced King David II had taken the opportunity to invade northern England[26] but had already been captured near Durham.[27] This astounding double victory greatly boosted English morale.

Eventually, Philip himself made an appearance but then he turned round and deserted the desperate soldiers of the besieged garrison. Edward, who was capable of hideously cruel acts, was then free to vent his fury upon the rebellious inhabitants. The famous incident where six brave burghers marched out of their crushed city and walked barefoot – ropes around their necks with the castle keys in their hands – to plead for mercy has passed into legend.[28] Queen Philippa, who had inhabited a prefabricated palace built under the walls of the besieged town throughout the protracted siege, is supposed to have pleaded with Edward to spare their lives.[29] Edward, predictably, relented. He established an English garrison at Calais and could now claim to be to be 'Lord of the Narrow Seas' (the English Channel). More importantly, he moved the lucrative Wool Staple to Calais.[30] This meant that the newly acquired French port was now the only place where English wool was imported, inspected and taxed before being sold to markets on the Continent.

Winter was never a time to keep an army in the field and so Edward ordered his troops to return home. The strength of Edward III's fighting force during this first foray into Northern France is estimated at around 20,000. There was a strict hierarchy. First in importance were the men-at-arms, the mainstay of the army, which consisted of earls, barons, knights and esquires, all of whom were hereditary landowners. They fought clad in armour and rode powerful war horses. The knights were divided into two groups. A 'knight banneret' was higher than a 'knight bachelor' (who fought under another's banner) but lower than a duke or an earl. He was expected to bring into the field a number of lesser knights, esquires and mounted archers, which would entitle him to display his own banner. This was square shaped in contrast to the tapering pennon flown by the lower ranking knight, who might be responsible for his own retinue of esquires and archers.

Among the great lords who displayed their banners at both the Battle of Crecy and Siege of Calais was Sir William FitzWaryn, brother of Fulk V, Lord FitzWaryn. He appears in the muster roll as a knight banneret commanding his own modest company. The muster roll records Sir William's company as banneret (1) knight (1) esquires (10) and archers (9); a total of 41. The King had granted him the English possessions of the alien Nunnery of St Leodegar or Leger of Normandy in Stower Provost, Dorset, to enable him to maintain his status of banneret. His company fought in the first division under the nominal command of the Prince of Wales, but which was really commanded by the Earls of Warwick and Oxford and Godfrey de Harcourt.[31] Later, the FitzWaryns would play an important part in the domestic life of London's famous Mayor.

The same muster roll lists a certain William de Whytenton, who fought under the banner of Hugh le Despenser (*c.*1308-1349). Hugh was the son of the ill-fated Hugh Despenser the Younger who had risen to prominence as Royal Chamberlain during the lifetime of Edward II. A personal favourite of the King, his own corruption and unjust behaviour resulted in his gruesome execution at the start of the reign of Edward III. Hanged in armour, he was then beheaded and his body cut in pieces and fed to dogs.[32] His valiant son[33] is named among the principal knights who fought on this momentous French campaign.

Hugh had been summoned by writ on 14 May 1346 to hasten to the King's assistance with as powerful a force as possible without waiting for the shipping of his horses.[34] All horses at the personal disposal of the men-at-arms were appraised by the sergeants-at-arms at the place of rendezvous. The larger 'destrier' or war horse was a very expensive part of a knight's equipment and he received compensation for it if lost in the king's service. Speed was imperative since the King's adversary was already assembling a great army to oppose him at the Feast of Pentecost.[35] In fact, Hugh commanded one of the largest companies on the French campaign, which combined the counties of Hereford, Warwick and Gloucester. The muster roll records 2 bannerets, 40 knights, 86 esquires and 105 archers.[36] Sadly, after his undeniable loyalty, Hugh became a victim of the 'Great Pestilence'.[37] His wages for war, which amounted to £2,770, were still partly owing to him.

Oddly, Walter de Wetwang, the Treasurer of the King's Household who was responsible for compiling the muster roll, was doubtful of Hugh le Despenser's actual rank. He had been summoned to Parliament as a Baron in 1338. This cannot explain exactly why his name is recorded separately from two other bannerets who served under him, because traditionally an hereditary Baron himself served as a banneret. Further, it is puzzling that William Whittington should be recorded without the knightly title, 'Sir'. It might be assumed that he fought as one of the bannerets or knights unless, of course, at that time he still remained an 'esquire'. Whatever his rank, he was definitely present at both Crecy and Calais. Possibly he was knighted after this successful campaign. Certainly, he will have returned a hero to Gloucestershire with exciting tales to tell his young sons at his manor of Pauntley: William, Robert and Richard Whittington.

Pauntley, Gloucestershire

The birthplace of Richard Whittington was first positively identified by a tenacious Victorian scholar, Rev. Samuel Lysons (1806-1877). He was Rector of Rodmarton, South Gloucestershire, and Canon of Gloucester Cathedral. His biography, *The Model Merchant of the Middle Ages* (1860), is a lively, although moralistic account of Mayor Whittington. He attempted to compile a pedigree of Whittington's ancestors, a task hampered by the profusion of firstborn males bearing the name 'William'. There is further confusion in that they had a propensity for marrying women called 'Joan'.

Pauntley is a tranquil hamlet that lies in a loop of the River Leadon, ten miles north-west of Gloucester. It lies just north of the Forest of Dean, where coal and iron had been profitably mined since Roman times, on the borders of Herefordshire and Worcestershire. Probably, the name derives from 'pent' (valley) and 'ley' (meadow). Traditionally, this desirable arable land divided itself naturally into two parts: the upper parish, which is sandy soil, was planted with rye and the lower part, that inclines to clay, with wheat. Today, although wheat and maize remain, the ryelands have been claimed by Cotswold sheep prized for their sweet flesh and fine wool. There are only remnants of cherry orchards but an abundance of cider apple trees. Horned cattle graze and plump pigs forage on the rich red farmland. This countryside dips and swells, valleys and hills are crowned with oak and lime groves. Six centuries have hardly changed the landscape.

Walter de Laci, one of the noblemen who accompanied William the Conqueror to England in 1066, was rewarded for his loyalty with numerous manors, including Pauntley. His niece married Ansfrid de Cormeilles, who thus acquired as part of her dowry 'Pantelie'. The extent of this desirable land was meticulously recorded in Domesday Book (1086). When their descendant Walter de Pauntley died in 1248, it was inherited by his daughter, Margery, who had married John de Solers (born *c.*1155). Thus Pauntley came to the Solers family of Hope Solers (now 'Solers Hope'), Herefordshire.

The village after which the Whittingtons were named has never been precisely identified.[38] One a mile south of Worcester is possible. The family emerges from the shadows with an elusive William Whittington I who lived sixteen miles eastwards at Upton by Haseler, South Warwickshire. This attractive village, which retains a few Medieval timbered cottages, is divided into two parts with Upton below and Haseler above, with its later church situated dramatically on the hilltop. His son, William II, married Hawise, sister and heir of Hugh Aquillon, Lord of the Manor of Upton between Stratford-upon-Avon and Alcester. These early Whittingtons must have been wealthy farmers or merchants to have secured this prestigious union with the last member of the ancient line of Aquillons. William I died in 1283 and his son continued to live at Upton until 1311. This was a humble property, later recorded as a house with land, a dovecote and wood. Clearly this did not compare with the larger estates held by the Whittingtons when they moved across into Gloucestershire.[39]

Pauntley remained with the Solers until the death of a later John de Solers (*c.*1235-1311). An Inquisition Post Mortem of 4 May 1311 taken by the King's Escheator[40] at Gloucester upon his demise lists the main features of Pauntley Manor. There was 'a certain capital messuage (dwelling) with a garden ...100 acres of arable land ... 6 acres of meadow, a park ... pastures (and) a watermill'. An impression is given of a rigidly structured, self-supporting community consisting of 'tenants, villeins, customars and cottars' who all had their rents and duties carefully defined. All the same, it was hardly a prosperous manor because it was valued at only £8 16s 11d.

These distant estates were inherited by John's daughter, Maud (or Mathilda), wife of William Whittington III. The date of the marriage is unknown but William is named in the Sheriff's returns as 'Lord of the vill of Pauntley' in 1280.[41] Their son, Sir William Whittington IV, married Joan, daughter of Robert (or Roger) Linet (or Lynet) of Haseler. Upon his untimely demise in 1331, he was succeeded by his son, Sir William Whittington V, who had fought in Northern France with Edward III. (He may have been knighted on the battlefield since such titles were not hereditary.) He now became Lord of the Manors in three counties: Upton (Warwickshire), Solers Hope (Herefordshire) and Pauntley (Gloucestershire).

Sir William Whittington had been a tearaway in his youth. In 1333, Sir William and three accomplices were indicted for hunting game on the chases of William la Zouche while he was absent from his estates at Corse, Hartbury and Hasfield, Gloucestershire.[42] Ironically, William's second son, Robert, was eventually appointed Head Forester for the private hunting ground of wooded hills and open spaces between Corse and the River Severn in 1400.[43]

The discipline of army life must have had an effect on Sir William who settled down, a contented lesser landowner, to family life on his own preferred estate, Pauntley. He married Joan, daughter of William Mansel (or Maunsell), a wealthier landowner in Gloucestershire. (His father, Sir William Mansel, had attended Edward I on his assault on the Scottish Marches in the winter of 1298, but after his brief military career he became a local administrator, most notably High Sheriff of Gloucester in 1308.)

William Mansel, born 1295, had inherited land at Bisley, probably at Frampton Mansell, comprising a house, vineyards, wood and ploughland, near Sapperton, South Gloucestershire. Later, he acquired the Manor of Lypiatt, near Stroud, which he held of John de Bohun, the Earl of Hereford. Lypiatt is a district, not a parish, to the west of Bisley consisting of Upper, Middle and Lower Lypiatte with 'Lypiatte Farm' near Miserden. 'It is easy to get lost in this rather inaccessible area' warns Michael Whittington, the family historian. This land was later acquired by the Whittingtons, not through inheritance, but by debt incurred through Philip Mansel, Joan's irresponsible younger brother, who was considered by an earlier researcher, Stratham, as 'either a very unfortunate or a somewhat dishonourable man'.[44]

A repeatedly rehearsed story demonstrates Philip Mansel's naivety. In 1360, he was placed in charge of the English garrison at La Rochelle, a busy port on the Atlantic coast in the combined region of Poitou and Aquitaine. The town had been restored to England as part of the Treaty of Bretigny. He maintained a close acquaintance with the Mayor, Jean Condorier, who gave a dinner for Philip and his officers. A messenger arrived during the entertainment with a sealed letter from Edward III. Philip, unable to read French, asked the Mayor to read it to him aloud. Philip was instructed, so he learned, to parade his soldiers outside the town walls on the following day for an inspection by senior officers. Foolishly, Philip complied. He ordered the drawbridge to be lowered and marched out ahead of his men into the open countryside. He was swiftly ambushed by troops who compelled him to make an ignominious surrender. The French, through subterfuge, made themselves masters once more of their fort.[45] The story of this French ruse is apocryphal. But it does point to Philip's gullibility. The details are at variance with the facts concerning the capitulation of La Rochelle. The town was at this time besieged by the French and yielded, together with Poitiers, after an abortive attempt at relief by a fleet under the Earl of Pembroke. This was the first major defeat of Edward III's reign.[46]

Sir William and Lady Joan's first son, William Whittington VI, was born in 1335/6. Their second son, Robert, was probably born shortly after in 1337/8. The date of the birth of their third son, Richard, remains a mystery. His father died in 1358, which leaves a possible time gap for the birth of their youngest child of about twenty years. Sir William was away fighting in France under Edward III in 1346-7. This narrows Richard's birth down slightly to two periods: 1339-1345 and 1348-1358. The first time Richard comes to the notice of the chroniclers is when he was affluent enough as a merchant to make a loan to the City of London in 1379. He would not have been allowed to be apprenticed as a Mercer, which was his chosen career, until he was eleven years old and his apprenticeship would have lasted seven years. It is reasonable to allow a further ten, fifteen or twenty years for him to build up his business before he was wealthy enough to make this modest loan. An early date for Richard Whittington's birth would be 1340, therefore, and a later one 1350. When he died in 1423. his executors omitted his age from their epitaph. Quite simply, they didn't know it and maybe Richard didn't either. But he died aged between 70 and 80 years of age, which was a remarkable achievement for a Medieval gentleman.[47]

There are innumerable variations of his surname: Whitingdon, Whityngton, Whytington, Whytingdon, Whytynton, Whytinton, Wytingdon, Whitindon, Wityndon, Witinton, Wittington, Wittingdon, Wityngton, Whyttyngton, Whytingtone and Whettenton.[48] His future colleague and companion, John Carpenter, spelt it as 'Whytyngton' throughout his legal tome, 'Liber Albus', which Richard personally gave his approval. The epitaph on his tomb, preserved by John Stow, includes the phrase, 'Albificans Villam',[49] which is a play on his name, 'Whiting - ton', meaning 'making the town white.' This indicates that it was pronounced with a short first 'i'. The recognised modern spelling is invariably 'Whittington'. His famous moniker is, of course, 'Dick', but when he was a child, he may have been called 'Dycon'. (This affectionate diminutive was also applied to his future sovereign, Richard II.)

Pauntley Court

The present Pauntley Court, which is privately owned, is believed to date mainly from the late eighteenth or early 19th century. Wonderfully restored, this building represents three sides of a courtyard house. Little or nothing remains, however, of the Whittington's Medieval manor house apart from a half-timbered west wing, with its internal charred beams, which served as a granary, *c.*1500. The cobbled courtyard, with its enclosed well, mounting block and dog kennel, was transformed by a recent owner into a delicate white garden. A crisp, manicured lawn slopes gently down towards the ancient watermill with its static undershot wheel formerly powered by natural springs. Tall hollyhocks brush and hardy roses climb the plaster and timber walls of the triple-gabled east wing, whose tiny latticed windows overlook fertile farmland.

Manors, originally, were not necessarily houses but areas of jurisdiction in the Medieval feudal system. They were transferred through the male line, but in the absence of a direct heir, sometimes by will, marriage or purchase. A 'Lord of the Manor' was not a peer but a holder of an office who could derive his title from the Crown or even a superior nobleman who might, in return, demand homage. His territory was strictly defined but his ownership of land entitled him to collect rents and dues from tenants. The Lord of the Manor would hold a regular court, presided over by his steward, to collect his fees and this was generally a convenient time to settle disputes. The Lord's main residence, therefore, was often termed a 'Court' rather than a 'Manor'.

Pauntley Court is, alas, not the building that Whittington knew as a boy, although the manor itself was owned by the family until Tudor times. They occupied it until 1546 when the estate was divided among the six daughters of a descendant, Thomas Whittington. The last male of the line, Thomas's burial is recorded in the register of Pauntley Church.[50] One of these daughters, Elizabeth, predeceased her father and her portion of the estate, which included Pauntley Manor, went to her husband, Sir Giles Poole of Sapperton.[51] At the Restoration of the Monarchy in 1660, the last male heir of the Poole family sold the manor to Henry Somerset, a member of the Beauforts. The Duke of Beaufort, through various heiresses, retained an interest in Pauntley until the close of the 18th century.

Sadly, Pauntley fared poorly in the Stuart and Georgian periods. Exploring the area in 1667, a certain Walter Nourse observed 'a great piece of stonework building by the Somersets which was never finished'. Worse still, Samuel Rudder, a county historian, commented in 1779: 'The large manor house at Pauntley Court is taken down, having been long deserted by the owners.' According to Lysons, 'The Manor of Pauntley was only worth about twenty pounds in about 1860 and the parish was mainly moorland and chase which had hardly improved since the Norman Conquest.'

When the Whittingtons finally left their country estate in the mid-16th century, it was leased to a succession of tenants, the last of whom, John Stokes, purchased the property in 1810. By 1821, David Ricardo owned the property, although the Stokes family continued to reside there until 1832 and they retained an interest in the estate until 1921. In 1933 it was conveyed to the Gloucestershire Home for Wayfarers. Poet Laureate John Masefield, who hailed from Ledbury, recited poetry in the present ballroom to raise funds for those desperate men who had been forced on the road to look for work in the Great Depression. Afterwards, Pauntley Court, passed into private hands.[52]

More recently, Pauntley Court was purchased to create a wedding venue. The walls of the house are painted in a rich rose colour while the interior is decorated in a truly enchanting style. The gardens are arranged in a sequence: a formal 'sunken' garden has intricate box hedges surrounding an ornamental pond with medlar trees at each corner; a 'ruined' garden allows yew hedges to prosper among remains of that proposed 'Great House' to be constructed of stone. Guests can relax in the dappled shade of the Quince Orchard. Beyond, the River Leadon meanders gently. The whole complex exudes warmth, intimacy, romance.

Dovecote

Midway between the church and the house is a substantial sandstone dovecote whose size indicates the scale of the original manor. Built by the Whittingtons at the height of their prosperity in the 15th century, it was remodelled in the 17th century,[53] yet its plain, square, gabled structure remains characteristic of dovecotes in the Cotswolds. Doves and pigeons were an important source of winter meat but in Medieval times only influential families were permitted to keep them because they are notoriously destructive of crops. This monopoly was resented by the peasants. Flocks of these birds descended upon their own crops, yet if they retaliated by trapping them, they faced a heavy fine in the manorial court.

The practice of keeping doves and pigeons in specially constructed houses for the larder probably originated in the Middle East but it was introduced into Britain by the Romans. In Norman times, the building of a dovecote was a feudal privilege restricted to barons, abbots and lords of the manor but later extended to the parish priest. Their right remained unchallenged since constructing a stone dovecote was beyond the purses of ordinary countrymen.

The terms 'dove' and 'pigeon' were interchangeable and, although there is now little resemblance between the domestic white dove and the feral street pigeon, both descend directly from the blue rock pigeon that inhabit the rocky cliffs of coasts and inland heights of several countries. Dovecotes or pigeon houses were also known as 'columbaria' ('columba' being the collective name for their species) or 'culver houses'. ('Culver' is Anglo-Saxon for pigeon.) They often formed a trio of live food stores along with rabbit warrens and fishponds. Hares and adult rabbits were called 'coneys'.[54] The ponds, which stocked carp (a luxury) and pike (fairly common) were termed 'stews'.

Customarily, most animal stocks was slaughtered at the approach of the winter months when fodder became scarce. Their meat was preserved by salting or smoking, but this became monotonous to consume. Fresh doves and pigeons were considered a welcome delicacy. Particularly prized were the young 'squabs' or 'squeakers'. Early cookery books reveal the versatility of the flesh and the imagination of the cooks. There are quaint recipes for preparing a variety of dishes ranging from humble pigeon dumplings to 'Grand Patty of Pidgeons Royal'.[55]

Keeping doves and pigeons was of course economical because they are foragers and only needed to be fed supplementary grain when snow and frost covers the hard ground. The return was manifold. In addition to their meat, the birds offered further potentials to the farmer. Their feathers provided stuffing for mattresses and pillows while their waste supplied fertiliser. Their dung was also used for softening leather in the tanning industry and later it became a major source of saltpetre for the manufacture of gunpowder. Mature birds were used as quarry for the ancient sport of falconry and, much later, for live pigeon shooting matches on country estates.

The Whittington's substantial dovecote fell into disuse around 1790 when it was converted into a workshop but in 1990 it was completely renovated to make a novel dwelling.

Pauntley Church

The infant Richard Whittington would have been baptised in the adjacent church dedicated to Saint John the Evangelist. The baby would have been immersed into the stone font[56] three times to secure a blessing from each member of the Holy Trinity by a parish priest with the immediate members of his family present. At baptism he was given his Christian name, which was introduced by the Normans into England, meaning 'powerful leader'. (It combines the Germanic 'rich', deriving from the Celtic meaning ruler or king, and 'ard', from Old French, indicating hardy or bold.) Presumably, the Whittington family had high hopes for their third son from the very start!

The Norman church, which was, by then, approaching two centuries old, is believed to have been built about 1150 by Walter de Cormeilles (or Pauntley). William the Conqueror founded the Benedictine Abbey of Cormeilles in Normandy while his son, William II, presented the Manor of Newent, in Gloucestershire, to this alien foundation. The Abbot, in gratitude, despatched a Prior and monks to Newent, where they built a Priory, intended as an adjunct to their Abbey in Normandy. In addition, the Abbot was entitled to appoint a priest at the newly built church of Pauntley. One of the Benedictine monks that administered divine service would also be required to teach the three young children at Pauntley Court.

St John's stands on a knoll which lifts it high above the Leadon Valley, giving it a panoramic view of the rolling countryside of Gloucestershire. This sturdy country church is constructed of local red sandstone that blends in perfectly with the beautiful scenery. Although this is a fairly modest ecclesiastical building, the parish church which Richard Whittington attended would have been far smaller in size. It probably encompassed only the present nave and chancel. There is now scant indication of the richness that once lay within that would have been appreciated by the Whittington family. The exquisite craftsmanship of the interior, however, confirms that masons from the Abbey of Cormeilles who built the Priory at Newent were also despatched to build Pauntley Church.

Two striking features of the Norman Church remain: a sweeping, decorated chancel arch with chevron moulding and a superb doorway with its tympanum carved with rippling fishscale ornamentation.[57] This latter presents a problem. The main church door for the congregation and the chapel door for the priest (now bricked up) clearly gave access from the south side, whereas the present Court House is on the north side. Family historian Michael Whittington speculates that the Norman and Medieval Manor House – now lost – was actually on the south side of the Norman Church and that a Tudor porch was added to the little 13th-century north door when a later Court House was built.

A short path alongside spreading yews with their bulbous bases and lichen-encrusted tombstones huddled against the biting wind leads to a lantern-lit timbered porch with a pitted, weathered oak door. It is a short step down into the wide, plain, dark interior with its flagstone floor and and honey-coloured box pews, each with their own narrow doors and wooden latches. Among the treasures of the interior are a 13th-century pillared piscina, a 16th-century altar triptych depicting the Adoration of the Magi, an 18th-century wooden chest for vestments and the royal arms of George III.

The late 15th- or early 16th-century low, square tower is built in the late Perpendicular style. It has diagonal buttresses, wide embattlements and gruesome gargoyles guarding each corner but an indifferent weathercock. It contains two 14th-century bells plus a third, a large treble (dated 1676) inscribed 'MAR – RETA' 'Margareta'). They are all suspended from a rare Medieval oak bell frame, capable of accommodating a fourth bell, considered to be the oldest in the shire. It is tempting to think that the oldest pair once summoned the boy, Richard, and his family to worship.

Possibly, the tower was constructed or rebuilt while the later Whittingtons still held the Manor. This is evidenced by the fact that the west window bears a pair of stained-glass coat-of-arms relating to John Whittington, Sheriff of Gloucestershire in 1525. The arms are impaled with those of his two wives, Elizabeth Croft and Elizabeth Milbourne. A stained-glass shield set into the tracery of the north window in the chancel carries the Whittington coat-of-arms.[58] Unfortunately, one of the top panels was replaced with white instead of red glass when restored in the postwar period by the Mercers' Company.

To celebrate the approximate 600th anniversary of Richard Whittington's birth, a grand ceremony was held at Pauntley Church. The Lord Mayor of London, the Mayor of Gloucester, officials of the Mercers' Company and members of the present Whittington family gathered at St John the Evangelist's for a memorial service in 1959. The City of London presented a large silver alms dish to the church and this is now displayed in the Treasury at Gloucester Cathedral.[59]

Whittington's Boyhood

Unsurprisingly, nothing is recorded of the boyhood of the third son of Sir William Whittington. His life, as yet, was undistinguished. Younger sons of knights who had returned from the French Wars were then termed 'esquires'. In wartime, knights and esquires combined to form the cavalry; in peacetime, esquires were made liable for all the duties of knights, by holding local offices and attending national Parliament. But all this responsibility was a world away for the young Richard, competing for the fireside in the great hall, listening to endless tales of his father's stirring military exploits while fighting in Northern France under the banner of the marcher lord, Hugh le Despenser; his comrades' courageous crossing of the River Somme at Blanchetaque Fort despite heavy fire from Genoese crossbowmen and his own part in the daring raid on the coastal town of Le Cretoy to secure provisions for the starving English troops that gave them strength to fight the decisive Battle of Crecy.[60]

The King, he knew, expected knights and esquires to be financially secure, especially if they were to be involved in his costly campaigns on the Continent. There were restrictions concerning their dress: they were prohibited cloth-of-gold, silver or silk if their income was less than one hundred pounds per annum. That appeared far beyond his reach... Esquires, however, were generally of noble blood and therefore entitled to display their own coat-of-arms.[61] That, at least, was within Richard's grasp, although his eventual choice of emblem would confuse future biographers and historians.

Edward III's reign marked an increased awareness of national identity and a developing pride in personal achievement. Opportunities were created whereby the humblest tradesmen might be elevated to high status in public service. Merchants were beginning to form themselves into societies specialising in particular trades or crafts, identified by their sumptuous liveries. Originally founded to protect and foster honest craftsmanship, they developed from the established City Guilds into exclusive chartered Companies, famed for their lavish hospitality, elaborate ritual and colourful pageantry.

Traditional roles for the sons of gentlemen were a military career for the eldest son, the church or law for the second son while the third was left little alternative than to become a merchant. Richard was the only one of his siblings destined to follow this established order, although this chosen lifestyle now held undeniable advantages and attractions. Merchants, whose grandfathers or fathers had been simple craftsmen, might swiftly be raised to important positions, civic and commercial, where they wore scarlet robes and costly furs and were addressed by their fellow townsmen as 'Worshipful Sire'. Such a career presented attractive possibilities, thought the young boy, as he sat dreaming, finding pictures in the beckoning flames of the roaring open fire...

Edward II's Tomb

Sir William Whittington, swelled with patriotic pride, cannot have failed to take his young family the short distance from Pauntley to Gloucester to visit St Peter's Abbey (now Gloucester Cathedral). There they would have joined the thousands of pilgrims who filed past the ostentatious tomb of Edward II. After his imprisonment, enforced abdication and alleged murder at Berkeley Castle, presumably on the instructions of Roger Mortimer, Edward III arranged an elaborately staged funeral for his father on 20 December 1327. The body of the deposed king, dressed in his coronation robes, was placed in a lead coffin and laid to rest under flagstones in the north ambulatory near the high altar. The King's body had not been taken to London for fear of an inimical reaction from the fickle citizens. This therefore remains the only example of a monarch's tomb in south-west England.

Edward III afterwards commissioned the innovative alabaster effigy and intricate canopy from either the royal mason, Thomas of Canterbury, or his successor, William Ramsay. Carved from local limestone, it is a wonderful confection of gothic arches and spires rising above a solid base faced with Purbeck marble. After his salvation from shipwreck, Edward III presented a gold model ship to stand on a plinth in front of the tomb and members of his royal family donated precious jewels to adorn the tomb [62] (Richard II held a Parliament around this tomb in 1378 and, as a tribute, adjacent thick columns are painted with bands of his emblem, a white hart.)

Edward II's coiffured hair, forked beard and fulsome moustache under his broad nose are exquisitely sculptured. His sad, haunting eyes stare sightlessly, from his head that rests on a tasseled cushion, supported by angels. Interestingly, this is the first instance of an orb, which the king holds, on an English sepulchral effigy. Once glittering with fresh paint, this magnificent tomb has been incised over the centuries with schoolboy graffiti. Despite this minor defacement, Pevsner's *Guide to Gloucestershire* describes Edward II's burial place as having 'arguably the most thrilling of all tomb canopies'.[63]

For a brief period, a cult of sainthood sprang up around the King. His effigy was presented as deliberately Christlike. His sarcophagus was venerated as a shrine. Visitors packed around the tomb and the subsequent crush necessitated deep recesses being cut into the surrounding columns to allow access from the sides.[64] Apparently, Edward III ordered the complete refurbishment of the Abbey to convert it into a splendid 'Chapel Royal'. Highlight of these improvements was the spectacular stained-glass window which today appears to float over the east end.[65] When the east window was revealed, it was the largest ever seen and it flooded the quire with dazzling light. Built in the Perpendicular style and a very early example of the use of bar tracery, the marvellous window's centrepiece is the Blessed Virgin Mary and Jesus Christ in majesty, flanked by twelve apostles. Tiers of figures rise from behind the High Altar, reaching from Earth to Heaven. They represent, row by row, a great hierarchy: angels, apostles, saints, abbots, bishops, nobles and kings, with at the centre, the Virgin and Child. At the top of the window, the position normally reserved for God the Father, appears a replacement panel representing Saint Clement who was Pope around 100 A.D. Curiously, he may be the only image of a Pope in a Medieval window to escape the wrath of Protestant Reformers in an Anglican Cathedral.[66]

At the lowest level are the shields and coat-of-arms of knights and noblemen who supported Edward III during his French Wars. For this reason it has often been hailed as 'the first war memorial'. Indeed, one scholar observed that these same heraldic families also fought alongside the Black Prince in his greatest victory and that the window therefore commemorates the Battle of Crecy. The romantic notion is belied by the fact that the figure of Saint George is attired in a style of armour dating from the mid-14th century.[67] The

Whittington family would almost certainly have been astonished, whenever they visited the Abbey, by the shimmering, silvery spectacle of the great East Window.

Disgrace

Disaster then struck the Whittingtons and Sir William fell from grace. The family unity was shattered. A formal complaint was made against him at the Husting Court in London.[68] He was required to answer a plea of debt brought before him by William de Southam, Vicar of Arrow from 1354 to 1361.[69] Nothing is known about the cause of this debt. It may have concerned the estate at Upton which lay only four miles from Arrow. Unfortunately, Sir William ignored the summons and this brought dire consequences. The Court declared him an 'outlaw'.

This dramatic pronouncement brought certain penalties. An outlaw could no longer claim the protection of the law and he forfeited all his civil rights. He lost the right to sue in any court or to defend any action against himself. This was the inevitable consequence of failure to appear before the courts in either civil or criminal proceedings. The Sheriff of the County would be authorised to apprehend an outlaw and bring him to justice. He could kill him if he offered resistance.[70] Technically, any citizens could arrest an outlaw, although for Sir William there was always the opportunity to conceal himself, with the aid of trusted friends, in the depths of the enveloping Forest of Dean.

The reason Sir William failed to attend court to face the charges concerning his debt cannot now be known. It seems out of character for a courageous soldier who had fought for his country and a responsible gentleman who had represented his county in Parliament. (The last time Sir William represented Gloucestershire in this capacity was at Westminster in 1348.) Maybe he was in poor health and physically unable to travel; but whatever the extenuating circumstances, a harsh penalty was imposed. This is revealed in an Inquisition Post Mortem on the deceased knight, 'William de Wetyntone, chivaler', held by the King's Escheator, Henry de Prestwood, 'taken at Kemperleye, Tuesday after St Katherine' (23 October 1358/9):

> The manor of Paunteleye was seized into the King's hands by the said escheator by reason of his outlawry promulgated against the said William in London on Monday the Feast of St Gregory (3 September) at the suit of William de Southam, clerk, in a plea of debt. This manor he held jointly with Joan, his wife, under a fine levied in the King's court. It is held of the honour of Clyfford and is worth 8 marks. He died on Saturday after St Gregory (8 September). William, his son and heir, is aged 23.[71]

Sir William died only five days after his sentence was pronounced. Possibly, he suffered a heart attack brought on by shame and stress. The litigious cleric perhaps felt that at last he was compensated for his outstanding debt. The circumstances had a traumatic effect on the family. It seems the older Whittingtons were never quite able to manage their finances. This public disgrace left a profound impression on the young Richard who resolved, in future, to invest his own money wisely. Dame Joan and her family surrendered Pauntley to the King's administrators and removed to their alternative abode across the border, Solers Hope.

Today this pretty hamlet retains a strong tradition that Richard Whittington spent much of his childhood there. Yet clearly such a modest estate was not sufficient to support three bereft young gentlemen. They could no longer expect patrimony and would need to seek financial security outside their immediate family. Maybe this situation caused tension between the young siblings. This might be the time that Richard – not an orphan but the youngest son of an impoverished and now deceased country gentleman – contemplated travelling to London to seek his own fame and fortune.[72]

2

The Apprentice Mercer

The Black Death

At the height of England's military triumphs the country had been plunged into the depths of despair by a deadly disease which swept across the whole of the known world: 'the Black Death'.[73] This most lethal epidemic in recorded history had a calamitous effect on the economy, commerce, government and the defined order of Medieval society. From 1348-50, it raged across the country killing perhaps almost half of the population and it seemed to contemporaries to herald the end of the world.[74]

The pestilence is often referred to as 'Bubonic Plague'. (Bubonic was the most common, though in fact there were three types of plague at work during 'the Great Mortality'.) The most characteristic symptom was the swelling of the infected person's lymph nodes in the armpits, groin or neck that resulted in small, dark pustules or 'buboes' on the skin. Known as 'God's tokens', these heralds of death were accompanied by a fever, headaches, convulsions, vomiting, giddiness, delirium, foul breath and excruciating pain. Death resulted from internal hemorrhaging, extreme exhaustion and heart failure. The disease was swift: few people who contracted it lived to a third day.

Plague is primarily a disease caused by a bacillus transmitted by fleas (Xenopsylla cheopis) from infected rodents and then, once firmly established, it is passed on from person to person to person.[75] It was carried abroad by ships at sea and wagons on land. It flourished alike in overpopulated towns and remote villages where rats and mice inhabited the straw and thatch of timber cottages and where country folk dwelt in close proximity to their animals. (In cold winters they were sheltered inside not just for their protection but to help heat the family home.) During the summer months, the opportunity for trade contributed greatly to the dispersal of the disease. Fairgoers gathered at markets and pilgrims crisscrossed the countryside, inadvertently spreading the disease at peak periods of warm weather.[76]

Traditionally, the Black Death is thought to have originated in the Far East. The overland caravan trade – silks and cloths, spices and drugs – provided a rapid means of transport for the disease westwards from Asia. It crossed the Black Sea from China and India, then into Europe. There it left between one third and half of the population dead. The first shock wave of the pandemic reached Britain from Northern France in the late summer of 1348. It was carried by rat-infested trading vessels, probably carrying wine from Gascony or Bordeaux, across the English Channel. Chroniclers disagree over its first port of call, but it seems likely to have been Melcombe Regis, a little coastal town that grew to become Weymouth, lying almost midway between Dartmouth and Southampton, Dorsetshire.

Encouraged by the incessant heavy rainfall from midsummer until Christmas, the contagion raged through the hinterland stripping entire counties – Dorset, Devon, Somerset – of a great number of their inhabitants. By mid-August it was definitely reported in Bristol. The citizens of Gloucester tried in vain to contain the infection by shunning its inhabitants, thinking they might be infected themselves by inhaling victims' infected breath.[77] They shut the gates in the high walls against travellers from the south as a wise precaution, although this self-imposed siege could lead only to privation and ruin. Alas, this was to little avail because the infection sneaked into the city aboard fishermen's barges able to negotiate the shallow bend of the River Severn. As winter approached, the epidemic slowed to a crawl, although its potency remained undiminished, which meant that it might still leap from town to town by tradesmen, leaving 'miles of disease-free countryside untouched'.[78]

The pattern was repeated throughout the country, whereby the plague started in the towns and spread outwards to the countryside. By late November, the pestilence had taken hold of the hamlets on either side of the Bristol-Gloucester Road. Sir William Whittington, home from the wars, would have closed ranks and sheltered his young family from the spreading disease; because of the remoteness of the manor, they stood a slim chance of avoiding the catastrophe.[79]

Causes of the Plague

Medics and Scientists were baffled by the spread of the 'pestilens'. Experts claimed it was connected to a wide variety of causes: swarms of flies, frogs huddled together, rotting fruit, large spiders, mad dogs, the birth of conjoined twins… Portents of its approach numbered birds restless at night, ravens circling in pairs, shooting stars, comets, a lunar eclipse, thunder and lightning out of the south. (Curiously, none of the assiduous observers mention a plague of rats.) The most learned opinion was that it was the result of planetary influences. Doctors at the University of Paris, citing Aristotle, pointed to a conjunction of Saturn, Mars and Jupiter at 1 p.m. on 20 March 1345. People blamed indecent clothing, corrupt clergy and disobedient children. Their wrath fell upon immigrants, drunks, beggars, gypsies and lepers. Jews were victimised on the Continent where they were accused of poisoning wells and fountains to spread infection among Christians.[80] It was widely believed by fundamentalists that the disease – like the HIV virus – was a deserved punishment for immorality by a vengeful God. The conundrum for the ecclesiastical hierarchy in England was how to explain to their puzzled parishioners the reason why God so favoured them in warfare yet punished them so terribly in peace.

An erudite Bishop of Aarhus of Denmark who practised physic in France suggested further causes: 'wymmen' and 'bathis'. He bravely ministered to the sick while holding a pomander to his nose to ward off germs and wrote practical advice that showed him to be far ahead of his time: wash hands with vinegar, fumigate the sickroom, sprinkle with sweet herbs, keep the windows open – north and east – for fresh air but be particular to keep closed the windows facing south for it was widely believed the warm southerly wind brought the plague.[81] When it occurred to people that the infection might be transmitted purely by touch, the sales of gloves rocketed and they fetched high prices in London.[82]

The poet, Langland, in 'Piers Plowman' conceded that 'this pestelences was for puyre synne' but blamed the Pope for his lack of intervention in the spread of the disease:

For, sith he hath the Power that Peter himself had,
He hath the pot with the salve, soothly as me thinketh.

Monks and nuns who had a duty of care for the sick of their parish would have had access to the physic garden in their monastery or convent. Medicinal plants and herbs grown with the purpose of healing included rhubarb, peonies, fennel, squills and opium poppies, and these might be supplemented by costly drugs and spices obtained from abroad.[83]

Edward III had no army to combat this silent enemy, which had not yet marched against the capital. He and his courtiers were resolved to carry on as normal: extravagant Christmas celebrations; feasts and dances; jousts and tournaments. But it was not exactly 'business as usual'. Parliament was prorogued; the Law Courts were postponed.[84] At first, the king refused to seal the ports to appease the merchants whose mercantile trade should not be disrupted.[85] They seemed untroubled by the fact that Europeans were dying by the millions. This lack of action proved fatal. The effects of the disease worsened. It was only when the epidemic hit Edward personally that a pall was drawn over courtly celebrations. First his infant son, William, was carried away,[86] then his youngest daughter, Joan, while journeying through Bordeaux. Edward ordered prayers and processions to seek divine protection from this disease, which, like the Magi, 'came from the East'.

The Plague in London

John Stow, the Elizabethan antiquarian, relates how the Black Death inevitably arrived, after spreading from shire to shire, in the capital: 'A great pestilence entering this island, began first in Dorsetshire, then proceeded into Devonshire, Somersetshire, Gloucestershire and Oxfordshire, and at length came to London and overspread all England, so wasting the people that scarce the tenth persons of all sorts was left alone, and churchyards were not sufficient to receive the dead.'

The pestilence made its appearance in the City about the feast of All Hallows, 1 November 1348, but developed rapidly between Candlemas (2 February 1349) and Easter (12 April 1350). All through winter it raged amid the narrow filthy streets. It was said that over two hundred corpses were buried every day in a newly consecrated burial ground in Smithfield.[87] The Abbot, Simon Bircheston, and half his monks of Westminster Abbey perished; the newly ordained Archbishop of Canterbury, Thomas Bradwardine, survived forty days from his consecration. In London, the greatest of the city's religious houses, Greyfriars, lost about one hundred brothers.[88] And then it ceased abruptly – no one quite knows why – having spent its force around the time of the church's celebration of the coming of the Holy Spirit at Pentecost on 31 May.[89] It left the capital in chaos.

The plague slew its victims with such speed the worst was over in London before it spread to the Midlands and the North. Eventually, Scotland, Wales and Ireland were affected. Entire families had been swept away, along with their domestics and labourers. The clergy were the most vulnerable since part of their vocation was to minister to the sick and dying. Indiscriminately, the pestilence carried off both priest and penitent to one shared shallow grave. Bishops delegated sacramental powers to the laity, which, extraordinarily, extended to women.

Villages were left desolate; swathes of land neglected. Widows might remarry twice in a matter of months; properties could be bequeathed twice on the same day. Agriculture suffered grievously. Fields were untended, crops were unharvested. Windmills and watermills ceased turning. Forges went silent. Highly prized horses and cattle fell in value. There was a widespread shortage of labourers.[90] For the first time ever, women and children took up the plough or drove ox carts. Food was in short supply. Inevitably, this dire situation resulted in a great change in the method of farming from labour-intensive land tillage to widespread animal husbandry. Sheep farming required few hands to tend flocks and this great advantage ultimately brought vast fortunes to landowners as consumption of meat[91] and export of wool escalated. Whittington himself would eventually dabble in the wool trade.

For the peasants who survived, the devastation brought real benefits. After this massive depopulation,[92] the scarcity of workmen resulted in wages doubling, trebling. This sudden possible acquisition of wealth through employment or inheritance resulted in the mobilisation of young men from failing manors and deserted villages to flourishing towns and cities. Bondsmen, previously tied to their overlord, sought alternative employment countrywide, despite repeated government restrictions. Edward III introduced a 'Statute of Labourers' in a feeble attempt to cap workmen's wages but this unenforceable act only provoked hostility.[93] For survivors of the plague, these startling modern times offered striking chances to thrive and flourish. Folk became prosperous as a result of an unexpected inheritance; ample land was available for mercantile investment while sheep farming contributed to the wealth of landowners. And for the nouveau riche there was a superfluity of money to spend on luxuries, clothes and imported merceries.

The impact on the Whittington family closeted in their remote hamlet in those shadowy days can only be imagined...

Recruitment Drives in the City

This 'dark destroyer of Medieval life'[94] had left London's industry and commerce paralysed. Trades and guilds suffered untold losses among their members. Wardens of companies – the Cutlers and the Grocers, the Hatters and the Goldsmiths – died in large numbers at the height of the Plague. The Mercers, who dealt in small goods and rich cloths, relied upon constant replenishment by apprentices to maintain their increasingly powerful position in the City. A poignant letter from the Mayor informed the Pope that 'a dreadful mortality had cut off our merchants' in 1350.[95] Their company halls were left deserted.

Edward III's government may have stuttered and stalled but it certainly did not collapse. It is a credit to his powers of delegation that, although the King and his chief ministers retreated into the country, their staff at Westminster Hall demonstrated remarkable resilience and continued to function despite the threat. These dedicated government clerks and officials, although daily depleted, dealt with an enormous mound of paperwork – petitions, charters, accounts – throughout the crisis. The King, conspicuous by his absence, confined his concerns with ordering and defending, at a distance, his disease-ridden realm.

Once the pestilence had abated, there were countless opportunities created by sudden vacancies and city companies instigated a recruitment drive among able young people countrywide. King Edward sternly rebuked the Corporation of London for actively avoiding his directive to discourage this inevitable migration from town and country to the City. The Black Death, presented unparalleled opportunities to the lower gentry who might be strongly tempted to send their sons to be apprenticed to a reputable city trade.[96] Richard Whittington, encouraged by his family, may have been among the numerous youths who showed enterprise and seized this unparalleled opportunity to explore his future and his fortune as an apprentice merchant Mercer.[97]

London and Westminster

Richard Whittington, by tradition, walked from Gloucester to London, a distance of one hundred miles, but this story assumes falsely he was a pauper. As the son of a former knight, he must have had access to horses and would have been accompanied, most likely by his brother, Robert, with servants for protection against thieves and robbers. Journeys were slow and tortuous. On foot a man might average fifteen miles a day whereas a mounted rider would manage twenty-five. A four days' journey, then, for the Whittington brothers, passing through the sequence of Cotswold wool towns – Northleach, Burford, Witney or perhaps dropping down to Fairford – with their mellow stone cottages and majestic country churches.

The inexorable growth of trade and the increasing centralisation of government was evidenced by the multiplication of roads in Medieval England.[98] Maps – Matthew Paris (*c.*1250) and Gough (*c.*1360) – that fairly accurately described the counties[99] would have been unavailable to the Whittingtons. Their meandering route through Gloucestershire, Oxfordshire and Berkshire would have been unfamiliar territory but they could not have become lost if they travelled in company with the teams of packhorses making their regular cross-country journey to the capital.

Richard's first impression of the City would probably have been of a small market town. He must have felt instantly at home among the stalls laden with country produce in the winding streets, particularly Eastcheap and Westcheap, where traders cried aloud their wares, selling everything from apples to lavender, shoes to onions, oysters to cherries, live eels, caged birds, meat pies.[100] There was a multitude of domestic dwellings in the maze of narrow lanes that criss-crossed the City, although timber and thatch had given way, because of the risk of fire, to stone and tiles.[101] Horses, dogs, pigs and poultry, mingled among the crowds and the accompanying farmyard smells were reminders of the proximity of the countryside.

The population of the metropolis was relatively small, depleted even further by the recent pestilence. According to the poll tax returns for 1377, it was approaching 40,000, far fewer than Paris, Venice, Florence, Naples, Ghent and Milan. Nevertheless, it was still three times as large as Bristol or York, the next in rank among English towns. There was now a steady flow of aspirant apprentices from the country, as evidenced by the surnames of provincial towns and villages born by its new arrivals – 'Northampton', 'Chichester', 'Sevenoke', 'Twyford' and even 'Whittington' – who spoke a variety of dialects. Indisputably, the City of London had become recognised as a great commercial centre which benefitted from the diversity of its trades. Quite simply, it was by far 'the most wealthy, prestigious and populous town in England'.[102]

Modern 'London', of course, evolved from two separate cities, London and Westminster, connected by a riverside roadway, 'The Strand'. Famously, the City of London comprises one square mile, defined from earliest times by its stone walls pierced by a series of gates. Although this was predominately a commercial centre, it was distinguished by its numerous religious foundations, Inns of Court and magnates' mansions, whose tranquil gardens provided a patchwork of havens among the bustling business premises. It was also proud of its ability to govern itself through its elected Mayor, Sheriffs and Aldermen, a right it jealously guarded. This was focused upon the Guildhall, which Whittington, through his deathbed bequests, would vastly improve architecturally.

Edward the Confessor created the second adjacent city when he moved his palace upriver from London to Westminster. Effectively, he separated the seat of royal power and justice from the nucleus of mercantile trade in the capital. The City of Westminster soon became distinguished by the towers of Westminster Palace and Westminster Abbey. Originally built along the River Thames by Edward the Confessor, the Palace of Westminster was commandeered by William the Conqueror and enlarged by his son, William Rufus, with the addition of the Great Hall. Thereafter, it became the main residence of successive kings of England and their courts until the reign of Henry VIII. Parliament, when summoned, assembled in the Painted Chamber where the Lord Chamberlain directed the Lords to withdraw to the White Chamber while the Commoners were relegated to either the Chapter House or the Refectory of the adjacent Westminster Abbey.[103]

During the reign of Edward III, Westminster Hall, cavernous and labyrinthine, became the hub of the monarch's power. Here was the Chancery, the government administrative department whose numerous clerks were responsible for distributing formal letters of instruction and charters conferring rights. Next were two Royal Courts of Justice, the Common Pleas (the highest civil court in the land) and, when it was held in London, the King's Bench. (It must have been confusing at times to find two law courts conducting their complicated legal business simultaneously in the same hall.) The Exchequer was the second largest office in the King's administration, which supervised the receipt of taxes and relevant revenues or audited both civil and royal accounts. Instructions to all these departments – Chancery, Courts and Exchequer – were authorised through the office of the Privy Seal, which ensured that the King's commands were communicated to the appropriate administrative department. Exercise of government on a daily basis was not, of course, by personal direction of the King but through his chief ministers: the Chancellor (who oversaw the Chancery), the Treasurer (the Exchequer) and the Justices of the Courts. These elite figures formed the royal council who met regularly, often without the sovereign's presence, to formulate uncontroversial instructions in the King's name.

Westminster Hall was damaged by fire in 1291 but restored by Edward II. Richard II, recognising that this was this was the administrative centre for his kingdom, enhanced its dignity by commissioning the wonderful oak hammer beam roof. Undoubtedly, Whittington would later marvel at this new construction – hailed as the widest unsupported span in the country – each time he was required to take his oath as Mayor of London before the Barons of the Exchequer.

Westminster Abbey evolved from the modest Benedictine Monastery that occupied unhealthy marshland just north of London's river. Edward the Confessor promised Pope Leo IX that he would restore its dilapidated Church of St Peter, which is faithfully represented in the Bayeux Tapestry. (There a workman is shown fixing a weathercock as a final touch to the lead roof.)[104] Edward the Confessor died a week after its consecration in 1065 and upon his canonisation his tomb beside the High Altar became a place of pilgrimage. When William I was crowned in the restored St Peter's Church, which later came to be known as Westminster Abbey, on Christmas Day 1066, he set a trend which has been followed faithfully by English sovereigns up to the present time.[105] Henry V venerated the sumptuous building recreated by Henry III and prior to his French campaign he commissioned Whittington to supervise the complete reconstruction of the north aisle of the Nave.

The Tower of London, although physically located within the City, remained directly under the jurisdiction of the sovereign. This imposing structure already appeared so ancient and venerable that studious citizens attributed its construction to Julius Caesar. Fortifications were strengthened in the 14th century by the addition of a curtain wall and a series of watch towers. This facilitated the safe storage of valuables for the Exchequer and accounts for the Wardrobe. The Tower also contained the royal armouries and the King's mint. Additionally, an office was provided for the keeper of the King's ships who commanded a modest royal fleet that could be augmented, in wartime, by impressed merchant vessels. Most importantly – and this would become of immense concern for Whittington – the Tower housed the Great Wardrobe, which purchased and stored bulky commodities: groceries, spices, furs and fabric.[106]

Young Whittington would have been instantly struck by the number and splendour of the parish churches. There were around one hundred and twenty, more, probably, than any other city in Christendom.[107] As he strolled through the streets, he would have heard the murmur of a parish or chantry mass through the open door of a church and said or sung masses at the altars of the side chapels for the members of the various fraternities and city guilds. As a merchant, he would become a prominent member of one of these companies and attend divine services on a regular basis in the church that it patronised. Moreover, he would create one of the finest churches within the City – St Michael Paternoster Royal – in gratitude for his phenomenal civic and financial success.

The crowning glory of the City was Old St Paul's Cathedral. This spectacular building was far larger than the present edifice created by Christopher Wren (which is, in fact, an audacious illusion, when viewed from above the body of the church is seen to be encased by a free-standing facade). Originally conceived during the reign of William the Conqueror, it was the fourth to be built on this sacred site on Ludgate Hill. Cruciform, Old Saint Paul's was one of the largest and most admired buildings in Medieval England.

At the west end were two great bell towers, which doubled as prisons, while in the centre was the square stone tower topped by a tapering timber spire that soared heavenwards.[108] An exquisite rose window at the east end bathed the interior with light in the early morning, illuminating the thirty side chapels and altars displaying holy relics, elaborate shrines and royal tombs. Young folk, at times, lacked respect for this extraordinary centre of devotion, for Bishop Bybrook complained that apprentices threw stones and fired arrows to bring down jackdaws and pigeons nesting in the rafters, or kicked footballs that smashed the exquisite windows.

St Paul's served a dual purpose, religious and secular. Its bell that marked the hours of service also summoned citizens to arms, while the open-air pulpit at the north-east corner of the walled churchyard was not only the platform for sermons but the place where proclamations were read and statutes proclaimed. Inside, the wide transepts north and south were regarded as a convenient thoroughfare for pedestrians and a marketplace for tradesmen who bartered their wares in competition with the priests declaiming masses. By Whittington's time, the nave might easily be compared with the Biblical 'den of thieves' and it was dismissively referred to as 'Paul's Walk'.[109]

The River Thames also linked the two cities, east and west. This was the main highway for an inconceivable number and variety of waterborne vessels between the City and the open sea. Directly across the river was Southwark. Despite its close proximity, this was a forbidden stretch of land with a dark, dishonourable reputation. Whittington, when Mayor, would strive manfully to bring it under his jurisdiction. London Bridge offered the only viable means to travel from the north bank over into Kent. This was a splendid structure with its narrow thoroughfare flanked by myriad shops and houses that formed its own nigh impenetrable tunnel for road traffic. Whittington one day recognised its prime location and would lease a grand shop there for his sale of mercery.

From Westminster, all the way along the water's edge to the Tower, lay the entanglement of docks and warehouses for the Steelyard, Billingsgate, Wine Wharf, Haywharf and Timberhithe. Pepperers and grocers, fishmongers and cordwainers, leatherworkers, goldsmiths, pewterers – almost every business save farming, quarrying and mining – took place within the city's boundaries. But London's primary business, then as now, was trade. Hides, cloth, iron, alabaster, gold, spices, almost every single kind of tradable commodity and finished product passed through London's docks, wharves and merchant houses. Whittington would one day supervise the Customs for the City of London which would encourage him to diversify his business as a wool merchant.

This is perhaps an ideal, picturesque portrait of the great metropolis: in reality there were intractable problems caused by the sheer scale of that massive immigration after the Black Death. Among the arrivals genuinely seeking the offer of work, there were scores of men interested only in pursuing a life of crime. Empty streets invited burglary; abandoned houses tempted squatters. The government acknowledged the challenges facing the Sheriffs who were striving to maintain law and order in the capital. A writ was issued to the City authorities on 29 December 1349 offering them full powers to control 'the many evil doers and disturbers of the peace who have come armed there ... and others of whom there is notorious suspicion or [are] found wandering by night ... as well as others who have broken the peace there, and in the present great concourse of aliens and denizens to the city and suburbs'. It reaffirmed the bounden duty 'now the pestilence is stayed' for the city officials 'to cause the King's peace to be inviolably kept'.[110]

London, though, for Richard Whittington, fresh from the country, was a magical city, 'bustling, chaotic, full of promise and the object of dreams'.[111] William Dunbar, the 15th-century Scottish poet, hailed it as the 'Sovereign of cities', largely inhabited by 'merchauntis full of substance and myght'. From this time onwards, it seems, Whittington lived and worked almost exclusively in the City throughout his long and eventful life. Indeed, there is little evidence that he ever left the capital, once he had made his mark as one of those substantial, mighty merchants of the City.

Mercers

Edward III recognised the value of commerce, which became crucial to the security of his realm. He encouraged the wool trade, which was heavily taxed in order to finance his wars with France. Undeniably, the King exploited the industry and encouraged its merchants who acted as his agents for collecting revenues. When the wool staple was established in English territory at Calais, a consortium of London merchants gained control of the lucrative trade on the Continent. They became prosperous, powerful and a prime source of loans to the Crown when the preferred supply from the Italian bankers inevitably failed.[112] The escalation of royal taxation, however, meant that this indigenous trade became troublesome and prohibitive to speculative dealers, while the expansion of the cloth industry offered the perfect alternative as a career. Astutely, Whittington grasped its realistic possibilities and decided to apply for an apprenticeship as a Mercer.

Mercers – although they might have been reluctant to admit the fact – evolved from peddlers who roamed the countryside, setting up their trade stalls at village fairs, markets and innyards.[113] The word, mercery, derives from Old French, 'mercier', meaning a dealer in small wares. All their wares were portable because they often sold simply from trays hung by cords slung around their necks. Peddlers displayed an array of items: gloves, purses, mufflers, stockings, buckles, buttons, girdles, combs, mirrors, ribbons, laces, thimbles, pincushions, moulds, spoons, pipes, soap, paper, scissors, knives, tweezers, razors, toothpicks, bells, whistles, toys, reliquaries. There was an abundance of accessories for headwear and dress and swatches of materials, particularly linen, that might furnish a home. Itinerant salesmen, alas, had the undeniable reputation of being rogues and vagabonds.

Gradually, peddlers increased their trade and invested their money in businesses in towns and cities, particularly London. Once established, they could rely upon traders travelling from the provinces to the city to make important transactions.[114] At first, the most affluent merchants invested tentatively in a diversity of commodities while carefully avoiding the risk of trading in expensive fabrics that might involve considerable capital and continental contacts. Nominally, their goods were intended for retail at fixed prices and were defined as small objects 'weighed by the little balance'. Gradually, they abandoned the majority of minor merceries, which were adopted by the drapers or haberdashers, and started to deal more specifically in expensive materials acquired from foreign exporters.

Since a great variety of headwear counted as mercery, Whittington would have become familiar with the range and types of popular designs for caps, chaplets, coifs, hoods and hats, although this trade brought conflict with the Chapelers or Cappers, who were the specialists in this particular field. His knowledge would also extend to the fur trade – marten, otter, badger, weasel, squirrel, fox, polecat, hare, kid, coney and the domestic cat – although this trade was the domain of the Furriers. His eventual focus would become luxury materials of which he became an expert in their texture, quality, purpose and versatility.

Apprentices

Richard Whittington, nervous and excited, arrived in the City with the express purpose of securing an apprenticeship with the Guild of Mercers. Obviously, Sir William's youngest son considered himself above the craftsmen that made objects in order to sell them from a common street stall. He was setting his aims high with a strong ambition to become a merchant involved with the trade in luxury goods and costly materials, eventually owning his own shop, perhaps travelling overseas. He had chosen wisely. By the close of the reign of Edward III the 'folk of the Mercery', along with the Grocers, would become 'the wealthiest and most powerful bodies in London'.[115]

The Mercers were particular about their acceptance of apprentices. Like rival fellowships, they insisted that an applicant must not be halt, lame, half blind or leprous. They only accepted able young men between the age of fourteen and sixteen.[116] And they insisted that their apprentices must have had no previous contact with itinerant peddlers who were suspected of handling stolen goods (although perhaps they were attempting to disassociate themselves from their own humble beginnings). Further, they agreed in 1404 that possible apprentices must be proven not to be a bondsman but 'a free man born and fremannes son'.[117] Whittington came from a firmly established county stock of gentlemen and his application would definitely be encouraged and welcomed. The common people – those bound to the soil – had no part in the share of the fortunes of the City of London.[118]

London apprentices spoke a variety of English dialects and they came from a mixture of social groups, but it must not be imagined they were composed of simple country folk. Before a master enrolled an apprentice, he extracted a premium from the boy's family which was expected to cover the cost of board, lodging and education. The master duly presented the applicant to the clerk who entered his name in the records of the guild and paid his indenture, which varied from one shilling for the Carpenters to two shillings for the Skinners. The wealthy Mercers commanded an even higher fee: two shillings and sixpence on entry and three shillings and fourpence on closure.[119] The length of term for apprenticeship was fixed at seven years.[120]

Next, the privileged youth swore a solemn oath before witnesses at Guildhall. He was bound not to reveal the secrets of his trade, to be totally loyal to his master, to spurn taverns and brothels, to refrain from dice and gambling, to be courteous towards women and not to marry without permission. He must obey his master implicitly, work diligently, and refrain from idle gossip or foolish chatter. For any breaches of these restrictions he was liable to be fined, severely beaten or in extreme cases have his term doubled.

The master then made his pledges in turn. He promised to feed and clothe his apprentice, to provide him with suitable accommodation and, above all, teach him all the skills of his trade. He was obliged to provide everything appropriate to the boy's age from stout shoes to short haircuts. Annual inspections by the Wardens would ascertain that the masters behaved impeccably towards their charges. Mercers who neglected their sworn duties were liable to have their apprentices taken away from them and handed over to a new master. A tailor was sent to prison on a charge of neglecting his apprentice who was forced to sleep in a makeshift bed, 'foule shirtyd and full of vermin'.[121]

These pledges were strictly regulated. Indentures stipulated that the apprentice should never be involved in demeaning tasks.[122] If the boy's parents considered that the master had been too harsh or lax in his duties they could complain directly to the City officials, the law courts or to the Wardens of the Guild. Cases are recorded of fathers protesting that their sons had not been educated properly or that they had been required to perform menial tasks: 'a keeper of horses or a bearer of tankards'. City regulations stipulated that the system should never degenerate into cheap child labour. They insisted on adequate training and suitable living conditions, restricting the number of apprentices a master might accept so that he could concentrate on his commitment to train a young man during the full term of his apprenticeship. Generally, a close bond developed between the master and his apprentice and at the completion of the full term the majority of masters were proud to present their apprentices for the freedom of the City.

The Mercers realised it was important that their apprentices should be able 'to rede, write and lay Accomptres sufficauntly'. These skills were essential for business transactions. It is unlikely that a boy would have been considered for apprenticeship unless he had already acquired these rudiments. Probably, Whittington was taught these basics by a private tutor, the parish priest or even a member of his family. As an apprentice Mercer, he would have been given the option of attending one of three established grammar schools: St Paul's, St Martin-le-Grand and St Mary-le-Bow. There he would have been tutored in English and Latin by a competent Master of Arts. He would also have acquired a knowledge of the scriptures and an ability to follow church liturgy. Whittington acquired a strong social awareness and adopted a high moral code of conduct at an early age, which is evidenced by his subsequent impeccable behaviour as a responsible citizen.

Besant and Rice identify a great number of strange and forgotten trades followed in London: plumier, fettermonger, wympler, tabourer, knyfesmith, imageur (maker of church images), selmeker (maker of seals), dishere (maker of dishes), saucer (dealer in salt), bureller (maker of a type of coarse cloth called 'burel'). Tradesmen or craftsmen tended to congregate in certain areas which today can still be identified: bakers in Bread Street, dairymen in Milk Street, fishmongers in Friday Street and poulterers in Poultry; hosiers in Hosier Lane, beekeepers in Honey Lane, ironmongers in Ironmonger Lane and goldsmiths in Goldsmith Street.

The main commercial street was Cheapside (from 'cheap' meaning to barter). This was the centre of trade. Customers were served from stalls set up in the middle of this wide thoroughfare which resembled a country market. Close by were St Paul's Cathedral and the imposing St Mary-le-Bow Church. Here stood the great cross, which rose three storeys high and was adorned with religious statues, one of a series marking each of the twelve resting places of the funeral cortege of Edward I's consort, Queen Eleanor of Castile, as it wended its way from Nottinghamshire to Westminster Abbey. The Great Conduit was at the east end and the Little Conduit at the west end, which on special occasions – royal weddings, coronations and christenings – flowed freely with red wine. Opposite Bow Church was a fountain, the Standard, that was sometimes the focus of riots and rebellions and the location of brandings, beatings and beheadings. And of supreme significance to the Mercers, here, too, was the Hospital of St Thomas of Acon or Acres. This is where the Mercers had their shops and where Whittington served his apprenticeship.

An Apprentice's Day

The anonymous Mercer to whom Whittington was apprenticed would have certainly owned a shop in Cheapside. He may, in this case, have attracted aristocratic customers and forged court connections. His young apprentice would have followed an arduous daily routine. He would probably have lived with his master who ensured that he was kept busy from six in the morning, when the bells of St Paul's sounded the hour of prime, until curfew (the time of which fluctuated between eight o'clock in winter or nine o'clock in summer) when the bells of St Mary-le-Bow signalled that trading should cease, the taverns should close and the city gates be locked. At dawn, the apprentice was expected to prepare the shop for trade by taking down the shutters and unfolding the flap boards in the front of the window where goods might be sold straight onto the street.

For most of the day an apprentice stood at the shop door crying out his master's wares through cupped hands: 'What d'ye lack? fine felt hats or spectacles for reading.' 'Pewter pots and green rushes.' 'Pepper and saffron.' 'Strawberries and cherries.' 'Cod and mackerel.' 'Velvet, silk, linen' – like barkers at a fairground. 'Buy fine cloth of lawne, Paris thred, coton and umple.'[123] (London Lickpenny' verse 10.)

During the day, he would also have been kept occupied by carrying messages to customers or running errands to suppliers. On Sundays he would be expected to accompany his master and mistress to church while in the evenings he escorted them through the dimly lit streets with a lantern.

At night the apprentice replaced the wooden shutters (literally, 'shutting' up shop), swept the shop floor and stored all the bales of cloth in the workroom at the back. The most expensive materials would be stored in large wooden chests. All this time his master would be checking the day's takings with the aid of tally sticks before locking the money away in a strong box. Then the master would retire for the night with his family while his tired apprentice curled up to sleep under the money counting board or 'counter' to safeguard the property. (Later, though rarely, apprentices were allocated their own separate 'prentisechambre')[124] At the end of each day, candles and rushes were extinguished.

Apprenticeship was tough. Young men sacrificed their liberty in return for prospects and security. Though a full stomach, a warm fire and a comfortable bed seemed a far more tempting option[125] than the 'freedom' to roam the streets, cold and hungry. He was distinguished by his austere clothes: a flat, round cap over close-cropped hair and a coarse, long coat.[126] For most of his life he would be confined indoors subject to the control of his master, dwelling in his house and working under his strict guidance.

To lighten the tedium of an apprentice's life there was entertainment aplenty centred round the Cheap. Even on ordinary weekdays the stalls were crowded with buyers and sellers, citizens flocked to the makeshift booths, men-at-arms rode up and down, prisoners were escorted to the pillory. But on special days knights rode at tilts to impress spectators while grand tournaments attracted the attention of the king and his court who watched from a stone gallery high on the wall of Bow Church. These exciting occasions provided excellent training for war.

On ecclesiastical days there were processions of priests, monks and choristers accompanied by minstrels to mark saints' days or church celebrations while the liveried companies arranged parades to honour their patron at their own parish church. The Mayor's Riding was the highlight of summer but even this could be eclipsed by the sovereign leading a military march-past to sing a Te Deum at St Paul's in gratitude for a great victory. But the festive mood might rapidly change when witnessing a state funeral or a horrific public execution. Whittington, up from the country, would have peered tentatively through the windows or stepped outside the shop to feast his eyes on these pageants and processions.

Chaucer relates in his uncompleted 'The Cook's Tale' how one rascally apprentice named Peterkin, who often had his hands in his master's till to pay for his gambling debts, skipped away from work to watch weddings:

He loved better the taverne than the shoppe,
For whan ther any ryding was in Chepe,
Out of the shoppe thider wolde he lepe,
Til that he hadde al the sighte y-seyn,
And daunced wel, he wolde nat come ageyn.
(lines 4,376-4,380)

Sports and Recreation

After the strict regime of a long working day, City apprentices turned their attention to the pursuit of pleasure, particularly on high days and holidays. 'It was their common costome to followe their maisters upon Sundays to the church dore and then to leave them, and hie unto the taverne.' Frequenting taverns was expressly forbidden because, then as now, boisterous youths and strong drink were a volatile combination. Nonetheless there were a host of taverns where apprentices frequently assembled: 'Salutation' in Billingsgate, 'Boar's Head', in Cannon Street, 'Swan' at Dowgate, 'Mermaid' on Cornhill, 'Three Tuns' at Newgate, 'Windmill' at the Exchange, 'King's Head' at New Fish Street and 'The Mitre' of Cheap. The most popular venue was the latter's rival, 'The Dagger', also in Cheapside.[127]

After a few too many drinks the intoxicated lads spilled onto the streets for a riotous game of football with an inflated pig's bladder. 'Fotebal', because of the violence that erupted during impromptu matches, was banned by the City officials. Edward III, in fact, had decreed that archery must be practised instead of such sports because this had the advantage of training young men for warfare. Cock throwing was another prohibited sport – the idea seems to have been to throw stones at a cockerel and the one who killed it took the carcass home for his dinner – discouraged not for its cruelty but because it attracted gambling disputes.

Sports, naturally, reflected the seasons. On Fridays in Lent there was horse riding and racing outside the City walls while at Easter there were water sports, including rowing full tilt against a shield hung upon a pole, along the fast-flowing River Thames. On May Day there was dancing around the maypole – a chance to flirt with the females – decorated with flowers, foliage, ribbons and streamers, accompanied by Morris dancing and hobby horses. All through summer there was archery, racing, wrestling, hockey, quarter staff, competitive activities that would be welcomed by the Mayor and Sheriffs. Cruel sports that invited rowdy spectators numbered bear or bull baiting and cock fighting, generally restricted to Southwark. In autumn the lads would go a-nutting in Epsom or Hainault Forest or Hornsey Wood, while in the frosty season lads could skate (with bones attached to their boots) over the frozen ponds of Moorfields. At Christmas, there was traditional indoor entertainment – feasting and dancing, singing and suppers, carolling and canoodling – by their master's crackling log fire in the hall decorated with evergreen. The greatest fun was reserved for Twelfth Night when havoc reigned with frolics and antics prescribed by an elected 'Lord of Misrule'.[128]

Street fights among apprentices bound to rival trades – Tailors and Drapers, Spicers and Pepperers, Saddlers and Lorimers[129] – were frequent and vicious. A cry, 'clubs', rallied mates who proceeded to attack a hostile gang with stout wooden clubs carried by all apprentices as weapons for personal defence (or attack). No one was permitted to walk about the City streets armed with a sword or dagger unless holding the rank of a knight. These vicious brawls were intercepted by officers of the law and offenders were rigorously punished. Occasionally, apprentices were engaged in less serious pranks. The watch arrested a group of apprentices who had filled a barrel with stones and then rolled it downhill from Gracechurch St to London Bridge 'to the great terror of the neighbours'.

It is hard to imagine that Whittington, when an apprentice, took part in such raucous activities as he appears serious and sober throughout his adult life. Certainly, he applied himself to his tasks and remained dedicated to the pursuit of his chosen career. We know Mercers were strict regarding training and qualification because between 1391 and 1464 nearly half of their enrolled apprentices failed to complete their seven-year course.[130]

Whittington, after proving himself to have been an apt and able pupil, must have been impatient to set up his own shop, which needed to be stocked with enticing goods to attract the attention of wealthy customers. Lacking an inheritance, Whittington needed to secure the attention of a patron whose identity can only be guessed: Sir Ivo Fitzwaryn, his future father-in-law, perhaps, or more likely Thomas of Woodstock, Duke of Gloucester. But there is a further possibility. It might have been his older brother, Richard, who had originally paid his premium to an unknown master and then continued to sponsor his career as a merchant.[131] Certainly, the two brothers, Robert and Richard, remained on amicable terms throughout their lives.

The Black Prince

Whittington would probably have been in London either serving his apprenticeship or setting up his shop as Mercer when news of a most astonishing victory at 'Peytes' or Poitiers (19 September 1356) was relayed via a personal letter from the Black Prince. Now a veteran commander, Prince Edward had employed almost identical tactics as the Battle of Crecy when marching northwards through the reclaimed Duchy of Aquitaine and confronting the new French King, John II. The Prince had chosen the battlefield with immense care, arranging his troops in a strong defensive position on a wide plain with a winding stream at one side and a dense wood to his rear, where he cunningly concealed part of his cavalry. The main body of his men-at-arms fought dismounted with rows of longbowmen protecting them on both sides in a V formation. This time the Prince was commanding his army, half the size of the opposing side, without direction from his father the King.

At the start of the battle the English simulated flight to provoke a hasty charge by the French cavalry, who were instantly ensnared by the narrow funnel of Edward's archers. Their speeding mounts were targeted by the bowmen, realising equestrian armour was likely to be weaker at the sides, and they shot them in their flanks. Falling horses, inevitably, destroyed the cohesion of enemy lines. The English, however, confused by the carnage, panicked and prepared to abscond. Prince Edward rallied his terrified troops and ordered them to advance, wielding their swords, maces, spears and axes, towards the taunting Oriflamme.

The Dauphin (later to become Charles V of France) pressed an advance by his formidable fighting force but then the Prince's mobile army emerged from the woods and joined the combat, encircling the French. Almost five thousand elite French knights and men-at-arms were either killed or captured. King John, after a memorable resistance, yielded around midday and became England's most illustrious prisoner. King Edward was jubilant. His son's victory had transcended his own at Crecy. He had prevailed against all odds and inflicted this crushing defeat on the French through sheer command, indomitable courage and inspired leadership. The result was the highly favourable Treaty of Bretigny (1360) in which Edward's French territories, Aquitaine, Ponthieu and the newly won Calais, were secured while relinquishing Normandy, Anjou, Maine, Brittany and Flanders.[132] England had been raised to a new pinnacle of glory. According to Froissart: 'Solemnities were made in churches ... great fires and celebrations were held throughout the land.' The suitability of the Prince of Wales to inherit the English throne had been confirmed.

After his capture King John was brought as a hostage to England. John's huge ransom of three million gold crowns was never fully paid. He lived in luxury at John of Gaunt's Savoy Palace, the most magnificent residence in London. There is some suggestion, in view of this, that he preferred the comfort of captivity in his gilded cage rather than the burden of a troubled reign. The defeated King was often paraded in royal robes mounted on a splendid white charger, accompanied by the Black Prince who modestly bestrode a black palfrey (or hackney), as living proof that Edward III had broken the power of the French monarchy. Whittington would surely have at one time set eyes on King John, known as 'le Bon', when he was escorted, with due respect and courtesy, yet still a 'trophy of war', through the crowded streets of London.

Decline of Edward's Reign

After almost a quarter of a century fighting, King Edward III retired from the active military life. In warfare, there seemed little more at that time he could accomplish. He had recovered the coveted land his ancestors had held in France. Through successful overseas campaigning he had ensured that his kingdom could enjoy a period of 'domestic peace, national unity, strong government and foreign glory'.[133] He had won spectacular victories over the French and Scots. His eldest son, Prince Edward, had achieved astounding success. Now both John II, King of France and David II, King of Scotland, were his prisoners. England was indisputably 'the foremost military power in Western Europe'.[134]

Latterly, King Edward became a patron of art and architecture. He concentrated on building projects: the expansion of Windsor Castle, evidence of which remains, and the creation of Queenborough Castle, long since vanished, on the Isle of Sheppey. Minor innovations are amusing to rehearse: baths with running hot and cold water were installed in royal palaces and a mechanical clock, lacking a face but which chimed the hours, was constructed at Westminster Palace.[135] Hallmarks were introduced whereby Goldsmiths were required to identify their work and standard weights and measures were implemented in England. Moreover, Edward was the first English king to sit for his portrait and also the first English monarch whose handwriting has survived. (It appears as a signature on a letter to the Pope.)[136]

Edward III's most enduring achievement was the development of the two Houses of Parliament. Former sovereigns summoned only leading noblemen and churchmen to discuss major national issues but the Crown's increasing demands for money caused representatives of two distinct groups – the landowning knights of the shires and the wealthy merchants of the towns – to gather occasionally for consultations on finance. They were instructed to meet separately from the Assembly of Lords Spiritual and Temporal – the Painted Chamber of the Palace of Westminster or the Chapter House of Westminster Abbey – and they were not consulted on every matter of state. Crucially, however, they were permitted to appoint their own Speaker.[137] Edward's principle of encouraging popular representation and inviting commoners to his periodic consultations evolved into our modern Parliament with its dual House of Commons and House of Lords.[138] Although Edward welcomed the participation of London merchants at these assemblies, Whittington, throughout his life, avoided proffered knighthoods, politics in general and – apart from one occasion – Parliaments.[139]

Another remarkable aspect of Edward's reign was his encouragement of the London merchants. His government was constantly in debt. The King had made incessant demands for funds to finance his foreign campaigns. The interminable French wars had sapped the resources of foreign bankers. Heavy taxation and private loans became his limited options. During the last decade of his reign, the King turned for assistance to the Londoners. The citizens gave a guarded response at first because he was a notoriously bad debtor. The Mercers, perhaps more than any other City company, came to his rescue and made a tremendous number of collective loans to King Edward. And, since they dominated these royal business loans, their members became exceedingly wealthy. Whittington, an astute apprentice, would not have failed to notice this.[140]

King Edward III far outlived his purpose, strength and wisdom. The lands that had been ceded to him at the Treaty of Bretigny had been whittled away so that only Calais and its marches plus the Gascon coastal strip south of Bordeaux remained by the end of 1375.[141] Beset by international turmoil and domestic strife, he virtually retired from active public life. His public appearances were limited to token gestures, such as the Opening of Parliament. Government of the country fell largely to Edward's third son, John of Gaunt.

After burying seven of his children, Edward, a devoted family man, was further devastated, first by the death of his devoted wife, Queen Philippa in 1369, and then by his eldest son, Edward, Prince of Wales, in 1376. His last expeditions into France had resulted in disaster and disillusionment while his excess of cruelty towards his captives had tarnished his reputation for martial glory and Christian chivalry. Worn out by war, this 'chief flower of chivalry' died a heroic invalid at his Palace of Kennington.[142] Edward III's grandson, Richard of Bordeaux, now became the heir apparent and would be groomed for kingship.

After a glorious reign of over fifty years, Edward's health and strength declined. A lonely, isolated, senile figure, he ended his days shuffling between three palaces – Eltham, Havering and Sheen – shunning the company of anyone apart from his despised mistress, Alice Perrers, Lady Windsor, the 'evil enchantress'.[143] Around midsummer, 1377, the King, after suffering a series of strokes, slipped into oblivion at Sheen Palace, Surrey.[144] Alice surreptitiously slipped the rings from his cold fingers…

One of Edward's last acts had been to dub two young boys with his sword as they knelt before him prior to their admission to the chivalric Order of the

Garter on St George's Day: Richard of Bordeaux, son and heir of the late Prince of Wales, and Henry of Bolingbroke, son and heir of the powerful Prince John of Gaunt. On the next day, these two auburn-haired boys took their place, trailing their blue mantles embroidered with versions of the insignia, in the high stalls of the original chapel at Windsor Castle. The future rivalry of these cousins, who were both destined to rule England, would have a drastic impact on the life and career of the aspirant Mercer, Richard Whittington.

3

The Later Whittingtons

Three Brothers

When Sir William's eldest son, William Whittington VI, inherited Pauntley Manor, it was still encumbered with a fine relating to his father's outlawry. Presumably, he managed to raise funds to settle the debt claimed by the Vicar from Arrow because in time he became the new Lord of the Manor. He did not inherit the knighthood of his disgraced father but remained an esquire.

William represented Gloucestershire in the first Parliament of Richard II at Westminster in 1377. He married Catherine, sister and heir of John de Staunton.[145] This was an excellent match whereby the considerable estate at Staunton, near Hereford[146], was enveloped by the Whittington family. It must have proved welcome to both parties: the Stauntons, who lacked a male heir, were content that their estates passed into the hands of friends while the Whittingtons benefitted by a considerable extension of their modest holdings at Pauntley, three miles distant. He survived his wife but died intestate and, since the couple were childless, William's heir was deemed to be his younger brother, Robert, who acquired Pauntley, Staunton and Solers Hope upon William's death in 1399. It appears that he was already dealing with these combined estates during his elder brother's lifetime. This presents another unresolved mystery in the early history of the Whittingtons. Perhaps William suffered a disability, either in mind or body, which idea is supported by the fact that he left no will, had no children and held no permanent public office. The 'Calendar of Inquisition Post Mortem' (12 August 1399)[147] reveals that Pauntley was held by William de Whityngton of Roger Mortimer. Gentry did not necessarily own their lands but this connection is interesting because Mortimer, Third Earl of March, was Richard II's heir presumptive – and the King had by then developed a friendship with Richard Whittington. Had Richard a hand in the return of the estates to his family?

Already, certain lands owned by the Stauntons – a free warren at Staunton Manor and Hawkeshurne Park in Hawgrove – had been directly transferred to Robert by Richard II. But Robert was thwarted in his claim to the Manor of Berrow which lay a few miles to the north of Staunton. The land still forms part of a desirable district of woods and open spaces, dotted with small hills which is less intensely cultivated. When Simon de Berrow died in 1377, his son was still a minor, although there was an older sister, Margaret. The Prior of St Mary's Abbey, in Worcester, carried her off by force, married her and assumed the title Lord of the Manor. Margaret, quite possibly, had appealed to Robert but her case faltered and the duplicitous Prior remained triumphant.[148]

Robert had a distinguished civic career but his successes have been overshadowed by his younger brother, Richard. He declined the honour of knighthood by paying a fine, which enabled him to avoid the responsibility of military service.[149] He did, however, represent Gloucestershire in Parliament attending successive monarchs on five occasions. Among his prestigious appointments in the county were High Sheriff of Gloucestershire (1402-3; 1407-8; 1411-12), Escheator to the Crown (1392-4, 1401-2 and 1409-10), Knight of the Shire (1391), Commissioner of Array (1377, 1380, 1392, 1399), Collector of Taxes (1384) and Justice of the Peace (from 1382 onwards).[150] It was this latter role that caused him the most problems.

In the closing decades of the 14th century, Ralph Greyndour and his son, also called Ralph, dominated the bandit country west of the River Seven. Their large gang of roaming ruffians constantly harried Robert in his official duties and always managed to evade capture in the wide expanse of the Forest of Dean. Ralph junior and his kinsmen even plotted to kill Thomas de Berkeley of Berkeley Castle when he dared to hunt under the King's licence through their declared territory. When an attempt was made to bring the outlaws to justice, they were acquitted because of their enormous band of sympathisers. Robert Whittington J.P. was repeatedly thwarted in his determined attempt to check their murderous activities. At one point Ralph and his kinsmen stormed the courts and seized Richard Ailberton, who was in Robert's custody, and detained him until a ransom of one hundred pounds was paid to John Dene, an accomplice of Greyndour. Their ferocious activities, father and son, towards law-abiding foresters continued at least until the 1390s.[151]

Sollershope, Herefordshire

There is a strong tradition that Sir William Whittington just before his outlawry retreated for a few months to Sollershope and that he brought his wife, Joan, and youngest son, Richard, to live there in solitude. They would have passed along the track known as the 'Stone Road' that leads via Dymock and Much Marcle over the wooded hills to cross the border of the two shires. A gentle, pleasant ride, eight miles as the crow flies. It is easy to imagine the sounds of snorting horses, creaking saddles and clattering hooves that announced their arrival and alerted the servants to welcome their master at the secluded manor house in Herefordshire.

Sollershope, lying about nine miles south-east of Hereford, is an even more remote hamlet than Pauntley. It consists of a farm, a Court House and a 14th-century church, overshadowed on the east by the imposing Marcle Hill. The present Court House, with its exquisite magpie-timbered facade and ornate twisting chimneys, is essentially Elizabethan. Behind is a stone barn with a dovecote built into the south wall. The adjacent farm is alive with activity: tractors, dogs, sheep and horses. The picturesque group of buildings, reached at the end of a winding lane, now belies Lysons' dismissive description of Sollershope as 'an isolated and, to this day, uninviting estate'.

The manor of Hope, which lies in a secluded valley,[152] was owned in the turbulent 11th and 12th centuries by the de Solers, powerful knights who had supported Duke William of Normandy. When Simon de Solers (1215-1259) inherited Pauntley from his father in the mid-13th century, and his wife, Isobel de Stokes, inherited Hope from her mother, Solers Hope became united with Pauntley. When their distant cousin, Maud de Solers, married William Whittington III, Pauntley and Sollers Hope were absorbed by the Whittingtons into their own estates and thereafter the family divided their time between these manors.

Robert Whittington probably spent a great deal of his time at Sollershope. He assumed the patronage of the church and presented rectors to the living in 1387 and 1421. On the first occasion he was described as 'domicellus' (or 'heir apparent'), his elder brother being then still alive, but on the second as 'Lord of the Manor'. This confirms the view that he was regarded as head of the family even in William's lifetime. It is undeniable from the scant remains of the manor and its estate, however, that Sollershope was vastly inferior to the family's chief residence at Pauntley. And perhaps it is significant, too, that although Robert chose to be buried at Pauntley, he left funds in his will for the fabric of the churches at Pauntley and Staunton yet nothing to that of Sollershope.[153] The reason, it seems, is because he completely rebuilt the little Saxon church whilst in occupancy of Sollershope Manor, around 1390.

St Michael's Church, Sollershope, is a humble sandstone structure. It has a wide, solid porch, a wooden bellcote with louvred shutters and a shingled spire surmounted by a gilded weathercock. There are remains of a Medieval preaching cross, which now serves as a war memorial, where open air services took place during the Black Death.[154] The trim churchyard, studded by robust yews, is bounded by a rippling brook where snowdrops grow on its banks in early spring, crossed by a narrow wooden footbridge. The meadow beyond, where mares and their foals gambol, has never been ploughed and is known as 'Church Green'. Behind the church are the remains of a lofty mound, once enclosed by a moat, known as the 'Tump', which may have been the site of the original castle or keep of the de Solars family.[155]

The interior of the church is a trifle sombre with its bare stone walls. There is a drum-shaped Norman sandstone font, a fine 14th-century barrel-vaulted ceiling, an open double-sided 17th-century pulpit, exquisitely carved 20th-century musical angels on the choir stalls and salvaged stained glass patching the plain windows. (These mutilated fragments of glass in the south wall of the chancel appear to show the arms of Whittington quartered with Staunton.) Hidden treasure, casually propped up against the south wall of the choir, is a 13th-century sandstone sarcophagus lid engraved with the image of a knight in profile wearing complete chain mail, a scalloped surcoat, ball and spike spurs, a flat-topped pot helm and carrying a shield bearing the arms of the de Solers family. It is regarded as the earliest incised military effigy in Britain.

There is one startling anachronism. Victorian restorers peppered the choir floor with ceramic tiles bearing the arms of Richard Whittington and the City of London. They assumed that the famous Mayor, rather than his older brother, was the patron of this secluded church. Indeed, this fallacy is rehearsed in a document in the Harleain Manuscripts:

> Sir Richard Whytington, knight, was sherife of London ye 17 yeare of Richard II and Maior 20 and 21 yeares of ye same King's reign and ye 8 yeare of Henry IV. He founded Whyttington Colledge, builded Newgate, a great part of St Bartholomew's, ye East End of Guild Hall, the library of Grey Fryars. He builded ye church of Solers-Hope in Herefordshire where he was born.

After this catalogue of worthy causes, it is little wonder the chronicler misattributed the work on the church of Solers-Hope.

Robert's Will

Robert Whittington died just months after his younger brother, Richard. His will, dated 29 April 1423, was proved on 13 February 1424.[156] It lists his personal acquisitions and gives a rare glimpse of the sumptuous furnishings eventually acquired at Pauntley Court. It reveals the comfort and privacy enjoyed by the lesser gentry at the beginning of the fifteenth century. Robert asked for his body to be buried in the Church of St John the Evangelist, Pauntley. One hundred shillings were allotted for the chaplain there to pray for the souls of himself, his father and mother, his mother and father-in-law, John and Sybil Browning, for a period of one year. The actual solemnities should last for a week and every mourner attending his funeral was promised one penny. He left 6s 8d for Pauntley Church and 13s 4d for Staunton Church. Intriguingly, he bequeathed a further 3s 4d to Hereford Cathedral and 'four shillings besides for the penance enjoined upon me'.

Over his privileged lifetime Robert had amassed an impressive collection of silverware. He bequeathed to his wife, Margery, a silver cup with a cover engraved with the Whittington coat-of-arms, a cup of silver gilt also with a cover, a silver-gilt standing cup, four silver cups without covers, a dozen silver spoons, a silver salt cellar and a silver urn decorated with a face in profile. His surviving son, Guy, acquired a silver cup with the Whittington arms on its cover, a silver cup with the initials 'E & S' engraved on its cover, two more pieces of silver and another covered salt cellar. His daughter-in-law, Cicely, was presented with a charming silver cup whose cover was 'yngraved' with roses and eagles. His daughter, Isabel, who had married Robert ap Eynon, received a superb gift in memory of her father, a silver cup and cover with a finely engraved silver-gilt knop, plus ten marks besides.

Further bequests to close family and friends reveal Pauntley to have been amply and comfortably furnished. Generally, though, the emphasis was not upon robust furniture but sumptuous materials, which must surely have been sourced by Robert's merchant brother. The whole household was adorned with bright banners, painted panels, opulent cushion ('quishines') and woollen tapestries ('costers').[157] It was decorated with vibrant colours – red and white, black and green, blue and grey, checked, striped or plain – against the bare stone or plastered walls.

Lowliest members of the household sat for their meals on a pair of robust forms or trestle tables. These could be stored after their use as the servants began their domestic chores. Robert and his family occupied two permanent heavy carved tables with matching benches on a raised dais at one end of the long hall. They could savour their leisurely meals at the 'top table' while keeping a careful watch on members of the household whose tables were set at right angles to their own.[158] (This seating plan is retained at formal dinners today.)

There were two meat safes and a long chest for napery. Table linen, a true sign of affluence, included two delicate linen Parisian ('paris werk') tablecloths with four best towels and four plainer, everyday tablecloths, with four towels, and six napkins. Tableware included two pewter salt cellars, three brass candlesticks, three copper pots, a large chafing dish and a basin marked with the Whittington arms.

Robert's will mentions three beds.[159] At this time, the term 'bed' referred to the complete set of soft furnishings – mattress, bedclothes, curtains and canopy ('testor') – while the wooden frame that supported them was known as the 'bedstead'. The bedstead consisted of four low rails drilled with holes through which cords were threaded to form a framework for the mattress stuffed with horsehair or plaited rushes. A canopy was suspended from the rafters and from this impressive 'hung' bed, positioned against the wall, heavy curtains were draped on three sides, which, when drawn, ensured warmth and privacy for its occupiers. Bolsters and pillows were filled with feathers or down and perfumed with lavender. It would not have been surprising for all three beds to have been placed in the same chamber because they would have formed extra seating for business meetings during the daytime.

Robert's largest bed was covered with broad green and black striped cloth with three curtains hanging below tapestry pelmets. A second bed consisted of red worsted[160] 'embrowdyd' with white stags while a third, also of red worsted, was embroidered in black and complete with cornice, testor and curtains. Guy inherited this last magnificent bed, which was evidently the principal one because it was emblazoned with the family coat-of-arms. The heraldic themes in the bedroom, which doubled as a withdrawing room from the main hall, were intended to impress important visitors. All these beds were positioned where the occupiers would be warm and cosy beside the chimney breast, complete with 'rekkys' (rakes), 'fyerpykes' (pokers) and 'andyrys' (andirons) in the 'new chamber'. Robert's granddaughter (Isabel's daughter) received the majority of the household bedding and linen. She was fortunate to be presented with two horses, 'Cook' and 'Dor'[161] complete with their best saddles and bridles. Presumably these were working farm or riding horses rather than warhorses. Another relative, John ap Eynon, who may have been her brother-in-law, would probably have been less impressed by his small bequest of two cows. (Livestock often feature in countrymen's wills.)

Medieval country houses were basic and comprised one large, single room, open to the roof, known as the 'hall'. This gave shelter to both family and livestock at night, winter or rough weather. Here all the domestic activities – cooking, eating and sleeping – took place although in summer most work was carried on outdoors. The hall accommodated a substantial number of servants, from the bailiff of the estate down to the humble scullion in addition to the lord, his lady and their children.

During the reign of Edward III and his successor, Richard II, there was a steady rise in the standards of home comfort for the 'middle classes', as evidenced by Robert's will. Manor houses and merchant's dwellings acquired private bedrooms with plastered walls in place of crumbling fortresses where men and beasts lived and slept together on filthy earthen floors in draughty halls full of smoke and stink. At the beginning of the fifteenth century Pauntley Court had both a main hall and a separate bedchamber.

Furnishings remained fundamental. Domestic tables were trestles, canopied beds served as couches but floor carpets were absent. Robert paraded his wealth by following trends – painted wooden panelling and an abundance of tapestry – at Pauntley. As Lord of the Manor, Robert would have presided at important functions by sitting on that raised bench under his personal standard in his grand hall. Invariably, his silverware would have been overtly displayed on an open 'cup board' when Robert hosted a festive meal for his country neighbours. At night the polished silver would have glistened with the flickering glow of the rush lights, oil lamps, horn lanterns and tallow candles made from clarified mutton fat saved in the kitchen.

Originally, the hall lacked a chimney. The fire was placed on an open stone hearth in the middle of the rush-strewn earthen floor and the smoke was left to meander upwards through openings or louvres in the thatched roof, leaving the occupants to work and sleep in an unhealthy fug. Charred timber rafters in the ancient roof indicate that the hall was situated in the present west wing of Pauntley Court. This is now three bays long. Richard would have been familiar as a boy with this primitive hall although perhaps he would have have no firsthand knowledge of Robert's modern improvements. From the exterior there is now little indication of the antiquity of the building.

Robert was at the forefront of fashion by installing fireplaces with a shared chimney reaching from the hall to his chamber above.[162] This allowed a ceiling to be installed and a first floor added, which could be divided up into bays – or chambers – for the lord and his immediate family. For the first time they could enjoy the privilege of complete privacy by retiring into their private quarters free from the hustle and bustle of their household. It appears that extensions were made to the extant west wing, north and later east, so that the hall was converted into a substantial, comfortable dwelling.

Gradually, Pauntley developed into a grand complex. Apart from the family's private parlour or sitting room there would have been multiple service and store rooms consisting of stone and timber buildings arranged around a modest courtyard. The kitchen would have been a separate structure placed apart from the main house to reduce the risk of fire. The Manor, with its farm, outhouses and cottages, if not particularly prosperous, was virtually a self-sufficient community by the end of the 14th century. The Whittington's country residence would have become the administrative centre for the estate dealing with domestic affairs and business matters. Here would have been held all the official civic and legal meetings of the immediate locality; hence 'Pauntley Court'.[163]

Sir Guy Whittington

Robert Whittington married Margery Peresford who bore him two sons, William and Guy. They also had a daughter, Isabella, who married Robert ap Eynon, presumably a Welshman. William died without issue and Guy, his nephew, inherited the family estates. He made a brilliant marriage to Cicely (or 'Cecilia'), sister of Richard Browning and sole heir to a further three manors, Rodborough, Notgrove and Leigh (or 'Lye') in Gloucestershire. Apart from these estates, Guy also inherited Eldersfield, Birstmorton and Little Malvern in South Worcestershire and small parcels of land around Lypiatt, through his grandmother.[164] There was also property in Gloucester that remains unidentified. The couple married in 1405 and had seven sons and one daughter: the eldest was called Robert after his grandfather and the second son was named Richard after Guy's favourite uncle.

Sir Guy Whittington was an experienced soldier who commanded a company under Humphrey, Duke of Gloucester, at Agincourt in 1415. Following in his father's footsteps, he, too, pursued a civic career. He became High Sheriff of Gloucestershire in 1426/7 and 1432/3 and also High Sheriff of Herefordshire in 1423/4. When Sheriff, Guy incurred the censure of the church. One of his officers, Thomas Solers, perhaps a relative, arrested a priest during the celebration of Mass at Gloucester Cathedral. After due apologies and a suitable donation to ecclesiastical funds, this transgression was tactfully forgotten.[165]

The empire of manors that Guy eventually held is impressive: Pauntley, Solers Hope, Staunton, Upton, Lypiatt, Rodborough, Notgrove, Leigh, Harford and Staveton. But his heart was at Pauntley. When he died in 1440, he was buried, according to his wishes, in the 'new chapel' dedicated to Saint George – the patron who had watched over him in battle – at St John the Evangelist's Church. Guy built the chantry, which from the exterior is obviously an appendage to the tiny church, about 1430. A priest was employed to attend daily, 'praying for the founder's ... and all christen sowlez'.

Inside, there are a few interesting features including two small plain brass memorials to Elizabeth Pole (died 1543) and William Pauncefoote (died 1616). Elizabeth was one of six daughters and sixth coheiress of Thomas Whittington who died in 1543. Pevsner[166] notes 'an impressive architectural monument of grey, black and white marble' commemorating two gentlewomen, Anne Somerset (died 1764) and her sister Anna Brickendine (died 1770). Henry Somerset (died 1708) was the last Somerset to be Lord of the Manor of Pauntley.

Guy's eldest son, Robert, became a soldier like his father. He served in the protracted campaign in France where he died, probably of fever, in 1437. He married Elizabeth, daughter of Baldwin Rowse, and the couple produced three sons, Robert, William and Guy. Today, the line of Whittingtons descends from Robert's youngest son, Guy, including Michael Whittington, chronicler of the family history.[167]

Guy's Will

Guy Whittington made his will on 21 April 1440. This would have been taken to London by one of his executors to be proved at the prerogative Court of Canterbury in Doctors' Common. After a grant of probate was obtained on 12 June, a fair copy was then made and transferred into a register of wills that was held for security in the City. Will registers were mighty tomes with parchment pages of sheep or goatskin and oaken board covers. Unfortunately, this surviving copy is greatly damaged, which means that most of Guy's personal bequests are difficult to discern.[168]

Guy Whittington, 'knight, of sound mind', left instructions and bequests which, as might be expected, betrayed a certain military preoccupation. He appointed his wife, Cecilia (or Cecily) and his oldest surviving son, Richard, his chief executors. He instructed his body to be buried in 'the new chapel of the Blessed George of Pawnteley'. He left bequests to Hereford Cathedral (13s 4d) and country churches including Pauntley (20s), Staunton (20s) and Hope Sollers (6s 8d). His eldest son, Robert, had predeceased him while fighting in France, and therefore the several bequests fell to his remaining sons.

The few bequests that can be deciphered include one hundred marks to his daughter, Margery, upon her marriage; six oxen and seven cows at Staunton and his flock of sheep at Pauntley to his wife, Cecily; and a rich red cloak to his son, Richard. Three sons Thomas, Guy and William received sumptuous beds with various accoutrements. Silverware was similarly distributed among family and friends including a gilded goblet to Cecily, a silver goblet bearing the family coat-of-arms to Richard, and a goblet decorated with roses to a neighbour, John Cassy.[169]

More interestingly, Guy distributed his armour among his sons. Richard was bequeathed his father's principal suit of armour that had been left purposely in 'John Picheford's official keeping'. Thomas acquired a coveted item: 'a hauberk called a gesserant'. Jeserants were magnificent mail coats padded with fabrics over which was worn a colourful robe made of silk brocade.[170] Armour was custom-made and extremely expensive; consequently it was a common occurrence for certain pieces to be handed down, especially from father to son, in English wills. Guy's armour would have seen distinguished service at Agincourt.[171]

Cecily lived on until 1452. She was buried beside her husband although not a trace of their tomb remains. Her will (13 October 1452) mentions several interesting items: 'one pair of trussyng coffres, one pair of lesser trussying coffres, a red chest, a pair of cophardis (cupboards), a tourne with le hechell (spinning wheel)'. Obviously, Pauntley was expanding, although the Medieval hangings might have become a little tired.[172]

Whittington Town Houses in Gloucester

Richard and Robert Whittington, along with three gentlemen – Thomas Kemell, Richard Kemell and Robert Mattesdon – later owned land and tenements in Gloucester. This is confirmed by damaged documents held at Gloucester Cathedral Library. The relevant deed is dated 'Monday before the feast of St Gregory, Pope, in the reign of Henry V' (although the regnal year is illegible). It is so badly worn that neither the location of the properties nor the names of the witnesses can be deciphered: John [illegible] and [illegible]) Blake, both 'militibus' (knights), Robert Gylbert plus two other illegible signatories. The grant, which was made by John Girold (or 'Garold') of Mettesdon (Matson) is warranted in perpetuity.[173]

It is known that the later Whittingtons owned a town house in Gloucester. According to Robert Cole's 'Rental', 1455: 'The prior of Lanthony holds all those houses and buildings with their appurtenances in the aforementioned lane, called Abbey Lane, up to the common highway adjoining the chancel of the Church of St Nicholas, and also the tenements of Richard Whitynton, Lord of Staunton, which are called Rotten Row and Ashwell's Place.'[174] This property would have been most convenient for business purposes and for avoiding the long trek home into open countryside in inclement weather to Pauntley Court.

The Whittington's house stood at the lower end of the steep hill, Westgate Street, leading to the River Severn. It was adjacent to the church of Saint Nicholas. Constructed of white sandstone, this splendid church, dedicated to the patron of sailors, dockers, fishermen and merchants, was built in the 12th century, enlarged in the 13th century and improved with a magnificent west tower in the early 15th century. This tower, which leans alarmingly, is surmounted by a graceful spire. Originally, it was twice its present height but it was truncated when it was deemed unstable after a direct hit from a royalist cannon during the Siege of Gloucester in 1643.

The 15th-century townhouse was built by Richard Whittington, the great-nephew of London's famous Mayor. Originally known as 'St Nicholas' House', the Whittingtons entertained their important guests there after they had arrived by river and entered the city by the West Gate (since demolished). The house received a substantial makeover in the early 18th century when a symmetrical rich red brick facade was added. Today, the building is most impressive with its stone rustication, sash windows, arched pediment, dentil cornicing and decorative stone urns on the balustraded parapet.

Queen Elizabeth I is supposed to have stayed there overnight during a tour of Gloucestershire in 1574. A spectacular carved wooden fireplace, featuring the lion and unicorn supporting the royal coat-of-arms, once adorned the main panelled room on the first floor. Unfortunately, both the panelling and the fireplace were exported to Chicago in 1907. (They were acquired to grace the walls of a high-class brothel.) A late 16th-century dado with a primitive design of fruit, flowers and foliage, hailed as 'a rare and significant survival', still decorates a first-floor back parlour in this historic property, 100 Westgate Street.

The building boasts an interesting history with a rich variety of owners. In the early 17th century, it was leased to John Taylor, a dubious character who, despite being imprisoned for embezzlement, became Mayor of Gloucester. In the 19th century, the house became a non-conformist chapel; in the 20th century it was converted into a leather factory. After reverting to a private dwelling, it was more recently turned into a public house, called, inevitably, 'The Dick Whittington'. The rambling interior retains its historic atmosphere with high ceilings, authentic beams, wide sweeping staircase and frosted glass panels in the Victorian saloon bar. The narrow coachway, squeezed in between the church and the pub, reveals the Medieval facade with jettied plastered walls and stout exposed timbers resting on a stone foundation. And the pub boasts a ghost, a servant girl who contracted the plague and was condemned to die, miserable and alone, confined to the cellar.

Great excitement was generated when workmen unearthed an ancient limestone tablet in the cellars of a private house, 34 Westgate Street, in 1862.[175] The surviving fragment of a longer frieze is in two sections and may have been intended as an ornament over a door or chimney. It presents a chubby, barefoot youth with curly locks, wearing a rippling cloak with its hood around his shoulders, fastened with a button. The lad is cradling a small animal that resembles a cat. The house above had belonged to a certain Mr Bonner, cabinet maker, but was later occupied by a Mr Compton, upholsterer, in Westgate Street.

Rev. Samuel Lysons, upon examination, immediately assumed that the figure of the boy represented Dick Whittington.[176] After acquiring it, he was thrilled when the panel was authenticated by scholars and antiquarians who assured him that it had been carved in the 15th century by an anonymous Italian sculptor.[178] Reverently, he presented it to London's Guildhall Museum, where it was prominently displayed. Unfortunately, Lysons in his excitement had mistaken which house the Whittingtons had owned.[179]

A reputable author, H.B. Wheatley, who later edited Pepys' diaries, viewed the sculpture with strong suspicion in 1885. And when a team of experts examined the bas-relief in 1920, they considered it to be a perfectly respectable Roman carving of a shepherd boy holding a lamb, and discreetly returned it to Gloucester Folk Museum. There, it is now displayed merely as a curiosity. A further speculation might be that it did, indeed, come from the Whittingtons' town house but was discarded when the Elizabethan fireplace was installed. In either event, it predates Richard Whittingtons' actual departure for London...

THE REIGN OF
RICHARD II

4

London Fashion

RICHARD II came to the English throne as a mere youth with insufficient training or experience of leadership. Although, laudably, he pursued a policy of peace, particularly with neighbouring France, his own country was blighted by internal strife in every quarter of his realm. The high levels of taxation and enforced loans imposed upon his subjects funded his own frivolous lifestyle.

King Richard, 'consumed with burning ambition and insatiable vanity',[1] was intent on developing an autocratic government. His perception of his divine appointment found expression in an array of bizarre and extravagant clothes. He was the first Medieval king to create a sequence of dazzling costumes to proclaim his unique power, position and privilege. Dismissed as 'a monarch so fond of tinsel and display',[2] he surrounded himself with a circle of courtiers who were themselves tempted to spend vast fortunes on their own attire, purely as an expression of their own vanity.

This colourful period of high fashion at the English court coincided with the early career of Richard Whittington as a London Mercer. His intention was to pander to the upper classes by supplying them with superior fabrics: damasks, velvets and cloth-of-gold. This brought him to the attention of the royal household and inevitably to the foppish King himself. Their acquaintance, it would appear, developed into a close friendship.

For a time the lives of the two Richards, contrasting in character and ideals, became entwined: the mercurial monarch and the ambitious Mercer. At first, their association reaped rich rewards for Whittington who was honoured by being made Mayor of London. But even this connection came at a price and as Richard Whittington's career soared, King Richard's reign careered inexorably towards disaster. His sovereignty was challenged and he was ruthlessly deposed.

Whittington was to experience firsthand how spectacular pageantry overlaid dark treachery at the royal court.

Richard II

Richard II was the grandson of Edward III and Philippa of Hainault and the younger son of Edward of Woodstock, the 'Black Prince'. This true 'flower of English knighthood' married his cousin, Joan, daughter of Edmund Woodstock, Earl of Kent, who because of her famed beauty was known as 'The Fair Maid of Kent'. The couple lived in extravagant style in Aquitaine where they brought up their two sons, Edward, born in 1365, and Richard, in 1367. Richard was born at Epiphany (6 January) in Bordeaux, which was then the capital of the English Duchy of Aquitaine and was consequently known as 'Richard of Bordeaux'. Little is recorded of his childhood except that he was provided with a personal 'rocker' for his cradle and that his wet nurse, Mundina, married his tailor, Walter Raufe[3] and that his companions foolishly played games with him using dice loaded in his favour so that he 'did alwayes winne when hee cast them'.[4]

When his brother Edward died prematurely in 1371, Prince Richard was catapulted into prominence as the Black Prince's surviving heir. Immediately, he was brought over to live in England. His father, Prince Edward, also died in 1376 and he was buried in the Trinity Chapel adjacent to the Shrine of St Thomas the Martyr at Canterbury Cathedral. There his marble tomb is surmounted by a gilded effigy that depicts him lying in battle armour, his hands encased in gauntlets clasped across his breast in fervent prayer. His achievements – armorial jupon, poplar shield, empty scabbard, spiked gauntlets and crested helm (formed of a leopard with an impossibly long tail) – are preserved in a nearby display case at the bottom of the Pilgrims' Steps in the South Choir Aisle.[5] Richard's grandfather, King Edward III, expired the following year. These deaths made Richard, while still a minor, the rightful King of England.

Richard's coronation took place on 16 July 1377 at Westminster Abbey. This momentous event, which involved spectacular pageantry, would have been a tremendous ordeal for the nine-year-old boy. Prior to the religious solemnities, Richard, dressed in white to convey innocence, riding a stallion but led by a knight, was paraded through the City streets from the Tower, along Cheapside, Fleet Street and the Strand to Westminster Palace. He was escorted by the Knights of the Bath, who were, by tradition, the close companions of the monarch. The next day, Richard, wearing white robes and red shoes, trotted down the scarlet cloth laid down for him along the short path from Westminster Palace to the Abbey. Dukes, Lords and Earls preceded him with the emblems of sovereignty: the sword of state, gilt spurs and a sceptre surmounted by a dove.

Richard was crowned by Simon Sudbury, Archbishop of Canterbury, and when seated upon the coronation chair, the Barons of the Cinque Ports held high over him a canopy of pure silk supported by four silver staves ornamented with silver bells.[6] Exhausted by these tedious ceremonies, the pampered boy was carried back to his Palace on the shoulders of his favourite tutor, Sir Simon Burley. On the way he lost one of his jewelled red slippers – a pair that had belonged to Saint Edmund which formed part of the coronation regalia – among the excited pressing crowds.[7] If this was interpreted by superstitious folk as an ill omen it was soon forgotten in the excitement of welcoming a new king. From the first, the citizens took this second son of their admired Black Prince to their hearts, dazzled by his youth, feminine grace, perfect poise and quiet composure. Immediately, Richard II was hailed as 'The Londoner's King'. It wouldn't last:

> At this lord's coronation, three symbols of royalty had foretold three misfortunes which would befall him: firstly, during the procession he lost one of the coronation shoes, so that to begin with the common people rose up against him, and for the rest of his life hated him; secondly, one of his golden spurs fell off, so that next the knights rose up and rebelled against him; thirdly, during the banquet a sudden gust of wind blew the crown from his head, so that thirdly and finally he was deposed from his kingdom and replaced by King Henry. (Chronicle of Adam of Usk)

Though admittedly the Welsh chronicler was ever hostile to King Richard II.

A Shop – Perhaps

Whittington, meanwhile, had completed his apprenticeship. He would have been required to swear an oath of loyalty to the King and to the City and its governance before the Mayor and Alderman at the Guildhall. Further, he was expected to show evidence that he was a man of good reputation and capable of earning his living in his chosen trade, mercery. Only then would he be acknowledged as a 'Freeman of the City of London'.[8] (The unenfranchised were termed 'foreigners', even though they might have been born in England, whereas those born overseas, unless they had been naturalised, were deemed 'aliens'.) Afterwards, Whittington would be assessed for national taxation and public duty. For a freeman, he soon learned, there were both privileges and obligations.

Whittington's next step would be to acquire a shop where he could display his wares and attract possible customers. There is no evidence that he actually owned a shop in the City but it is worthwhile speculating. The most likely area where he sought suitable premises would be in the Mercery, located on the south side of West Cheap (which distinguished it from East Cheap), later known simply as 'Cheapside'. As mentioned earlier, the name originates from the Old English word, 'chepe', meaning a market, from which is derived the term for an inexpensive purchase, 'cheap', and also a street vendor with knockdown prices, a 'cheapjack'. This was a vibrant commercial centre where the Mercers clustered together, separated from nearby Goldsmiths, Drapers, Cutlers, Saddlers and Pepperers.[9] For centuries, this was the most desirable location providing the opportunity for citizens and traders to live and work in harmony in the City. In Medieval times, the area resembled a country market but later it became a fashionable shopping centre equivalent to London's West End.

This wide, bustling street was lined with rows of shops, huddled together, vying for space and competing for custom. The smaller shops, wedged into tight corners or packed between rival stores, measured as little as five or six feet by ten. Larger ones that commanded attention from the street took up perhaps ten or twelve feet with a depth of about twenty. There might even be a separate place for their owner to work but the majority only had one separate living room with maybe a top floor and attic.[10] Stow notes that these rows of narrow, lofty buildings were 'formerly sheds or shops with solars above them... but these sheds are now largely builded on both sides outward and upwards, some three, four or five stories high.'

At the rear were larger covered markets called 'selds', containing a number of selling stations, identified by their decorative signs, where mercers traded from chests, cupboards and collapsible stalls. Behind, beyond and above these overcrowded shops and selds were warehouses, workshops, dwellings and gardens. The 'Broad' or 'Painted' Seld was the grandest in the Mercery, owned in the late 13th century by Walter le Brun, probably a mercer, who, with his wife, Rose, founded St Mary Spital, Bishopsgate.

Whittington, always alert to business opportunities, will have taken pride in displaying his wares to the public and in paying his first customers his personal attention. His newly acquired stock of materials may have been supplied by an anonymous sponsor or a silent partner in return for a share of the profits. While serving his apprenticeship, he would have developed a trained eye for the intrinsic beauty of the colour and texture of cloth, the smoothness and sheen of fine fur and the splendour of woven, striped or patterned fabrics. Drab colours and coarse cloths were associated with poverty and servitude. The customers he targeted were those with taste and discernment, and a sense of their own grandeur, the hallmarks of the gentry. At this, he was phenomenally successful for he rapidly made his mark as a merchant providing exquisite fabrics – silk, linen, fustian, worsted, velvet, damask and, most particularly, cloth-of-gold – to the royal household.[11]

What is certain is that two years after Richard II came to the throne, Whittington, as a Freeman of London, was required to contribute five marks towards the defence of the City. Indeed, 1379 marks the first instance of Whittington's name appearing in the City Letter Books. This was the lowest assessment, which he shared with a large proportion of the ordinary citizens.[12] Ten years later his contribution had doubled. The amount would be payable to the Chamberlain acting as the City's Treasurer. These two figures are positive indications of Whittington's rise in wealth and stature.[13]

Between the two dates a second devastating national event was played out in Whittington's lifetime.

The Peasants' Revolt

Richard II came to the throne at an explosive time when his subjects expressed their numerous grievances that had been brewing over several decades. Their resentment against authority focused upon the servile manorial system introduced by William the Conqueror. Peasants – 'serfs' and 'villeins' – were compelled to work for the Lord of the Manor without access to rights or representation in Parliament. Serfs[14] worked for their Lord in return for his protection and a plot of land to cultivate. Villeins, who were of slightly higher status, rented humble homes, with or without land, from their Lord who, as part of the contract, compelled them to perform agricultural tasks – harrowing, haymaking and harvesting – at certain seasons each year. Serfdom generally involved performing menial tasks for an overlord – tilling his land, grinding his corn, baking his bread and brewing his beer – in return for little reward and a total absence of prospects for self improvement. Recipes, every one, for resentment. Many dreamed of becoming freemen.

The Black Death had irrevocably overturned traditional modes of employment and changed the pattern of country life. There was a massive fall in population which had resulted in the scarcity of cheap labour nationwide. Consequently, the demand for labourers increased and workmen realised for the first time their true value in terms of wages and conditions. Parliament, in desperation, attempted to control spiralling costs by introducing a series of harsh labour laws – the Ordinance of Laborers (1349), Statute of Labourers (1351) and a later Statute of Labourers (1388) – in an effort to restrict both the increase in wages and the relocation of workers. 'No labourer,' decreed this last draconian statute, 'was allowed to be taught a craft if required to serve at the plough or on the land.' These measures merely escalated a recession in the country's already fragile economy.[15]

The Peasants' Revolt which followed was the greatest and most serious national uprising in the Middle Ages. Although, inevitably, it was a tragic failure, it resulted in the gradual abolition of serfdom and the introduction of basic rights to protect the labouring classes.

England's peasant population were stirred into action by priests and poets. William Langland (*c.*1332-1400) penned a portrait of his age in his allegorical poem, 'Piers Plowman'. The scholarly poet, who was born at Ledbury beside the Malvern Hills, was a near neighbour of the Whittingtons. He presented the stark contrast between the wealth of the rich overlord and the dire poverty of the peasant toiling in the fields. Langland celebrates labourers as good and honourable. His controversial poem, consistently revised, helped to rouse the peasants to rebellion, encouraging them to fight for their basic rights.

Langland's themes were echoed by the Oxford scholar, John Wyclif (1324-1384) who further inflamed the minds of the common people with revolutionary notions of equality. His disciples were known as 'Lollards' (probably derived from the Dutch word 'lollen' meaning 'to mumble' prayers). Richard II was an orthodox churchman yet he tended to tolerate this bluff, learned Yorkshireman because many influential courtiers and relatives – his mother, Princess Joan, and his uncle, John of Gaunt – were impressed by his simple philosophy.

Another radical priest from Kent, John Ball, travelled around the country, whipping up the disgruntled peasants into vociferous discontent. He preached incendiary sermons on equality and posed the rhetorical question:

When Adam delved and Eve span,
Who was then the gentleman?

The time was ripe for rebellion in Southern England.

The catalyst for the outbreak of popular unrest, however, was the series of crippling poll taxes – 1377, 1379 and 1380 – introduced ostensibly to finance military campaigns in France. That third poll tax, which followed immediately upon the conventional levy of tenths and fifteenths according to possessions and property, was bitterly resented across the entire country. Rather than being sensibly graded according to means and status, these taxes were levied upon every male, from lord to labourer, indiscriminate of wealth or circumstances, at one flat rate. And that rate trebled from an initial one groat to three groats (one shilling) per head, which was a 'manifestly unfair and inequitable imposition'. The peasants, supported by some of their superiors, responded with insurrection. Moreover, these militant tax evaders were joined by disillusioned veteran soldiers who were left wandering aimlessly around the countryside after the recent failure of the French wars.

In the summer of 1381, two rebel factions pitched their camps on the outskirts of London. Peasants from Kent assembled under the leadership of Wat Tyler of Maidstone – this soldier-cum-brigand was by trade a 'tyler of roofs' – at Blackheath while those from Essex rallied to fight with their champion, Jack Staw, at Stepney. Apparently, this was not a spontaneous uprising by angry dissidents but a highly organised and well coordinated rebellion supported by responsible members of the community – reeves, bailiffs, jurors, constables.[16] Clearly, this was not a rebellion restricted to the poor and downtrodden but also involved the more ambitious and assertive in society.[17] They targeted John of Gaunt (Regent), Archbishop Sudbury (Chancellor),[18] Robert Belknap (Chief Justice) and Sir Robert Hales (Lord Treasurer) who were responsible for the introduction of the hated poll tax. These corrupt agents, they believed, were preying on the inexperience of their King. The combined force of 60,000 men marched peacefully from north and south upon the City, now 'shadowed in a troubled sleep'. There they were joined by more insurgents, intending to appeal for justice directly to their young sovereign. Their resounding cry: 'For Kynge Richarde and the Trew Communes'.

Richard II was in deadly peril. He was removed for safety from Windsor Castle to the Tower of London. Yet while his councillors deliberated the situation, which was completely out of control, the teenage King took action.[19] He commanded the royal barge to escort him at dawn along the River Thames towards Greenwich where he attempted to address the rebels from Kent. They responded by hurling missiles from the banks and the conference was abandoned. The King had shown resolution and resourcefulness, but he was forced to return to the Tower where he sought further advice from his experienced councillors. Meanwhile, the rebels crossed London Bridge and broke through the gates of the City.

The authorities were ill prepared for armed resistance as the rebels went on the rampage. They burned down the Savoy Palace, the riverside mansion of the haughty, autocratic magnet, John of Gaunt, after quaffing his wine and casting his silver into the river, where his son, Henry, another target of the rebels, had been hiding from the frenzy. Prince John, First Duke of Lancaster, the fourth son of Edward III, was blamed for the recent lack of military success and it was rumoured that he had embezzled sums intended for the French wars. Robustly supported by the Londoners, the mob set then fire to Highbury Manor, Sir Robert Hales' magnificent house, and, since he was also the Prior, attacked the Hospitallers' Priory of St John of Jerusalem at Clerkenwell. Next, they destroyed the despised legal documents at the Inns of Temple before turning their attention to the prisons – Marshalsea, Westminster, Newgate and Fleet – where they killed the guards and released the prisoners, who joined their bloody revolution. Even the bawdy house of William Walworth, Mayor of London, was razed in Southwark. Their most brutal act was the arbitrary slaughter of Lombards and Flemings whom they despised as foreign bankers, merchants and moneylenders.

Inside the Tower, King Richard's councillors and courtiers were paralysed with fear as the violence escalated. London apprentices now joined the fanatical rabble and surrounded the fortress. The King displayed exceptional fortitude after his abortive attempt at appeasement by riding out the following day to confront the Essex peasants at 'Mileend'. There, the renegades, after pledging their allegiance to the King, presented a petition that effectively demanded the abolition of serfdom. The King heartily agreed to every request and the mob – for a time – disbanded.

During this confrontation a group of rebels stormed the Tower. They entered the Great Wardrobe where they insulted Princess Joan, who had interrupted her pilgrimage to Canterbury and raced to be at her son's side in her speedy 'whirligig'. They dragged Archbishop Sudbury[20] and Treasurer Hales into the streets and beheaded them on Tower Hill. Innocent victims included a Franciscan Friar, who was John of Gaunt's physician, and the Grand Prior of the Hospital of St John.

Once more, the King took the initiative. The next day (15 June), he rode out with a train of nobles, citizens and men-at-arms to encounter the Kent rebels at Smithfield. This area was normally the scene of horse fairs and cattle markets, games and tournaments. Before leaving, he took the sacrament as a precaution. The rebels made further impossible demands, including the abolition of lordship beyond that of the sovereign, the confiscation of the extensive ecclesiastical estates, the expulsion of all high clerical positions, apart from a single Bishop. Predictably, the King acquiesced to all these terms but this time the peasants did not disperse quietly.

Tyler, the rebel leader, behaved belligerently, wielded his dagger and insulted the King. Incensed, Sir William Walworth, Mayor, who wisely wore a mail shirt under his cloak, reacted by pulling Tyler from his pony and attacking him with his own dagger. At the same time, Sir Ralph de Standish pierced him with his sword. Tyler staggered and fell wounded as the crowd surged forward, demanding vengeance. The King, rashly but heroically, spurred his horse and confronted the rebels. In a moment of high drama, although sensing their dangerous mood, he made a solemn promise: 'You shall have no captain but me!' Everyone would be pardoned if they dispersed peacefully to their homes, he declared. The mob was duped by his spirited performance and false promises. The volatile situation was temporarily defused.

King Richard II's impulsive behaviour, regarded at that moment as courageous, increased throughout his long and turbulent reign...

The King knighted Mayor Walworth for his gallantry. This was a rare honour and still rarer for not being bestowed for deeds on the battlefield. Indeed, there was not a single Alderman, not even Whittington, who was knighted in the fifty-year period following the Peasant's Revolt. Walworth was a leading member of the powerful Fishmongers' Company.[21] (The Church allocated 'fissche-dayes' and 'flesche-dayes' which were strictly adhered to by Londoners.) His dramatic statue, carved in yew by Edward Pierce in 1684, graces Fishmongers' Hall at the approach to London Bridge. At the base of this statue is the inscription:

Brave Walworth, knight, Lord Mayor, he slew
Rebellious Tyler in his alarmes.
The King, therefore, did give in lieu
The dagger to the Cityes Armes.

The dagger (or 'basilarde') is displayed in an illuminated presentation case in the vestibule with this confident assertion: 'With this dagger Sir William Walworth Lord Mayor of London Citizen and Fishmonger slew the rebel Wat Tyler in Smithfield, reign Richard II.'

Alas, the dagger, a prized possession of the Fishmongers' Company, has since been declared by armoury experts to be a composite. The hilt derives from a parrying dagger dating from either the late 16th or early 17th century. It would have been held in the left hand in tandem with a long-bladed rapier when engaged in combat. (A large oval ring protected the hand and could be used to engage the opponent's blade.) The dagger's blade also dates from the 17th century.[22]

Mayor Walworth had slipped away while the rebels were distracted by the action of the King and hesitant after the death of their leader. He activated the City militia, which surrounded the unsuspecting peasants at St John's Fields. This reserve force pursued, captured and executed the leaders, including John Ball and Jack Straw. After the collapse of the revolt, the King's concessions were revoked and his pardons were repudiated. Surprisingly, although the great officers of state – the Primate, Treasurer, Chancellor and Chief Justice – had all been eliminated, his justice was tempered with mercy. The London revolt was effectively terminated.[23]

There is a misapprehension that Wat Tyler's dagger features in the City arms. The shield of the City of London features the red cross of Saint George on a white background. In the uppermost canton (top left quarter) is a drawn sword. There is a common belief that this represents the dagger that slew Tyler. This is refuted by the College of Arms. It is an incontestable fact that the design of the City arms predates the rebellion by two months. The sword depicted, therefore, probably represents the one that beheaded Saint Paul in Rome. (St Paul is the patron and protector of London.) Incidentally, the City of London arms were only officially confirmed in 1957.

Whittington could not have failed to have been witness to the unfolding crisis from behind the barricades of his shop in Cheapside. Always an observer rather than a participant, he would still have been disturbed by firsthand accounts of the violent clashes among angry demonstrators in the streets. The bitter hostility during this time of anarchy and strife was a world away from the peaceful hamlet in Gloucestershire. He would have absorbed tales of Mayor Walworth's impulsive action in the bitter affray, which would temper his own behaviour when he was elevated to that high civic office. He would have noted that the main target of the dissidents was the financiers, which just may have affected how he apportioned his own amassed wealth. And he would have registered the courage, guile and subsequent treachery of his new sovereign, who was destined to become a close confidant and valued customer.[24]

City Guilds

Whittington completed his apprenticeship, gained his Freedom and entered into business when the Mercers were still technically a City Guild. The Guild system, formed for the protection of certain crafts and trades, is supposed to have existed even before the Norman Conquest. Certainly, by Medieval times, this had become an organisation of immense significance for the whole fabric of society. London Guilds or 'Mysteries' multiplied as the commercial and industrial importance of the City developed. Further, they tended to become exclusive[25] with the increasing incentive for fostering trade and industry in the rapidly expanding capital. Brethren of fraternities assembled regularly for the purpose of controlling trade, regulating prices, recovering debt and, optimistically, gaining wider powers from the Crown. Regrettably, there was intense rivalry between the various Guilds that sometimes erupted into violence. For instance, there was a particular rancour between the Goldsmiths and the Pepperers. The Fishmongers quarrelled constantly not only with rival Guilds but also among themselves. In general, though, the Guild system, traditional but unofficial, worked effectively with business in the City divided fairly among them.

There is no record extant of when Whittington was accepted as one of the brethren of the Mercers' Guild. Although as a prospective businessman he would have had little choice of membership of this fraternity, there were obvious benefits from belonging to a Guild. Their declared aim was to combine the strict regulation of work with parish duties and religious observances. Moreover, a brother was convinced that he belonged to a community of both the living and dead: consequently, the welfare of his soul would be cared for both in this world and in the afterlife. A common obligation of a City Guild was to attend Mass on the day of the patronal festival and the funeral of one of his fraternity. There was a strong social awareness which ensured that benefits were often paid to ailing or elderly members. And there was a strong bond between tradesmen, which meant that they would generate work strictly among themselves, while their officials offered to adjudicate in matters of dispute between brothers, thus saving the expense of a lawsuit.[26]

The City Merchant

Richard II's reign was characterised by a positive period of 'opportunity, competition and experiment' in England.[27] Whittington, swept along by this surge of speculation, progressed at some point from being a tentative novice shop keeper to an established London merchant. Indisputably, he would then have joined the dominant class in the City. 'To be a merchant', proclaims Thrupp, 'was to be known, wherever one went, as belonging to a group with a distinctive economical position, referring to the conduct of wholesale trade, and with a distinctive political position, that of controlling government.' Generally, though, Medieval merchants did not aspire to a political career. Rather, they sought tangible rewards in the form of business from wealthy citizens, military contracts and civic appointments that promised social advancement.

Whittington was assisted in his steady rise to success in commerce by the statute that decreed foreign merchants could only sell on a wholesale basis in London. Wholesalers bought and sold in bulk. They would have been importers or manufacturers. Their greatest concern was for rival companies that might undercut them. City merchants, alone, could buy and sell wholesale goods and, if they chose, keep retail shops. Retailers, as shopkeepers, were free to set their own prices: should they favour a regular customer they might reduce their price or, conversely, if they were certain of a wealthy customer, they could increase it. Effectively, this cancelled out competition from foreign traders. Whittington became one of the Medieval 'men of mixed enterprise' because throughout his life he combined a number of business interests: Mercer, banker, wool merchant.

King Richard abolished the monopoly of the victualling trades, allowing free trade in flesh, fish, corn and food, including spices, fruit and all sorts of 'small merceries' such as gold, silver and silk thread, fur and headwear. 'Great merceries' – velvet, damask, silk, linen and cloth-of-gold – continued, like wine, to be reserved for sale by 'strangers' strictly as wholesale. Certainly, the custom of London affirmed the right of every citizen to buy and sell wholesale whichever commodities he pleased – wine, wool, cloth, fruit and fish – and, since their demand was universal, anyone whose credit was good was free to experiment.

For a time, the Mercers retained a virtual monopoly in textiles in the City of London. Whittington mirrored the trend of the majority of Medieval Mercers who progressed from the retail of small goods to dealing with wool and cloth until they finally gained control over the sale of luxury fabrics. This monopoly had completely ceased in the reign of Queen Elizabeth I, by which time Mercers were unable to supply luxury fabrics to Her Majesty. When Queen Bess wrote to enquire why silk had become expensive she received an evasive reply because at that time not a single member of the Company traded in that commodity. By the Elizabethan age, the Mercers' Company had become preoccupied with the management of charitable trusts and extensive property put into to its care by benefactors, most notably Richard Whittington.

Anne of Bohemia

Richard II, young, personable and handsome, was the most eligible bachelor in Europe.[28] At fifteen, he was considered ready for marriage. It was swiftly settled that the most suitable choice for his consort was Anne of Bohemia. Princess Anne was the daughter of the Holy Roman Emperor, Charles IV, and the sister of King Wenceslaus of Bohemia and Luxembourg. She was extremely cultured after spending her childhood in her father's elegant palace in Prague. A perfect match for the English King, although just how his government would provide Anne's dowry, with the poll tax abandoned and the Exchequer almost empty, posed a major problem.

After a perilous voyage from Prague – pirates roamed the English Channel – Anne arrived safely at Dover. Immediately after embarking, Anne's ship was wrecked in a sudden storm, supposedly an evil omen. At Blackheath, Anne's entourage was awarded a magnificent reception by the Mayor of London and the Goldsmith's Company. As she processed across London Bridge and along Cheapside, she was delighted to find that the towers of a fairytale castle spilled red wine. On 14 January 1382, Richard and Anne were married in St Stephen's Chapel and afterwards Anne was crowned by Archbishop Courtenay in Westminster Abbey. Richard and Anne were a devoted and contented couple although they remained childless throughout their twelve years of marriage.

Richard II was a patron of the arts: literature, music, painting, sculpture and architecture. Highly intelligent, cultured and creative, he was an accomplished dancer and composer of 'lays, ballads, songs and rondels'. A true connoisseur, he amassed a valuable collection of tapestries depicting jousting, religious or courtly scenes. Foremost was his passion for books, learned early from his tutor,[29] which he could read in English and French. He kept his collection in a private closet where each volume was bound in red, blue or white satin covers with gold clasps and blue silk markers. His 'Great Bible' survives in the British Library, his 'Condemnation of Lollard Heretics' is kept at Trinity College, Cambridge, while his illuminated 'Book of Divinations' is held at the Bodleian Library, Oxford.

Queen Anne, although not beautiful, was admired for her generosity and compassion. She shared her husband's literary tastes for she was noted for her diligent study of 'godly books', which she could read in English, Latin and German. Lighter reading for the royal couple consisted of French or English romances featuring King Arthur and Guinevere or Percival and Gawyn. Richard became patron of Geoffrey Chaucer, 'father of English poetry'. A pleasant custom was for Chaucer to mount a pulpit in the palace gardens to read aloud his love poems to the courtiers and their ladies as they strolled across the lawns on summer days.

Anne was an excellent horsewoman and introduced riding sidesaddle to her ladies at the English court. King Richard improved his substantial stables by putting Anne's renowned Bohemian horses to stud in Prague. Interestingly, the Queen also influenced fashion. She is credited with introducing the horned or mitred cap, the long train, peaked shoes and the humble pin ('espingle').[30] Richard, who was extremely fastidious, invented the handkerchief to wipe his nose. (His courtiers were content to use their sleeves.) In fact, his effect on the style and fashion of clothes worn in England was truly astonishing...

Heights of Fashion

Richard II, following the example of his grandfather, Edward III, was determined to transform his court into a civilised centre of leisure, elegance and entertainment. He introduced women into his intimate circle and invited them to accompany him and his courtiers as they rode from one palace to another. Their presence softened the previously male-dominated household and their manners and graceful dress became the focus of courtly love.[31]

After the victories in France during the previous reign there was a sudden craze for French fashion among the gentlefolk in England. The surrender of Calais in 1347 had resulted in the mass shipment of plunder from sacked towns and cities across the English Channel. Noblemen's wives and mistresses began to flaunt the latest type of garments recently modelled in French cities. Their bright, sweeping, silken gowns may recently have hung in aristocratic Frenchwomen's wardrobes until seized by knights and esquires returning home from a foreign campaign.[32] Clothes now become remarkable costumes. Dresses, that had simply covered the body to prevent indecency, suddenly encompassed style and fashion. Now their purpose was primarily to allure.

Hitherto, the universal apparel of both sexes was loose and flowing, which disguised the natural shape of the body. Now, tailors and dressmakers had learned the skill of cutting cloth 'on the bias'.[33] Here was an exciting, innovative method of shaping clothes to fit the lines of the human form. It greatly extended the range and appeal of garments they could offer their wealthy customers. Suddenly, the 'cotehardie' was all the rage. This close-fitting outer garment – hip length for men, full length for women – was the first tailored costume in Europe. The tightly buttoned sleeved tunic, often with streamers hanging from the cuffs, flowed freely for women from just above the knee.

Men who followed fashion were far more conspicuous in their courtly attire. 'Brilliant as butterflies',[34] they sported short jackets, with broad shoulders and padded chest, over a short skirt that (hopefully) showed off slim hips below. The addition of clinging hose, which left little to the imagination, was further intended to emphasise the wearer's masculinity. Women, who owned fewer garments then men, shared in this daring trend for flaunting their sexuality by wearing tight bodices with loose sleeves and dresses dyed in rainbow colours. Women wore white makeup as fair skin was much admired. Their loose or braided hair was bound in netted buns or tucked under cauls, leaving the neck uncovered, inviting stolen kisses... Men employed barbers to trim their forked beards and curl their hair with tongs. Ostentatious clothing, predictably, drew condemnation from the clergy, who were concerned not only that it distracted from the service, but that tight fitting garments prevented men and women from kneeling in church.

The intricacies of fashion were mainly restricted to court circles where, over the decades, styles of dress and accessories, particularly among young men, became exaggerated. Shoes called 'crackowes' had extended points, stuffed with moss, which might be attached to the knee with silver chains or silk ribbons. The traditional hood acquired a peak with bonus material twisted around the head in a turban with a trail flopping over the shoulder called a 'liripipe'. Sleeves, cut or 'carved' to reveal a contrasting colour underneath, became impossibly long so that they, too, had to be wound round the arm while cloaks were tongued or 'dagged', fastened with a jewelled clasp, and thrown over one shoulder to reveal an expensive lining.[35] A popular unisex garment was the 'houpeland'. This was a full-length gown, with a high collar and flared sleeves, whose skirt reached either to the knee, the calf or the ground. Worn with a jewelled girdle, it was trimmed with fur while its edges might be cut into a decorative pattern, scallops or leaves. They came in an assortment of shades: blue, green, scarlet, mulberry and, charmingly, 'faire violet'.

Extreme fashions, which depended upon an excess of material, were encouraged by the Mercers. The constantly moving court and noblemen's households inevitably returned to the City where their members enquired about the latest styles. They visited the shops in the Mercery to examine the newest imported cloth, which they ordered for recommended City tailors and dressmakers to turn into flattering garments. Medieval costume invited excitement, secrecy, intrigue and rivalry among the gentry. London, rather than Paris, now became the centre of 'haute couture'.

Londoners began to pride themselves on their appearance. Gentlemen and their ladies strolled nonchalantly, resplendent in embroidered tunics, velvet robes, silk-lined hoods or hats trimmed with fur: ermine, beaver or marten. They drew attention to themselves with imaginative accessories: abbreviated doublets embroidered with exotic birds and flowers; leather girdles from which hung crystal-hafted knives, silk purses and taffeta bags; male garters that drew attention to the stockinged legs; gold, silver and jewelled rings, clasps and brooches in feathered hats; hoods and sleeves sewn with silver bells that tinkled with the slightest shake of the hand or head... Poets and chroniclers delighted in describing the variegated colours of the costumes worn by the citizens as they crowded the streets on days of royal progresses or civic pageantry.

Costume was an accepted indicator of wealth and power in Medieval England. It was one of the most effective means of visually expressing the social hierarchy. Clothes became extremely complex so that tailors confidently charged astronomical prices for their services knowing that their customers would invest a small fortune in keeping up appearances. Consequently, there was great consternation among court circles when the working classes attempted to imitate their superiors by adopting clothing above their allotted station. After the Black Death, particularly following the second wave of the pestilence, English peasants achieved a modicum of emancipation. Their newly acquired 'wealth' and mobility meant not only that there was an improvement in living conditions but that they began to afford modest luxuries. One priority was superior clothes.

Obviously, certain styles adopted by peasants prevented them from performing their daily menial tasks. This was considered not only to adversely affect the economy but blurred social distinctions. Defiantly, peasants abandoned their loose-fitting smocks and simple caps in order to emulate their superiors with tightly fitting gowns, pointed shoes, furs, hose and even jewellery. Previously, a series of laws attempted to govern the number of meals served, the type of food consumed and even the value of drinking vessels owned by the lower classes.[36] In 1363, Parliament had introduced the first in a series of sumptuary statutes restricting 'the outrageous and excessive apparel of many people, contrary to their estate and degree'. Everything – from length, style, material, colour and adornment – was carefully graded according to accepted rank and status.[37] Obviously, this ludicrous law was unenforceable, and it was quietly abandoned. Its most harmful effect was to penalise the burgeoning trade of the Mercers whose interest lay, naturally, in supplying materials to whoever could afford them.

Royal Costume

Richard II was the first king to turn costume into an art. His gregarious grandfather had comprehended that extravagant clothes were an important expression of kingship. Towards the end of his life, he was determined to affirm publicly that his grandson was now in the direct line of accession. He took care to spend freely on Prince Richard's formal attire, which initially followed court protocol. The task of choosing his wardrobe would have been shared by his mother, Princess Joan, and his tutor, Simon Burley. And whilst he was still a minor, invoices for these purchases were directed to his mother's treasurer, William Packington, who recorded them as 'expenses of the household'.[38] When Richard became Prince of Wales, he was allocated his own establishment with a separate wardrobe allowance appropriate to his royal rank. As he advanced towards adulthood, however, Richard will have formed his own opinion and made his individual choices about clothes and fashion.

As he grew to maturity, Richard II became remarkably handsome. His features were delicate, slightly feminine. Generally, he was clean shaven; his hair was long, fair and wavy. His eyes were blue and his milk-white skin blushed readily. He was almost six feet tall and so he cut a slight, yet imposing figure.[39] He had a speech impediment and stammered when excited, but this trait was deemed fashionable and imitated by his fawning courtiers.[40] He was interested in geomancy and astrology and he consulted that 'Book of Divinations', which offered him both solace and guidance in troubled times. He was an accomplished horseman, with a particular penchant for the chase.[41] Secretive, suspicious, calculating and capricious, he was also prey to tempers and tantrums, a characteristic inherent in all Plantagenet kings.

Richard II was also a renowned gourmet. A 14th-century cookery book, compiled by his master chef, survives: 'The Forme of Cury'.[42] In the introduction, he is described as 'the best and ryallest vyander of alle cristen kynges'. This tiny volume contains over two hundred recipes handwritten on vellum in Middle English. The recipes, which display the influence of French cuisine, lists methods and ingredients but lack times and quantities.[43] Main courses include minced pheasant spiced with cinnamon, cloves and ginger; oysters with hare's flesh and honey; roasted goose stuffed with quinces, pears and grapes; turbot and eel in gelatine and even a cheese 'loseyns' (lasagne). Courtiers attacked these delicacies with knife, spoon or fingers. All these delicacies were washed down with a choice of wines from La Rochelle and Bordeaux or even, in a good year, from the King's own vineyards at Windsor.

King Richard, in the tradition of his grandfather, spent a fortune on clothing. During his first regnal year his tailor, Walter Raufe, provided him with eighty-seven outfits with matching hoods, hose, underwear and accessories; in the second year there were approximately another eighty. This, apparently, was the minimum requirement for the royal calendar of Parliamentary sessions, court functions, religious festivals, seasonal activities, sport and travel. His costume was often startling. For his first Christmas, Richard wore a tunic and hood of 'scarletta' embroidered with ships fashioned in pearls and gold thread. At Epiphany, he attended a joust sporting a tunic of red silk stamped with gold suns and a matching helmet with a crest formed of ostrich plumes.[44]

Members of the royal household would not necessarily buy from common shopkeepers but deal directly with favoured merchants who supplied quality cloth before it even reached the shops. At intervals, Walter Rauf, the King's tailor, and Thomas Lytlington, his costume designer, consulted their royal master over his personal preferences and anticipated orders for certain materials to be stored for future requirements at the Great Wardrobe at Baynard's Castle. According to custom, the King claimed the right of first choice of all imported merchandise and so his Sheriff or Chamberlain would inspect the bales of cloth as they arrived by ship and were laid out on the quayside.

Costly materials imported from the Continent would be shipped in convoys to protect the cargo from pirates and marauders, particularly at those times when England was at war with France. Assistant tailors and minor clerks without a special royal directive would also be regularly despatched to visit the London Mercers, notably Whittington, at their stores or warehouses to select quantities of materials for distribution among the array of embroiderers, seamstresses, milliners, costumiers, even armourers. There was always a flurry of activity among the Mercers and merchants at the approach of royal christenings, weddings, funerals, state occasions, military campaigns, sporting activities, national progresses and City pageants, plus all the major feasts of the Christian calendar.

Richard II established his personal preferment for clothes which, on state occasions, were, frankly, outlandish. At the Feast of the Purification of the Virgin on 2 February 1386, he chose a long gown and matching hood of red velvet, embroidered with white harts worked in pearls and crowns in gold thread, with a miniver lining and ermine trimmings. For Easter that same year he sported a long gown and hood of blue velvet embroidered with harts lying beneath trees stitched in gold and coloured silks, with scrolls bearing mottos, curled around a tree.[45] His steed was attired in complementary trappings.

Another bizarre outfit consisted of a white satin gown embroidered with silvergilt cockles, mussels and whelks under rock pools, interwoven with white silvergilt trees and a doublet with golden orange trees bearing a hundred silvergilt oranges.[46] When the King appeared in a crimson satin gown with gold and silk suns, plus a crest of a large gold sun above a silver cloud atop his crowned helmet, his horse was covered in a matching cloth of red silk stamped with gold suns and silver or blue clouds within a border of crowns.[47] (The King's armourer, William Snell, provided a saddle and harness.) The white hart was Richard's personal emblem. The intention of Richard II's dazzling costumes were to reinforce visually his divine role as England's king.

From boyhood, then, Richard had been dressed in sumptuous materials for formal occasions but during the course of his reign cloth-of-gold became acknowledged as the supreme indicator of his royal blood. His spectacular costumes were further embellished by precious stones: 'besants', 'beralles', 'calsydodynnes', 'dymandes', 'saphirs', 'emeraudes', 'amatistes', 'rubyes'. They sparkled in the candlelight at the ancient royal palaces. The King's visible display of wealth did not always achieve the desired effect, however, because it brought sneering criticism from his subjects, and even his peers, who accused him of squandering his inherited fortune.

Noble Customers

Richard II, in his desire to rule across his kingdom and embrace the citizens of his realm, travelled extensively. Fifty towns, at least, played host to the King in the course of his reign which boosted their economy as his courtiers spent lavishly. His purpose was to win support from his subjects – from the knights and gentry in the shires to the merchants and craftsmen of the towns – and proclaim his royal presence.

King Richard, it would seem, was probably better known to the English people than any of his predecessors and they marvelled at his stylish – and startling – appearance.[48]

Richard II's zest for fashion in clothes was emulated by his servile courtiers. Men flattered their monarch by imitating his outrageous styles. In their desire to follow court fashion, they patronised a coterie of merchants in the City – Mercers who supplied materials and accessories, Drapers who specialised in heavier fabrics, skinners who provided fashionable furs.[49] This presented the perfect opportunity for Whittington to flourish as a merchant supplying superior fabrics to wealthy courtiers. In a short space of time he established his reputation and expertise for buying and selling luxurious fabrics. There seems little probability that he ventured abroad but certainly he cultivated superior suppliers on the Continent.

None of Whittington's accounts survive but there are occasional glimpses, even during his early days as a Mercer, of his transactions with certain privileged customers. Among the members of the royal court who patronised Whittington, Sir Simon Burley, King Richard's boyhood tutor and trusted friend, appears to be the most prominent. According to the 'Kirkstall Chronicle' he had no 'peer in the splendour of his apparel'.

He owned an extensive wardrobe that included a cloth-of-gold tabard embroidered with roses and lined with green tartarine, a second scarlet tabard embroidered with the sun and gold letters and lined with white tartarine, a white leather coat decorated with over fifty gold buttons, an ermine cape and a cloak of minever.[50] It would seem, therefore, that he instilled his great love of fashion in his royal pupil.

Burley rose to become one of the most powerful and influential noblemen in the realm. Positions conferred upon him included Lord Warden of the Cinque Ports, Constable of Dover Castle, Vice Chamberlain[51] and Castellan of Windsor. It is doubtful, however, whether this Knight Banneret achieved his coveted ambition to become an Earl.[52]

Burley remained close to the King and would have been consulted on appropriate costume for official state appearances. In this, he was ably assisted by his nephew, Sir Baldwin Raddington, who was Keeper of the Wardrobe. He became vastly unpopular because his influence on Richard II was considered excessive and undesirable.

Robert de Vere, Ninth Earl of Oxford, Chamberlain of England and Duke of Ireland, was probably Whittington's most loyal customer. Richard II had created him Marquis of Dublin[53] which gave him precedence over the Earls. During his heyday as a royal favourite, he purchased mercery to the tune of almost £2,000.[54] Whittington may also have provided materials to the household of the King's uncle, John of Gaunt, and to the Earls of Stafford.[55]

Later, Whittington was patronised by Richard II's cousin, Henry Bolingbroke. Henry, named after his birthplace in Lincolnshire, was the oldest surviving son of John of Gaunt and Blanche of Lancaster, a descendant from a younger branch of Henry III. He proved another enduring customer, although neither indiscriminate nor lavish, since his purchases of velvets and cloth-of-gold appear comparatively modest:[56] in 1390, one, in 1393, four and in 1395, six. Henry's household spent £169 on drapery, £444 9s 10d on furs and £668 15s 6d and 1/2d on mercery.[57]

It must be remembered that exquisite costume was regarded as a worthwhile investment. It was viewed as portable capital that might be readily offered as security on loans and it was often bequeathed to family and friends.[58] Burley was reported to have raised money from six amenable citizens on the security of his own clothes.[59] John of Gaunt bequeathed expensive fabric – twelve lengths of cloth, red satin striped with gold – to his reigning nephew, Richard II.[60]

The Common Council

'Status was a major preoccupation of the London Mercer throughout the Middle Ages,' writes Anne Sutton. 'They mostly denied their low birth and, by adopting civic responsibilities escalated to important positions within the ruling classes, and aligned themselves with their superiors.'[61] Whittington's remarkable civic career began modestly in the penultimate decade of King Richard II's reign.

In the later Medieval period, the Mayor of London was elected exclusively from the affluent liveried companies. Few of their members, however, were eager to accept this prestigious office because of the exacting duties it involved, particularly regarding time and expense during the profitable years of wartime trade and finance.[62] The Mayor was assisted in his capacity by two Sheriffs and twenty-four Aldermen, one for each of the Wards into which the City was divided. The 'Shire Reeves', or Sheriffs, were the oldest recorded civic posts in the country, charged with the maintenance of law and order and the collection of revenues, existing from Norman times. It was to simplify their onerous tasks that London had been divided into precisely defined Wards that may have evolved from privately owned estates whose landlords were required to supply armed men for the defence of the City.

The Common Council, which had considerable powers of administration and legislation, existed to provide an element of democracy to the government of the City.[63] Members of the Council were selected from the Wards, each one sending from four to eight members according to its size.[64] When the Guildhall was rebuilt in the 15th century, their meeting place was the Upper Chamber, although if attendance was high, members were obliged to remove to the lower floor generally occupied by the Court of Husting. This last elite assembly met separately to consider matters of commerce – trade, debt, measurement and land – relating to the City of London. The word 'husting' derives from the Danish where 'hus' means house and 'thing' an assembly.[65] This implies that from its inception a building existed in which to hold the court, and that perhaps it previously occupied the site of the present Guildhall.

The Mayor was the leader of a smaller executive body of civic government, the 'Mayor's Court'. This comprised the Mayor, the Recorder, Sheriffs and Aldermen who eventually gathered in an inner room of the Guildhall. It dealt with matters arising from common law such as debt, slander and assault, in addition to established customs, including apprenticeship and orphanage. Inside this private chamber the ordinary administrative business of the City was conducted: ordinances were approved, freedoms granted, elections ratified and expenditure affirmed. Additionally, this secure room may also have served as the repository of the City's records and documents.

City Wards varied greatly in size and character. According to an assessment made in 1339, Cordwayner was the richest while the poorest, by far, was Aldgate Ward. The second appearance of Whittington in the City Letter Books was when he was chosen to represent 'Colmanstret' (Coleman Street), the second wealthiest Ward, in 1384.[66] Coleman Street was probably named after the charcoal burners who occupied the area. According to Lambert: 'It begins on the east side, upon the course of Walbrook, in Lothbury, and extends to the end of Ironmonger Lane, on the south side of the street, and to the end of Bassinghall Street to the north side: and in a north and south direction, it extends from Moorgate to the garden belonging to Grocers' Hall.'[67] Most importantly, this Ward encompassed Guildhall.

That same year an Ordinance limited the number of councillors to ninety-six to ensure that meetings were conducted in an orderly manner. Furthermore, it was ordained that councillors should be chosen from the Wards and not the crafts or companies, as before, 'fifteen days after the feast of St Gregory' (3 September). Councillors met quarterly to deliberate over the affairs of the City. Their most important concern was to nominate two people to serve as Mayor and two more to serve as Sheriffs, although the actual election rested with the Aldermen. Previously, the Common Council was dominated by eminent members of the most prominent Companies and the Ordinance sought to stem their power in civic government. There could be little improvement, however, because only wealthy and successful businessmen found themselves in a secure enough position to offer themselves for election. Whittington breached this change of rule and even repeated his role, intermittently, for the next two decades.

The Lords Appellant

Now it was the turn of the barons to rebel. Ostensibly, they complained about Richard II's ostentatious, licentious and profligate behaviour which resulted in burdensome taxation without apparent benefit to the country. In reality, they were seething with jealousy and bitterness over his patronage of favourite courtiers – talented and venturesome but inexperienced – and their elevation to powerful positions in government. Five noblemen combined forces to confront their tender young sovereign. This formidable faction were Richard II's uncle, Thomas of Woodstock, Duke of Gloucester, Richard FitzAlan, Earl of Arundel, whose wealth derived from the wool trade, his brother, Thomas Arundel, Bishop of Ely but later Archbishop of Canterbury, and Thomas, Earl of Warwick. Their avowed intention was to prosecute or 'appeal' certain noblemen they accused of being traitors. Subsequently, they became known as the 'Lords Appellant'.

These five senior lords confronted the King at the 'Wonderful Parliament' in 1386. Their vociferous complaint focused on Richard II's extravagant household and young noblemen he had unwisely promoted above veteran and venerable statesmen. Their hostility was directed towards his five councillors: Robert de Vere, Marquis of Dublin, Michael de la Pole, Earl of Sussex, Alexander Neville, Archbishop of York, Robert Tresilian, Chief Justice, and Nicholas Brembre, former Mayor of London. When the lords demanded the removal from office of Michael de la Pole, the King's intimate friend, he famously countered that he would not even dismiss, at their behest, a common scullion from his kitchen.

But Richard capitulated under duress and he reluctantly dismissed Suffolk as Chancellor of the Exchequer.

King Richard commanded Nicholas Exton, Mayor of London, to summon troops to support him in his confrontation with the Lords Appellant. The Mayor prevaricated. He responded with the feeble excuse that the City's militia was formed mainly of craftsmen and merchants whose military role was confined to the defence of the City. The King was forced to scour the country to secure alternative military protection, although now he lacked the authority – after surrendering the Great and Privy Seals – to raise an official army. Instead, he formed a sizeable bodyguard from among the Welsh pikemen and Cheshire archers, the sons of seasoned soldiers who had fought for his father, the Black Prince, at Crecy. He instated the despised Robert de Vere as Justice of Chester and placed him in charge of the army that comprised approximately five thousand men. It marched southwards towards London to confront the Lords Appellant who had illegally retained their own private armies. England was now on the brink of civil war.

De Vere was confronted by the combined armies of the rebel lords who forced him to fight at Radcot Bridge, near Eynsham, below the Vale of the White Horse. The Lords Appellant had been joined by Henry Bolingbroke, the King's cousin, and Thomas Mowbray, Earl of Nottingham. At the sight of their formidable army, De Vere's men deserted him. He, too, although courageous, was reluctantly forced to flee and he was soon enveloped by the midwinter fog. For Richard, the defeat of his friend was a cruel and humiliating experience.

Upon his return to London, King Richard was confronted by Gloucester, Arundel and Warwick, who brought their absurd 'appeal' of high treason against Robert de Vere, Michael de la Pole, Robert Tressilian, Chief Justice, Alexander Neville, Archbishop of York, and Nicholas Brembre.

Brembre, a member of the Fishmongers' Guild, had resorted to subterfuge to secure the coveted office of Mayor of London in the autumn of 1383. Richard, with the loss of his army, had little alternative than to comply with every one of the lord's demands, or he would be deposed. Brembre and Tressilian were executed while de Vere and De la Pole (who had both fled abroad) were sentenced to death in their absence at the aptly named 'Merciless Parliament' of 1388. The most cruel blow was that the King's former tutor, Sir Simon Burley, was also condemned and summarily beheaded. This Parliament has been denounced as one of the most bitter, brutal and bloody in the history of England.

The Lords Appellant insisted on a complete reform of Richard II's household. His personal staff, courtiers and clerics, were dismissed.[68] Richard's close circle of friends was destroyed. A Council of Regency was organised from older statesmen headed by the Duke of Gloucester who would govern the country while Richard remained a minor. Further, the King was informed that a commission would be set up to review royal finances and curtail extravagant expenditure. Indeed, the commissioners in their first year of office reduced spending by the

Royal Wardrobe by five thousand pounds,[69] 'a not inconsiderable achievement', comments Saul.

King Richard – deprived of his closest companions and at the mercy of ruthless lords – was left defeated, bereaved and simmering in the Tower. Whittington had lost two of his most valued customers and influential friends: Sir Simon Burley and Robert de Vere. It seemed that his career as a City Mercer had stuttered and stalled. Along with his young sovereign, he had fallen at the first hurdle.

5

The Court Mercer

ONE YEAR LATER, King Richard II, approaching the age of majority, made a dramatic statement at the Great Council of Westminster on 3 May 1389. He announced his intention of reclaiming his 'dignyte, Regalye and honourable estate' in order to resume the sole government of his kingdom. 'For every heire of my realme havynge xxti yere in age after the dethe of his fader is permitte to govene hymselfe and his londes,' reported Ralph Higden in his 'Polychronicon'. The King curtly dismissed his uncle, Thomas of Woodstock, Duke of Gloucester, as Regent. Richard was determined he would no longer be muzzled and reduced to a mere cypher. He was resolved to appoint personally the five chief officers of state: chancellor, treasurer, chamberlain, keeper of the privy seal and the steward, who, with the King's councillors, would govern the country.[70] Above all, he would regain control of his own expenditure since he regarded the previously imposed restrictions as a trespass on his royal prerogative. The Lords Appellant had increased their own influence and amassed a fortune during that one year they had taken charge of the kingdom. But they were not skilled statesmen and their lack of political success resulted in widespread disillusionment and condemnation in Parliament.

Richard endeavoured forthwith to establish a regime of royal absolutism. Optimistically, the King promised his subjects in return that they would experience lower taxes, fairer justice and better governance.[71] On a personal level, he harboured deep grudges against those senior Lords who had hastened the deaths of his intimate friends. According to the 'Kirkstall Chronicle', he 'vowed to avenge the executions and exiles of his closest friends'. This he would attempt when he felt the time was ripe and, even then, not through brute strength but through guile – 'ffeynyng'.

In celebration, Richard II made a generous gift to Westminster Abbey, which had always been of immense significance to him. It was the burial place of his patron, Edward the Confessor, and the focal point of his own kingship.[72]

During the latter period of his reign, he patronised the embellishment of its furnishings and fabric. At regular intervals, he presented liturgical banners, altar pieces and magnificent vestments to the venerable monks. During the same month he reclaimed his throne, Richard donated a set of splendid vestments consisting of a chasuble, three copes, three albs, three maniples and two stoles to the Abbey. The chasuble – an ornate sleeveless outer garment worn by the priest when celebrating Mass – was exceptionally fine. It was woven of cloth-of-gold with orphreys (embroidered bands) featuring the figures of the Virgin Mary, St Edmund and St John the Baptist. King Richard and Queen Anne's coats-of-arms were prominently incorporated into the design.

Whittington's first recorded sale of goods to the crown came at the same time as Richard II's assumption of direct responsibility for the realm. In May 1389, the King ordered two splendid cloths-of-gold as rewards for a couple of Scottish knights who apparently had acted as welcome messengers. It would hardly have been coincidence that he had turned to the Mercer who had constantly supplied his former friends in order to acquire those exquisite fabrics. The King was enchanted by his purchases and more orders swiftly followed. Whittington was assured that in Richard II he had found 'a patron of taste'.[73]

It is surprisingly difficult to find a definition of cloth-of-gold or silver in books on Medieval costume. It would appear that it was a silk fabric through which was woven an additional weft of metal thread, either gold or silver, secured by an almost invisible binding warp.[74] Plain gold cloth had a yellow base while silver cloth had a white one. Both were referred to as 'baudekyn' or 'baldechin'. Variant colours were also employed to produce purple cloth-of-gold or, one especially favoured by Richard II, a red one called 'samite'. Its acquisition was reserved for royal robes or church vestments, but this expensive fabric could cover primers, psalters and gospels.

Richard II's Cult of Majesty

From this time onwards, King Richard II betrayed an almost obsessive concern in projecting, through a variety of mediums, his own perceived 'Majesty'. This is demonstrated by two famous contemporary paintings: the Coronation Portrait (*c.*1395) and the Wilton Diptych (*c.*1395-99).

In the Coronation Portrait the youthful Medieval monarch, crowned, enthroned, appears swamped by the heavy vestments that engulf his fragile frame. He holds aloft the coronation insignia – sceptre and orb – that seem as though they might at any moment slip through his slender fingers. As they did...

Richard's delicate features are exaggerated: disdainful eyes, mournful mouth and bunches of curling golden locks. The overall effect is of a willowy and distant, lonely and vulnerable, Christlike figure. Painted by Gilbert Prince in about 1394, its purpose appears to have been to reassert Richard II's sovereignty after he achieved his majority and claimed his exclusive right to rule. It was intended to hang prominently in Westminster Abbey. Restored in Victorian times, the original gesso background was removed and the portrait was enclosed in its oppressive ornate frame [75] This is arguably the earliest surviving portrait of an English King.[76]

The Wilton Diptych[77], which is a portable altarpiece, is another priceless piece of propaganda. It was designed to be unfolded and positioned on an altar as a focal point for Richard II's private prayers. These exquisite paired paintings accentuate the relationship in Medieval minds between Heaven and Earth. The sophisticated European artist presents 'a complex web of allusions criss-crossing from one panel to the other'.[78]

The artist depicts the King clean-shaven, whereas, by then, he sported a moustache and goatee beard, in an attempt to present him as fresh-faced, young and innocent. He is dressed in a long gown of rich red samite[79] decorated with medallions of his personal emblem, the white hart[80], and a golden collar of broomcods, *planta genista*.[81] He kneels with open hands before the Virgin Mary who is surrounded by angels who also sport the King's badge or 'favour' and broomcod necklaces.

King Richard is attended by a trio of saints: King Edmund the Martyr[82], King Edward the Confessor[83] and his own special patron, John the Baptist, dressed in camel skin, who places a protective arm around him. Mary stands cradling the infant Christ, wrapped in gold tissue, in an English meadow planted with roses, daisies, violets or irises and, charmingly, a fairy ring. She is attended by eleven angels wearing chaplets of scarlet and white roses[84], one of whom holds aloft the banner of Saint George.

Recently, it was observed by skilled conservators that the flagstaff is surmounted by a tiny orb, finely painted, featuring a white castle with twin turrets on a fertile island surrounded by a silver sea on which bobs a twin-masted ship under full sail.[85] The inference of this hidden detail, intended for royal eyes only, would have been noted by the King at his daily devotions. Richard appears to be offering his kingdom as a dowry to the Virgin.[86] Or, alternately, he is receiving it. The Christ Child is confirming King Richard's divine right to rule England.

It is tempting to consider that the artist worked in a similar vein to modern portrait painters. Presumably, King Richard posed for his head and hands to be sketched in detail. Later, the artist, back in his studio, worked at leisure, building up the fine details of both paintings. He would also have required a reference for the costly furs and apparel of the earthly kings.[87] Lisa Monnas,[88] who has made a study of the silks depicted in the Diptych, doubts the notion that the King's robe would have been woven in Italy to a pattern submitted by a royal tailor, even though the superlative fabric displays a quintessentially Ricardian design. She does, however, concede: 'It is possible to confirm from documents that such garments were typical of what was being worn by Richard and that these specific robes could very well have existed.' And if they did indeed exist, they could have been supplied only by a close circle of court Mercers, the most prominent of whom was Whittington. Is it possible that the anonymous artist has captured actual samples from Richard Whittington's stock of superlative regal fabrics?

Together, these two paintings reveal not only Richard II's vanity but also his aloofness from his subjects, who he deemed mere mortals. On formal occasions, the King sat isolated on his throne, watching everyone summoned to his presence. When his eyes alighted on a courtier, he was expected to kneel three times in acknowledgement of his inferiority. This pair of artistic images were adjuncts to the verbal elevation of the narcissistic King. In the last decade of his reign formal modes of address were introduced at court. Commons' petitions were now addressed to 'your excellent and powerful prince' or 'your highness and royal majesty'. Richard II was the first English monarch to insist upon being addressed as 'Majesty'.[89]

Alderman Whittington

Originally, the City's governor assumed the title 'Ealdorman', later born by the chief citizen in each of the Wards.[90] In Saxon, 'alde' means old while 'alder' means older, although this indicates respect for maturity of mind rather than an ageing body. Indeed, an Alderman was expected to be honest, discreet, able-bodied, financially secure and, naturally, a Freeman.[91] They assembled in a communal hall located in Aldermanbury, which means 'fortified residence of the Aldermen'. Records of Aldermen reveal that the majority were chosen from the powerful merchants, predominantly Mercers, Drapers or Grocers. They presided over quarterly 'Wardmotes' at which citizens, apart from knights or clerics, over the age of fifteen were obliged to attend. These were held bi-annually in the principal church of each Ward at which current civic regulations were made known and public enquiries were held into breaches of the law. They were also the occasion when a varying number of 'good and discreet citizens' were chosen as their representatives on the Court of Common Council.

Aldermen, too, were elected annually at 'Wardmotes'. An Alderman took his title from the Ward over which he presided: 'Alderman of Chepe', 'Alderman of Bridge' or 'Alderman of Quenhithe'. (In former times the reverse was the rule: 'The Ward of Thomas de Basyng' was actually the Ward of Candlewick Street, while 'The Ward of Henry le Frowyk' was the Ward of Cheap.) On 12 March 1391, Whittington was elected 'Alderman of Broad Street Ward'.

The main responsibility of an Alderman was to keep the peace and to guard the walls and gates of the City. They were expected to assess their male inhabitants to arms, set the watch at nighttime and levy the trained bands during disturbances. Moreover, they were responsible for the highways and byways, fire regulations, street cleansing, sanitation and trading, which involved fixing wages for journeymen, examining conditions of apprentices, and testing weights and measures. They were endowed with considerable police and judicial powers and were assisted in their duties by Beadles.[92] Their authority and dignity was protected by law and they had powers of arrest in the absence of the Sheriff, and they could even order the loss of a hand for anyone who insulted him.[93]

The duties of an Alderman could not be avoided. There were hefty fines for late or non-attendance at Wardmotes. Ill health, however, provided a valid excuse for resignation. 'Alan of Bredstrete' was dismissed from office 'by reason of his dulness of hearing'.[94] A cautionary tale concerns John Gedeney, draper, who tried to avoid his responsibility by declaring inadequacy. The Court reminded him sternly of his oath as Freeman by which he was made partaker of Lot ('liability to take office') and Scot ('liability to taxation'), and yet he stubbornly resisted. Gedeney was gaoled, his shop was impounded and his stock sequestered. Unsurprisingly, after these drastic measures, Gedeney acquiesced. Surprisingly, he rose to become Mayor of London (1427 and 1447).

In 1394, Richard II, for purposes off administration, ordered that Farringdon Ward should be divided into two, Farringdon Within and Farringdon Without, thus increasing the number of wards to twenty-five.[95] Effectively, this brought a large, unruly area beyond the walls into the jurisdiction of the City. The new ward, entered from the City through Ludgate, terminated at Fleet Street where a barrier across the road marked its boundary at Temple Bar.[96]

Richard II's Quarrel with the Londoners

During Richard II's personal rule he quarrelled with and confronted the City of London. His Court was now excessively expensive and could not be maintained without constant recourse to moneylenders. When the King applied for a substantial loan in May 1392, he was curtly refused by the Londoners. Richard had not forgiven the citizens for supporting the Lords Appellant and he retaliated by revoking all their ancient liberties. He progressed now from the brief phase of something like democratic government to a period of absolute personal rule.[97]

Richard's first thunderbolt was to command the Mayor, Sheriffs and Aldermen to attend him at Nottingham on 25 June in order to answer charges of misgovernment. Whittington, certainly, was among the twenty-four commoners 'of the second rank of wealth' delegated by the City to face the fury of the slighted monarch.[98] The King ordered that the Chancery, the Exchequer and the Law Courts should be removed from Westminster to York and Parliament to Shrewsbury. This was calculated to cause immense disruption and inconvenience to the citizens of London.

The King imprisoned, on the flimsiest of pretexts, the Mayor, John Hende, and deposed the Sheriffs and Aldermen. They were all replaced with a compliant Warden, Sir Edward Dalyngridge (or 'Dalyngrigge'), a Knight of the Shire for Sussex,[99] who was commanded to govern London on the King's behalf.[100] The liberties of the City would only be restored once its citizens had agreed to pay a revised loan of £100,000 – ten times the sum initially requested![101] The Mayor and Corporation had little alternative but to comply and attempt to pacify their megalomaniac monarch.[102] Richard accepted the invitation 'to ryde through his chaumber of London' accompanied by Queen Anne from Sheen Palace. It was a rare occasion for royalty to travel along London's noisome, congested streets as the preferred mode of travel at that time was the River Thames.

The royal couple arrived in state, preceded by the newly appointed Warden. They were welcomed by the penitent civic officials who proffered the sword and keys of the City. They were then escorted through the streets by the Aldermen – Whittington among them – attired in red and white, and the prominent members of the Companies wearing their finest liveries, including the Mercers, sporting 'Lucchese patterned silk called baldekin'. Houses and shops lining the route were bedecked with colourful tapestries, choice silks and rich gold or silver cloths. At intervals there were pageants calculated to please their Majesties. Musicians played joyful tunes on their cymbals, lyres, cytherns and viols. At Cheapside fountains flowed with wine... at St Paul's heavenly music played... on Ludgate Hill angels strewed flowers while at Temple Bar a religious tableau depicted John the Baptist leading the Lamb of God in a desert inhabited by wild beasts.[103] The pointed theme to the Londoner's choreographed pageant was the Second Coming of Christ to the New Jerusalem.[104] When the cavalcade crossed the newly repaired London Bridge[105] Richard was presented with 'a mylke-white stede, saddled and brydilled, and trappid with white cloth of golde and red parted togadir'. Anne graciously accepted 'a palfreye alle white trappid yn the same aray'.[106]

King Richard, placated by presents and pageantry, magnanimously forgave the Londoners and confirmed their liberties 'in perpetuity'. Moreover, he directed that the Chancery, the Exchequer and, most importantly, the Court of Common Pleas should return to Westminster. Triumphantly, he rode away unaware that behind their smiles the citizens harboured a deep, brooding resentment of their duplicitous sovereign. The King had obtained his money, but the price he paid for this high-handed behaviour was an irretrievable loss of popularity and goodwill among the citizens of London.[107]

Alderman Whittington most likely played a significant role in mollifying his moody monarch. He may even have choreographed the whole charade by organising the pageant, perhaps supplying the sumptuous materials for this royal extravaganza. He possibly acted as a mediator between the King and the City. As an astute financier, he may also have negotiated the terms of the loan[108] that had been adjusted to one tenth of the sum originally demanded from the King. Certainly, the contract benefitted the King, the Londoners and, indirectly,

Whittington. It also greatly advanced his own Company, which thereafter rose steadily in stature to revel in its ebullient success. Mercers, from this moment onwards, 'basked in the splendour of his reputation'.[109]

A Royal Spending Spree

After his acquisition of the money from the citizens of London, Richard II went on a wild spending spree.[110] The expenditure on the Great Wardrobe suddenly doubled. It appears the King dissipated the fines imposed on rich furnishings and clothes. A solitary roll of purchases by Richard Clifford, Keeper of the Great Wardrobe,[111] survives covering the years 1392-4.[112] This comprises ten membranes – sheets of parchment sewn end to end – written with a flourishing, legible hand in Latin. Acquisitions were first ordered under general headings, 'Drapery', 'Pelletry' or 'Mercery', and then subdivided under materials: 'velvett', 'satyn', 'taffati', 'damasc'.[113] The first name under the heading 'Mercery' is 'Ricardo Wytyngton, Mercer, London'. It reveals that Whittington had achieved his aim to become a major supplier of textiles to the Crown. Indeed, out of a total expenditure of £13,243 9s 11 1/2d (for which £6,204 15s 7 1/2d was for 'mercery') an incredible £3,474 15s 9d was owed to Whittington. (The same roll reveals that John Hende, draper, charged £4,144 for woollen cloths and William Horscroft, skinner, £1,709 for fine furs.)

Whittington's rolling total reveals the wide range of his available merchandise. His finest fabric was velvet, a most desirable and expensive silk, that was hugely popular among the fashionable Medieval noblemen. Silk cloth was exorbitantly priced which, although in great demand by ecclesiastics, aristocrats and royalty, was only available from a few merchants. Whittington's charges for plain tabby woven silks were: velvet (£505 17s 6d), satin (£80 10s), tartarin (£185 18s 6d), damask (£140 15s), taffeta (£53 5s 7d) and sindon (£13 7s 6d). These latter silks were in great demand since they could be easily stamped with emblems in gold or silver leaf for heraldic banners, chapel curtains, military tunics, jousting apparel and theatrical costumes. Whittington's principal supplies to the Crown, however, involved gold enriched figured silken cloths referred to as 'baudekyn' or 'baldachin': cloth-of-gold of Cyprus (£1,308 16s 8d), cloth-of-gold 'Racam',(£205 3s 4d) and cloth-of-gold 'Sigaston' (£14).[114] Such exquisite fabrics, for which Whittington gained national fame, might be transformed by the royal embroiderers John de Strawesburgh or his successor, William Sanston into splendid bed hangings and chamber drapes for King Richard and Queen Anne.[115]

Whittington's ability to supply Richard II and his courtiers with such large quantities of superlative Italian silks remains an intriguing mystery. It indicates that over a short period of time he had carefully cultivated his contacts with the Venetian warehouses. There is, of course, the slight possibility that he had travelled himself to Italy while still an apprentice for that unidentified master.[116]

But this extraordinary achievement for a London Mercer from comparatively humble beginnings remains remarkable.

Whittington was also responsible for supplying vast quantities of cheaper materials for mundane purposes to the royal household. 'Wurthstede' was available from established suppliers at Worsted, North Norfolk. This versatile fabric was produced when fine yarn was spun from long strands of combed wool. When dyed or painted in primary colours, the result was a smooth, shiny surface resembling silk. It was highly esteemed as a furnishing cloth, particularly for covers, curtains and canopies for beds. It was also in demand for military purposes, flags, banners and tents, or in a coarser version for soldiers' tunics. Equivalent materials were fustian for pillows, bolsters and cushions; buckram for linings of curtains and clothes; canvas suitable for packing possessions; carde (or muslin), ideal for protecting clothes when travelling and bolting cloth fashioned into costumes and headdresses for court entertainments.

He also provided linens of varying weight, price and quality and invariably, these were all imported from the Continent. Most expensive was linen from Reims (£111 1s 8d) required for the King's own sheets, pillows and underwear. Sturdier linen cloth used to line padded doublets and leather saddles was ordered from Flanders, Brabant and Westphalia (near Lake Constance), Germany. Fine Paris linen was reserved for hand towels and table napkins (£13 9s 6d). ·

Whittington must have regarded these substantial royal commissions as a windfall for they represented a massive increase in his private fortune.[117] Indeed, his business success is confirmed by the number of apprentices he now employed. This is evidenced by the Wardens' Accounts of the Mercers' Company. In 1391-2, when these accounts commence, he enrolled five apprentices; in 1395-6 he paid to enrol a further two apprentices and he acquired two more in 1400-1. The fact that he ceased to enrol apprentices after this date indicates his interest in alternative projects, both civic and commercial.[118]

The apprentices were Edmund Peyton, John Weston, Nicholas Lemyng, Edmund Brigge, John Empyngham, John Pychard, William Cavendish, Henry London and Thomas Roos. The last three mentioned – they eventually entered the livery of the Mercers' Company – occur later as partners in Whittington's business or property transactions. Thomas Roos, in particular successfully traded in his own right and his name appears twice in that extant roll of purchases by the Royal Household (1392-4). The City Guilds and Companies restricted the number of apprentices their members might enrol. Among those whose Ordinances set a firm limit were the Bowyers, Brewers, Cutlers, Glovers, Plumbers and Woolmen. The Mercers never seem to have subscribed to this ruling.

Sheriff Whittington

Obviously, the Mayor and Common Council, who firmly controlled the 'Sheriffwick', retained confidence in Alderman Whittington. Shortly after this latest crisis between the King and the City was averted, they elected him to the Shrievalty of London.[119] On St Matthew's Day (21 September 1393) the Mayor, Recorder, Aldermen and Commons duly assembled at the Guildhall. Their purpose was to elect two Sheriffs for the ensuing year. The Mayor, John Hadley, grocer, who was entitled to choose one candidate, selected 'of his own free will' Richard Whittington. The Common Council voted for Drew Baryntine, Goldsmith. Once again, there were heavy penalties for avoiding this high office: 'And if any one of those then chosen to be Sheriff shall refuse or absent himself, so as not to be ready at the Guildhall on the Vigil of Saint Michael next ensuing, at ten by the clock, there to receive his charge, there shall be levied forthwith from the goods, lands, and tenements of him who absents himself, one hundred pounds.'[120]

Whittington duly presented himself on Michaelmas morning (29 September) at the Guildhall where the retiring Sheriffs handed over all the legal records held in their possession. Whittington would then have received the keys and cocket (seal) of Newgate Gaol. This would have been the first time he came into contact with the infamous prison of which he would become a zealous benefactor. He was then escorted to Westminster Palace where, upon Richard II's insistence, he was required to swear his oath of allegiance before the Barons of the Exchequer. This contravened the rights of the Mayor and Aldermen who vigorously protested against the King's innovation. Once again, the crown prevailed.

One of the main responsibilities of a Sheriff, there being no electoral system, was to select representatives from the County and larger towns to serve in Parliament whenever one was summoned by the King. A Sheriff of London was also responsible for Middlesex.

Formerly, London Sheriffs were styled 'Bailiffs'. They acted as judges hearing personal pleas in their own courts at Guildhall. In the Court of Hustings, they were not only judges but additionally executors of the Mayor's judgements and precepts. Should a dispute arise, however, this was to be resolved by the Mayor and Aldermen because 'the liberties of the City have forbidden the Sheriff to be judges in their own cause.'[121]

Towards the end of his term of his office as Sheriff, Whittington was indeed sued by Thomas Spencer, 'golochemaker', on 14 October 1394.[122] Spencer claimed that Whittington had allowed his apprentice, John Toky, to be released from Ludgate Gaol, where he was held as prisoner for debt, on Whit Sunday. The plaintiff successfully proved that Toky owed him £11 10s plus 3s 4d damages. Whittington, curiously, appointed the gaoler, John Bottesham, to be his attorney although, in the event, neither appeared for the defence. Whittington was ordered to pay the debt, himself, while Spencer was awarded his costs.

During this period, the law was becoming increasingly complicated and professional lawyers were readily available after their intensive training at one of the City's Inns of Court. It appears odd, then, that Whittington chose rather to avail himself of a former gaoler, presumably untrained in legal matters, to plead on his behalf. This indicates a certain diffident attitude in this instance and also an obvious compassion for debtors and prisoners. It was an integral part of Whittington's character to show sympathy for prisoners that culminated in his bequeathing funds for the rebuilding of Newgate Gaol.

That aside, the fine awarded was 'not too weighty a sum'[123] for a merchant who supplied thousands of pounds of material for the Royal Wardrobe.

A New Queen

Tragedy struck the royal household in the summer of 1394. Richard II's beloved consort, Queen Anne of Bohemia, died, possibly due to a reoccurrence of the plague,[124] at Sheen Palace. The distraught King delayed her burial for six weeks to allow preparations for her funeral, which he commanded should be the lavish, at Westminster Abbey. Grief-stricken, he ordered the demolition of Sheen, which had been their favourite palace among the seven or eight that they possessed.[125]

After Anne's death, Richard's health deteriorated and he suffered intense bouts of depression, although his spirits were raised when Charles VI of France 'delivered unto Kynge Rycharde dame Isabell his daughter'.[126] Isabella of Valois was just six years old when she married the royal widower at the Church of St Nicholas at Calais in the autumn of 1396. The elaborate ceremonies were enormously expensive and subsequently viewed as a veritable Ricardian 'Field of the Cloth of Gold'.[127] The weeping princess was permitted to pack her dolls in her wedding trousseau when she sailed to her new home. The following year she was crowned Queen of England. This strange union ensured an extended truce with France but there was inevitable criticism over the enormous expense incurred in the wedding ceremonies, particularly by the Londoners.

State funerals became increasingly elaborate during the 14th century. They numbered Richard II's mother, Philippa of Hainault (1369), his father, Prince Edward (1376), his grandfather, Edward III (1377) and his mother, Joan of Kent (1385). Whittington's warehouse must have been one of those scoured for black silks and cloths to be turned into mourning garments edged with marten (black fur) for distribution among the members of the royal household and peerage who were expected to attend.

Mourning, incidentally, extended to furnishings, which included bed hangings and wall hangings. The period of mourning might extend for the greater part of a year. His precise contribution, of course, is impossible now to determine.

The Mercer's Charter

By the end of the 14th century, the leading Guilds were applying for royal charters in order to become limited companies, which would increase their power and influence over trade. Initially, the Goldsmiths, Skinners, Taylors and Girdlers had taken the lead by successfully obtaining their prized charters in 1327. They were followed by the Drapers, Fishmongers and Vintners in 1363-4.

Charters allowed these new companies a monopoly of their trade and the right to regulate standards of craftsmanship, a privilege that previously was claimed by the Mayor and Sheriffs. At the beginning of the 15th century, the majority of the London trades and crafts had secured their Charter of Incorporation, which entitled them to employ a common seal and a suit of livery. Confusingly, Medieval Guilds or Mysteries became 'Companies' and 'Fellowships'.[128]

Originally, the Mercers formed themselves into a fraternity in order to support their brothers and regulate trade. The antiquity of the Mercers' Guild is unrecorded although there are scattered references in documents indicating that it was already a recognised body early in the 13th century. Records of the Mercers commence from 30 June 1348. Their first Ordinances date from 6 July 1376, when their principal objectives were revealed to have been to promote the spiritual welfare of their brethren rather than to foster trade. Curiously, despite their brethren being immensely rich and powerful, they were inordinately late in obtaining their Charter of Incorporation, and even more dilatory in acquiring their Company seal and livery.

Richard II, true to character, was instinctively distrustful of the City Guilds. He regarded them, not without reason, as being potentially subversive. He issued an alarming royal writ on 1 November 1388. This ordered them to make returns to the Chancery before the following spring. They were required to set out their rules of government, oaths taken, details of licences or charters and – ominously – lands held. Obviously, this was a determined attempt by the Crown to gain control over influential and affluent Mysteries, particularly with regard to their commonly held property. Until that time, the Mercers had existed without charter, licence of property, although they had formulated their Ordinances and they held a common chest overfilled with funds from fines and fees that financed their fraternity.

The King's purpose was to reinforce the 'Statute of Mortmain' of 1279. This forbade the alienation of land to the 'dead hand' of the Church or formal institutions that lacked heirs, whereby the King or feudal lord was deprived of 'his' dues from a possible heir upon his accession. Richard II comprehended that during his reign vast areas of land had already been artfully absorbed by towns, parishes and guilds, prominent among whom were the Mysteries of London. Invariably, they had reserved their accumulated rents from these properties to fund priests, feasts and charities, the cash being locked securely in communal chests.

Eventually, the Mercers responded by seeking to purchase a Royal Charter confirming their commonalty and a licence allowing them to acquire lands worth twenty pounds a year to support a priest and alms. The application could hardly have been made at a more fraught time. After the King summoned the prominent citizens of London to Nottingham, he ordered the arrest of several leading Mercers. He commanded two of their Wardens to attend him personally, which coincided with their annual meeting when the accounts were presented and new Wardens elected. There were further complications. One elderly

Warden died, another was imprisoned while the two remaining were involved in a bitter feud when their accounts were disputed in June 1393.

During this difficult year, the 'Mystery of Mercers' called a special meeting at which all their members were obliged to attend. Unanimously, it was agreed that five persons should sue the King 'to be granted special commonalty of themselves' by letters patent passed under the Great Seal. The names of the elected representatives are not recorded but possibly they included the pair of harassed Wardens. Most probably, they numbered the recently appointed Sheriff for that year who could guide them adeptly through the complicated and sensitive legal process of application – Richard Whittington.

The coveted 'Charter of Incorporation' was duly obtained on 13 January 1394. Previously, the Mercers had existed amicably without a charter, hall, fraternity or property. Now they acquired physical proof of their corporate identity and gained their 'perpetual commonalty'. This defined the government of their select Company by a Prime and three Wardens plus their assistants who were permitted to possess property to support a priest and maintain their own charity.[129] Forthwith, they invested the accumulated contents of their common box and purchased 'The Pye' (cost £277) which comprised three dwellings with eight shops in St Martin Outwich, Bishopsgate. This proved to be a liability since the properties constantly needed repairs. The annual income, which amounted to about half the permitted twenty pounds, supported the new Company's chaplain and alms for distressed Mercers. Later, they spent their surplus funds on purchasing the 'Crown Seld', which cost in excess of two hundred pounds. This arcade occupied a prime site on Cheapside, which was immediately hired out to respectable tenants, mainly Mercers. This proved a far sounder investment. The Mercers' Company were demonstrating their initiative by becoming competitive property investors in the City of London. These rentals, indeed, contributed to the fact that, until a great misfortune befell them in the 18th century, the Mercers remained the richest of all the City Liveries.

Warden of The Mercers' Company

In the summer of 1395, Richard Whittington received the highest civic accolade when he was elected Prime or Upper Warden of 'The Commonalty of the Mercers of London'. The four Wardens who were responsible for the administration of the Company were elected by their predecessors at a formal meeting on Midsummer Day. The most senior Warden was generally an Alderman, of which, evidently, the Mercers enjoyed a superfluity! There was a rule that a Warden could not hold another term within five years that sensibly enabled younger men, such as Whittington, to be given a fair chance of election. Whittington, in fact, was to hold office on three separate occasions: 1395-6, 1401-2 and 1408-9. Each time he made it his job to call in late apprentices' fees, two shillings each, which improved company finances.[130] At a full assembly in March 1409, he chided his fellow Wardens for their late presentation of accounts.

After election, Wardens of a City Company was required to swear a convoluted oath before the Mayor, Sheriff and Aldermen at Guildhall. 'Extortion or wrong unto no one, by colour of your office, you shall do; nor unto anything shall be against the estate and peace of the King, or of the City, you shall consent.'[131] He vowed to be honest, impartial and careful to administer all the approved Ordinances of his company or craft. Funds were handed over to the new Wardens and the accounts were submitted for audit the following day. A City Ordinance of 1364, which decreed that there should be from four to six wardens for each Mystery, had set forth penalties for Wardens who were found to be 'rebellious, contrary and disturbing', ranging from a ten shilling fine and ten days in prison for a first offence to a forty shilling fine and forty days in prison for the fourth offence.

The Master or Wardens exercised great powers. They sanctioned new members; they rigorously inspected the quality of the materials offered for sale and they checked the accuracy of all weights and measures. For this purpose, they carried a silver yardstick for measuring the cloths displayed. They forbade any brother to secure a shop or house from another by offering a higher rent and they ensured there should be no cheating by underweight or undermeasure. They even controlled the hours of work, from daybreak until curfew.[132]

But there was another most laudable aspect to the Company. From its inception, the Mercers' Company became actively involved in the welfare of their less fortunate brothers who had fallen on hard times. This might be through accumulating debts, becoming the victim of fraud or, because of trading abroad, from 'misfortunes of the sea'. It offered practical assistance to their poorer brethren, the decayed and infirm, the widows and orphans, by supplying alms. Membership of a City Company was positively 'an insurance against old age or mischance'.[133] A newly appointed Warden would be allocated the responsibility for these charities and was known as Fourth Warden or 'Renter'. He was charged with collecting the weekly rents, supervising repairs to properties and paying the almsmen's pensions. Undoubtedly, Whittington proved indefatigable in exercising these particular duties early on, as he rose through the ranks to become Master of the Company.

In Merchant Companies, it became the custom to address veteran Wardens as 'Master', not only for the period when they were presiding but for life. Apparently, the title was a genuine distinction reserved for skilled professionals: doctors and lawyers, and chief masons or carpenters. Their wives assumed the corresponding title, 'Mistress', and were addressed politely as, 'My Lady'. (Wives of Wardens in lesser companies, apparently, were content to be called 'goodwife'.)[134]

Master Whittington presided over the Mercers' Court, which met quarterly. Members were summoned by a 'Bedel' who was charged with calling together the 'Felliship'. For this task, he was provided with his livery and received a modest recompense: four pence a week. Absence from meetings carried a heavy fine. Also in attendance were a priest or chaplain and a clerk to record the minutes. The Ordinances were read aloud to the assembly so that everyone became familiar with them. Originally, these were recorded in the form of rolls but later they were bound in books by the stationers. This was important, as rules – which ranged from drawing a knife against a member to speaking after the Master had struck his mallet – constantly changed.

Surprisingly, the Mercers', despite their accumulated wealth, lacked their own Company Hall in which to conduct their business and provide entertainment. During the 14th century, most rival companies had acquired administrative headquarters of 'rambling spaciousness'.[135] A Hall was not merely a social centre but a visible sign of the status of the company. It was an essential building where company officials could administer its laws, dispense its charities, supervise its properties and collect its rents. Possibly, the Mercers hired an accommodation they deemed adequate for their assemblies. Alternatively, they might have met at the mansions of magnates or Wardens. One suggestion is that they met at a large tavern, 'The Tumbling Bear', which offered superior facilities, often frequented by Mercers trading in nearby Cheapside.[136]

At the time of Whittington's first Wardenship, the Mercers began to assemble in a rented room at the Hospital of St Thomas of Acon, on the corner of Cheapside and Ironmonger Lane.[137] The Hospital, served by a Master and brethren of the Military Order of Saint Thomas the Martyr, was founded on the site of the birthplace of the saint by his devoted sister, Agnes, in 1220. (Thomas of Acon is an archaic name for Thomas Becket.) Agnes was the wife of Thomas Fitz Theobald de Helles who, around 1190, had founded a band of crusading knights after the miraculous intervention of the saint during the invasion by Richard the Lionheart of the seaport, Acon, in the Holy Land.[138]

From its inception, the Mercers were sponsors of the Hospital, conveniently located in the centre of the Mercery, Cheapside.[139] 'Gilbert Bekkettes', father of the martyred 'Erchebysshope', was himself a Mercer who became Portreeve of London.[140] Originally, this was a modest foundation inhabited by humble secular canons who dedicated their lives to the service of the poor, the burial of the dead and especially the ransoming of captives held in the Far East. After Becket's canonisation in 1173, it developed into a far larger complex with cloisters, chapter house and library, served by Augustinian Canons.[141] The Hospital gatehouses presented an image of Saint Thomas looking down favourably upon the markets of Cheapside.[142] Mercers' shops and stalls nearby would have benefitted greatly from the constant passage of pilgrims who wished to pay homage at the birthplace of one of the two patron saints of the City of London.

The adjoining Chapel of St Thomas of Acon, slightly east of the Hospital on the corner of Old Jewry, also became a focus of civic ritual. Master Whittington would have worshipped at this Chapel on countless occasions. The Mayor and Aldermen assembled there on the day the new Mayor took his oath, processed alongside Cheapside to St Paul's to worship at the tomb of Becket's parents, and then returned to the Chapel by torchlight if it was late, where they made offerings of 'single pence'.[143] This short pilgrimage was repeated on Saints' days. The Chapel was a grand affair with nave, choir and side aisles with the 'aulter of Seynt Thomas the Martyr in the north parte of the Chyrche'. It was set attractively among the Hospital's courtyards and gardens. The ringing of the Chapel bell for the early hour of prime was the signal for the City gates to be opened and the market trading to begin at Cheapside.

For the Mercers, an even more impressive ceremony took place at the Chapel of St Thomas on the Feast Days of their patron saints, the Virgin Mary and St Thomas. All the brethren, from the highest to the lowest, gathered there in their smart livery. The whole day was regarded as a holiday. The procession to the Chapel was attended by the Master, Wardens and frequently the Mayor, sometimes members of the royal court, occasionally even the royal princes.[144] In 1406, the Mercers' Company was referred to as the 'Brothers of St Thomas a Becket'.[145]

After Mass, the whole assembly would return either to the Master's house, or later, the Mercers' Hall. There, the Company cook would have prepared 'toothsome dishes' for a banquet. Every sense was gratified: banners fluttered, minstrels played, sweet scents filled the air... The master presided over the top table with his invited guests while below sat the brethren and their consorts. There was an interval while the serious business of the day was transacted, including the election of officers for the coming year. Once over, the loving cup was passed around to 'refresh and cheer'. Finally, a fanfare announced the entertainment; allegories and interludes, players and mummers.[146] These regular feasts offered a chance for the members to socialise with their distinguished guests, who, naturally, were regarded as potential customers. Whittington, for one, would relish this opportunity.

Early in the sixteenth century, the Mercers acquired a substantial plot from the Hospital to build their Company Hall over their own private chapel. This was commonly referred to as 'Mercers' Chapell'.[147] According to Stow: 'Before the Hospital, towards the street, was a fayre and beautiful chapell arched over with stone, which stood before the great olde chapell and over which was the Mercers' Hall, a most curious piece of work.' The furnishings of the interior of both the chapel and the hall were sumptuous. An altar piece was later purchased from a Flemish carver and probably the early 16th-century statue of Christ, now displayed in the modern Mercers' Hall. The elevated Hall with its elaborate 'sylling' was enriched with wonderful tapestries, 'bankers' (seat covers) for the benches and twelve plump cushions from Arras. Apparently, further sets of these valuable hangings were presented to the Guildhall but they were surreptitiously 'borrowed' by members when entertaining at their own homes. Agas's 'Copperplate

Map' includes a rude sketch of Mercers' Hall and Chapel with its impressive battlemented stone facade, central entrance and adjoining shop.

After the Dissolution of the Monasteries, Henry VIII allowed the Mercers to purchase the redundant buildings and continue to worship in their Chapel. Sadly, these were all engulfed in the Great Fire of 1666. Determinedly, the Company rebuilt its Hall in Cheapside. This was a grand, symmetrical building with a central ornamented doorcase flanked by a row of shops 'unshashed', rented out to Mercers, Goldsmiths and Booksellers. The main entrance was tucked away in Ironmonger Lane, where the elevated Hall was supported by Doric columns above a spacious piazza. At the far end stood the Chapel, 'neatly pewed and wainscotted and paved with black and white marble'. A long flight of stairs led to the Hall which was 'a very lofty apartment, handsomely wainscotted and ornamented with Ionic pilasters, and various carvings in compartments.'[148]

Mercers' Hall and Chapel remained occupied and substantially unaltered until their destruction by enemy action in the Second World War.[149] Fortunately, the Hall's interior was recorded in a series of photographs that reveal it to have been a truly magnificent building. It was a long room with two entrances on the south and east sides, two fireplaces centred in the north and south walls and a gallery running the width of the west end. It was panelled throughout in English oak, carved with armorial crests and adorned with heraldic tapestries. All the stained-glass windows dated from the mid-Victorian period. They featured past worthies of the Mercers' Company.[150] One window in the north wall depicted Whittington. Alas, this was shattered by enemy action in the London Blitz of 1941.[151] A delicate watercolour survives to show this beautiful room with a grand banner disporting Whittington's coat-of-arms. His portrait, dated 1536, once hung in a prominent position, revealing, apparently, a middle-aged man wearing a free livery gown and black cap, stroking a black and white cat. Richard Whittington's portrait is now lost.

Richard II graciously accepted the invitation to become an honorary member of the Mercers' Company. Whittington's hand is surely seen in the initial invitation extended to this capricious sovereign? The King was following in the footsteps of his grandfather, Edward III, who, realising the economic importance of fostering the trade of the City, consented to the invitation to become an honorary member of the Merchant Taylors (formerly the 'Linen Armourers'). The tradition of welcoming the sovereign as an honorary member of a City Company continues to this day. Queen Elizabeth II was a Freeman of the Worshipful Company of Drapers from 1947 and Patron of the Worshipful Company of Shipwrights from 1952.[152]

6

The Mayor of London

DURING THE SUMMER of 1397, Adam Bamme, the Mayor of London,[153] a wealthy Goldsmith who was serving a second term, died while in office. The King made an arbitrary decision to replace him with a close, trusted and subservient friend, who also happened to be his chief supplier of luxury goods. 'Ande that same Adem Bamme mayr stylle tylle the vj day od Junij and then he dyde,' records William Gregory, Mayor and Skinner, in his 'Chronicle'.[154] 'Ande Richarde Wedynton was chosse for the resydewe of the yere.' The King's choice of Whittington was surprising in view of the fact that he had only been an Alderman for four years. His rash action, in any case, was in breach of the right for the Londoners, confirmed in Magna Carta, to elect their own Mayor. The Barons, therefore, refused to swear him in office and instead this solemn duty was undertaken personally by the King.

Richard had twice before interfered in the election of a Mayor, most notably when he resorted to force in 1383. His most influential friend was the magnate, Nicholas Brembre, fishmonger, grocer and wool merchant, who had made an advantageous marriage to an heiress by which he had acquired six manors in Kent and three in Middlesex. Brembre's ardent opponent was the radical John of Northampton, also a man of considerable wealth and property but one who championed the poor in London.[155] Further, his patron was John of Gaunt, he was a disciple of Wycliff and a member of the Drapers' Guild. When a riot erupted after Brembre's dubious election, Richard contrived for Northampton to be imprisoned. The inevitable result was intense disillusionment among the Londoners with their novice King.[156]

King Richard issued a royal mandate on 8 June 1397:

Know ye, that whereas Adam Bamme, late Mayor of our City of London, and our Escheator within the same city, has gone the way of all flesh...

We, wishing therefore, as unto us pertains, duly to provide for the sound governance and happy rule of the said city, and of our people therein, until the accustomed day of the next election that shall be of our Mayor of the City aforesaid, with the assent and advice of the Council, have appointed our well-beloved Richard Whityngtone, in whose fidelity and circumspection we do repose full confidence, to be Mayor of the City aforesaid, and our Escheator within the same City.[157]

It would appear from this effusive statement that the King, isolated from his friends and betrayed by the magnates, had formed a close attachment to Whittington, who declined to criticise or meddle in politics. Immediately, he was transferred to the Aldermanry of Lime Street left vacant by Bamme, where he remained until his death a quarter of a century later. (The affluent Ward of Lime Street, named after the lime burners and seller who lived there, incorporated Leadenhall Market.)[158]

As Mayor – the alternative title was 'Warden' – of London, Whittington would have been expected to wear an official livery which changed with the church or civic calendar. For the attendance at open air divine services, according to Stow, 'At these sermons, severally preached, the Mayor, with his brethren the aldermen, were accustomed to be present in their violets at Paul's on good Fryday, and in Scarlets at the Spittle (Spittlefields Cross) in the (Easter) Holidayes, except Wednesday in Violet, and the Mayor with his brethren on low sonday[159] in scarlet at Paul's Crosse.'

An indication of the finery habitually worn by London's Mayor is gained from a description by Stow of a later civic procession to welcome the young Henry VI after his coronation in France:

The 10 of Henry the sixt, hee being crowned in France, returning into England, came to Eltham towardes London, and the Mayor of London, John Welles, the aldermen, with the commonalty, rode against him on Horsebacke, the Mayor in Crimson velvet, a great velvet hat furred, a girdle of gold aboute his middle, and a Bawdrike of gold aboute his necke trilling down behind him, his three Henxemen, on three coursers following him, in one sute of red, all spangled in silver, then the aldermen in Gownes of scarlet, with sanguine hoods, and all the Commonaltie of the citty in white gownes and scarlet hoods, with divers cognizances embrodered on their sleeves.

Mayor Whittington, despite his supreme authority, would still need to obtain the consent of the Sheriffs, Aldermen and Councillors before affixing the Common Seal to official documents. This seal was kept under six locks, the keys being distributed among the Aldermen and leading citizens. The Mayoral Seal was redesigned in 1381 to incorporate conventional and religious imagery. It was created by the same Goldsmith responsible for the Great Seals of Edward III and Richard II. Surviving impressions of Mayoral seals are rare but one attached to a charter dated 2 July 1399,[160] although imperfect, remains incredibly detailed. This can be compared with a far later, large red wax imprint, cut from a Tudor document, which presents the complete picture.[161]

In a wide central niche of three canopied bays appear Saint Thomas Becket, Archbishop of Canterbury, complete with mitre and pall, his left hand holding a crozier, his right hand raised in benediction, and Saint Paul, Patron of the City of London, his left hand holding the Bible, his right hand a drawn sword, amicably sharing a humble pew. Overhead, the Virgin Mary, enthroned, presents the Christ Child, attended by winged angels, all of whom appear in their own canopied niches. They are guarded on either side by a Sergeant-at-Arms, bearing a mace and wearing a 'kettlehat'. Below are the arms of the City of London – the cross of St George and, in the first quarter, that same drawn sword of St Paul – supported by a pair of demi-lions. (Incidentally, this seal is one of the earliest authorities for the City arms.) The tracing and vaulting of the canopies, the folds of the ecclesiastical robes and, exceptionally, the kindly face of the elderly apostle, are immaculately realised. The legend surrounding these splendid seals reads (incomplete in the first example): 'SIGILL * MAIORATUS * CIUTATIS * LONDON'. Alas, although the official seal would have been attached to hundreds of documents, none remain from the periods when Whittington was Mayor.[162]

Mayor Whittington's West Country burr must have jarred in the trilingual world of Medieval London. Although English was his native tongue, he would have learned more than a smattering of French words and phrases from his father who had fought in France. Edward III and his knights had spoken French but that language became unfashionable amongst English courtiers as the wars with France progressed. Richard II, born in France, spoke English fluently and he encouraged its cultivation at his court and in Parliament. Latin was fast becoming confined to the written word in legal departments, whereas English was embraced by cultured authors and poets. Whittington's career in the City coincided with the transition from French and Latin to English as the accepted language of Londoners.

Pleshey Castle

Whittington's high civic appointment soon proved to be a double-edged sword. He was Mayor of London at a period when its noble citizens faced acute peril. Richard II had been biding his time but as he approached his thirtieth year he felt confident enough to strike back at his former enemies. He had never forgiven those who had publicly humiliated him and hounded his companions. His revenge was concealed by cunning. In the summer of

1397, the King began to pick off the Senior Lords Appellants one at a time. He invited Thomas, Earl of Warwick, to attend a banquet at Westminster Palace, but after a sumptuous repast he was arrested and imprisoned. Richard, Earl of Arundel, was apprehended at Reigate Castle, Surrey, and brought to the Tower. His brother, the former Chancellor, Thomas Arundel, Archbishop of Canterbury, was deprived of his primacy and banished for life.

Yet the real bane of Richard II's life was his bellicose uncle, Thomas of Woodstock, Earl of Buckingham and Constable of England. The King had also created him Duke of Gloucester. Religious, austere, censorious, Gloucester, although himself highly cultured, despised his nephew for his extravagant lifestyle. His constant criticism and scornful reproaches were calculated to undermine Richard's authority and wound his pride. His private scorn turned to open hostility, which led to the interpretation that he coveted Richard's throne. Far too often, while in attendance on the King, he had 'checked him too sharply'.

The Duke of Gloucester's stronghold was Pleshey (or 'Plashey') Castle. This must have been a splendid residence since the Duke was one of the richest men in the kingdom. The castle is located above the village of Pleshey in the parish of High Easter, about six miles northwest of Chelmsford, Essex. The name derives from the Old French word 'plasseis', meaning 'an enclosure'. Although long stripped of its stonework keep, it remains one of the largest Norman motte and bailey castles in England. The massive artificial wooded mound or 'motte' (50 feet high, 900 feet in circumference) is certainly one of the highest. The vast sweeping inner enclosure or 'bailey' is surrounded by an even bigger outer bailey that encompasses the present sleepy village. The steep, tilting, buttressed brick bridge that traverses the moat is supposedly the oldest in Europe.[163]

Richard II plotted to arrest his uncle the Duke. How far Whittington was involved is debatable. Contemporary accounts of Gloucester's entrapment, imprisonment and demise offer conflicting dates, times and circumstances. According to Gregory, the King summoned a contingency of his men to meet him at 'Myles Ende' from whence they rode straightaway to Pleshey in the early morning. Froissart relates how the King assembled a small retinue on the pretext of hunting at Havering-at-the Bower before riding out to Pleshey later that hot afternoon. Both chroniclers condemn the King's subterfuge. The anonymous author of the unreliable 'Chronique de la Traison et Mort de Richard II', however, relates how Richard's arrival with his men-at-arms and archers was announced with trumpets blaring.

The most convincing record is the Kirkstall Chronicle.[164] This graphic account, untainted by later Lancastrian influence, was penned in the closing years of Richard II's reign by the monks at Kirkstall Abbey in Yorkshire.

The King set out from his manor at Kenington round the Feast of St John the Baptist [24 June] having issued a proclamation that all members of his court should immediately prepare themselves to accompany him and journey to a place and for a reason of which they were quite ignorant. The King met with his court and retainers on the London road, and after entrusting the security and safeguarding of the city to the Mayor and Sheriffs,[165] immediately set off, riding by night and reaching Plasghe manor, the property of Thomas of Woodstock, Duke of Gloucester. In the early morning, the Duke being suddenly warned of the King's speedy arrival set out with his lady Duchess, his household and his chaplain in procession to bow before the King and to show him all customary reverence.

Certainly, Whittington was ordered to raise the militia, but whether he accompanied the King on his thirty-five-mile ride across country to Pleshey is doubtful. His presence would then have been intended as a decoy with the aim of tempting the Duke from the security of his castle. The Kirskstall Chronicle presents the Mayor of London in a passive role, remaining to seal the City against a possible rebellion.

The arresting party entered the protective bailey from the east, rode over the double bridge, crossed the outer moat and climbed the steep, inclined brick bridge over the inner moat to the castle keep. The Essex landscape is fairly flat and the commanding view from the top of the dominant stone tower must have stretched almost as far as London. The Duke and Duchess would have had ample warning from the sentries of the approach of the royal party, even in the early morning mist. Roused from their prayers, they would have prepared to greet their sovereign.

The King, after taking refreshment, invited his uncle to return with him to London, bringing the minimum of attendants, because he sought his expert advice in dealing with its troublesome citizens. Unsuspecting, the Duke complied and accompanied his nephew along the rambling country roads to the City. When they reached Stratford-le-Bow, the King suddenly galloped ahead after leading the Duke into an ambuscade on the remote Essex marshes. The Earl Marshal, Thomas Mowbray, seized Gloucester's reins and arrested him. He was bundled aboard a waiting boat anchored on the Thames, which was rowed across the Channel. The Duke was secretly imprisoned at Calais.[166] Mowbray, who was also Constable of Calais, was ordered to kill his noble prisoner, which he refused to do. All the same, that September, the Duke of Gloucester was smothered to death under a 'feder bed' in the back room of a common inn at Calais.

Immediately after the arrest of Gloucester, his property and possessions were forfeit to the Crown. Richard II's officials were ruthlessly efficient in impounding 'all that might be found in his bailwick' and storing everything to await instruction for their disposal from the King.[167] One of the most efficient and ruthless agents of Richard II's tyranny, Clement Spice, Escheator of Essex, was placed in control of the liquidation of Gloucester's estates. He compiled an inventory, written in French but with occasional interpolations in English, on a long roll, with headings relating to library books, church vestments, personal garments, tapestries, silverware, arms and armour. The most impressive furnishings listed are sixteen sumptuous beds with trappings of blue or white satin, green double samite and black baudekyn, exquisitely embroidered with designs of blossoming lilies, roses, eagles, falcons, owls, popinjays, greyhounds, lions, unicorns.[168] These are perfect examples of the rich fabrics that Whittington specialised in providing to noblemen's households.

Whittington must have been perfectly aware of the misery and humiliation this situation caused to the Duchess of Gloucester. She was determined, however, to weather the storm and threw herself into the management of her estate with all the vigour she could muster. The purpose of the inventory was to value the property for their resale to the benefit of the Crown. Duchess Eleanor was provided with the opportunity to redeem her late husband's personal possessions, which she did to the total of £1,136. This amount included £260 spent at an auction conducted by Whittington in London.[169] It seems she was made a ward of the teenage Queen Isabella, which must have added insult to injury, before she spent her last days of brief widowhood in a nunnery at Barking. Pleshey Castle fell into decay and became a desolate place – 'empty lodgings, and unfurnish'd walls, Unpeopled offices, untrodden stones' – according to Shakespeare. (*Richard II* Act 1 scene 2.)[170]

Richard II recalled Parliament at Westminster where it met in a grand marquee erected in the Palace Yard on St Lambert's Day, 17 September 1397. Its main purpose was the appointment of fresh Lords Appellant whose views the King would find more conducive. Their role was to appeal Arundel, Warwick and Gloucester of treason after rescinding their previous pardons. The atmosphere was fraught with tension and everyone present, including Henry Bolingbroke, feared for their lives. They realised that to deny the King his unfettered right to rule was now tantamount to treason. Arundel was beheaded, Warwick imprisoned, but the fate of Gloucester, apparently, hung in the balance. The King kept up the pretence that his uncle was at that time still alive. When news of his death filtered through to the populace, the exact circumstances were shrouded in mystery. Chronicler Gregory, shaking his head in perplexity, penned a blunt statement: 'God wote howe, but ded he was.'

Eventually, the Duke's embalmed body was brought back by boat to England. The coffin was transported along the River Thames to Hadleigh Castle and then overland to Pleshey where it was buried in the tomb previously prepared in the Collegiate Church dedicated to the Holy Trinity.

The Duke had founded this country church after surviving a sudden storm on his homeward journey from one of his campaigns in Brittany. When Henry IV ascended the throne, he conveyed the bodies of his uncle and aunt to London, where they were respectfully reburied in the Chapel of St Edward the Confessor in Westminster Abbey. The pictorial brass commemorating Eleanor of Bohun, Duchess of Gloucester[171] is considered to be the finest in the Abbey.

Richard II had made a dramatic leap forward in his aim to rule as an absolute monarch. After he had vanquished his enemies – a step that included the clandestine murder of a high ranking member of his royal family – his commands went unquestioned, unopposed. He remained blinkered, completely oblivious towards the bitter resentment brewing among his subjects. Instead, he retired into a dream world where he 'werid his croune, and went in his rial array… and make in his chamber, a trone wherynne he was wont to sitte… spekynge to no man.'[172]

Whittington, too, had become adept at keeping his own counsel. Indeed, his reaction to the horrific treatment of Gloucester that fateful summer is difficult to interpret. Duty bound to obey his monarch, he acted, like everyone else, in a climate of fear. The Duke's arrest and ignoble death must surely have been repugnant to him and he lived the rest of his life in the shadow of these harrowing events. Curiously, the Duke of Gloucester was described as his 'promoter' (or patron) in the 'Ordinances of Whittington College', which he founded towards the end of his life. He had been among Whittington's most diligent and appreciative customers,[173] which would account for those luxurious furnishings at Pleshey Castle. Whittington, full of remorse after tacitly accepting Gloucester's inevitable fate, forever afterwards remembered Gloucester in his prayers.

Blackwell Hall

Whittington's first Mayoralty was more positively remembered for his organisation of Blackwell (or 'Bakewell') Hall, a market reserved exclusively for the sale of broadcloth in the City. English wool commanded high prices abroad because it was regarded as the finest in Europe. Raw wool was available in this country at lower prices and it was this which encouraged the expansion of a thriving native cloth industry. During the fourteenth century, exports of woollen cloth were negligible but by the end of that century there was a marked rise in overseas trading when as many as 20,000 cloths might be exported in a single year.[174] And as the cloth trade developed rapidly in the provincial towns, the number of clothiers and drapers who wished to expand their business by selling in London increased. City merchants were adamant that a concerted effort should be made to control sales of imported wares and restrict their prices to avoid unwelcome competition by these intrusive clothiers from the country.

Blackwell Hall, which became the focus of the cloth trade in the capital, was conveniently situated east of Guildhall. It originated from a private residence centred upon a vast open hall belonging to a nobleman, Roger de Clifford. In 1280, Clifford granted his Hall to the Mayor and Commonalty of London. About 1292, the City sold the property to Sir John de Bankuell ('Bacquelle' or 'Banquelle'), Alderman of Dowgate Ward, from whom it acquired its name, and later it passed to a descendant, Thomas Bakewell. According to deeds, the estate with its 'gardens and appurtenances', extended from Bassishaw (now Basinghall Street) to Guildhall Yard.

In 1396-7, Richard II granted a licence for certain 'Citizens and Mercers' to reconvey 'the said Messuage called bakewellhalle' back to the Mayor and Commonalty.[175] The building was soon established as the location of a thrice weekly market – Thursday, Friday, Saturday – for broad cloths brought there from all parts of the kingdom.[176] Mayor Whittington, the following year, drew up Ordinances (21 September 1398)[177] to ensure that 'foreigners' and 'strangers' were restricted to selling their cloth at Bakewell Hall, that they were limited to fixed days and hours in the week, and that their cloths or half cloths should be listed at both ends, 'upon paine of forfeyture therof'. These regulations were strictly enforced. The supposed justification for such strictures was that 'foreign drapers bringing woollen cloths to the City of London, do sell the same in divers hostelries in secret, where they make many disorderly and deceitful bargains.' Later, in the same document, the real reason is revealed: '... and also, that our said Lord the King may be the better paid his custom and other duties upon the said cloths.'[178]

Blackwell Hall was administered by two rival Companies, the Drapers and the Tailors. From 1405, the Keeper of the Hall was nominated by the Drapers, although his 'admission, confirmation and removal' remained in the power of the Mayor and Aldermen. It was his responsibility to collect the rents of the chambers, cupboards and chests ('hucches'), which might be hired for the year, the month or even the day, on behalf of the City Chamberlain.[179] By providing this central covered market, where bales could be rigorously inspected, safely stored and conveniently sold, the Mayor and Corporation ensured that London became established as the national market for the sale of English broadcloth.

Apart from the 'Copperplate' (*c.*1555-8) and Agas (*c.*1560) maps, there are no surviving representations of the Medieval building once described as 'the greatest woollen cloth market in the world'.[180] When it was renovated in 1588, Stow commented: 'The Bakewell Hall ... hath been long since imployed as a weekly market for all sorts of Wollen clothes, broade and narrow, brought from all partes of this Realme, there to be solde.' He recalls it was 'builded upon vaultes of stone, which stone was brought form Cane (Caen) in Normandie, the like of that of Paules church'. Admittance was by payment of reasonable tolls or dues but 'aliens' were strictly barred from entry.

Eventually, Blackwell became so 'ruinous and in daunger of falling' that it was completely demolished and a new hall was built on the same site. Richard May, a merchant tailor, financed most of the project, which cost two thousand five hundred pounds. The building was opened in 1658 but was destroyed by fire in 1666 and rebuilt in 1672. Lambert describes this elegant replacement:

> It is a square building, with two courts in the middle, surrounded with warehouses and has two spacious entrances, or gates for carriages: one from Basinghall-street and the other from Guildhall-yard, where is the principal front, and a door-case adorned with two columns of the Doric order, with their entablature, and a pediment, in which are the King's arms, and, a little lower, the city arms, enriched with cupids.

Inside the open arcaded edifice were large chambers or 'halls' where cloth was displayed, pitched or stored ready to be sold by the merchant's agent. Each linked hall bore an appropriate name – 'Devonshire', 'Worcestershire', 'Kentish', 'Gloucestershire' – indicating the province of the cloth or clothiers. Interestingly, the profits were claimed by Christ's Hospital whose governors managed the warehouses.[181] Blackwell Hall was demolished in 1820 and the site is now occupied by Guildhall Art Gallery.

King Richard's Fundraising.

Richard II's extravagant lifestyle continued to gain momentum. His father, Prince Edward, his grandfather, Edward III, and his great-grandfather, Edward II, had all been reckless, financially. The closing years of Richard II's reign were marked by his ingenious, irresponsible and illegal methods of amassing money. He had learned a sharp lesson when he had introduced a poll tax to raise funds nationwide that had resulted in the insurrection of his subjects. Instead, he turned his attention to targeting the Londoners. Ultimately, this unwise measure, too, would lead to his downfall.

It was an acknowledged truth that when a sovereign was weak or his title doubtful, he sought the alliance of the City of London. Its citizens were primed to raise a trained army at a moment's notice. At such times, it was comparatively easy for the citizens to gain charters and privileges from a compliant Crown. Once the sovereign felt himself secure – and Richard II now betrayed signs of being a megalomaniac – Londoners tended to be regarded as an 'inexhaustible treasury'.[182]

King Richard attempted to accrue funds from the Londoners in several ways. First, he tried to raise a loan on the security of a valuable jewel. The

Corporation declined to oblige him on the grounds that he had allowed so many 'foreigners' to trade in the City that they had become impoverished. Next, he revived that tried and tested method of conferring a knighthood – from which he was entitled to receive a substantial fee – on every subject who possessed property to the value of £40. London merchants, he knew, would opt to pay a fine rather than accept an honour both costly and time-consuming. Thirdly, he instituted an audacious measure which played on the citizens' insecurity. He reminded anyone who had supported the Lords Appellant in the previous decade that they were guilty of treason but then graciously offered a 'free pardon' upon their paying an exorbitant fine. Ironically, this last piece of chicanery was known as 'La Pleasaunce'.

When Parliament resumed at Shrewsbury in 1398, its members felt compelled to grant the King the duties of wool, woolfells and hides for life. This generous gesture, worth £30,000 per annum, would bolster Richard's fluctuating finances. Perhaps their decision may have been influenced by the presence of the King's bodyguard, the Cheshire archers, who stood with bows drawn and arrows loaded.[183]

Anne Sutton considers that 'Whittington realised from an early age that loans to the King remained the key to worldly influence and profit.' Earlier, in fact, Whittington had lent the King's former tutor, Sir Simon Burley, 400 marks for which he received silver vessels as security. He managed to retain them, although with great difficulty, after Burley's condemnation, execution and the forfeiture of all his possessions. Now, in the last decade of Richard II's reign, Whittington started to lend money to the Crown. And, since he was the only citizen to do so, this would confirm that close relationship with his increasingly despised sovereign.

At first, these loans were trifling: £4 in 1388; £4 in 1389, which had jumped to £10 in 1390. This last larger sum must have attracted the attention of the Exchequer because from this time onwards these loans became substantial. In 1397, Whittington lent approximately £1,600, a huge amount. The date is significant. Richard II, it would appear, positively favoured Whittington after he had supplied him with fabulous materials and promised him phenomenal loans. Undoubtedly, this influenced his choice of the Mercer as Mayor.[184]

Whittington proved an excellent choice for Mayor – dutiful and subservient – despite his dubious 'election'. Whatever Londoners thought about his financial exactions during the summer or his participation in the autumn Parliament of 1397, they obviously appreciated the advantage of having a man who could pacify their unpredictable King. Accordingly, Whittington was invited freely by the Aldermen to continue as Mayor in October 1397. (They may, of course, have decided not to risk the King's further displeasure by voting for anyone other than the current royal favourite.) The actual voting, however, was conducted with such clamour that a change was made whereby in future no one was to be admitted to an election except the Mayor, Sheriffs and Aldermen.[185]

This time the Barons, too, were content.

On Saturday, the Feast of St Edward the King and Confessor [13 October] the aforesaid Richard Whityngtone was elected Mayor for the following year; and afterwards, in the Guildhall of London, on the Feast of the Apostles Simon and Jude (28 October), he was sworn ... and on the following day, on the morrow of the Apostles Simon and Jude, he was presented before the Barons of the Exchequer of our Lord the King, admitted and sworn.[186]

The Sheriffs chosen to support him were John Woodcock and William Askam.

Blank Charters

Richard II at least demonstrated an enlightened foreign policy. He betrayed no appetite for warfare. He fostered cordial relations with England's former antagonist, France. Consequently, there was a marked absence of war throughout his reign. This approach should, theoretically, have reduced the burden of taxation upon his subjects. Instead, the King lavished gifts on his close circle of cherished companions and this abundant generosity proved far more expensive than warfare – but without the attendant potential benefits.

Devastating news was received which would plunge this spendthrift King into greater debt. Richard II's Lord Lieutenant of Ireland, Roger Mortimer, Earl of March, had been defeated and killed by rebel Irish chiefs at the Battle of Kells in 1398. Mortimer was recognised as the heir presumptive and, upon learning of his demise, the King declared Roger's infant son, Edmund, to be his heir in his late father's stead. He then announced that he intended to avenge Mortimer's death and subdue the rebel chieftains by invading Ireland in 1399. This was a reckless decision at this uncertain time, compounded by the intention of taking his loyal companions with him, thus leaving his kingdom virtually defenceless. It was a doomed venture for a King little versed in warfare.[187]

After squandering a vast amount on luxuries, Richard needed to raise even more money if he was to fund his Irish campaign. Direct taxation was only to be levied in wartime, which presented the King with a dilemma. Rashly, he now resorted to forced loans, which involved supposed offenders buying back – at a price – his royal favour. He targeted counties, shires and, inevitably, the capital, known to have supported the Lords Appellant in their challenge to his sovereignty in 1388-9. His method of extorting money from its principal citizens were once again intimidating, iniquitous, illegal...

The King 'thorughe wyckyd consyle' ordered his clerks to prepare documents which they were instructed to distribute among high-ranking officials. These baffling depositions were not filled in at the time of the deposition but might be completed at a later date with convoluted statements amounting to admission of guilt for unspecified past crimes.[188] Acting as proctors, the officials were themselves required to sign them, acknowledging their consent and placing themselves and their possessions at the King's disposal. Spaces were left in each copy of the document allowing Richard to insert a random fine for these supposed transgressions. In the City, the King demanded this formal submission be signed by the Archbishop of Canterbury, the Bishop of London, 'Richard Wedyngton, Mayre' and his two 'Scherevys' (William Askham and John Woodcock).

Gregory records the tenor of the despised documents in his Chronicle:

And then anon, aftyr the presentacyon of the sayde supplycacion, there were made many blanke chartours, and all ye men of any crafte in the cittie, as welle servauntys as maysterys, were chargyd for to come to the Yelde Halle to sette hyrselys to the sayde blanke chartours... And soo dyd also for the moste parte of Inglond, and no man wyste what hyt mente.

Yet the immense funds that these documents, equivalent to modern 'blank cheques', intended to raise were insufficient for Richard's military purposes. Further loans were sought from wealthy citizens and the King's unpopularity escalated.

During this traumatic time Whittington applied to the Vatican for a papal licence to appoint his own confessor. This was granted to him on 15 June 1398 by Pope Boniface IX. The licence expressly stated that he could gain absolution, being penitent after his private confession, at any time he pleased and not just upon the approaching hour of his demise. A personal confessor was a luxury indeed! Perhaps this application reveals Whittington's true state of mind. Guilt-stricken, he sought absolution for the despicable tasks he had been required to perform on behalf of his unscrupulous monarch as London's Mayor.[189]

Henry, Duke of Lancaster

Political as well as financial motives were behind the final financial scheme to which the King resorted in desperation. Late in his reign, he began to bear great enmity towards John of Gaunt, the Duke of Lancaster, widely acclaimed the most powerful subject in his kingdom. He also happened to be the richest nobleman with vast estates and over thirty castles at his disposal. But in the spring of 1398, the health of the old warrior was visibly declining and this prompted King Richard to put into practice his wildest tactic: the absorption of the great Lancastrian inheritance.

John of Gaunt, born in 1340, was the fourth son of Edward III. His son, Henry, although Richard II's cousin, was not, in fact, the immediate heir. By tradition, if not the law, the throne of England passed by primogeniture. Should Richard remain childless, the succession would pass to young Edmund Mortimer, Earl of March, who was descended in the female line from Edward III's third son, Lionel, Duke of Clarence. Inevitably, this created rivalry between the Lancasters and Mortimers, which King Richard fully exploited. It also occurred to him that if Henry was exiled prior to his father's demise, then Gaunt's vast wealth would replenish the royal coffers.

After the elimination of the senior Lords Appellant, Richard II had created five new Dukes. These included Henry, Earl of Derby, who became Duke of Hereford, and Thomas Mowbray, Earl of Nottingham, currently Earl Marshal, now Duke of Norfolk. A chance encounter between this antagonistic pair led to a sequence of events that altered the course of history. The Dukes met on horseback and quarrelled just before Christmas, 1397. Their dispute is difficult now to disentangle. Mowbray informed Henry that the King plotted to kill both him and Gaunt. Henry raced to inform his father, who left directly to confront the King. The King summoned both Dukes before him at Windsor Castle – only Henry dared attend – both men feared his vengeance, realising they were the last two remaining Lords Appellant.[190]

Henry and Mowbray, arrested and imprisoned, taunted each other with charges of treason, since their accusations implied King Richard's prior knowledge and personal involvement of the intended assassination. All three men were cornered. Henry, who had simply reported a plot to kill him and his father, found himself accused of being a traitor; Mowbray, who had conspired in the murder of Gloucester, was deeply implicated in the King's duplicity, while Richard had, indeed, twice before secretly planned to kill John of Gaunt. The King adjudicated their conflict should be resolved by a 'Court of Chivalry' that following autumn at the cloth town, Coventry. Hereford retorted wryly: 'It's a funny old world.'[191]

It was indeed an extraordinary pronouncement. A tournament, lances uncapped, was advertised between two Dukes, both accomplished jousters, who represented the two major families in England. The King would personally preside. The whole realm was gripped with excitement. Nothing on this scale had taken place before. It would be a fight to the death because, if not killed in the tourney, the defeated contestant would be liable to be either hanged or beheaded. Thousands of spectators flocked to Coventry on 16 September 1398, where they anticipated witnessing what promised to be the 'greatest chivalric event of the age'.[192]

King Richard entered the arena protected by his royal bodyguard, the Cheshire archers. The combatants watched as their lances were measured before they advanced from their decorated pavilions – Henry's with roses, Mowbray's with mulberries – and approached the lists. Mowbray donned his armour, fashioned from German steel, and mounted his courser, caparisoned in crimson velvet embroidered with silver lions and mulberry trees. Henry emerged, protected by Italian armour, and climbed onto his white charger, draped in blue and green velvet, embroidered with swans and antelopes. The Constable of England, the Duke of Aumale, accompanied by the new Marshal of England, the Duke of Surrey, signalled jousting could commence. Visors down, shields aloft, lances raised. The crowds were ecstatic. There was a mighty hush. The noble opponents prepared to advance ready to 'break spears'... Suddenly, King Richard, stealing this rare moment of drama, threw down his staff and shouted, 'Hold!' Instantly, the tournament came to a halt.

Henry and Mowbray, the King commanded, were banished from the realm. Perhaps he could not afford to let either nobleman win? There was an uproar from the crowds. Denied their sport, the spectators were angered their champions had been insulted and humiliated. The King, once peace had been restored, ordered the rivals to swear obedience before he swept, imperiously, from the green. Henry sailed from Dover, attended by thousands of supporters, where he sought refuge at the court of Charles VI in Paris. The French King was impressed by his charming manners – Henry was adept in disguising his simmering hatred – although it might be expected that his real concern lay in supporting the husband of his daughter, Queen Isabella. For 'time-honoured' John of Gaunt, banishment of his eldest son was a bitter blow and he expired the next year at Leicester Castle.[193] Callously, the King sequestered Henry's inheritance, as he secretly intended, and extended his banishment from ten years to life.

King Richard II, now marked as a tyrant who had thrust a nobleman out of his inheritance, was racing inexorably towards the climax of his turbulent reign...

King Richard in Ireland

Richard II left England, leaving his ineffectual uncle, Edward, Duke of York, as Regent. Here was a public refutation of Henry's claims to the throne because he had clearly favoured the House of York over that of Lancaster.[194] After antagonising almost every section of the community, from nobleman to peasant, he departed his kingdom, attended by his most loyal fighting men. This was surely an appalling error. The Londoners, he might have understood, lionised the banished Bolingbroke and welcomed his speedy return. Foolishly, the King had left his realm wide open to invasion.

King Richard landed with the royal forces, composed mainly of Cheshire men-at-arms and archers, at Waterford on 1 June 1399. He had at least the forethought to take with him Henry's eldest son, Henry of Monmouth, who was, in reality, a royal hostage. Richard created John of Gaunt's impressionable grandson a knight while he was in Ireland. The future Henry V fell permanently under the spell of Richard's charismatic personality.[195] After an inordinate delay waiting for his sly cousin, Edward, Duke of Albemarle, Richard and his hastily assembled army marched towards Kilkenny.

Ahead, the King sent 'Robert de Whytnton of the County of Gloucester' who nominated his younger brother, Richard, as one of his two attorneys until his safe return.[196] Their eldest brother, William, had died that year. Curiously, this is the only instance where the two brothers Robert and Richard are mentioned in the same document. It proves not only that they stayed in close contact but that they had complete trust in one another. And it disposes of the myth that Richard left Gloucester after a lifelong dispute with his two siblings.

Henry's Invasion of England

Henry Bolingbroke seized the opportunity to return to an unguarded kingdom. He assembled ten small ships and with a modest army – fifteen knights and three hundred 'other ranks' – crossed the English Channel.[197] His loyalty had turned to loathing for his reckless cousin and childhood playmate. Henry had lost everything he held dear – family, status, dignity, royalty and self-respect – and he now viewed his cousin's actions as motivated by malice, envy and spite. He regarded King Richard as a vicious man and an incompetent ruler. Henry's aim was high. He resolved to take the throne of England.

Henry was joined by a large fleet which escorted him on his zigzag course around the north-east coast where he disembarked at Ravenspur (or Ravenspurn),[198] on the Humber estuary, near Hull, Yorkshire. Prominent in his company was Thomas Arundel, the defrocked Archbishop of Canterbury. Henry marched northwards through his reclaimed Lancastrian strongholds – Pickering, Knaresborough and Pontefract – where thousands of soldiers supported his armed rebellion.

Richard was enraged when he heard of his cousin's invasion and ordered his army to return instantly, but there was a problem locating suitable ships. When Richard finally reached North Wales he learned with dismay that his own supporters had deserted him or had been killed and that Henry had gained control over his kingdom.

King Richard took refuge in Conway Castle. A communication from Henry convinced him that he would be wise to surrender his crown. Richard, tempted by reasonable terms, was lured from his impregnable stronghold and returned to the apparent safety of the capital. As he rode along the coastal path, he was ambushed and taken prisoner. Triumphantly, Henry escorted his captive cousin from Chester Castle to London where, he was informed, he would be judged by Parliament.

The King, dressed in a plain black gown and mounted on a lowly mare, was paraded through the City to the Tower. The Londoners, who had officially renounced their fealty to Richard under the City's Common Seal,[199] were rapturous and hailed Henry as their saviour. Crowds jostled and jeered. 'And the bells of the churches and monasteries rang so merrily,' trilled an anonymous French author, 'that you could not hear God thundering.'[200] Only a few citizens showed remorse – was Whittington among them? – and wept openly as they watched this public humiliation of their sovereign. The mighty fallen.

Deposition

Richard II's abdication speech was read aloud in his absence before an incredulous Parliament at the Palace of Westminster on 30 September 1399. The King was accused of violating his coronation oath and ruling without reference to the established laws and customs of the country. Further, after squandered his own wealth, he had burdened his subjects with high taxation. More serious accusations included his employment of enforced loans, tampering with justice and the recourse to blank charters in order to extort fees from his subjects. Richard must therefore forfeit his crown in favour of 'Henry Duc off Lancastre' who claimed his 'right of decent' from Henry III.[201]

The deposed King, in close confinement, reflected upon his inglorious fate. 'My God, a wonderful land is this, and a fickle, which hath exiled, slain, destroyed or ruined so many kings,' wrote the Lancastrian Chronicler, Adam of Usk. Richard II was spirited away, disguised as a forester, with a hunting spear and a horn slung around his neck, by boat 'in the silence of dark midnight'[202] along the Thames to the coast of North Kent. He was first imprisoned at Leeds Castle, near Maidstone, before being whisked away to a secret destination. 'None,' whispers Wylie, 'knew where.'

Mystery surrounds the death of Richard II. He was reduced to the rank of a knight, Sir Richard of Bordeaux. Tormented by his jailors, he was served 'starving fare' and mercifully expired after days and nights of hunger, thirst and cold at the secure fortress of Pontefract Castle, Yorkshire. Early that spring, Richard's body, embalmed and coffined, was transported to London where it was paraded along Cheapside to St Paul's.[203] A multitude of torch bearers, dressed alternately in black and white robes, attended the hearse. It was estimated that 20,000 people witnessed the solemn procession and were convinced that Richard II was, irrefutably, 'unking'd'.[204]

Fortune, after emboldening King Richard to raise his crown to dizzying heights, turned her wheel. Towards the close of his 'paradigm of misrule',[205] he spectacularly crashed from power while Richard Whittington, by stark contrast, enjoyed a meteoric rise to success. As a Mercer, his talents had been recognised by his own Liveried Company and he became its Warden and Master. He rapidly rose through the ranks of the three supreme civic offices of the City of London – from Alderman, to Sheriff and finally Mayor of London. On a personal note, he had dutifully complied in the arrest of the Duke of Gloucester and the subsequent confiscation of his property, for which he expressed private remorse. This would explain how he found it perfectly possible to transfer his allegiance to Richard II's bitter adversary, the future King Henry IV.

THE REIGN OF
HENRY IV

7

The Royal Financier

HENRY IV was a vastly different character and personality to the cousin he deposed. The only legitimate son of John of Gaunt, he became the first King of the House of Lancaster, a junior branch of Plantagenet. This resolute founder of a new dynasty was tentatively open to introducing a more democratic form of government. Magnanimously, he invited onto his council noblemen who had previously opposed him and, disdaining revenge or malice, he listened to their advice or criticism and embraced their wisdom.

At the start of his reign, however, Henry's authority was challenged by rebels in Scotland and Wales and also former allies who revolted, through jealousy, against his regime. His declared intention to reduce taxes was overturned almost immediately when his resolve to counter rebellions in remote regions combined with his determination to protect English possessions in France sapped his limited resources. Later, a special commission ruthlessly curtailed royal expenditure that had spiralled alarmingly after Henry spent lavishly on three royal marriages, in which Whittington was prominently involved as Court Mercer.

For Whittington, it was a time to consolidate his own civic career – he was again elected Warden of the Mercers' Company and Mayor of London – but he was also encouraged to diversify in business, progressing from Court Mercer to wool merchant. As an astute financier, his loans to the Crown increased and the rewards from a grateful monarch were tangible: he was made Collector of the Customs in London and Mayor of the Staple in Calais.

King Henry, surprisingly, was a private man devoted to his home and family. Whittington was never welcomed into that sphere and, although the King recognised his worth, he discouraged an intimate relationship. Everything from this time onwards was kept on a business level, which perfectly suited the London Mercer who was rarely tempted into revealing his own emotions.

For Whittington, the new reign was a time of both personal success and private tragedy. Occasionally, there are glimpses into the secret world of this celebrated merchant who married late in life the daughter of a Devonshire knight, Sir Ivo Fitwaryn. When his wife, Alice, died prematurely, Whittington devoted his time, energy and wealth to the first of his enduring charities, the Church of St Michael Paternoster Royal. Today, rebuilt, it remains a magnificent monument to Whittington's fabled success in the City.

Henry IV's Coronation

King Henry's ascension, 'based on undisputed conquest yet unconvincing descent', was confirmed at the shortest Parliament in history held at Westminster Palace on Tuesday 30 September. When Henry arrived at the Great Hall and stood before the vacant throne, draped in cloth-of-gold, the Archbishop of York confidently assured those present that Richard had 'cheerfully' acceded his kingship to his beloved cousin. This implausible news was greeted with thunderous applause. Throughout his short reign, however, he would be known in certain quarters as 'the Usurper of England'.

Henry IV's coronation – 'the culmination of his revolution' – was timed for midday on 13 October. Coincidentally, this was the Feast of St Edward the Confessor, Richard II's personal spiritual benefactor, now audaciously commandeered by his successor.[1] Although the ceremony was hurriedly arranged, scrupulous attention had been paid to detail. Henry made the traditional procession from the Tower of London to Westminster Abbey, mounted on a white stallion, accompanied by Prince Henry and six thousand supporters. Undoubtedly, Whittington was invited to ride among the company as a prominent member of the Mercers' Company.[2] Resplendent in a 'shorte cote of clothe of gold', Henry rode bare headed on his white courser to proclaim his humility. There was light, autumn rain.[3]

Henry was escorted into Westminster Abbey by two Archbishops – York and Canterbury – although the latter was yet to be reinstated. He was attended by his four young sons,[4] three of whom Henry had knighted the previous evening in an innovative ceremony, the Order of the Bath. His eldest son was created Prince of Wales, Duke of Aquitaine and Earl of Chester.[5] Henry received the insignia, swore the oaths and was crowned with a closed crown, an imperial one with arches in the shape of a cross. Then he was anointed with sacred oil poured from an ampulla, cunningly concealed by Richard II, that had been entrusted to Thomas Becket while in exile by the Virgin Mary herself.[6] Alas, this was the moment it was noticed that the King had head lice.

There were four swords of state instead of the usual three, the most prominent being the magnificent jewelled 'Lancaster Sword' borne by the Earl of Northumberland. Henry wore the signet ring that Richard had surrendered the previous day while languishing in the Tower. The supreme moment was when the outlawed Archbishop of Canterbury led the outlawed Duke of Lancaster by the right hand and seated him on the throne of England. Henry surprised everyone when he addressed the company in English. He was the first Medieval king to do so at a coronation.[7] He publicly asserted his double royal descent from 'the gude lorde kynge Henry therde'.[8] Previously, French was the language of the nobility, translated into Latin for legal documents, but by the beginning of the fifteenth century English was acknowledged as the language of the nation.[9]

When the new Plantagenet King was presented to his people, the crowds were ecstatic. He had been swiftly transformed from an exiled traitor to a national saviour. Londoners, particularly, welcomed this sovereign who understood the importance of encouraging their trade and respecting their charters.[10] He was most careful to treat the merchants with their due respect. This, then, promised to be 'the most popular usurpation in English history'.[11]

Henry's First Parliament and Council

Parliament[12] resumed its session on the day after the Coronation. Henry defined his aims as king. They were magnanimous, to say the least, because he was about to reign over powerful noblemen, some of whom had recently plotted against his life. He expressed his firm intention of terminating his cousin's style of autocratic rule and he immediately repealed the proceedings of the 'Revenge Parliament'. Inevitably, this reduced the power of the monarchy. It cancelled the perpetual grant of the wool subsidy and annulled the iniquitous blank charters.[13] Henry vowed never to levy direct taxation in peacetime. Ominously, he promised the prelates that he would not tolerate heresy.

When Parliament reassembled later that month – the day following the King's ceremonial bath – Henry ordered the arrest of all six surviving Counter Appellants. They were the Dukes of Aumale, Exeter and Surrey; John Beaufort, Marquis of Dorset; Thomas Despenser, Earl of Gloucester and John Montagu, Earl of Salisbury. Expecting the worse at a time when Richard was still alive, they were surprised to be treated leniently. Although they were stripped of their recent titles, recklessly awarded in the previous reign, they were allowed to keep their former titles and inherited land, while half of them were absorbed in his own government or allocated royal appointments. Imitating his role model, Edward III, Henry promised to be considerate even to his enemies.[14] Historians later termed this the 'Merciful Parliament'.[15]

And Henry, in his munificence, ordered the repayment of one thousand pounds owed to Whittington by Richard II. He was authorised to recover the sum in three successive annual installments from the customs and subsidies of wools, hides and fells[16] shipped by him through the Port of London.[17] His generous treatment was a wise precaution because throughout his turbulent reign Henry would be compelled to approach the amenable Mercer for further loans to finance his own projects. Whittington responded to the King's frequent appeals for pecuniary aid and was persuaded to open his purse on numerous occasions, convinced that he would be rewarded by either position or power, or if not, in ready cash.

Soon after his accession, Henry IV appointed three prominent citizens to be members of his council.[18] Thus, he effectively acknowledged the active role Londoners had played in his usurpation. At this time they regarded him as their champion. Men selected were Richard Whittington, Mercer, William Brampton, Fishmonger, and John Shadworth, Mercer, who had himself been vindictively imprisoned by Richard II.[19] Their fee was fifty marks per annum each, although there appears to have been a problem obtaining it! Certainly, Whittington held office for the first year but he may have attended further councils unofficially. He must have felt relieved that he had emerged from the change of dynasties unscathed.[20] More, he would have felt immense pride that he had been chosen personally to advise the new King. It confirmed that he was already held in high regard.[21]

Catalyst for Richard II's Death; and the French Threat

As mentioned earlier, Richard's death is shrouded in mystery. Henry's assumption of the throne met with an immediate challenge. A consortium of Ricardian supporters, including the replacement Archbishop of Canterbury, gathered secretly at Westminster Abbey to plan the assassination of Henry and his four sons at a New Year tournament planned to take place at Windsor Castle in 1400. The rebel leaders miscalculated the fervent support the new King would receive from the London citizens. Their plot was revealed and Henry successfully ambushed the leaders, who, this time, were severely punished. One large problem was that one of the plotters, Richard Maudeleyn, intended to impersonate the deposed King until he could be released and reassume authority. This 'Epiphany Rising' sealed the fate of Richard II.

Richard had pleaded with Henry not to parade him before the Londoners while he was being held a prisoner at Whitehall. Henry declined to execute Richard but instead ordered his perpetual confinement in Pontefract Castle, West Yorkshire. The King realised that while Richard lived he would be a catalyst for rebellion and probably arranged for his cousin to expire, expediently, of starvation. Richard's emaciated body was brought to London and publicly paraded through Cheapside prior to ignominious burial at the Dominican Priory of King's Langley, Hertfordshire. This avoided the threat of imposters.[22] Further, to allay the fear of invasion from France by King Charles VI, determined to reclaim part of his childless daughter's dowry,[23] Henry's council advised that Queen Isabella should be returned home, along with her own jewellery and possessions. Dressed in deepest mourning, the plucky young widow, sullen and morose, was conducted to the ship that would carry her across the English Channel.[24]

Throughout Henry's reign, an invasion from France posed a real threat. Wisely, he took the precaution of protecting the vulnerable southern coastline. Southampton's defences were placed in the capable charge of a renowned Devonshire knight: 'Appointment during pleasure of Ivo Fitz Waryn as keeper and governor of the town of Southampton, with full power to fortify the town with walls, towers, loups, gates, garrets, ditches and other defences with the advice of the mayor with all speed and to cause the inhabitants to contribute according to their means.'[25] Moreover, Sir Ivo was ordered to summon 'workmen, stone-cutters, carpenters and labourers' to strengthen the fortifications of this strategic port with stone quarried on the Isle of Wight.[26] Whittington was a member of the council responsible for the allocation of this important task to the man who was soon to become his father-in-law.

Character of King Henry

At first glance, Henry might present an unprepossessing figure, short, stocky, red-haired and with a forked beard, yet he commanded authority. There are only a few authentic representations of his appearance apart from miniatures illustrating documents and his splendid effigy on his tomb at Canterbury Cathedral.[27] Indisputably, he was a curious admixture of character: pious, studious, conscientious. He was intelligent, articulate, logical, calculating and conservative. Courtiers were impressed by his impeccable manners, retentive memory and impressive energy. Generous to a fault, he was loyal to his friends and obligated to his kingdom.[28] He could read and write in English,[29] Latin, French and Spanish and he constructed a study with cupboards for his valuable books at his cherished residence, Eltham Palace. He sought the company of literary figures and awarded three veteran poets – Gower, Chaucer and Hoccleve – generous pensions.[30] He owned the earliest recorded portable clock, an enviable possession at a time when timepieces were displayed on turrets. 'He was,' considers Ian Mortimer, 'the nearest to an intellectual among all the Medieval kings.'

A military leader, Henry excelled at active sports – riding, jousting, fencing, hunting and hawking – and he collected wild animals, lions and leopards. Generally, though, he was a private person who relished musical evenings in the company of his family. They sang to the tune of a guitar or harp while Henry played the first known recorder.[31] He loved playing cards, chess and board games, sitting at a silver table drawing pieces from a cloth bag while sucking sweets that rotted his teeth[32] and sipping rose water from a flask from Damascus. His first wife, Mary de Bohun, although still a minor, was one of the richest heiresses in England.[33] She worked hard to create a comfortable home for her warrior husband. Before a roaring fire she toyed with her popinjay and played with her greyhounds sporting livery collars of green and white check with tinkling silver bells. Mary bore him four sons, Henry (later Prince of

Wales), Thomas, John and Humphrey, but died giving birth to her sixth child, Philippa, without knowing that she was the wife and mother of future kings of England.[34]

Henry's Religion

Henry was completely conventional in his religious beliefs. He had even made his own pilgrimage to the Holy Land. In 1392, he had travelled from England to Venice, via an overland roundabout route through Poland, Bohemia, Austria and Italy, before crossing the Mediterranean to Cyprus and finally Jerusalem. Previously, Richard I and Edward I had ventured upon this perilous journey by land and sea but Henry had distinguished himself by actually stepping into the Holy Sepulchre.[35] This pilgrimage magnified his reputation and presented him as an exemplary knight 'combining the spiritual and chivalric values of his age'.[36]

Henry's reign was a time of religious persecution. Influenced by his close companion, Thomas Arundel, Archbishop of Canterbury and Chancellor of the Exchequer, Henry became extremely intolerant of religious dissenters. Arundel was the declared arch enemy of Lollards. Among their revolutionary beliefs were that the church should not be dedicated to amassing riches, priests ought to be allowed to marry, prayers should not be offered for the dead, images of saints were idolatrous and – the greatest blasphemy – that the bread and wine were not miraculously converted into the actual body and blood of Christ after a priest's blessing at the Eucharist.

Henry's council passed a statute on 10 March 1401[37] legalising the ultimate sanction of burning heretics. This infamous act was at variance with his cousin's laudable tolerance in matters of religion. It was, in effect, the first law for the suppression of religious views enacted in England. Richard II resisted pressure from the church authorities for capital punishment for heretical beliefs, and penalties invoked during his reign were comparatively mild – brief imprisonment and confiscation of property. On 2 May 1401, Henry issued the order for the Mayor of London to publicly burn a relapsed heretic, William Sawtre, a saintly country priest, who, after being 'degradyd off his pressethode', was packed in a barrel which was set alight at Smithfield. This horrific sentence was meant as a warning to Londoners – usually tolerant of diversity – who were largely sympathetic to the tenets of Lollardy.[38] Sawtre thus gained an unenviable place in history as the first man to suffer death by burning for heresy in England.

In 1410, John Bradby, a craftsman, was declared 'ffals Loller and an herytyke' and suffered the same terrible punishment merely for expressing his doubts concerning transubstantiation. Prince Henry was present at this cruel execution. As King, Henry V did not hesitate to inflict suffering on his enemies, but here he baulked at the appalling sight and called a halt, temporarily, to the horrific spectacle. This was a turning point in history. Until this time, no commoner had been burnt for merely stating what he believed. Furthermore, this terrible incident reveals an inhuman side to Henry's character at complete variance with his tolerance of dissension politically.

Fortunately, Whittington was not concerned in any of these sordid religious events. His own beliefs were conservative but he managed to avoid involvement, even in his civic career, in religious quarrels. Supporters of Lollardy, passive at first, became increasingly aggressive during the following reign when Whittington and members of his immediate family would be personally affected by their violent activities.

Henry's Taste in Clothes

Henry, in comparison with his predecessor, was more indifferent to fashion, although he realised that it was important to 'dress to impress' as King of England. There were gifts of costly cloths to visiting dignitaries and his court was draped with rich hangings on formal occasions. He had become established during the previous reign as a prominent customer of Whittington.

As a royal Duke, Henry had worn striking apparel each time he appeared at the court of Richard II. He was determined to present himself as the natural heir to his cousin's throne. He looked handsome wearing the long blue damask tabard, a present from his stepmother, the Duchess of Lancaster, when he appeared at Richard's wedding to Anne in January 1382. Later that month, he took part in a tournament to celebrate Anne's coronation when his dazzling armour was enlivened with silver spangles in the form of roses. On his pilgrimage to the Holy Land in 1392, he acquired rich gold cloths, baldekin and velvets plus three ducats' worth of gold ribbon that he purchased direct from the warehouses at Venice. His clerks ordered quantities of wool, silk, damask, satin, linen, cotton[39] and cloths of every hue: his tailors turned these into gowns, mantles, tunics, paltocks, tabards, kirtles and hoods for everyday wear.[40]

There must have been one startling moment at Richard II's court when Henry arrived for a Christmas banquet. The guests were invited to attend wearing 'the gayest desgysing that they could devys'. Henry, inexplicably, chose a gown 'broderyd al abowte with toadys'. (The King, highly superstitious, had been warned by an astrologer to beware of toads...)[41]

In the first four years of his own reign, Henry sported splendid outfits. Despite these turbulent times, an account of the regular provision of magnificent garments for the King is recorded in the Livery Rolls. The task of obtaining suitable cloths and presenting them for the approval of the sovereign remained the province of the clerks of the Great Wardrobe. Records exist listing expenses incurred for transporting precious velvets and cloth-of-gold,[42] accompanied by an armed escort, specifically 'to show to our lord the king', wherever he was residing. At first glance, the budget for Henry's clothing appears lavish although it is, in fact, moderate compared to the profligate spending of Edward III and

Richard II.[43] There can be little doubt that the main source for these sumptuous materials was again, Richard Whittington.[44]

The fourth Parliament of his reign (30 September-5 November 1402) passed a statute whereby every man was compelled to wear clothes suitable to his own estate. None below the rank of banneret, for instance, was to wear gold cloth, velvet motley, large hanging sleeves nor long trailing gowns, not even fur. Interestingly, this law did not apply to Mayors of London, York and Bristol, or their consorts. Churchmen, esquires, varlets and their wives were forbidden to deviate from their regulated costumes for fear of forfeiting the finery and paying a fine of £5.[45] This edict confirms that Whittington's customers were drawn exclusively from the upper middle class and above, people who could well afford such opulence.

Free Hats

The earliest surviving Account Book of the Merchant Taylor's (1398-1445) supplies a fascinating snippet: Whittington was a regular recipient of complimentary headwear from that illustrious Company.[46] Under 'Expenses', is the subheading 'Drap allowe par la Companie', which lists the hats or hoods presented annually to worthy citizens. The King, naturally, heads the list but senior civic dignitaries also honoured include the Mayor, Chamberlain, Recorder and Sheriffs. Among the miscellaneous recipients are Thomas Knollys, Alderman and Mayor, a member of the Grocers' Company; the Incumbent of St Martin Outwich, the Merchant Taylors' Church near their Company Hall; several noblemen, assorted widows and even 'le garderobier',[47] all of whom the Wardens felt it worthwhile to cultivate. The value of these hats increased until they reached 5s per 'chaperon'. A further detail is noted in 1413-14 when the hats that year were described as 'chescun contenaunt viii entier raies' ('each one composed of eight whole stripes'). This apparently was the last time Whittington accepted this welcome free gift of headwear because that year the Mayor and Aldermen decreed that in future no officer was permitted to 'take livery or vestment from any craft or fraternity within the City, save only that one craft of which he had been made free'.[48] Alas, the actual style of the hats Whittington sported is not recorded.

The Visit of an Emperor

As noted, Henry was the son and heir of by far the richest nobleman in England, John of Gaunt. As King, he was determined to live off the revenue from customs duties, the royal estates, the royal treasury and, privately, his own great Lancastrian inheritance. After vowing not to levy taxes except in wartime, he was compelled all too soon to renege on his promise. Insurrections in Scotland and Wales had sapped his reserves and placed him in dire financial straits. His early reign was blighted by terrible harvests that resulted in high food prices and the simultaneous collapse of revenue from the wool trade. This resulted in his declining popularity, evident by the increased lawlessness in the country. Londoners protested at the soaring price of bread while the merchants complained about their inability to make profitable investments through their exports.

Henry's impoverished condition came to the fore with the impending visit of the Emanuel or 'Manuel' II, Emperor of Byzantium, on 21 December 1400. It was painfully obvious that the King could barely afford to entertain his illustrious guest, let alone help fund the Holy War that he was proposing to defend Christendom against the Muslim Turkish Sultan, Bayezid I, nicknamed 'Yldirim' (thunderbolt), who had surrounded his capital city, 'Constaignynnople'.[49] The Greek Emperor from the mysterious East had travelled thousands of miles across Western Europe seeking assistance and at last he arrived in England to plead in person with Henry for financial and military support for his religious crusade.

For two months these shadowy strangers were royally entertained with sports, tournaments, processions at vast expense at Eltham Palace. Princess Blanche, Henry's eight-year-old daughter, presided over the New Year's Day tournament where, fortuitously, the lances were blunt. Henry struggled to donate the embarrassingly low sum of £2,000 towards the Byzantine defence fund from his depleted Exchequer. Whittington had come to his rescue by lending a third of that sum in the first of his 'national' loans: £666 13s 4d. Fortuitously, by the time the Emperor returned with Henry's miserly offering, the danger threatening the Christian capital had already dissipated. A crushing defeat had been inflicted on Bayezid I at Angora by Timur the Lame ('Tamerlane') in 1402.

A Comet before the Battle of Shrewsbury

Europe was alarmed by the appearance of a comet in the spring of 1402.[50] 'Stella comata' was first noticed at the beginning of February and, thereafter, at intervals until Easter. Chronicler Adam of Usk observed the comet in the daytime. Its tail streamed to the west, then to the north. Astrologers interpreted it as a presage of doom. Each country read into the phenomenon a supernatural warning 'written in characters of blood'.[51] To England, it foreshadowed disaster in Scotland and Wales.

The French King Charles VI, who had welcomed Henry as a fugitive, declined to accept him as England's King. Henry thought that Charles might be pacified through negotiations but his ally, the Scottish King Robert III, also stubbornly refused, at first, to acknowledge his sovereignty. Henry decided to lead an expedition into Scotland – he was the last English King to venture there in battle – in an effort to compel Robert to pay him homage. Henry amassed a vast army consisting of soldiers, mariners, archers and gunners, conversant with single and double cannon, at York. This speculative military campaign cost a fortune. Artfully, the King ordered that every subject holding a fee under the King should present himself with all haste to do service in the Scottish

Marches. But in a council held on 11 June 1400, certain persons were excused from this service and exempted from the penalties which would be incurred by non-attendance.[52] Whittington was one of those duly released from military service upon paying a tenth of his income to the state. Sensibly, the King recognised that Whittington was a businessman rather than a soldier and that his loans to the Crown were indispensable.

The scale of Henry's army alarmed the Scottish King, who sought to avoid confrontation through delaying tactics. He sent his ambassadors to negotiate with Henry to deflect him from his determined march on Edinburgh Castle. Henry swallowed their honeyed words and returned home mollified by the promises of a peace treaty. But he had been fooled and he was publicly humiliated by his abandoned – and expensive – venture into Scotland.

Henry's struggle to gain control and assert his authority over his kingdom was further exacerbated by the charismatic leader, Owen Glendower ('Owain Glyn Dwr'), who claimed independence for Wales. This self-styled 'Prince of Wales' repeatedly organised armed insurrections and systematically besieged regional towns and castles, constantly evading capture by the English. His frequent forays into the West Country, plundering and pillaging, burning and looting, were initially fuelled by a secret alliance with the French.

Glendower in a mock Parliament announced his intention of being crowned 'King Owen I of Wales'. His declared intention was to restore Richard II (if still alive) to the English throne or, failing that, to replace Henry with Edmund Mortimer, Earl of March. In anticipation of this momentous event, Glendower devised his own seal, which featured himself crowned with a sceptre in his right hand. After a series of rapid, inconclusive campaigns to subdue the rebels, Henry delegated this responsibility to his eldest son, the rightful Prince of Wales. Although he failed to draw Glendower onto the battlefield, Henry did at least ensure he remained a fugitive, skulking in the dense woods of North Wales.[53]

The greatest challenge to Henry's supremacy, however, came from an unexpected source – his companions and councillors. The powerful and influential Percy family – Henry, First Earl of Northumberland, Thomas, First Earl of Worcester and Sir Henry, whose impulsive nature had earned him the nickname, 'Hotspur' [54] – had been Henry's staunch supporters in his own rebellion against Richard II. In return, they had all counted upon rich rewards upon his accession for their loyalty. Yet the King, strapped for cash, had been inordinately slow to reimburse their considerable expenses in defending his realm from the Scots and Welsh. Now, in the summer of 1403, they reversed their allegiance and joined forces with his arch enemy, Owen Glendower, and their prisoner, Sir Edmund Mortimer, in rebelling against Henry's authority. Sir Edmund, an uncle of the young Earl of March, had become entangled with the Welsh revolt by marrying Owen's daughter, Catherine, while he was a prisoner in Wales.[55] England was once more on the verge of civil war.

Henry was forced into taking decisive action to combat the Percys' betrayal and treason. The nation, after all, could not have failed to notice the contrast between the Percys' brilliant victories in the North and the King's miserable retreat from Wales. Henry recalled the Prince of Wales, where he was relieving the siege of Harlech Castle, and summoned the Earl of Stafford, while his own army of around two thousand men marched on Shrewsbury. Henry's aim was to engage Hotspur, who was recruiting archers in the palatine of Cheshire, some of whom were formerly members of King Richard's bodyguard, and engage him in battle before he was joined by the combined forces of Northumberland and Glendower. After sealing the town on all three sides, it was left to Hotspur, upon his eventual arrival, to select the site of the inevitable combat. This would be the first time ever that two massed companies of archers with longbows were pitted against each other on English soil.[56]

The battle took place on St Mary Magdalene's Eve (21 July).[57] Hotspur, advised by his allies, the Earls of Douglas and Worcester, selected a dominant position at the top of a gently, sloping plain, overlooking a vast field of tangled peas and vetches.[58] From there, his thousand bowmen could fire on Henry's approaching army, struggling to attack while marching uphill. Henry approached the rebel army – 'numerous, skilled and motivated' – with resolve and fortitude. He organised his marching men into two battalions; the Prince leading a third force to the south of the town. The vanguard, incorporating the company of archers, was headed by the young Earl of Stafford, leaving Henry in charge of the main division. He did, however, take the precaution of arranging two decoys – knights dressed in his own livery – although, since arrows cannot discriminate between ranks, the King and the Prince faced equal dangers as their men-at-arms.

Henry ordered Stafford, as Constable of England, to advance with the royal vanguard in the early afternoon. An experienced campaigner, he knew that longbows were deadliest when facing an oncoming charge, particularly when archers had the advantage of firing from a stationary position on high ground. His army moved swiftly but was crushed by 'a rapid reign of sharp iron'[59] that blackened the summer sky. Douglas, seizing the moment, charged down the hill with his men, wielding swords and axes. The conflict was intense. Trumpets blaring, men screaming, horses whinnying... Stafford was among the first to fall, dying bravely among his confused men who fled in terror to avoid the inevitable carnage.

Unbelievably, the rebel archers rapidly ran short of arrows! They were reduced to running down the slippery slope and ripping arrows from the dead and dying men before they could reform, reload and fire. Prince Henry learned a vital lesson from this experience and ensured that he had sufficient arrows for his future French campaigns that culminated in Agincourt. But he made his own life-threatening mistake when he raised his visor to gasp for air in the scorching heat and was scarred by an arrow that penetrated his skull below his left eye.[60] According to the chronicler, Gregory: 'And in that same bataylle was the prynce shotte thorowe the hedde wyth an arowe.'[61] Prince Henry later recovered through the skilful efforts of the Physician General who applied honey, alcohol and used his own specially designed surgical instruments to tend the deep wound.

King Henry took the initiative. Stafford's banner was down, his vanguard in flight and the rebel troops charging towards him. He gave the order for the Prince to advance and attack Hotspur's army on the flank while he would lead the main body of the army in a determined, desperate charge. The opposing armies met in bitter conflict at the foot of the slope, in hand-to-hand fighting: 'kin against kin'. Henry showed that he had lost none of his skills in leadership and fought valiantly, his presence intensifying the vicious slaughter. Hotspur, realising his position was weakening, watched horrified as his infantry was demolished. He ordered a concerted charge towards the King. It was his final, fatal mistake. His courageous knights fell to the swords of the royal men-at-arms and somewhere in the thick of this slaughter the impetuous 'Harre Hottesporre' lost his life, struck down by an unknown hand. It seems that Hotspur, too, had lifted his visor and an arrow pierced him through the mouth.

The Percys conceded defeat now that they were without their leader with his perverse cry: 'King Richard is alive.' The Earls of Douglas and Worcester were captured; their demoralised armies turned and fled. Punishments were horrific. Hotspur's mangled body was publicly displayed, impaled on a spear and propped upright between two millstones in the market square at Shrewsbury.[62] The rebel leaders anticipated no mercy: they received none. One exception, surprisingly, was Henry's leniency towards that turncoat, the Earl of Northumberland, who was pardoned after his abject submission.

'The bataylle of Shrousbury' is still regarded as the bloodiest on English soil. It was 'one of the wyrste bataylys that ever came to Inglonde', pronounced Gregory, 'and the unkyndyst'. The fearful conflict had raged from midday until nightfall when there was a total eclipse of the moon.[63]

Whittington may have been one of the magnates who were approached to sponsor the military operation, which had further drained Henry's Exchequer. There are huge sums recorded by the Exchequer, including two unspecified loans for £1,000 each, repaid in cash to Whittington during that momentous year.[64] Henry ordered the construction of a chapel to mark the site of the battle against the northern nobles. Battlefield Church, dedicated to St Mary Magdalene, was reconstructed in Victorian times. Above the east window appears a rare statue of King Henry IV in full armour.[65] Henry's 'little work at Battlefield,' caustically comments Wylie, 'is but another evidence of how he managed to give to the Lord of that which cost him nothing.'

Henry's mercy towards the Earl of Northumberland was misplaced. It was reported to the King that he was conspiring with the northern nobles to renew his rebellion. He reacted swiftly. While he travelled across the Midlands, his council responded with an urgent appeal to send troops for a surprise attack against the rebels who were preparing their castles for armed resistance to their King. The rebel army – high in numbers but lacking in strategy – was defeated by subterfuge. The Earl of Westmoreland invited the leaders to dine while loyalists persuaded their armies to disband. This time, capital punishment was inevitable. The rebels, the Earl of Northumberland and the Earl Marshal, Thomas Mowbray, Earl of Norfolk, were executed. They could no longer be allowed to attempt to drive Henry from his throne.

Archbishop Scrope, who expressed grievance concerning taxation of the clergy, stirred up a second rebellion among the citizens of York. Eight thousand armed men amassed at Shipton Moor. When Henry arrived to confront these further rebels, the Archbishop courageously challenged him at Pontefract. Henry's rage – 'at white heat' – railed against the citizens of York.[66] Against the sound advice of Archbishop Arundel, Henry sentenced Scrope, without trial or inquiry, to death. The King was determined not to flinch from punishing a traitor in his realm. And while Henry and Arundel enjoyed a convivial breakfast, Scrope was beheaded near York. Henry's execution of an Archbishop stunned all Christendom. The mangled corpse was entombed at York Minster where it soon became a place of pilgrimage. Henry IV's sacrilegious deed was compared to King Henry II's involvement in the murder of the martyred Archbishop Becket. This was not a good omen for the troubled reign.

The Wool Subsidy

Parliament freely granted Henry IV the subsidy on wool for the next three years to fund the wars in Scotland, the protection of Calais and the subjugation of Ireland. Richard II, it should be remembered, had made the iniquitous demand that Parliament surrendered the wool subsidy for his lifetime. Stress was therefore laid on the fact that this lucrative grant had been made for a limited period and for a specific purpose. Henry was wise enough to submit to these conditions. Inevitably, this three-year grant on the customs was renewed for a further two years and a sizeable wool subsidy was confirmed, plus an extra levy of 3 shillings on every tun of wine and 1 shilling in the £1 on all commodities entering or leaving the country by sea.[67] Further strictures accompanied these grants. Two War Treasurers were appointed in October 1404.[68] Answerable only to Parliament, they were charged with ensuring that all monies collected, apart from that half a mark on every wool sack, were expended exclusively on the defence of the realm.[69]

The idea of entrusting the nation's finances to War Treasurers met with general approval because the system appeared fair and reasonable. Immediately, there was a significant reduction, under their strict vigilance, on the amount drawn on the King's Great Wardrobe.

Inevitably, the original pair were soon replaced by two officials considered more amenable to the wishes of their King. As a Mercer, Whittington had suffered temporarily by this tightening of the belt in the Royal Household.

8

Whittington's Life
in London

Henry's Second Marriage

Henry sought to strengthen his tenuous position abroad by marrying his children into influential foreign families. At the same time he turned his attention to his own second marriage. His choice of a second wife, Joan (or 'Joanna') of Navarre, a prominent member of the French royal family, was curious, considering the current enmity between the two countries. Yet since Henry had produced an heir and spares – enough to secure a dynasty – by his first wife, he could now afford to indulge in a love match. Henry and the Duchess of Brittany 'plighted their troth',[70] albeit by proxy, at Eltham Palace on 2 April 1402.

England could hardly wholeheartedly rejoice in their union. In addition to the provision demanded for the King's four sons, who each received constantly enhanced grants of manors and lands, the country was now required to find 10,000 marks per annum for the dowry of Queen Joan. This prodigal grant – for which the country received no return – was made on 8 February 1404. Henry, it would appear, could be as profligate as his predecessor when it came to distributing money among his family and friends.[71]

Henry ordered a large consignment of gold cloth as a gift for his bride, at a cost of £200, charged to the country.[72] Whittington would be the natural source for this material although there is no record of his involvement in this particular transaction. And the King's intimate present to his consort was a fantastic bejewelled collar engraved with the motto soveignez and the letter S. Joan is depicted wearing a similar Lancastrian collar on her effigy at Canterbury Cathedral. Henry's extravagant gift was purchased from a London jeweller at an enormous cost to the country: 500 marks (£430).

Lancastrian kings adopted the French custom of presenting livery collars to their close male or female friends and supporters.[73] Henry adopted his father John of Gaunt's, distinctive style of collar – linked esses or 'SS' – and as a prince he was referred to as 'the one who wears the S'. Fancifully, the repeated 'S' has been interpreted as standing for 'Souveyne vous de moi' ('Remember me'.) Significantly, Henry's favourite floral emblem, embroidered on regal attire, was a forget-me-not which in the language of flowers is interpreted as 'Remember me'. Tantalisingly, quite who is to be remembered remains a mystery. Antiquaries have suggested that the word 'Sovereyne' or 'Soverayne' simply means 'sovereign' but since Henry sported this device while still Duke of Lancaster this would have been treasonable.[74]

Interestingly, the Lord Mayor of London has worn a royal livery collar of esses since 1545. This collar, however, has no origin in royal favour because it was bequeathed by Sir John Allen, thrice Lord Mayor, to his successors 'to use and occupie yerely at and uppon principall and festivall dayes'. Later enlarged, it has in its present shape twenty-eight esses and therefore comprises the Lancastrian S, the Tudor rose, the tasselled knots of the garter and the portcullis.

The marriage of Henry and Joan took place, amid joyous celebration, 'in the Abbay of Saynt Swithyn', Winchester,[75] on 7 February 1403. Afterwards, the royal couple gorged on a feast of such tempting dishes as roast cygnets, venison, rabbits, bitterns, partridges, woodcock, plover, quails, snipe, fieldfares. An elaborate wedding cake featured panthers firing flames.[76] Henry's marriage to the widowed duchess, according to Ian Mortimer, was 'one of the real surprises of his reign'.[77]

Henry owned property in the City and its suburbs where, according to Wylie, he had 'hostels, gardens and wardrobes' in Fleet Street, Coleman Street, Bishopsgate, Leadenhall and Aldermany. Joan was presented with 'a good town-house', recently forfeited by the Duke of York, beautifully situated in Thames Street. She would have been a neighbour of Whittington when he purchased a mansion in the near vicinity.

The King, happily married, now turned his attention to marrying his two prepubescent daughters, disregarding any personal choice, into royal families in order to heighten his own international influence and prestige.

Princess Blanche

Rupert III, Duke of Bavaria and Count Palatine of the Rhine, became Holy Roman Emperor after he had deposed Wenceslaus IV in 1400. (Wenceslaus, who remained King of Bohemia, had forged an alliance with England when his sister, Anne, had married Richard II.) Immediately, the new Emperor despatched commissioners to London to make formal arrangements for a marriage between his son, Louis, and Henry's eldest daughter, Blanche, who had been born at Walmsford, near Peterborough, in 1392. After their betrothal in February 1401, it was agreed that the princess should be conducted the following Easter to Cologne for their marriage in the Rhineland.

Although the account book for the royal wedding survives it does not record the names of the suppliers. Whittington was definitely approached to supply ten cloths-of-gold and other unspecified merchandise for the wedding at a cost of £215 13s 4d.[78] He was paid by Blanche's treasurer, John Chandler, who recovered the money from the Exchequer (19 April 1401). In return for this lucrative commission, Whittington lent £258 6s 8d to cover the expenses of Blanche's overland journey to Germany.[79]

At Cologne, the royal party was met, rather indifferently, by Louis, who was to escort Blanche to Heidleberg where their marriage was solemnised. The entourage included the Bishop of Worcester who was to perform the marriage ceremony. Her attendants were alarmed to find Louis so plainly dressed and poorly attended. The young princess, by contrast, charmed the courtiers and soon 'her winning English beauty secured for her a very kindly welcome in her German home.'[80] At her coronation, Blanche appeared dazzling in her golden wedding apparel. She wore an exquisite crown, fashioned in gold, adorned with sapphires, rubies, emeralds and pearls, that had previously belonged to Richard II's consort, Anne of Bohemia.[81]

Blanche's happiness was not long lasting. Sadly, she died while giving birth to her first child, Rupert, in 1409. She was buried in the Church of St Mary at Heidelberg. Henry was visibly shocked when he opened the Emperor's sealed letter giving news of her premature demise. Her promised dowry, amounting to 20,000 marks, was partially withheld from his son-in-law, who later became Elector Palatine Louis III. Blanche's fabulous crown passed to the Palatine Treasury in Heidelberg. Now held at Munich, it is the oldest surviving English crown.

Princess Philippa

Henry's second daughter, Philippa, was born in Leicester on 4 July 1394. She was his last child: his beloved first wife, Mary, had died in childbirth. Like her own father, Philippa never knew her mother. In 1405, when she was just eleven years old, she was betrothed to Eric, Duke of Pomerania, who had expressed an interest in marrying an English bride.[82] Upon her marriage, Philippa became heiress to three crowns and she later became Queen of Denmark, Norway and Sweden.

Whittington, high in royal favour, received the further commission to supply cloth-of-gold and pearls[83] for the juvenile princess's trousseau. His handsome fee of £248 10s 6d was authorised by Richard Clifford, junior clerk of the Wardrobe of Lady Philippa, on 28 July 1406. This is a rare recorded instance of Whittington's involvement in handling precious stones. In 1382, his opinion had been sought under oath, along with a fellow Mercer, John Woodcock, for the valuation of an assignment of pearls in a convoluted law suit that involved the Count of St Pol when still a prisoner in England.[84] And he was sufficiently regarded to be entrusted with the care of jewels valued at £600, to hold until an orphan, Thomas Pynchoun, reached his majority, without offering any security.[85]

Henry was annoyed to learn that this latest marriage was against his councillors' advice. There could be no justification, they insisted, for a second daughter to make extravagant claims upon the Treasury. Happily, Duke Eric demanded no dowry, at least in monetary terms. Yet funding was in short supply. Immediately, letters were despatched under the Great Seal to leading military figures and high-ranking clergy compelling them to advance money to their King. London merchants, upon application, needed little persuasion. Prospects were good and money lent freely. Whittington loaned one thousand pounds. The date recorded for his transaction – 18 May 1406 – coincides with Philippa's planned voyage to Scandinavia.[86]

Winter was spent acquiring purchases for Philippa's trousseau. At the same time that Whittington was measuring the golden cloth and examining the beautiful pearls, Clifford was earnestly overseeing the expenditure of the Wardrobe. His register records a tremendous array of garments: robes, hoods, mantles, kirtles, surcoats, copegowns with trains of white satin and crimson and trims of ermine and white fur, beaver caps garnished with silk buttons and tassels... The list of requirements considered essential for Philippa Plantagenet's future comfort was endless: folding chairs, leather cushions, a set of knives in a sheaf with jet handles tricked with silver and gold, an alms dish embossed with seven leopards, riding saddles with gold harness and silver spangles, a pair of beds, one of gold cloth worked with flowers, another of white satin embroidered with the King's arms, carefully packed in bear-hide cloth sacks, a 'whirl' (a fast, light carriage) beautifully painted, upholstered with red satin and fitted with 'draught reins, collars, dorsals and cappers', commissioned from the chariot makers, a tent painted with angels displaying the arms of England. Even mundane items – a dozen spoons, a pair of cruets, two saucers and a tiny bell – were of silver.[87] There could be little doubt where Whittington's loan was invested.

The King travelled to King's Lynn overland by road, either on horseback or in a litter, because he was suffering from a painful leg wound. This tortuous journey severely delayed his daughter's departure for her intended spring wedding in Denmark. From the quayside, King Henry and Queen Joan, Princes Harry, Thomas and Humphrey, watched the little squadron put out into the North Sea. Princess Philippa was berthed in one of the king's own ships, *Holy Ghost of the Tower*, whose captain was suitably named John Gold. Upon her arrival towards the end of summer, the twelve-year-old princess could expect a hearty welcome from her bridegroom – 'handsome, active, lusty' – although not, apparently, well mannered, prior to her marriage followed by her coronation in Lund Cathedral. But as the little princess waved gracefully before she skipped below into her royal cabin, bedecked with waxed canvas, red worsted and cloth-of-gold, she must surely have guessed that she would never see any member of her family again.

The royal ship was heavily armed and sailed in convoy. The voyage was long and the seas were dangerous. The English were in constant danger from attack by the French. Every hour brought real and present danger. Indeed, Don Pedro Nino, a Spanish pirate in the pay of the French, caught site of a little fleet, which he assumed was the royal squadron, and apparently guaranteed rich pickings he led an abortive attack.[88] The Princess Philippa arrived without incident in her new homeland where, in contrast to her unfortunate elder sister, her future happiness was assured. Late that summer she disembarked attended by her vast retinue – lords, ladies, grooms, pages, minstrels, clerks, chaplains, cooks – dressed alike in her clashing livery of scarlet and green. Her sumptuous wedding took place on 6 October when the petite princess wore 'a tunic and mantle with long train of white satin worked with velvet, furred with pured miniver[89] and purfled with ermine; and the sleeves of the tunic also furred with ermine'.[90] The colour of the tunic is unrecorded but it is tempting to think this might be the cloth-of-gold provided by Whittington. Philippa, incidentally, is thought to be the first royal bride in history to wear white at her wedding.

This succession of royal marriages came at a time of great disaffection among the English people. They had imposed great financial burdens upon the Exchequer. Henry's council advised the king that further foreign alliances and marriage portions should be indefinitely postponed. People were also beginning to express their disapproval at the marriage of young children. There was no legal age for marriage and but an acceptable age for both partners was around 14 or 15, considered a perfectly respectable age for cohabitation. There were further concerns when young girls were partnered with unseen mates. High-born girls, particularly princesses, were completely at their father's mercy when it came to choosing a husband.

Royal marriages were viewed from the outset as matters of political expediency. Kings were expected to ally themselves with foreign powers for political advantages and their daughters were regarded as highly marketable commodities.[91] The mood, however, was changing concerning the union of a young princess with her foreign husband who would have been a stranger to her until the wedding day. Lydgate and Hoccleve voiced this rising protest in poems composed around the time of the royal negotiations.[92] For Whittington, of course, royal weddings brought commissions for luxury materials that marked a pinnacle of his success and confirmed him as the official Court Mercer.[93]

On 8 December 1406, Henry's council met to resolves the problem of the strain on the country's finances this succession of royal marriages had caused. Unanimously, it was decided to appoint controllers with authority to drastically reduce the King's expenses. Tactfully, they waited until the Christmas festivities were over before requesting a private audience where they courageously confronted Henry. As the son of a wealthy nobleman, he was unaccustomed to balancing his books and he displayed a cavalier attitude towards his household expenses. 'Kings are not wont to render account,' he famously declared.[94]

Evidently, the tremendous privations imposed upon his subjects for constant warfare and court pleasures did not concern King Henry, Queen Joan or members of the royal family. Alarmingly, they continued to devour cash. It became increasingly obvious that a sharp check should be made upon their reckless extravagances.[95] A reshuffle of officials was needed to maximise savings. Sir John Tiptot, Speaker, was duly appointed to the plum positions – Treasurer of the Royal Household and Keeper of the Wardrobe – replacing Richard Kingston.

Whittington's Marriage

Whittington, too, flushed with success, turned his attention to marriage. In Medieval times merchants' marriages served practical purposes, to gain wealth, land or status and to forge bonds between families. Marrying merely for love was frowned upon, regarded as both foolish and wayward. A merchant might deliberately defer his marriage until his prospects were secure. Then he could command an even more favourable bargain regarding his fiancée's dowry, which might take the form of money, lands, jewellery, plate or even household possessions. To marry an affluent woman – a young heiress or a wealthy widow – was a surefire means of social advancement, particularly if the woman was equal to, or higher than, the suitor's own rank. Unashamedly, marriage was a means of obtaining capital to advance one's business, and on rare occasions it might even be hailed as a social triumph.[96] Whittington chose as his wife Alice, youngest daughter of Sir Ivo (Yvon or Hugh) Fitwaryn, an influential landowner with extensive estates in ten counties including Somerset, Wiltshire, Northampton, Dorset and Gloucestershire, but whose main residence was in Wantage, now in Oxfordshire but within the historic boundaries of Berkshire.[97]

There are several possibilities as to how Whittington could have become involved with Alice. Perhaps the two men met at the court of Richard II where Sir Ivo was one of the knights retained by the King.[98] Maybe there was a connection between them involving the wool trade on Fitzwaryn's estates in the West Country. A third consideration is that Sir Ivo may have have fostered a friendship with the influential Mansells – a daughter of whom was Dame Joan, Whittington's mother – who owned neighbouring lands in the West Country.[99] All this, of course, is speculation. Sir Ivo was born in 1347 and was possibly an exact contemporary of Whittington, which makes Alice a generation younger than her husband.

Medieval marriage was an informal affair among ordinary citizens. A couple might be espoused in the home of the bride's father or legal guardian, often after their union had been consummated. Consecration by the church, if desired, took place at a later stage which, for Whittington, a devout churchman, would have been performed according to the ancient rites of the Roman Catholic Church. Richard and Alice would have exchanged their vows in the church porch and these would have been followed by a nuptial mass before the High Altar. Two witnesses only were required to be present. The select company would return to the bridegroom's home where the religious ceremony was augmented by feasting, dancing and entertainment with invited guests. At the end of the evening, the sumptuous marriage bed would be blessed by a priest and the bride and groom would be escorted to their chamber by their friends and family to consummate – assuming they had not already done so – their now holy union.[100] The Whittington's wedding was probably held at the Thameside Church of St Michael Paternoster in 'The Royal'.

An inquisition on the death of Fitzwaryn[101] reveals that Richard and Alice Whittington were previously parties to deeds (August 1402) by which Sir Ivo granted them upon his demise the reversion of certain manors in Somerset and Lands in Wiltshire.[102] This may have been intended as a portion of Alice's dowry, which would indicate the approximate date of their union. Further, the inquisition reveals that Alice predeceased her father and that his lands and property descended to his eldest daughter, Alianor (or 'Eleanor') who had married John Chydyok, Lord Fitzpayn of Dorset.[103] It may have been that either Whittington had waived all rights to Alice's properties or, possibly, that he had exchanged them with his brother-in-law for cash. Neither Sir Ivo nor Richard had sons to inherit[104] and there must have been an agreement among them that Chydyok was the perfect choice to maintain Fitzwaryn's substantial estates.[105] Throughout his life, it must be noted, Whittington's interest in property remained almost exclusively in London.[106]

Whittington's House

Around the time of his marriage, Whittington had purchased a grand house in the City. Perhaps the property was purchased with Alice's dowry or even the proceeds from the recent transaction with her sister, Eleanor, and her husband. The timing is perfect. Whittington bought his house from Sir Baldwin Berford on 22 December 1401. Previously, it had belonged to Sir Nicholas Brembre, the disgraced Mayor of London. Associated with the conveyance were William Hedyngton, Thomas Fauconer, Thomas Roos and Henry London. All were his former apprentices who had become successful Mercers. Hedyngton had risen to become Chaplain to the Mercers' Company.

Whittington's mansion was situated halfway down College Hill leading to Thames Street. Probably built of stone rather than timber with tiles instead of thatch,[107] it was firmly set in the heart of the wine importing district known as 'The Royal'. Possibly, the name derives from the 'La Riole', a celebrated wine growing region of Bordeaux. The house was not only convenient for both Cheapside and Guildhall but also Lombard Street, where Whittington could make contact with the Italian bankers in order to transfer credit for his increasing overseas trade on the Continent. And his house was just a stone's throw from the Customs House and the busy commercial quays of London's River.

Whittington's mansion was, after all, not only to be a domestic residence for himself and his wife but his team of apprentices. All his mercantile business would be conducted either there or in his adjacent 'ware-chamber'. Whittington would regularly play host to visiting Italian counterparts who would expect to lodge there while business was discussed, amiably and advantageously.[108] Soon after this mansion was purchased and furnished, it acquired another most important use: as the residence of the Mayor of London.

Whittington's Coat of Arms

Prominently displayed outside his mansion, Whittington would have commissioned two carved and painted shields: one with his trademark, the other bearing his personal coat-of-arms. Merchants were most eager to adopt armorial bearings since they served a dual purpose in identifying families or individuals and asserting an undisputed claim to status. London's Mayors, Sheriffs and Aldermen increasingly assumed the right to bear arms in the same manner as a high-ranking military commander and this custom went unchallenged because their aim, after all, was to defend the City. Unauthorised, casual assumption of coat-of-arms was also fairly widespread among noblemen, but this practice was curtailed after a system of heraldic administration was introduced, supervised by the office of the Garter King of Arms, created in 1415. Merchants, before that time, acquired their arms by a variety of means: by inheritance from their ancestors, by grant from the King, by purchase of an official patent or simply by assuming them.[109]

As he came from a knightly stock, Richard Whittington inherited his established family coat-of-arms.[110] These are described as 'Gules, a Fess checky Or and Azure, in dexter chief an Annulet Or' – a chequered horizontal band in gold and blue on a red background with a gold ring or annulet in the top left corner.[111] Lysons misunderstood the gold annulet, which traditionally denotes a mark of cadency and therefore erroneously assumed that Whittington was the fifth son. Yet an annulet, at that time, did not denote the seniority of siblings because it was already an integral part of the Whittington coat and therefore must have had an earlier, unknown origin.[112]

Whittington's arms correspond with his family in Gloucestershire and correspond with those that appear on the Ordinances for Whittington College. There is, however, one marked difference. Whittington substituted the original crest of a predatory lion's head[113] for a gentler emblem, either a bee or a mayfly with gold-tipped wings. Either insect might be considered emblematical of his life. The first was a mark of his success through industry, the second exhibiting his ephemeral existence – he was the author of his own fortune, leaving no heirs. Guillum's 'Heraldry' describes the characteristics of bees in quaint terms: 'Bees have three properties of the best kind of subjects. They stick close to the king. They are very industrious for their livelihood expelling all idle drones. They will not sting any but such as provoke them, and then they are the most fierce.'

Upon his marriage to Alice, Whittington impaled his arms with those of his wife's family, the Fitzwaryns. These latter arms are described as 'Quarterly per Fess indented Ermine and Gules'. That is to say, the top left and bottom right quarters display ermine (as used in the robes of peers), the other two quarters consisting of a plain red background. The horizontal division of the shield takes the form of a zig-zag (indented).[114] This is the form of the coat-of-arms which would have been displayed on the double funerary monument commemorating Richard and Alice Whittington's in the Church of St Michael Paternoster Royal before its destruction in the Great Fire.

Thrupp considered it 'one of the commonplaces of English social history to remark upon the successful merchant's traditional ambition to become a gentleman'. Despite the fact that his father had been branded an outlaw, Whittington, throughout his life, remained a 'jentilman'. Whittington, possibly because of childhood traumas, never took the opportunity to return to his home county and live as a country gentleman but preferred to remain for the rest of his life in London. It must have been with a sense of pride and achievement, then, that Whittington displayed his coat-of-arms in the City which he had adopted and where he had made his mark. Certainly, the possession of a coat-of-arms, either through inheritance, purchase or acquisition gave the bearer credibility and made him more acceptable to the Royal Household.

Whittington's Seals

'Esquires from knightly families who simply did not wish to assume the superior rank would wish to employ a seal which bore the family arms,' writes Nigel Saul. Whittington employed a variety of seals for use in several capacities, although only a few samples of his sigillography are extant. For example, he authorised legal or official documents by affixing them with his own personal seal. Three examples survive, attached to documents in the London Metropolitan Archives and British Library. Merchants refined their seals and owned exquisite examples, featuring religious scenes or armorial charges surrounded with delicate tracery. By the fifteenth century, the art of seal engraving was evidently in decline and it became common for a merchant to employ a coarser cut design of a monogram or single initial, or figures and heads, culled from antique signet gems. Whittington juggled two impressive seals according to the circumstances and they are both, in some measure, an expression of his personality.

The earliest and most impressive surviving impression of Whittington's seal is the middle one of three appended to a vellum document dated 1402.[115] It is repeated in a letter dated 1410.[116] This distinct oval impression in red wax features a raised profile of a Renaissance youth on a rectangular panel inscribed:

'Ricardi Whityngton'. At the top centre appears a fleur-de-lis motif with the letter 's', signifying 'sigillum' (seal). Barron notes that 'the choice of motif more characteristic of the Italian Renaissance than that of early fifteenth-century England places it quite outside the normal run of merchant seals of this date'. The flamboyant design is a strong indication that Whittington was becoming a connoisseur of fine objects. He was by this time consorting with Lombards, Florentines and Venetians and was obviously influenced by the artistic trends of Northern Italy.

Later, Whittington became Mayor of the Calais Staple and he commissioned an alternative seal for exclusive use in this office. Only one impression of this seal survives. It authenticates a letter sent by the English Ambassadors, John Bourghope and Perrin le Loliarenc, with a proclamation of peace, to the Duke of Burgundy (29 April 1409). The new seal is larger, about the size of an old penny, and cannot, therefore, have been a signet ring. It is excessively damaged although the fine detail can still be admired. The inscription reads Ricardi (Whitting) ton with 'S' expanded to 'Sign' to occupy the enlarged circumference. The Renaissance bust has been replaced by Whittington's tilted heraldic arms surmounted by his crest of a bee or mayfly, while on either side are two 'lions or leopards facing', adopted from the original Mayoral seal of London.[117] Curiously, there is a slight variation of his coat-of-arms where the annulet is placed below the chequered bar.

Whittington also employed a simpler device of initials on seals for documents in later life. Two examples are extant. One is attached to a deed in the possession of the Skinners' Company.[118] The other concerns the transference of a lease on a tenement from the Mayor and Commonalty to William Est, in order for him to receive the annual rental of 20s from his tenant, Robert Cotyn, clothier, for a property in 'Candlewykstrete in St Swithin's'.[119] This small, simple seal, is enlivened with a sprig of foliage. Puzzlingly, there are two lower case letters, 'r' and 'b', which, Barron suggests may actually signify Sir Richard Beauchamp, for whom Whittington acted as attorney and mainpernor around this time.[120] These impressions appear to have been punched into a hot blob of wax with a clenched fist. Not Whittington's style at all!

Warden of the Mercers' Company

Whittington was elected Master of the Mercers' Company for a second term in 1401-2 and a third in 1408-9. Conveniently, his newly acquired mansion would have provided an excellent venue for their annual feast.[121] The Wardens often footed the bill themselves to celebrate their term of office but members also contributed about five shillings each. The Company might provide a lavish feast with entertainment, especially when special guests were present. Charmingly, it became the tradition for brothers to wear garlands of summer flowers on this auspicious occasion. Roses in summer with gillyflowers (pinks), lavender or sprigs of rosemary. Entertainment took the form of disguising and presentations.[122]

By the early 15th century, Merchant Companies began to divide their members into two groups, whereby the most senior, wealthy and experienced were entitled to wear an official uniform of 'livery'. Obvious pride was expressed in wearing a company's distinctive livery at public processions through the City. These might include daytime attendance at their parish church for their patronal festival followed by a splendid dinner or torchlight parade to celebrate a requiem Mass for the repose of the souls of deceased members of their fraternity. Livery, tippet and hood were obligatory when attending the Mayor and Corporation at St Paul's on Christmas Day, Twelfth Day and Candlemass, and on formal occasions including vigils, obits, offerings and assemblies. It was the aim of younger members to imitate their superiors by becoming successful and prosperous in business in order to be accepted, around the age of thirty, into their Company's livery. Generally, the group not admitted to the livery were those members who had not been commercially successful in the wholesale trade and had to depend on retail shopkeeping for their living.

Wealthier companies adopted the habit of changing their livery every two or three years, reserving their second best for less solemn occasions. The combination of colours was vivid and resembled modern day racing silks. The Grocers, for instance, sported scarlet and green, scarlet and black and scarlet and violet.[123] By 1423, it had become 'murrey and plunket' (dark red and blue).[124] Dyes were expensive and so too were the cloths,[125] but it was an unbeatable method of displaying both the importance and wealth of one's company. A 'full suit' comprised a coat and surcoat together with a cloak and hood, although a part dress, called the 'hooding', where just the head was covered, was allowed for members not yet eligible for the compete livery.[126] The Mercers' Master, Wardens and assistants marched in gowns 'faced with foins in their hoods' but the liverymen sported gowns covered with satin rather than the more common budge. Alas, their colour scheme is unrecorded. During Whittington's wardenship, the Mercers regularly changed their livery, which ensured a modest income, although liveries and hoods were presented to certain dignitaries, including, later, the Master of Whittington College.[127]

Liverymen led their brethren in public processions and presided over their splendid feasts. Only they were permitted to take part in the election of the officials of their Company. Should they become its Master and Warden, they would then enjoy the honour of having the 'cap of maintenance' (a velvet and ermine headband) placed on their brows by the retiring officers.[128] Liverymen were allowed to vote for the Aldermen, Sheriffs and Mayor and of course they might have the ambition to hold these offices themselves. The moment Whittington became a liveryman of the Mercers' Company, he had paved the way to being an Alderman, Sheriff and finally Mayor of London.

The Mercers, unlike rival City Companies, at first declined to assume a coat-of-arms. When Henry VI granted them their second Charter (14 February 1425), it allowed them a common seal. A few impressions survive. They bear the legend: 'Sigillum communitatus mistere mercerie Londonienses' and carry an image of a glamorous maiden. Generally, the young woman is depicted with long, flowing locks, a chaplet of roses and white lilies, wearing a crimson robe adorned with gold and appearing from a bank of clouds. The origin of this emblem is unknown. Perhaps she evolved from a tavern sign? Maybe she was employed as a trademark? Or was her role to demonstrate the sumptuous materials available for women to purchase? This secular device is often confused, because of her personal attributes, with the Virgin Mary.

In 1530, the Mercers' Company affirmed to the College of Heralds that it lacked arms although it employed a Maid's Head for a common seal. In 1568, this striking symbol was registered by the heralds as the Company's coat-of-arms: 'Gules, a demy-virgin, with her hair dishevelled, crowned, issuing out and within an orle of clouds, all proper'.[129] In 1911, the College confirmed the arms and granted the Company a crest and a motto: 'Honor Deo' (Honour to God). Today, maiden property marks carved from stone adorn walls and buildings owned by the Company. These signs are most prominent in the City of London, Stepney and Covent Garden.[130]

Whittington's Shop

About this time Whittington took rental of a shop in a prime position on London Bridge.[131] According to the rental book which was begun in 1404, but subsequently amended and updated, John Hert was the tenant for a shop 'on the east side beginning at the staples'. (These staples were wooden posts through which chains were passed to guard the entrance to the bridge in Southwark.) Properties on the bridge commanded high rents and this was one of the most expensive at forty shillings per annum. It can be conjectured that it combined a shop with storage above and living accommodation in the attic oversailing the River Thames. Apparently, people who worked there also tended to live there.[132] Several of these larger properties boasted a 'hautepas' or transverse gable connecting them to the building on the opposite side of the bridge. Additional floors across the narrow street created a dark tunnel, greatly restricting the flow of traffic across the bridge. Further obstacles were caused by the painted signs and projecting counters of the numerous shops.[133]

At an unspecified date, Hert surrendered his rental to Richard Whittington (who was in turn succeeded by Andrew Rede). Neighbouring shops were occupied by craftsmen, Cutlers, Stringers and even a 'brochemaker', John Spene, who took over from Whittington. At that time, however, Whittington was the sole Mercer in this premier commercial location, attracting travellers approaching the City from Kent. Stow noted the trend of shopkeepers following Whittington's initiative in moving from the City centre to the bridge in order to catch this custom. 'For where Mercers and Haberdashers used to keepe their shoppes in West Cheape, of later time they helde them on London Bridge, where partly they yet remaine.'[134]

Whittington's Third Mayoralty

Whittington became Mayor of London for the third time in 1406. His Sheriffs were Nicholas Wotton, Draper, and Geoffrey Brooke, Grocer.[135] The election, which took place on the Feast of St Edward the Confessor (13 October), was preceded by a High Mass with solemn music, during which the guidance of the Holy Spirit was sought, in the adjoining Guildhall chapel. This innovative service had been instituted by the retiring Mayor, John Woodcock. Indisputably, this time Whittington had been legally elected with the consent of the citizens of London. And since Whittington was the first Mayor to be elected with the assistance of divine inspiration, it was believed that he had won a far greater approval than a mortal sovereign.

Riley's 'Memorial' described the grand occasion:

> John Woodcock, Mayor, considering that upon the Translation of St Edward the King and Confessor, he and all the aldermen of the same city, and as many as possible of the wealthier and more substantial Commoners of the same city, ought to meet at the Guildhall, to elect a new mayor for the ensuing year, ordered that a mass of the Holy Spirit should be celebrated with solemn music in the Chapel annexed to the Guildhall, to the end that the same Commonalty might be able, peacefully and amicably, to nominate two able and proper persons to be mayors of the same city for the ensuing year, by favour of the clemency of our Saviour, according to the customs of the City.
>
> This was accordingly done, and the commoners peacefully and amicably, without any clamour or discussion, did becomingly nominate Richard Whytyngton, mercer, and Drew Barentyn, goldsmith, through John Westone, Common Counter of the said city, and presented the same. And hereupon the Mayor and Aldermen, with closed doors, in the same chamber chose Richard Whytyngton aforesaid, by the guidance of the Holy Spirit, to be Mayor of the City for the ensuing year.

After Woodcock's institution of a formal civic mass to assist the deliberations over a new Mayor, the Commoners unanimously entreated the Aldermen to make it a regular feature. They implored him 'that in future years, on the day of the Translation of St Edward the Confessor a Mass of the Holy Spirit ... should be celebrated before the election of the mayor.' Moreover, this was to be 'solemnly chaunted by the finest singers'. Thereafter the City's rituals became increasingly religious in character.[136] It soon became the custom for Mayors to attend Mass with their Sheriffs, Aldermen and Livery Companies at St Paul's Cathedral on at least seven occasions annually.[137] This trend continues to this present time when it is the custom to hold a religious service before the election of a new Lord Mayor.[138]

Traditionally, it was the custom for the Mayor, Aldermen and Sheriffs to process to the abode of the new Mayor and inform him of his election.[139] Whittington would have been delighted to receive the news at his recently acquired mansion in the City. The Mayor, Sheriffs, Aldermen and Commoners were summoned to Guildhall on the morning of the Feast of the Apostles of Simon and Jude (28 October). This date for country folk marked the end of fine weather and the commencement of gales and storms. The Common Crier or 'Serjeant-at-arms' called for silence while the Recorder[140] announced to the assembly that the Mayor Elect was about to take his civic oath on the Gospels.[141]

The Mayor's oath is preserved in 'Liver Albus'. First and foremost, Whittington would swear obedience to the King and his heirs and secondly, he would affirm that he would treat every citizen equally and fairly, no matter what their state or circumstance: 'and that neither for highness, nor riches, nor promise, nor for favour, nor for hate, wrong you shall do unto any one... So God you help, and the Saints.' The outgoing Mayor then handed the incoming Mayor the Seal of the Statute Merchant (with which he sealed certain bonds appertaining to London merchants) with the Seal of the Mayoralty, enclosed in two separate purses. After this brief ceremony the past Mayor, the sword proceeding him, escorted the incoming Mayor to his home, before returning to his own residence, the sword still leading him, where he tactfully remained.

A magnificent procession, known as the Mayor's 'Riding' (or 'chevauche'), signified the importance of the office and took place early on the morrow (29 October). The newly elected Mayor rode in procession from the City of London – Cheapside, Newgate, Fleet Street and the Strand – to the City of Westminster where he took his loyal oath before the Barons of the Exchequer.[142] This procession evolved from a mundane formality into a spectacular display of civic pride. The Mayor, sporting his ceremonial livery, a crimson velvet fur lined gown and velvet and ermine cap,[143] was preceded by his sword bearer.[144] He was accompanied by the Sheriffs and Aldermen and escorted by representatives of the City Companies dressed in their distinctive liveries, which on this auspicious occasion were permitted to be trimmed with fur. Among the proud participants were courtiers, apprentices and soldiers on horseback or foot attended with men bearing banners and minstrels playing music. All the houses in the streets were decorated with garlands, tapestries, bay and bunting.

After dismounting, the Mayor, Aldermen and Sheriffs, preceded by the mace bearer and the sword bearer, entered the chamber where the Chancellor, Treasurer, Keeper of the King's Privy Seal and Barons of the Exchequer were already assembled. The new Mayor repeated his oath. Afterwards, the illustrious civic company returned to the City, where the Mayor hosted a grand banquet at his own house, company hall or later the Guildhall. It became the custom for the Mayor to head a joyful procession from the Church of St Thomas de Acon to Saint Paul's Cathedral. Later 'Ridings' were criticised for being too raucous since they involved music, dancing and 'disguisings'.

Whittington, as Mayor, claimed the right for his sword to be borne upright before him, and not behind him, the same as an Earl.[145] Further, the dignity of the Mayor of London in his official capacity was confirmed by the attendance of ceremonial guards whose duty it was to carry both his sword and mace. They ranked as esquires or gentlemen and, although their fee was modest, they were supplied with rich liveries and were entitled to dine freely at the Mayor's expense. The Mayor jealously guarded other privileges. At a coronation he attended the Chief Butler, acted as honorary cup bearer and served the new monarch with wine, for which service he was entitled to retain the cup and ewer as his fee. [146] At ceremonial banquets he sat nine degrees above an esquire, higher than a knight, a knight banneret or an abbot without a mitre, with only the mitred abbots and the ranks of nobility above him. The Mayor of London took precedence over all nobles apart from those of the blood royal.[147].

For the first time, Whittington's jurisdiction as Mayor extended into the wild and unruly district of Southwark. For years there had been vociferous complaints that criminals, debtors and malefactors were sheltered from justice while living across the river from the City. In 1376, Londoners unsuccessfully petitioned Edward III in Parliament to bring Southwark completely under their control. Another constant concern was that the south bank waterfront proved convenient for burglary attempts on London by boat on moonless nights. In 1406, King Henry responded with a Charter (23 July) granting the Mayor and Commonalty the right to arrest, through their officers, miscreants seeking to escape from justice by hiding on the south bank, to try them in their courts and to imprison them in Newgate Gaol. Henry was probably influenced in his decision to take this action by his dependence upon London merchants such as Whittington anxious to protect their trade.[148] Craftsmen refused membership of a City guild or company often took refuge in Southwark and simply crossed the river to risk selling their goods illegally in London.[149]

Mayor Whittington, as the supreme authority in the City, might be addressed throughout his time of office as 'Lord' in legal documents, but variants were 'wise', 'gracious' and 'worshipful' and even, on one occasion, 'your high wisdom'.[150] A petition addressed to 'our worshipful Lord Mair of the Citie of London', appeared in 1414 although this title did not come into habitual usage until the mid-16th century. In fact, the title, 'Lord Mayor', was never officially conferred. Apart from York, the Lord Mayors of British cities have been granted their titles by royal letters patent, although, it seems, the title of 'Lord Mayor of London' is enjoyed 'by virtue of long usage'.[151]

Aldermen, in early civic records, were addressed as 'sire', a style later abandoned, apart for the Mayor. Their dignity was symbolised by a scarlet robe of office worn on ceremonial occasions and, on the streets, by a distinctive cut to their hood.

Apparently, tenure of judicial office as City magistrate, irrespective of how brief, entitled the wives of Aldermen ito be addressed as 'Lady', although their husbands were not entitled to a personal appellation. This affectation raised them to the social level of the spouses of knights and squires and they jealously retained it, even when widowed or remarried to men who held no public office! Thus, the Mayor and Aldermen were regarded as superior in status to ordinary commoners and this tended to blur the traditional three-estate system.[152]

A most important annual event in the City was the 'Marching Watch' that took place on Midsummer's Eve (23 June) prior to the Feast of St John the Baptist. The intention of this male-orientated parade was to demonstrate the strength of the City's defences. First recorded in the early 13th century this chivalric ritual was enhanced in the 14th century by a haunting, nocturnal march through the main streets. Bonfires were lit at dusk when the streets came alive with musicians, mummers and Morris dancers. Private houses were decorated with greenery and public buildings were illuminated with lanterns. London Bridge was garlanded with sweet-scented flowers and boughs of leaves: green birch, long fennel, summer roses, white lilies and St John's wort.[153] Evidently, this was the highlight of the calendar in Medieval London.

About two thousand citizens took part in these torchlight parades in those long evenings of summer. They were formed primarily of veteran soldiers, archers and pikemen, who marched abreast, in rank, carrying torches and cressets, with 'banners spread and clarions ringing'.[154] Military bands accompanied them led by drummers, pipers and trumpeters. Aldermen and Constables wore particoloured livery, red and white in Richard's reign and scarlet and green in Henry's, over their armour. Every ward was enjoined to provide representatives from their own standing watches 'all in bright harness'. Standard bearers held aloft the City arms, the Mayor's arms and the myriad arms of the City companies. Focus of the procession was the Mayor, dressed in full armour, who rode immediately behind his swordbearer, adding lustre to this spectacular occasion. After all, it was the role of the Mayor – Whittington knew this from recent experience – to muster men at times of rebellion or invasion.

Stow nostalgically recalled the glamour and excitement of later St John's Eve Watches:

> The waytes of the City, the mayor's officers, for his guard before him, all in a livery of wolsted or say jaquets party coloured, the mayor himselfe well mounted on horseback, the sword bearer before him in faire armour well mounted also, the mayor's footmen, and the like torch bearers about him, hench men twane upon great stirring horses following him. The Sheriffs watches came on after the other in like order, but not so large in number as the mayor's, for where the mayor had beside him his Giant,[155] three Pageants, each of the sheriffs had beside their Giants but two pageants, each their Morris dance, and one hench men, their officers in jaquets of

wolsted, of say party coloured, differing from the mayor's and each from the other but not having harnised men a great many.

A third pageant, organised by the Skinner's Company, was the procession to celebrate Corpus Christi. Stow, again: 'This fraternitie had also once every yere on Corpus Christi day after noone a Procession, pased through the principall streets of the Citie, wherein was borne more than one hundred Torches of Waxe (costly garnished) burning light, and above two hundred Clearkes and priests in Surplasses and Coapes, singing. After the which were the sheriffes servants, the Clarkes of the Counters, Chaplains for the Sheriffes, the maiors Sargeants, the counsell of the Citie, the Maior and aldermen in scarlet, and then the Skinners in their best Livereyes.' One can visualise the Skinners, brimming with pride, as they brought up the rear to receive the adulation of the cheering crowds. King Henry and Queen Joan did not disdain to watch these City processions and brought their honoured guests along to share in the festivities from the royal box. This took the form of an elevated grandstand attached to the north wall of St Mary-le-Bow in Cheapside, at the heart of all these proceedings.

London's civic pageantry revolved around this calendar of processions; patron saints days of the individual City Guilds and Companies, Midsummer and Corpus Christi. Focal point of these processions was often the Church of St Thomas Acon, where the venerated Archbishop had been born, on the north side of the Cheap and a little to the east of St Mary-le-Bow. After his martyrdom, his sister, Agnes, and her husband had donated the site for the foundation of a Hospital of the Military Order of St Thomas of Acon. This became a place of special devotion for Londoners and the City government was keen to emphasise its connection with its patron saint, so that in 1327 custody of the Hospital was transferred to the Mayor and Commonalty. In 1383, they ordered the church to be rebuilt on a grander scale.[156] In winter there was a series of civic processions to St Thomas Acon for mass and thence to St Paul's on important days in the church calendar. At Easter the Mayor, Aldermen and Sheriffs went to St Mary's Bethlehem Hospital outside Bishopsgate. On Whit Monday they visited St Peter's Cornhill and led by all the rectors of the city churches they then marched in procession to St Paul's to pray at the tomb of the parents of St Thomas Becket. There were further processions to the Cathedral on Whit Tuesday and Wednesday. Londoners valued these processions greatly and insisted on the correct uniform or livery.[157] Invariably, these public parades were led by priests holding aloft crosses and candles to emphasise the point that their purpose was to combine the religious with the secular in Medieval London.

River Thames Weirs

Whittington's jurisdiction as Mayor encompassed the River Thames. There was a major problem in Medieval times with illegal weirs and eel traps in the rivers of England. They were a cause of disastrous flooding across the country and a hindrance to navigation. King Henry IV ordered commissioners to investigate the state of the rivers and report on all 'piles, pales, pools, kidels (obstructions), trinks (dams) and races' that impeded the passage of boats. An important piece of legislation during Whittington's second mayoralty was the complete removal of these obstructions in London's river.[158]

'Ande that yere alle the werys bytwyne London and Mydway were drawe downe by the conselle of the kynge and of the mayre of London, and of the comyns of the same cytte, for they dyd miche harme in the ryver of Themys, for they dystroyed moche yonge frye, for the pepylle gaffe hit hir hoggys, and soo uncomely devouryd hyt.' (Richard Wytynton, Mayre of London. Endorsed by his sheriffs Nicholaus Wotton and Geoffrey Broke 1407.)[159]

Laws prohibiting the fastening of 'nets and other engines... to great posts, boats and anchors in the Thames' helped protect fish stocks. When nets of small gauge were attached to obstacles they trapped fish when far too young. The City's Water Bailiff organised armed excursions to police fishing activity and apprentices from the City companies were commandeered to destroy weirs and seize illegal nets and traps. The confiscated gear was publicly burned in Cheapside.[160]

Whittington's efforts to abolish these obstructions to navigation in the River Thames did not go unchallenged. 'Libus Albus' records bloody clashes between the officials and the riparians. On 9 February 1407, an officer, acting on the instructions of the Mayor, lifted sixteen nets with the intention of examining them to see if their meshes were too narrow. Straightaway, bells were rung from the church towers on opposite banks of the Thames. This summoned a multitude of angry fishermen who set off in boats armed with swords, bucklers, sticks, clubs, and bows, even doors and windows in place of shields, to pursue the officers from Barking to Erith where they secured the nets and carried them off in triumph.

Eventually, Whittington and the Londoners, after 'great plea and discord', approached the King in council where they asserted their chartered rights over fishing in the Thames and gained full authority to remove, burn and destroy all obstacles between Staines Bridge and the River 'Medewaie' (Medway).[161] This blight on illegal weirs continued into the next reign when Henry V ordered the City Companies to organise an extensive working party, two men from each Company, to ride in a barge along the whole river between Staines and Gravesend in Kent and Queenborough on the Isle of Sheppey.[162]

Illegal weirs were abolished because they ensnared eels which were an important source of food. Eels were eaten on prescribed fish days as a mark of religious observation. Fortunately, they were in plentiful supply in the River Thames. These fish first appear as larvae at the river mouth in the autumn and swim upriver once they have developed into baby eels, called 'elvers', in the spring. Elvers are considered a great delicacy and are the only other young fish, apart from whitebait (herring) permitted to be caught for food.

Traditionally, eels were fished on spring tides at night since they are nocturnal and lie buried in the mud during daylight hours. They were caught by long nets, wicker traps and pronged forks. Wicker baskets, three to four feet long, were woven from osiers cut from river banks. Small ones were called 'putcheons', large ones 'weels'. A piece of rabbit or lamprey was placed as bait inside the narrow end and the opening stopped with a wooden plug or handful of rag. The trap was then weighted with stones, tethered to the bank and laid in the water.

Later, eels were caught with spears. These consisted of a wrought iron head with closely spaced tines mounted on an extremely long ash handle. The spear was plunged vertically into clear, shallow water and the eels became wedged between the tines. Eels were captured in this way without harming them and they could then be sent live to markets. Use of spears to trap eels was only made illegal by Act of Parliament in 1911.[163]

Dispute with the Goldsmiths

During this third mayoralty Whittington incurred the wrath of the Goldmiths' Company. A memorandum in the Wardens' accounts explains the circumstances. William Chipstead, a hotheaded young member, accused the Wardens of misappropriating funds before the Mayor, Sheriffs and Aldermen of London. He denounced them for spending all their income from rents and tenements (which he claimed amounted to between £160 and £180 per annum) on maintaining 'false quarrels' to the detriment of younger members, diverting them from seeking worthwhile employment. It is difficult to understand the actual cause of Chipstead's outlandish complaints but it seems there was an argument over trade between some of his fellow members with a rival company, the Skinners. The Wardens of these two Companies entered into negotiations in an attempt to resolve this bitter dispute.

Chipstead took great exception to the Wardens' most sensible communication. He felt that his company should support its own members whatever the circumstances and his anger kindled rebellion. He incited his companions to attack and kill his own Wardens[164] when they next convened at Goldsmiths' Hall, a magnificent new building on the east side of Foster Lane.[165] Subsequently, Chipstead was arrested for rioting and placed in the custody of the Sheriffs. The Wardens vehemently denied Chipstead's accusations; they asserted he had grossly exaggerated their annual income and they submitted a counter claim of slander. Naturally, the Wardens of the Goldsmiths' Company looked to the Mayor of London for his positive support.

At this moment Queen Joan chose to intervene. From Kennington Manor, she despatched a letter which she addressed to 'our dearly and most well-beloved' Mayor of London, Richard Whittington, on 28 April 1407. At the same time she composed a beguiling letter to the master of the Goldsmiths' Company. A transcription survives at Goldsmiths' Hall. It reveals that, although Her Majesty concedes that William Chipstead behaved in a discourteous manner towards the Wardens, she recognises that there might be a certain amount of truth in what he contends. Indeed, she, herself, is prepared to overlook his 'over weening pride' because she feels a fondness towards this young man, who just happens to be a relative of her chaplain, Sir John Cleseby. Further, Her Majesty implores the Wardens to treat Chipstead with 'favour and leniency' so that he can be swiftly released from prison 'without fine or ransom'. The Queen then promises that, if the Wardens comply with her command, she will be inclined to look favourably upon any future requests from the Goldsmiths' Company. Thus minimising the recent very real threat to the Wardens' lives, she sweetly affixed her seal to this charming letter.[166]

Whittington, to his discredit, succumbed to the Queen's flattery and without consulting the Wardens ordered Chipstead's release. Characteristically, Chipstead renounced his Company, declaring that he would not wish to be under their rule, nor ever claim to be a Goldsmith, 'not for a thousand pounds!'[167]

Happily, Whittington must have renewed his good relations with the Goldsmiths' Company because later he made a successful appeal on behalf of a Dutchman, Frederick Malver, to be admitted to their Freedom. It was fairly unusual for an alien to be admitted to any of the City Companies but the Wardens complied with his request upon payment of the Customary fee: £10. (Goldsmiths' Accounts: 14 May 1423.)

A Case of Adultery

Mayor Whittington and his Sheriffs would have presided at the Court of Hustings held at Guildhall. This ancient assembly met every Monday but continued on Tuesday should it prove necessary. It transacted both legal and administrative business: deeds, wills and indentures were enrolled there and the court heard action by writ dealing with land and tenements, suits about rents or services and disputes about wills. It was busy with the usual privilege of enrollment and probate of wills. Indeed, it was so busy that the Sheriffs' Court had already started as an overflow which, along with the Mayor's Court, eventually superseded the Hustings Court.[168]

Whittington would also have presided there over the Mayor's Court comprising the Mayor, Sheriffs, Recorder and several Aldermen. This dealt with actions arising out of the common law such as theft, debt, slander, swindling, brawling and assault, in addition to matters relating to City customs including orphanage, apprenticeship, trading by women and offences against the City ordinances. In this same court, when held in the inner chamber, the administrative business of the City was conducted – ordinances of the mysteries were approved, and permission granted to orphans in the City's custody to marry – and it was here in this court that freedoms were granted and elections ratified and orders were made for the expenditure of the City. Occasionally, it was thought fit to involve the wider community and opinions were sought from the common councillors although, in truth, their advice seldom carried weight against that of the Mayor and Aldermen.

Evidently, it presented a high moral stance since it routinely deal with sexual misdemeanours involving adulterers, bawds, courtesans and whoremongers. One minor yet distasteful offence came before the Mayor's Court on 14 December 1406. This concerned Richard Dod, a tailor, who had connived at the adultery of his wife, Margaret, with a chaplain, Sir William Langford, for a paltry sum. The trio had been arrested by the 'bedel' of the Ward of Bishopsgate Without. Dod, it was ascertained, had received forty pence from the randy cleric in return for his wife's sexual favours. And for this shameful verbal contract, Whittington sentenced Dod to stand in the pillory for three hours on the following Wednesday.[169] The priest avoided punishment.[170]

9

The Wool Merchant

Whittington the Banker

Whittington's Massive Loans to the Crown can certainly be substantiated. Over his career, it is recorded he made almost sixty loans amounting to millions in today's terms to bale out the constantly insolvent Exchequer.[171] His largest recorded loan was for £2,833 6s 8d, a phenomenal amount, on 27 October 1408.[172] Certainly, it was expected that London's Aldermen made regular contributions towards their country's finances. Frequently they shouldered a loan between them since they were deemed to be among the wealthiest citizens of London. Chronicler Richard Grafton reminded them persuasively of their duty to be charitable: 'Look upon this, ye Aldermen, for thys is a glorious glasse' – holding the mirror up to their civic icon, Whittington.[173] The City, both as an institution and as a collection of individual wealthy merchants, was in effect expected to act as the King's bankers. And Whittington, famously, responded repeatedly to England's dire financial situation.[174]

Whittington amassed his fortune through mercery towards the latter end of Richard II's reign, 1379-1395. His loans at that time were minimal compared to those throughout the reigns of the next two Plantagenet kings. Thereafter, his brilliance in financial dealings was a direct result of the fact that rather than being tempted to hoard, he kept his money 'on the move'.[175] He declined to invest in land or property outside London. And, unusually, he did not have a large family to support. Presumably, he kept most of his capital in liquid assets, which enabled him to make frequent hefty loans at extremely short notice to the Crown.

Henry IV faced the continual problem of governing his realm with an empty Treasury.[176] Early in his reign a lack of funds became increasingly desperate and he felt 'hampered and embarrassed' with debt.[177] This meant he had little choice but to rely heavily upon the support of the City magnates. Occasionally,

Whittington made loans in conjunction with his colleagues: Thomas Knolles, Grocer, and Nicholas Wootton, Draper, and even a syndicate formed of Calais merchants (1406-7).[178] At intervals, he was required by certain individuals to fund their public activities: Lord Burnell for expenses incurred at the Gloucester Parliament (£258 6s 8d); John Beaufort, Earl of Somerset, after he enlisted in Henry's Scottish expedition (£666 13s 4d) and Sir Thomas Talbot, Keeper of Montgomery Castle 1403-5 (£180).[179] So high-ranking noblemen, although they might publicly despise the London merchants, did not hesitate to approach them privately when they found themselves strapped for cash!

Whittington lent money to Henry IV annually, except in 1412 (and in his son's reign, 1416, notably the year after Agincourt). The maximum recorded loan in any one year was £4,876, representing seven separate loans, in 1402.[180] Exchequer Receipt Rolls confirm that between 1400 and 1420 Whittington was in a position to lend sums of £3,000 and upwards annually. This was on a scale beyond any other contemporary London merchant. Whittington had become one of the country's most important sources of ready cash.

He played 'the dangerous market of the royal court'[181] on which no timorous man might then depend, since repayment was often long delayed. It is tempting to speculate as to his purpose and potential reward. Usury was illegal in Medieval England. The Bible explicitly denounces the practice.[182] Whittington may not have directly benefitted financially from his loans – but they were a sure means of gaining royal favour and this would lead, naturally, to more tangible returns. His interests, then, may have been to gain political influence and to play some part in national affairs, which he could only achieve as a member of the royal entourage.[183] Certainly, the frequent borrowing of the impoverished Lancastrian kings allowed the merchants, particularly the Mercers, privileged access to power, both in the Capital and the Council. And it must not be forgotten that these substantial loans exempted Whittington from military service at home and abroad.

By lending money to Richard II, Henry IV and Henry V and arranging their complicated financial affairs, Whittington became, in the course of his London life, tremendously wealthy. Richard II repaid his loans in cash but it became the tradition of the Lancastrian Kings for repayment to be made by assignment (an allocated task) and it was this method that consolidated Whittington's fortune. His loans, then, were repaid with interest, but this took the form of obtaining lucrative Crown contracts or appointments to profitable offices such as that of Collector of Customs.[184]

The Collector of Customs

King Henry appointed Whittington Collector of the Custom and Subsidy on Wool in London. He held this prominent and influential position from 1401-3 and 1407-10. This post lacked a salary but there were benefits. He could ensure that his licences to export wool without paying customs duty remained unchallenged and this privilege increased his tidy profits. Further, his appointment guaranteed his assignments made on the customs of London because repayment of his loans was given top priority. This security encouraged him to provide additional loans to the Crown. He was safe in the knowledge that they would be repaid even during the times – and they became increasingly frequent – 'when royal credit was running low'.[185]

The customs service boasts a long lineage, dating from at least Saxon times although it may even reach back to the Roman occupation when London began to emerge as a commercial centre.[186] Earliest documentary evidence for customs appears in a charter dated 743 AD when Aethelbald, King of Mercia, granted the Abbey of Worcester dues of two ships 'which shall be demanded by the collectors in the hithe of London town'. In 979 import duties were being collected at 'Belingsgate': '½d on a little ship, 1d on a larger ship with sails, a ship full of wood, one piece as tax... Men of Rouen who shall come with wine or large fish shall give a due of six shillings, men from Flanders, Normandy and France shall be free of tax.'[187] Additional duties were charged on cheese, butter, eggs and cloth. It seems a remarkable coincidence that from the early 13th century there has been a Custom House within close proximity to Billingsgate.[188]

King John instigated a national Customs Service in 1203. He placed a duty of one-fifteenth on all imports/exports and decreed that in future all the customary dues at the port should be accounted directly to the Treasury. The ports were thus placed outside local control and into a central system administered by the Exchequer. In 1275, Edward I introduced a further duty on exported wool, woolfells and hides which became known as the 'new customs'. In 1303, he revised the import duty on wool and introduced a further duty on imported and exported small goods by both alien and denizen merchants, 'petty customs'. Collectively, these new duties in his revised charter became the 'new customs' while the previous duties imposed were referred to as the 'ancient custom'.

At first the complicated collection of customs was deputed to the Italian bankers from Florence, Lucca and Genoa. Gradually, their dominance in the affairs of the customs dwindled and it was placed in the hands of merchants from the City. A trio of officials was introduced to assist the customs collectors: 'searchers', who examined imported and exported goods, made up appropriate accounts and ensured the correct duty was paid; 'surveyors', who became supervisors of the searchers' activities; 'customers', who safeguarded the duty received and transported it from the ports to the Customs Headquarters. This has always remained the case in London.

All these customs officials were constantly checked by an independent authority who submitted his own separate accounts, written on a roll, to the Exchequer. He was the most senior member of the team, the 'Comptroller'.[189] Comptrollers were appointed directly by the king and selected from minor officials in his court or household. Geoffrey Chaucer was appointed Comptroller of the Customs and Subsidy of Wool, Woolfells and Hides and the Petty Customs for the Port of London in 1374. He was awarded with a lifetime lease on a house with a suite of rooms built in an enviable position over Aldgate.[190] As Comptroller, the celebrated poet held a more senior post to Whittington's.[191]

Henry IV revised the collection of customs after Parliament admitted that thousands of pounds were lost annually by unscrupulous collectors who practised artful deceptions. Incompetent comptrollers were often found to be absent from their post and delegated responsibility for collecting dues to their deputies. Moreover, they were often suspected to be in collusion with the merchants in falsifying their accounts. Henry insisted that those who were appointed collectors of customs should reside in their designated area. Further, a pair of customers were to be stationed at each port, one to be nominated by the King and the other by the merchants themselves. Stringent laws were introduced to combat smuggling by merchants who attempted to conceal wool in empty casks and 'steal abroad with cargoes uncustomed'.[192] Members of Parliament were expressly forbidden to hold office, although reliable merchants were still deemed suitable to hold prominent positions in the revised customs service.[193] Whittington, honest and trustworthy, fitted the bill perfectly.

At that time the coast of England was mapped out into districts, each with a named principal port. Eastwards, for instance, there were seven districts whose chief ports were Newcastle, Hull, Boston, Lynn, Yarmouth, Ipswich and London. Wylie estimates that the yield for the whole country at the beginning of Henry's reign amounted to approximately £50,000 per annum.[194] Collecting customs and transporting them to the capital was a difficult and dangerous task, particularly at a time when the country was engaged in quasi civil war. The officers were repeatedly evaded by the rebellious inhabitants on the borders of Wales and Scotland. Charge of Customs in London, and also the ports, was still an onerous although less dangerous task, which could only be entrusted to a person of impeccable character. During the 14th century, the preference for collectors was former London mayors. Whittington was following in the footsteps of his worthy associates: William Walworth, John Philpott and Nicholas Brembre.

By the mid-14th century, the Exchequer was beginning to introduce a system whereby the collection of the three main areas of customs – wool custom and subsidy, petty custom and cloth custom, tunnage and poundage[195] – and relevant subsidies were consolidated. The administration process had been simplified in most ports with one body of officials (two collectors with a controller) rendering one account for all the duties collected in that area. In London, however, they remained distinctly separate, presumably because there was a far greater volume of cargo than at other ports around the country. Whittington would have concentrated on the Customs and Subsidy of Wool, Woolfells and Hides (without becoming involved in any other form of import or export duties) that conveniently combined the Ancient Custom, New Custom and Subsidies in the 15th century.

For Whittington it was a short walk from his mansion along the river bank eastwards towards the Custom House adjacent to Billingsgate, 'famous for fish and bad language'.[196] Headquarters of the customs service was ideally situated for the mooring of vessels and the landing of their cargoes below London Bridge. A first London Custom House was built in 1275 on the quayside to collect dues for Edward I's 'Great Customs'.[197] There was certainly a Custom House with a tronage (or weigh) house on the ground floor and a counting house on the first floor in 1381. This was replaced by a far grander building designed by John Churchman, Sheriff of London, at Wool Wharf in Tower Ward, completed in 1386. Churchman's imposing Customs House, intended to accommodate officials of the Great Custom on Wool and Woolfells but later extended to house officials of the Petty Custom, was the building which Whittington would have known.[198]

Whittington would have been responsible for overseeing the weighing of wool on scales, known as the 'tron', before export from London. He was assisted in this essential task by a 'troneur' who, at that time was John Shadworth, a former Mayor and fellow Mercer. These official scales took the form of a stout timber bar known as the 'king's beam' located outside every Customs House. Stow mentions a 'Wey house' where 'merchandizes brought from beyond the Seas are to be weighed at the king's beam' on Cornhill. It was situated in the churchyard of St Mary Woolnoth, which later became the site of the official residence of the Lord Mayor of London, Mansion House.[199] (The best preserved king's beam is outside the Custom House at Poole, Dorset.)

The Wool Merchant

Henry IV's numerous assignments entrusted to Whittington almost exclusively involved the collection of the wool subsidy, which was by far the most lucrative permanent source of royal revenue. This particular collection was authorised at England's six major ports: Chichester, Southampton, Ipswich, Kingston-upon-Hull, Boston and, most importantly, London. Obviously, these assignments would bring him into close contact with wool merchants across the country and the collectors of customs around the coast of England.[200] From thence, it would be a natural progression for Whittington, as Collector of Customs and Subsidies in London, to be tempted into investing in the precarious, yet often lucrative wool trade himself.

There was one strong enticement for Whittington to dabble in the commodity. Henry's recompense for loans occasionally took the form of a licence to export wool from London without paying the stipulated customs or heavy subsidy until the royal debt was absolved. This, in effect, meant that Whittington could export wool far cheaper than any other merchant. They simply could not compete with him...

Wool was considered 'the sovereign merchandize and jewel of the realm'.[201] Indeed, the country's finances and politics depended heavily upon the wool trade, which enjoyed a virtual monopoly abroad. It paid for Richard I's ransom after being taken prisoner while returning from the Crusades and it raised funds for Henry II to build the first stone London Bridge. (This fact explains the legend that the foundations of Old London Bridge were laid on woolpacks.) In 1275, Edward I negotiated amicably with merchants that first specific tax on wool, at 7s 6d per sack, which was subsequently known as the 'Great and Ancient Custom'. [202] Today, the Lord Chancellor plumps himself down on the 'woolsack' which is his official seat in the House of Lords at Westminster. This is a poignant reminder that the profits from wool were for four hundred years the main source of England's prosperity. Hilary Green points out in *International Trade in the Middle Ages*:

> The attitude of the merchants who profited from the wool trade can be summed up in lines inscribed on the window of one of their houses: 'I praise God and ever shall, it is the sheep hath paid for all.'

English wool commanded high prices as it was widely perceived as the finest in Europe. Incontrovertibly, sheep farming was the most important component of Medieval farming. It survived both war and pestilence, and greatly flourished when the population decreased and profits slumped after the Black Death. Sheep provided not only wool and meat but tallow for candles and hides for leather, parchment or vellum. Flocks were folded (penned with wicker fences) on fallow fields and also on the stubble after the corn was cut in order to manure the land, necessary in the absence of fertilisers. Tenants would be required to lend a hand at sheep shearing and gangs of clippers might be hired, although traditionally this was women's work. A 13th-century treatise on estate management exhorts a shepherd to be 'discreet, watchful and kindly' so that his sheep felt secure and that when he watched over them at night he should provide himself with 'a good barkable dog'.[203] They flourished especially on the springy turf of the downlands of southern England, but also in the West Country where the hills of the limestone Cotswolds[204] supported the most prized flocks of sheep, referred to as 'best Cottes'.[205]

Whittington, as a wool merchant, would have been most familiar with, and almost certainly dealt in, 'Cotswolds', with his links to Gloucestershire. This ancient, hardy breed is thought to have been established by the Romans during their occupation of Britain. They introduced both sheep and weavers to provide their soldiers with cloaks and blankets. The breed with which the Medieval merchants were familiar was probably smaller than today with a more compact frame, since they were farmed primarily for wool. Today, Cotswolds are one of the largest breeds of sheep, bred mainly for their meat, which has a sweet texture because of the lush pastures of herbs and grasses in the West Country.

Cotswolds are distinguished by their white purled coat but they may also have the occasional black spot on their face, ears, legs and hooves. Adult sheep have a wave, or 'crimp', on their long strands of wool (a single strand is known as a 'staple') revealing a yellowish tinge nearest the skin, and this gives rise to its moniker, 'Golden Fleece'. Traditionally, the top knot is left on their head once shorn to show the quality and length of their prized wool.[206]

During the heyday of sheep farming in the Middle Ages, flocks owned by great noblemen or powerful monasteries roamed (or 'hefted') in great droves over the hillsides.[207]

Around May or June, competitive merchants instructed their agents, 'woolmen' or 'woolmongers', to ride far out into the country to bargain for the new year's clip from farms, abbeys and markets. Frequently, wool was disposed of years in advance through contracts and this was invariably the practice of religious houses. Until the late 14th century, the best woollen cloth was manufactured abroad and there was a lucrative trade in exporting bales of wool to Flanders[208] and Northern Italy.[209] Whittington, as a wool merchant, would need to exercise his knowledge of different types of wool, the prices at which to buy and sell and, importantly, how to negotiate with shrewd Flemish and Lombard merchants. They obtained permission to purchase and transport wool, on condition that they, in return, lent money to the English kings. In this manner, the realm prospered.

At home, wool provided not only warm clothes and bedding but rich drapes and tapestries. Short wool produced by small sheep was prepared by 'carding' to make cloth while long wool from larger sheep was primed by 'combing' to make lighter worsted and serges.[210] Both types would have been woven undyed into homespun garments by women. Originally, this would have resulted in drab cloths but countryfolk began to experiment with plants and vegetables for dyes: brown from yew, indigo from woad, green from privet. Luxurious when handcombed, 'top notch' wool might be threaded with fine wires of spun gold to make special vestments for priests and kings. And this might have been the native source for Whittington's own trademark cloth-of-gold.

By 1404, Whittington was definitely exporting wool from London and Chichester, but he may also have exported from Southampton and Sandwich, Kent, the latter described as 'wool out, wine in'. In 1407, he monopolised the wool exports from Chichester when he exported six shiploads to Calais. His ships transported a total of 250 sacks on which he paid more than £360 in custom and subsidy dues. This appears to represent his maximum effort, at a time when it was rare for a single merchant to ship more than 300 sacks per year[211].

Whittington remained among the dozen most important wool exporters in England.[212] There is a suggestion, however, that he may have been the head of a syndicate formed from fellow Mercers.[213] Henry London, his former apprentice, who had been involved with him in several property transactions, appears to have joined his wool company.[214] Whittington would have depended upon reliable staff to operate the trade, so probably while he remained in his counting house dealing with the finances, working late into the night balancing the complicated exchange rates by candlelight, he employed a team of labourers for the more strenuous work. This involved loading the wool onto packhorses that ambled along the country roads, the tinkling of bells of the leading horses keeping the team together and warning travellers of their approach, and transferring the bales onto ships at the quayside. Whittington's renowned organisational skills would have been tested by this challenging land and sea trade.

Bundles of wool destined for export were packed in canvas sacks, known as 'sarplers', stamped with the merchant's distinctive mark. Wool merchants, highly competitive, became extremely wealthy and some built churches in their home towns to proclaim their commercial success and to honour God. Upon their demise, they were commemorated by elaborate memorial brasses that often feature their own merchant mark inside those same churches. The Cotswolds is famed for its magnificent 'wool churches' and one prime example is SS Peter and Paul, Northleach.

Whittington's Cargo Ships

Shipmen of the Middle Ages sailed vessels designed to be versatile. They carried a diversity of cargo – wheat and wine, spices and soldiers – that needed to be transported across stormy oceans into the tight coastal harbours and then along narrow inland rivers. Vessels were typically eighty feet long and twenty feet across the beam, with fore and aft castles and a single mast. Oars were used to propel the vessel down river to the sea. The master would then take his chance among the considerable traffic of cargo ships, fishing boats and sailing barges on the open sea with his limited knowledge of navigation.[215]

The type of ship that wool merchants employed was predominantly the 'cog'. Today, their design can be studied from Medieval coins, harbour seals, church wall paintings and maritime shipwreck excavations. These small, sturdy cargo ships were eminently suitable for transporting timber, grain, glass, furs, wine and wool to or from the Continent. Cogs were heavy-duty seagoing vessels distinguished by their short, high, boxlike hulls with steep, raked stem and stern posts. They were powered by a single square sail which was often gaily patterned with broad vertical red and white stripes. The cog was 'the classic sailing ship of Northern Europe'.[216]

Helmsmen, who navigated without charts or compass, preferred to remain within sight of the coast. This was perfectly feasible for the short run between the Kentish port of Sandwich and the English one at Calais. Even then there was the hazard of the treacherous Goodwin Sands to be negotiated. Ships might be becalmed in fine weather for days at a time in the natural anchorage known as 'The Downs'. Distant harbours could not be reached simply by hugging the land and masters were reluctant to cross a wide expanse of sea in poor visibility. They often preferred to await a clear night in order to navigate by means of the North Star.[217]

The crew travelled exposed to the elements, without any form of shelter. Cogs were economical since they required a modest crew. They wore a hooded coat called a 'gugel' that offered minimal protection against adverse weather. Often the hull would become waterlogged so some goods were packed in watertight containers – boxes, barrels or bales. This limited the capacity of the cog's already cramped hold. Whittington or his deputy must have been on hand to supervise the loading of his valuable cargo, achieved by removing planks to allow access to the hold and rotating cranes equipped with ropes, chains and hooks. A notable example are the 'three strong cranes of timber placed on the Vintry Wharf by the Thames side to crane up wines there', noted by Stow. They feature on Wenceslaus Hollar's 'The Long View' panorama of London published posthumously in *c.*1647.

The scale of Whittington's activities as wool merchant hardly compares with his rival Italian exporters who operated from London and Southampton. Their larger ships – galleys and carracks – arrived regularly from Florence, Genoa and Venice. Italian 'great galleys' were impressive merchant ships, about forty metres long with lateen sails and rowed by around one hundred and fifty oarsmen, sitting three to a bench. These were enormous vessels, capable of weathering Atlantic gales even in winter, in the Bay of Biscay. Italian galleys berthed at Galley Quay, just west of the Tower, adjacent to the Customs House, a visible reminder of their legal obligations. English merchants tended to despise Italian traders and resented the fact that they were welcomed by successive monarchs who borrowed from them large amounts of money. They imported sugar, spices, currants, raisins and luxury materials – silks, damasks and cloth-of-gold – obviously of great interest to Whittington.[218]

English or Italian cargo ships transporting wool faced many perils as they crossed the English Channel. Their Masters' worst fear was to encounter 'sea theeves' or enemy ships, particularly at times of uncertain peace between England and France. Chaucer's fictional Merchant whose ships operated on the route between Harwich and Holland declares: 'He wolde the see were kept for any thyng bitwixe Middleburgh and Orewelle.'[219] Crews were armed with guns, gunpowder and bows ready to defend their cargo. Safe arrival of a ship in harbour was a matter of fervent thanks to Almighty God. The Mercers' Company, mindful of the dangers that attended transportation of their goods, were granted permission to have a chaplain and brotherhood 'for relief of such of their companie as came to decay by misfortune on the sea' in the early reign of Henry IV.[220]

Inexplicably, Whittington began to dabble in wool when it was in serious decline. Customs receipts indicate that the average annual wool exports from

England decreased by 35,000 sacks in the early 14th century to 8,000 sacks in the middle of the 15th; even lfewer in the second half of that century.[221] The wool trade, obviously, was never Whittington's prime concern in the reigns of the two Lancastrian Kings. At this time, the decrease in the wool trade was compensated by a vast increase in the export of woolcloth.[222]

Merchant of The Staple

Wool merchants for convenience – from the late 13th century through to the 16th – exported from one authorised port known as the 'Staple'. Originally, there were a number of Staple towns across England although they were intended as collecting or cloth centres whereas London and Newcastle were ports specifically equipped for exporting wool.[223] English merchants who controlled this export trade were called 'Merchant Staplers' and they belonged to the exclusive 'Company of the Merchants of the Staple'. Merchant Staplers became extremely powerful and exerted their greatest influence in the early 15th century after Henry IV granted them a monopoly over the export of wool and the collection of attendant dues. Wisely, The King realised that he could tax monopoly profits by means of a heavy export duty and raise loans from the company of merchants on the security of the duty.[224] In London the Staple was settled at Westminster[225] and on the Continent the town appointed was Calais.[226]

From 1347, when Edward III captured Calais, until 1558, when Mary Tudor famously lost it, this European port remained English territory. For that pertinent period, Calais was ruled exactly as if it was an outpost of England. The town was inhabited by an imported English population[227] governed by an English Mayor aided by twelve English Aldermen. It had an English mint and an English prison. Even the outlying forts were manned entirely by English soldiers. The surrounding peasantry, according to Wylie, was 'bound to the English connection by no ties but fear'.

This garrisoned town provided an excellent base for cross-Channel traffic trading from Sandwich and Dover. The Merchants of the Staple established their headquarters there, from which they organised their thriving wool trade with the neighbouring Flemish markets.[228] Obviously, it was convenient for the royal officials to collect the customs and subsidy on wool and far easier to control the important trade if it was concentrated in one place. Furthermore, the merchants, acting as a single body, were in a strong position to secure excellent terms and trade concessions from their wily customers, the Flemings. The main concern of the Staple was to enforce the rules and regulations that ensured the high standard of English wool was strictly maintained when it was offered for sale at the mart in Calais.[229] English or Italian merchants, referred to as 'staplers', jealously guarded their connection with Continental cloth manufacturers who, they knew from experience, would pay high prices for their wool exports. The

Company of the Staple of Calais – first registered in a Charter dated 1313 – is thought to be the oldest trading company in England.

Whittington served as Mayor both of the Westminster and Calais Staples. His main duty in connection with the Westminster Staple was the witnessing of bonds between merchants. The Patent and Close Rolls refer to a number of these bonds and twelve of them were sealed in the presence of Mayor Whittington. The earliest is dated 24 October 1403 and the latest 26 February 1418. 'From these documents,' assesses Barron, 'it appears that it was the duty of the Mayor of the Westminster Staple to act as a kind of mercantile commissioner of oaths, witnessing recognizances for debt, bonds and general releases of actions.'

About 1406, Whittington also assumed the role of Mayor of the far more important Calais Staple. This was a difficult and dangerous time when the irascible Duke of Burgundy vowed to drive the English out of their barbican. The War Treasurers, alerted by intelligence, started to accumulate funds for paying and victualling troops in preparation for a seaborne attack. London merchants petitioned the King's council to abandon this risky and costly project but Henry was adamant that he would personally lead the offensive. He gave orders for 400 men-at-arms and 600 archers to stand in readiness to accompany him across the Channel.

Gunners, masons and carpenters were sent ahead to repair the fortifications at Calais, the condition of which was 'scandalous and deplorable'.[230] Twenty-four vessels of between 10 and twenty tons burden were chartered from around the south and west coasts to transport troops, ammunition and provisions from London, Sandwich and Dover. Henry's council ordered that half of the wool subsidy raised in English ports should be allotted for the wages of the garrison in Calais, although it was stipulated that the claims of the Merchants were first satisfied. Alas, when the quarterly returns were assessed they revealed that this yield amounted to precisely: nil.

The unpaid troops seized wool belonging to the Merchants of the Staple at Calais in order to recoup their back pay. The merchants duly complained to the King, who meekly replied that he wanted his money, too! The whole expedition was placed in jeopardy owing to lack of funds. After a remonstrance and delay, a consortium of staple merchants obliged with a loan of £4,000 on 9 May 1407. Whittington, naturally, was one of the principal lenders. Surprisingly, they were repaid in a matter of weeks, although in the event, the project was abandoned. Whittington must have realised the moment he was appointed to the lucrative post that he would be expected to make sizeable loans to the Crown. Artfully, he ensured that he would be repaid promptly by retaining both the customs stamp (or 'cocket') and the seal of the Staple in London.

Apart from these regular loans for the war effort, there are disappointingly few references to Whittington as Mayor of the Calais Staple. On 13 August 1408, Whittington was ordered to ignore a recent statute which stipulated that no new wool should be offered for sale until the old stock at Calais was disposed of first.[231] In July 1413, he was paid a minor sum for expenses incurred in bringing Robert Ekford from York to London to appear before the Barons of the Exchequer. Circumstances of the dispute are unrecorded, except that predictably it was adjudged to the Crown's advantage.[232]

Whittington found exporting wool from the English ports of London, Chichester, Southampton and Sandwich was a dangerous business. Cogs conveying his cargoes were often the target of pirates.[233] Generally, he arranged for his ships to leave in a tight convoy to cross the Channel to Calais.[234] At one point, he took the precaution of arming his hired ship, *Trinity of Tychefield*, as it sailed from Southampton. Presumably, this involved installing archers in the fore and aft castles.[235] Piracy on the high seas continued to be a threat to commerce in the subsequent reign of Henry V. The English stationed two armed ballingers in the Channel to protect merchants transporting wool over to France. King Henry compensated Whittington when his cargo was shipwrecked on the Goodwin Sands by ordering the Customs to waive the fee when the salvaged bales of wool left for a second time from Chichester.[236] While acting in this capacity, it can be assumed that Whittington never actually left London.

A Wool Ceremony

Coventry, the third largest city in the country, was hailed as the premier centre for the cloth industry in England. In its heyday, it boasted three miles of fortified stone walls, with twelve gates and three dozen turrets, enclosing a trio of churches – Holy Trinity, St John's and St Michael's – whose towers and spires soared over myriad houses, gardens and orchards.[237] There were also a series of flourishing guilds – St Mary's (founded 1340), St John the Baptist (1342), St Katherine (1343) and Holy Trinity (1363) – which amalgamated as the 'Guild of the Holy Trinity' in 1392.

The Trinity Guild drew its members from almost every corner of the land. Members gained great advantage in belonging to a fraternity that fostered a thriving trade in this principal city of the Midlands. Although they were primarily concerned with finance and politics, members were obliged to become involved in religious and ceremonial duties. London merchants appreciated the substantial benefits provided by the Guild, particularly the offer of cheap quayage at Bristol Docks from where ships regularly traded with Europe.

Richard and Alice Whittington were welcomed as honoured guests in Coventry when they were enrolled in the Guild of the Holy Trinity. Although undated, their names were entered in the register: 'Ricardus Whytington et Alicia'.[238] Whittington's coat-of-arms impaled with Fitzwaryn were included in either the east or west window of St Mary's Hall[239] but, they were both destroyed during the election riots of 1780.[240] The first two Lancastrian Kings,

Henry IV and Henry V, were enrolled in the Trinity Guild, for political rather than financial reasons. Illustrious members also included Whittington's late patron, Thomas, Duke of Gloucester, and his colleague, John Coventre, Mercer, Alderman and Sheriff, who became his executor. (His surname, presumably, indicates that he originated in Coventry.)[241]

Legal Advice

Whittington, because of his untarnished reputation, reliability and responsibility, was often involved in special royal commissions, both as a justice and an administrator, but also as an advisor and an arbitrator for private individuals. On at least four occasions he witnessed land transactions; he was four times appointed an attorney (including when his brother, Robert, was in Ireland); he was chosen on three occasions as an arbiter in disputes between individuals. He was the recipient of goods and chattels in a complicated case that appears to have been a ploy to forestall seizure of goods in lieu of a debt by a fellow Mercer, William Rody (31 March 1402). Earlier he had acted as custodian of the possessions of the politically exiled John More in 1384[242] and he was a Receiver General in England for Edward, Earl of Rutland and Cork in 1402.[243]

On almost a dozen occasions Whittington agreed to stand as surety or 'mainpernor' (guarantee of a prisoner's appearance in court). Legal cases involved Richard Clifford, King's clerk (16 January 1394); Richard Greneway, a prisoner in the Tower (16 March 1401); James Spersholt, King's alnager[244] in Berkshire and Oxfordshire (2 May 1403); Henry Somer, Chancellor of the Exchequer, 'under pain of 10,000 marks, that he shall answer in Parliament' (1 April 1413); and Thomas Podmore, a London ironmonger, who wanted to marry a widow whose six children were in the care of the Court of Aldermen (14 February 1419). Mysteriously, Podmore left London later that summer without enrolling his apprentice, Richard Colyn, at the Guildhall.[245]

Whittington had been made the ward of another young man, William Bonevyle, by Edward, Duke of York. (Calendar Inquisitions Post Mortem 14 October 1413). Surprisingly, he only twice acted as an executor: for Richard Clifford, Keeper of the Great Wardrobe in Richard II's reign and later Bishop of Worcester, 1401-7, who made his will on 20 August 1416[246], and for Sir Ivo Fitzwaryn, his father-in-law, who made his will on 6 November 1412. His younger companion, John Carpenter, often acted in this capacity.[247] All these responsibilities demanded concerted effort and financial risk without, it seems, offering much financial gain.

Whittington was appointed to fifteen commissions of 'oyer and terminer' ('to hear and determine') between 1401 and 1418.[248] The majority of these cases involved profits and plunder arising out of war, either on land or sea. His first case, in 1401, concerned the interminable and politically embarrassing quarrel over the Count of Denia, captured at the Battle of Najera in 1367.

Four of Whitington's commissions involved the seizure of ships and disputes about their ownership: *Matthew of Brittany* (20 November 1405); *Lawrence of Ipswich* (3 November 1407); *Trinite of Bayonne* (20 June 1409) and *Holygost* (13 December 1417). Two concerned rival claims on merchandise and cargoes. Appointment to these onerous tasks indicates that Whittington was familiar not only with merchant and civil law 'but also the laws of war and the relative jurisdictions of the constable marshal and admirals of England'.[249] In 1412, William Waldern, Mayor of London, Thomas Knolles and Whittington were appointed to investigate a quantity of French and Spanish merchandise that had been captured and stored in London. These worthy judges adjudicated that the Spanish goods were to be restored to their owners while the remainder were to be resold to the advantage of the King.[250]

Whittington was also appointed to supervise the papal revenues to be collected in England by the Bishop of Ancona on behalf of Pope Laurence in 1409.[251] Assisted by Philip de Albertis, a Florentine merchant, he was charged with ensuring that the Bishop collected no more than the stipulated £866 13s 4d. Half of that amount was to be forwarded to the College of Cardinals at Pisa. The project appears to have fizzled out because the bond in which the pair undertook to do this task was subsequently cancelled.[252]

Despite his legalistic mindset, Whittington forgave his debtors in certain circumstances. Ralph Burbugh of Somerset who owed Whittington £12 (1411); Richard Clifford, the parson of Stepney, Middlesex, £51 (1418) and William Butteler of Suffolk, 40 shillings (1419) were all forgiven their debt.[253] Although these were comparatively small amounts, this sympathy towards citizens who could not meet their financial responsibilities may have arisen from the personal experience of his own father's plight when Whittington was a minor.

A Question of Knighthood

Towards the end of his reign, Henry, short of money, revived the dubious scheme of imposing knighthood upon his wealthier subjects. Edward III habitually knighted his soldiers on the battlefield, either as an encouragement before or as a reward after a conflict, during the prolonged French Wars. Mortimer makes the astringent comment that newly made knights often died in their first engagement, attempting to prove themselves worthy of their great honour.[254] Wily Londoners, however, shunned this opportunity for elevated status because it imposed time-consuming responsibilities upon them for local government and national defence. The honour, invariably, came far too late in their lives to greatly affect their own social relations. City merchants preferred to pay a heavy fine to avoid the onerous chivalric title.[255]

On 20 November 1410, noblemen who had been for the last three years in receipt of an annual income of £40, whether from owning land or property, were ordered to appear before Henry's Council by Candlemass. They were then to be offered the choice of accepting the order of knighthood or, upon refusal, paying a fine of £3. The Receipt Roll of the Exchequer for this winter period contains over forty entries of gentlemen drawn from the counties of England. Interestingly, the only person prominent on this list who declined the honour at that time is Robert Whittington, previously Sheriff of Gloucestershire.[256]

Robert Whittington remained a shadowy figure compared to his famous younger brother. All the same he was certainly a formidable character in Gloucestershire. A Robert 'Whityngdon' or 'Whitingham' was raised to the Shrievalty in 1416 and, again, in 1419 (the year of Richard's last mayoralty) in London. In 1416, he was returned as Member of Parliament for the City. There is no evidence, however, that this was, in fact, Richard's own brother. Nor is there any suggestion that Richard was involved in nepotism.

Contrary to popular belief Richard Whittington was never knighted. Knighthood, in any case, was rarely bestowed on Mayors or merchants in Medieval times. True, Richard II had knighted William Walworth, Mayor and Fishmonger, for his bravery in defending him from the rebel leader, Wat Tyler, and he also awarded him with certain lands in order to sustain this unsolicited royal favour. Edward IV at his consort's coronation[257] knighted the Mayor, Ralph Josselyn, for his loyalty to the Crown. After this time it became customary for the Mayor of London to be knighted automatically in recognition of his services.[258] It was not until the reign of Henry VIII, however, that it became customary for the Mayor of London to be knighted upon acceptance of his term of office. By this time, of course, the high honour had moved far from the battlefield. Richard Whittington was never 'Lord' Mayor of London.

King Henry's Illness

'We now approach a time of much obscurity,' warns Wylie. The last seven years of King Henry IV's life were blighted by a terrible illness. First symptoms appeared after he visited York in the summer of 1405. The King was returning to London but the weather was wild and he was forced to seek shelter for the night. His sleep was disturbed by a hideous dream. He awoke with a burning sensation and cried out in alarm: 'Traitors! Ye have thrown fire over me!' At first his attendants thought that he had been poisoned but soon realised that he had contracted an infection resembling leprosy.[259] This was interpreted by the northerners as Henry being struck down by God – the weather reflected divine displeasure – punishment for the execution of Archbishop Scrope. Henry had already survived two ingenious assassination attempts: a poisoned leather saddle and a booby-trapped bed.[260] Furthermore, he had a narrow escape when his tent was blown down in a gale and was only saved because he slept in his armour.

From that time onwards, Henry suffered a disfiguring skin disease, first manifested by baldness, and a series of acute attacks not necessarily related to it. He began a series of pilgrimages across the country to healing shrines in search of a miraculous cure that cruelly eluded him. His English physician, Master Malvern, was baffled. Henry, following the prevailing trend, consulted the services of an Italian Jewish medic, Dr. David Nigarelis from Lucca. He made him Warden of the Mint to ensure that he received a high salary for his services. Known as 'Nigarill', he remained in this country as a naturalised subject until his death in 1412.[261] Henry also sought the ministrations of a second Jewish doctor, Elia di Sabbato from Bologna, who was permitted to come over to England and practise in December 1410. Afterwards, the career of this 'most illustrious of International Jewish physicians' saw a meteoric rise: he was knighted for his medical services by the Duke of Milan before he was appointed physician to Popes Martin V and Eugenius IV.[262]

Henry's health continued to deteriorate alarmingly and he became a 'majestic invalid'. Sensibly, he transferred the business of government to a council headed by his trusted friend, Archbishop Arundel. The Prince of Wales was appointment to act for a time as Regent.[263] The King remained mentally agile but his authority was severely curtailed, although he professed never to be an autocratic sovereign, and he retired from public life. (King Charles VI became mentally deranged at this time and his son, Dauphin Louis, was elected Regent.)

In anticipation of his demise, Henry made his will on 21 January 1409. Short and concise, this was notably the first royal will written in English. The Prince of Wales was named his executor. There is a marked absence of instructions for funds for feasting the poor, or religious houses, or an elaborate funeral, or even personal gifts to family or friends. Henry IV died so seriously in debt that his executors were unable to administer his estate.

Stormy Weather

Rumour was rife concerning the King's impending end and there was widespread discontent at the constant crises – violent rebellions, piratical attacks, harvest failures, recurrent plague... Writers revelled in the attendant doom and gloom:

> The vii year of Henry IV (1406/7): In this sommer the Pestilenciall plage so infected the Citie of London and the countrie roundabout that the King durst not repaireth nor yet nere to the confines of the same, wherefore he departyng from the castel of Ledes, determined to take ship at Quinboroughe in the Isle of Shepey over to Lye in Essex and so to Plasshey, there to passe his time till the plage were seased. (Hall's 'Chronicle')

Even his swift passage invited danger because 'certaine pyrates of Fraunce were lurkying at the Temmes mouthe waityng for their pray'.

The weather mirrored the mood of the nation. From December 1407 to March 1408, the country was covered with snow so that poultry and wildfowl, the staple diet of country folk, died in their tens of thousands.[264] These harsh winters were deemed 'the wildest that any man living had ever known'. Records abound in the annals of every country of its severity and the havoc caused by the subsequent thaw throughout Europe. Scribes found it difficult to write about the event because the ink froze on their pens. Nevertheless, the Greyfriars Chroniclers managed to compose this daunting contemporary account: 'Thys yere was the grete frost and ise and the most sharpest winter that ever men sawe, and it duryed fourteen wekes, so that men myght in dyvers places both goo and ryde over the Temse.'[265]

Terrible weather conditions prevailed month on month, with disastrous effects on the economy. The crops failed all over southern England. The price of corn rose. Hungry mobs rioted in the streets of London. The government acted with a series of restraining laws. In November 1408, it was ordered that no corn, barley, oats or malt should be sent out of the country, except for shipment to Calais. An unusual step was taken to allow Yorkshire and Lincolnshire wheat to be brought free of duty into the City. In January 1409, an order was issued that no person would be allowed to carry arms within the City boundaries. These extreme measures appear, in some ways, to have extricated the country from many of its difficulties.

Extraordinarily, in view of the situation, the Treasury could report it was now in credit. This was despite the fact that the clergy in certain parts of the country refused to pay their share of the taxes and violently resisted the officers who called to collect them. Archbishop Arundel, it was felt, could be trusted 'to ply the whip over his rebellious flock' and draw them into line with required taxation. Whenever money was scarce, the City magnates – Norbury, Hende and Whitttington – could still be relied upon to forward funds in their certain knowledge that they had a guarantee of prompt repayment through the customs.[266]

The years following his third Mayoralty were a time of personal tragedy for Whittington. Disease and death were never far away for the inhabitants of London. The first outbreak of plague in the new century occurred between 1405 and 1407, when thirty thousand inhabitants died in the City.[267] This spanned the year of Whittington's term in office. Intermittent bouts of summer plague were later attended by winter influenza, referred to colloquially as the 'sweating sickness'.[268] Alice fell ill, and her complaint may actually have been a prolonged one from which there was little hope of recovery. Generally, the task of ministering to the sick fell to the priests and friars because physicians were far too expensive for ordinary citizens.[269] Whittington could afford to pay for his wife to be treated.

Whittington acquired an official letter of safe conduct, dated 23 October 1409, for Master Sampson, a Jewish doctor, to travel from Mirabeau in Southern France to administer to the ailing Lady Alice. Evidently, he acted quickly:

> Know ye that our burgess and merchant Richard Whityngton concerning a certain illness which remains with his wife has made agreement with certain individuals, experts and counsellors in order to remedy the said

illness, and for the said remedy he intends to invite Master Sampson of Merbe Merbeawe into our realm without our safe conduct and licence, and after the deliberation of our said burgesses and their especial consideration of this said Master Sampson, they have authorised for him permission and licence to come to our city of London.[270]

Anti-semitism was rife in the 15th century and Jews were excluded from most professions in predominantly Christian Europe. Optimistically, Henry III had constructed a safe house for converted Jews, although this was turned into a depository for documents when they were expelled in 1290. Absurdly, they had been blamed for the existence of the Black Death on the Continent. Jews were still accepted as doctors or surgeons, however, and they were encouraged under licence to administer in England.

Merchants, who previously would have relied upon the Church to minister to them when sick, began to invest in private medical services. The Black Death had acted as a catalyst for modern medicine when the limited medical knowledge of priests was supplanted by the beginnings of scientific investigation into health and hygiene. Jewish doctors were highly regarded after their formal training and rigorous examination at the Italian Universities of Florence, Padua, Bologna, Siena and Turin. They commanded impressive fees for their impressive medical qualifications. There was a certain prestige in having a personal physician constantly in attendance.[271]

Whittington may have retained him as a member of his household, which was the custom, to proffer advice on health or diet. Despite all Master Sampson's remedies, however, Alice succumbed to the mysterious chronic illness and died in 1410, probably on 30 or 31 July, which were the dates of her obit. She was buried in the nearby church of St Michael Paternoster Church that her husband had been engaged in 'beautifying'.

'There is a hint of tragedy about the marriage of Richard and Alice,' observes Michael Whittington in his short history of his ancestors. Lady Alice, who was younger than her husband, was childless. Maybe the couple elected for chastity within marriage, as has been suggested for the relationship between Richard II and his young consort, Anne of Bohemia.[272] Another supposition is that Alice had been an earlier victim of the plague, which rendered some women who survived barren.[273] The strongest impression, however, is that this was a loveless match, lacking passion, even 'a cold marriage of convenience', according to Barron. Richard Whittington never remarried. He was not, it seems, a family man. He evinced little desire for an heir, something which drove his fellow merchants to multiple marriages. There was, however, one small consolation.

Whittington's close friends were Sir Richard and Mary de Sancto Mauro. His ancestor, Wido (or 'Guy'), came over from Normandy[274] with William the Conqueror and was rewarded for his services with lands in Somerset, Wiltshire and Gloucestershire. Sir Richard, the son of a valiant knight also named

Sir Richard, fought in Ireland and France. Summoned to Parliament 1402-1407, Sir Richard fils died the following year lacking a male heir. His wife, Mary, died giving birth to his only daughter after being taken into care by Thomas Cressy, Mercer, whose house was in Cripplegate Ward, on 23 July 1409. Alice Whittington was one of the two women who were invited to become the orphan's godmother when she was baptised at the Church of St Lawrence Jewry. The child was named 'Alice' in her honour.[275] When she came of age, Alice de Sancto Mauro stood to inherit the considerable family fortune in lands and property which eventually passed to her husband, Sir William le Zouche of Totnes.[276]

Around this time, Whittington acquired a new apprentice. Robert, son of Laurence Steven of Great Jernmouth (Yarmouth), was released from his apprenticeship to William Butte, a Mercer, who had been imprisoned in the Fleet. Clearly, in these circumstances, Butte was no longer able to instruct and provide for his apprentice who, with the approval of the Mayor's Court, was transferred to the care of Whittington for the remainder of his term.[277] The law provided in certain circumstances for an apprentice to be assigned to an alternative master who would provide for him and teach him his trade for the completion of his seven year's term.[278] Alas, there is no record of Robert Steven ever entering the livery of the Mercers' Company.[279]

Henry's Death

For a brief period towards the end of his life, King Henry made a temporary recovery from his debilitating illness. And in a final burst of energy, he emerged from his 'cloud of greatness'[280] to regain control of his Kingdom. But then, one day in about mid-Lent Henry was making his oblations at the shrine of St Edward the Confessor behind the altar at Westminster Abbey when he suffered a massive seizure. He was carried by his attendants through the cloisters to the newly erected Abbot's Palace. There, he was laid on a straw pallet near the fire and tenderly nursed while in great pain. By ancient custom, the crown was placed on a cushion of cloth-of-gold beside him so that his successor might access it the moment life departed. The Prince of Wales entered and, assuming his father was dead, prematurely removed the crown for security. Henry expired, aged only forty-seven, on St Cuthbert's Day (20 March 1413) in the room known as the 'Jerusalem Chamber'. Henry had been bitterly disappointed that he had failed to lead a pilgrimage as King to the Holy Land. It appeared that he had, at least, fulfilled the prophecy that he would 'die in Jerusalem'.[281]

After lying in state, Henry's embalmed corpse was wrapped in lead and placed in a rough elm chest, which was then packed with haybands to steady it as it was transported on a torch-lit barge along the River Thames. The three royal brothers, Princes Henry, John and Humphrey,[282] were part of the waterborne cortège of vessels, arrayed with lanterns, rowing at dead of night from Barking to Greenwich. The coffin was then transferred to a horse-drawn bier covered with cloth-of-gold and taken overland via Faversham to Canterbury Cathedral. Henry was buried in Trinity Chapel behind the high altar on the north side of the spectacular bejewelled shrine of Thomas Becket, opposite the tomb of the Black Prince. Thus, according to Wylie, Henry IV 'was laid to rest at one of the most hallowed places in the Christian world'.[283]

Down the ages, there was a persistent rumour that a sudden storm had arisen when Henry's body was being transported along the River Thames. The crew, fearing for their lives, ditched the body overboard to lighten their load and immediately peace was restored. This seeming miracle testified to the vengeance of Archbishop Scrope. The sailors then filled the empty coffin with stones and deceived the country into burying it, minus its illustrious body, in Canterbury Cathedral. In 1832, the Dean and Chapter decided to investigate the fantastical tale and ordered the royal tomb to be opened. When the lid of the coffin was prised open the undisturbed face of King Henry IV was revealed. His forked beard was still russet,[284] one tooth was missing while his cheeks were brown and moist 'like the leather of a shoe'. When Queen Joan died on 10 June 1437, she was buried in this double royal tomb. Her own effigy, which is markedly shorter, reveals a prim, demure figure and 'displays more than ordinary beauty of features and daintiness of dress'.[285]

Henry IV's Achievements

Wylie, the Victorian scholar, presents a damning view of Henry IV's 'aimless' and 'unthrifty' reign. It was, he adjudges, 'thwarted by the toils of disaffection that everywhere beset his throne'.[286] A modern authority, Mortimer, also admits that in contrast to Edward III's 'glorious kingship', the King's early years had been blighted by 'domestic unrest, national disunity, financial insecurity and foreign antipathy'.[287] Nonetheless, this author and biographer considers Henry ultimately to have been 'phenomenally successful'. The King of Scotland is his prisoner, the Welsh revolt is crushed, the French are in disarray and he can take pride in the fact that he had won every battle he had personally fought.

True, there is little that is tangible that remains of Henry's difficult and traumatic reign. In contrast to Richard II, Henry IV did not invest his time, money and effort in fostering art and architecture. Usurpers, by definition, are far too preoccupied in keeping their kingdoms to spend time in cultural pursuits.[288] Three surviving scattered building projects are Battlefield Church at Shrewsbury, the Castle Gatehouse at Lancaster and the Chapel of St Edward the Confessor at Canterbury Cathedral.

The King's finances were constantly in arrears and he was forever forced to borrow huge sums from the City's magnates. Whittington, as principal royal financier, took measure of this money wasted in warfare and determined to become involved in far more worthwhile projects that would mark his name for posterity. Undeniably, Henry IV's reign had given him the opportunity to accumulate and consolidate his vast wealth.

Shakespeare in his historical trilogy portrays Henry IV as a man plagued by self-doubt and ridden by guilt. For the dramatist, Henry's reign offered an excess of incidents that encompassed assassination, rebellion, duplicity, betrayal, kidnapping and murder. At the centre was a humane and cultivated warrior whose greatest virtue was his resolution to circumvent confrontation and avoid bloodshed, despite his sovereign authority being constantly challenged by his own previously trusted allies and supporters. He had successfully converted his ducal crown into a royal one and resolutely established the Lancastrian dynasty.

Whittington, the third son of a disgraced knight who had chosen a despised career in commerce, had risen in status far above his two elder brothers. Through his industry and efforts, he now exerted equal powers with landowning barons and warrior knights. The King greatly respected him and relied heavily upon his financial assistance and perhaps advice. In gratitude, Henry provided him with high positions of influence and authority, and authority he exerted politically, economically, socially and commercially at a period when England was about to experience a great change in power and prosperity abroad. Henry IV's bitter disillusionment and despair was eclipsed in his son's reign by the greatest military achievement – partly funded by Whittington – of the Medieval Age.

THE REIGN OF
HENRY V

10

Rumours of War

HENRY V inherited a stable throne but a depleted Treasury from his father. He was determined to unite his kingdom and establish his authority in France. Skilled in warfare, he stirred up patriotism and raised funds for a daring military campaign. Henry was young, active and demonstrative, with a zest for military adventure; Whittington was elderly, cautious and peaceful, with an abhorrence of excessive personal display. Yet both men shared a common concern for national prestige and religious orthodoxy.

Henry V's reign was marked by a period of religious fervour. He was determined to combat diversity in thought or expression of personal belief. The Warrior King was resolved to present a nation united in vision and purpose in order to prove to the world in battle that God bestowed his favours upon England. And in order to appease his Creator, Henry commissioned Whittington to supervise the restoration of the nave of Westminster Abbey.

Whittington continued – to a lesser degree – to act as Mercer and banker to the royal household. Regal ceremonies in the reign still required great quantities of luxury fabrics for dressing and drapes, including Whittington's hallmark cloth-of-gold. Henry's three successive French campaigns necessitated vast loans and Whittington obliged with funds for the initial assault, which proved decisive, the siege of Harfleur.

As the reign progressed Whittington emerged as a veteran of civic government – reliable, trustworthy, dependable – and a formidable force with a commanding authority. The impression of the historical Whittington as a remote, reclusive figure is erroneous, based possibly upon an absence of personal records. 'What has survived – to be cherished and turned into legend – is his great sense of civic pride and humanitarian duty,' writes Anne Sutton.[1]

Henry V's Accession

Henry V was tall, slender and athletic. He had a long, lean, clean-shaven face, straight nose, pale complexion and short cropped brown hair. He demonstrated a cold, reserved manner – his tendency was always to say little – but his piercing hazel eyes and low, quiet voice pointed to a confident, tenacious and authoritative character. His one disfigurement was a scar from the arrow that had penetrated his cheek when his visor was temporarily raised during the Battle of Shrewsbury. Perhaps this blemish, concealed by his only surviving portrait painted in profile, was obscured from his courtiers who were strictly forbidden to look their sovereign directly in the eye.

He could play the harp and gittern; he could speak and write in English, French and Latin and he enjoyed reading – he devoured books on hunting. From the first, King Henry exhibited a love of rich clothes – a trait that boded well for Whittington. He wore splendid attire: velvet cloaks, ermine trimmed robes, high-collared gowns or gold-embroidered tunics, their loose sleeves slashed to show gold linings or extended to reveal elaborate embroideries inside impossibly wide cuffs. He wore the Lancastrian collar, several rings and a golden crown.

After dutifully accompanying his father's cortège to Canterbury Cathedral – where his body was entombed next to the Black Prince – King Henry V returned to London where he was 'conducted with a great riding' through the streets. Ominously, it was blowing a blizzard with savage storms beating the surrounding countryside. On Passion Sunday (9 April) Henry was escorted in state through the sleet and snow by his nobles, lords, barons and newly created knights from the Tower of London to Westminster Abbey.[2] There he was dressed in cloth-of-gold and red samite and crowned by Archbishop Arundel.

The young King was then ushered into the Great Hall of the adjacent Palace for his Coronation Feast. He was seated on a marble chair on an exalted dais under a carved gable decorated with a luxurious cloth of estate. He was accompanied on his left hand by his brothers, Princes John and Humphrey. Thomas, who should have officiated as Steward of England, was absent in France. Whittington, who stood in high royal favour, must surely have been present among the distinguished guests to sample the sumptuous menu that included such culinary delights as 'blandesory', composed of hen brawn ground with rice and milk of almonds, and 'flampets', pork fat and figs boiled in small ale with cheese fried in clean grease and baked in a coffin of paste.[3] The conduit in the courtyard flowed red with Gascon and Rhenish wines.

Henry was attended by liveried servants precariously balancing steaming dishes on horseback.[4] The minstrels played; the choir sang. The Earl Marshal, also mounted, juggled his tipstaff while he huffed and puffed, hustled and bustled, among the standing spectators, smoothing the way for replenishing the jugs of wine and plates of delicacies. The royal champion, Dymock, dressed as Saint George, boldly issued the traditional challenge to fight anyone who dared to dispute the King's title. Despite all this frivolity, Henry, it was noted, looked pensive. He speculated that the English seemed far from being united in accepting his sovereignty. Pessimistic citizens predicted a reign, not of peace, but of civil war. Outside, the biting wind continued to blow across the land...

Henry's immediate problem was finance. His father had died seriously in debt so that his executors refused to administer his diminished estate. Strapped for cash, his son devised desperate measures to extract funds from his insecure subjects. Traitors and insurgents were encouraged to purchase immunity from further prosecution. Absent landowners in Ireland and Wales were offered insurance against threatened confiscation of their vacant property. Citizens and clerics were promised favouritism in return for substantial loans. The Treasury coffers began to swell.

Whittington, who was still Mayor of the Staple of Calais, responded amenably to Henry's 'money hungry' appeals. On 7 July 1413, he lent £2,000. This was an exceptional sum equal to the collective amount lent by the citizens of London. Encouragingly, Whittington's entire loan was repaid either by cash or by assignment on 15 November that same year. Indeed, true to his word, most of these enforced loans from wealthy laymen and influential clerics were repaid by Henry in less than three months.[5]

Restoration of Westminster Abbey

Henry V was passionately devoted to the Holy Trinity and he zealously supported the Church. He cherished a genuine affection for the Benedictine Abbey of St Peter at Westminster where he had been crowned King.[6] His purpose may have been to atone for the presumed wild excesses of his youth by venerating the place where his father had expired. Possibly, he wished to ensure divine approval of his intended foreign campaigns, which would bring him fame and glory for posterity. Throughout his reign Henry frequently bestowed favours on Westminster Abbey, he constantly donated treasures – valuable ornaments, devotional books, rich vestments – and he regularly attended services, particularly at Ascension and Whitsuntide. He sent the monks gifts of game after he had been hunting and he returned a priceless ring originally donated to the shrine of its founder, Edward the Confessor, by Richard II.[7]

Yet the Abbey itself, rebuilt by Henry III, a great patron of art and culture, remained 'a stunted fragment of height without length'.[8] The Chapter House, choir, transepts, apse, eastern chapels, north front, rose windows and just four bays of the celebrated lofty nave had been completed more than a century before. Alas, this extensive building programme had been abandoned when King Henry died in 1272, leaving the earlier Norman nave and west front in a dilapidated condition. The three Edwards lacked the money and commitment to bring this noble work to completion and the reconstruction was further delayed because there was an acute shortage of manual labour during the Black Death. Richard II ordered the demolition of offending structures, intending to rebuild them in harmony with the choir and transepts, although he was only able to make a start by the erection of the Purbeck marble pillars and the raising of the exterior walls.[9] During the reign of Henry IV, the 'new work' of the nave proceeded inordinately slowly and upon Henry V's accession it was described as having been 'long in ruins and undone'.[10] At that time the building fund stood at a miserly £3.

Henry V took command of the situation. Immediately, he donated one thousand marks per annum for the restoration of the Abbey.[11] On 24 August 1413, he commissioned, William Waldern, Mayor of London, to engage stone cutters, carpenters, sawyers and labourers to continue the work that had already begun the previous July. The building grant for completing the nave of one thousand marks per annum was payable quarterly. Funds were to be collected in equal amounts directly from the Chancery and also the customs raised from the subsidy on wool, leather and sheepskins in the Port of London. Sadly, the promised amount for this laudable project was not always forthcoming from either the hanaper at the Chancery nor the wool customs and it remained in serious arrears when Henry V died.

Nonetheless, the work was carried out with vigour under the supervision of Edward, Duke of York, and Henry, Bishop of Winchester, who was also Chancellor. Henry directed that all the disbursements were made through Richard Whittington, who was still Collector of Customs in London. Whittington was the obvious choice as accountant and supervisor because he had already made a personal donation to the new building works in the reign of Richard II.[12] He was assisted by a trusted monk, Richard Harowden (or 'Harweden').[13] Later, the Pope appointed Harowden Abbot of Westminster, doubtless through Henry's recommendation after his sterling efforts on the completed nave.

During his absence in France, Henry informed the new Mayor, Thomas Fauconer, that he was forbidden from demolishing any public building in the capital without the express permission of Whittington and three other persons in authority. This instruction followed an outcry over the recent demolition of the walls of the Augustinian Friary in Broad Street. Erroneously – his contribution was purely financial and administrative – Whittington has been hailed as 'the great architect of the age'.[14]

Actual 'werkemanschippe' was entrusted to William Colchester, the master mason who was currently involved in building York Minster. His fee was a respectable £10 per annum. His workmen provided their own tools but required aprons, gloves, clogs, board and lodgings and a warm coat at Christmas, in addition to wages at his expense. Stone was quarried at Reigate, Surrey, Bere, Dorset and Stapleton, Yorkshire, with Caen stone imported for fine detail. One stone-laden ship called a 'shout' crashed through the middle arch of London Bridge with loss of three lives and, by tradition, its wrecked hull was forfeit to the King.[15]

Meanwhile, work proceeded apace and the new section of the nave was carefully copied from the earlier design, yet it is less ornate in detail and its slight deviations may be easily discerned. Henry V continued to contribute to the building fund, although the total amount at his death (£3,860) was about half that promised (£6,330), which would have been one thousand marks for nine and a half years. At his demise, the walls to the extent of six bays had been carried through the triforium and extended towards the clerestory. Sadly, in Henry VI's reign grants ceased and work halted. He was more interested in his building programmes at Eton and King's College, Cambridge.

As a tribute to his industry, a tiny image of Richard Whittington appears at the foot of a stained-glass window in the eighth bay from the west on the north side of the nave of Westminster Abbey. This attractive double light was designed by J. Ninian Comper to commemorate the life of William Thomson, Baron Kelvin of Largs (1824-907). Lord Kelvin was an engineer, inventor and physicist whose numerous projects included a flexible wire conductor and the Atlantic cable. His memorial window was a gift of engineers from Britain and America. In the centre strides the majestic figure of Henry V in full armour, wearing a crown and wielding a sword. A scene above him presents Henry's coronation at the Abbey while opposite, the King appears visiting the resident anchorite to seek guidance on the night after his father's death. Perhaps this was the occasion when he vowed to continue the completion of the nave as a tribute to his late father? Whittington is depicted in mayoral robes, while at his feet strolls a plump ginger tom...

The Threat of Lollardy

Henry V was assessed by those astute historians, Wylie and Waugh, as being 'hard, domineering, over-ambitious, bigoted, sanctimonious, priggish'. He was superstitious and studied astrology and so possessed several astrolabes to chart the position of the planets. Above all, he was a spiritual leader who actively demonstrated his defence of the Church. Piety, it was recognised by his contemporaries, was the most dangerous side of Henry's character. His fanatical protection of the Orthodox Church soon came to the fore in his ruthless persecution of the Lollards.[16]

Lollards followed the teachings of John Wyclif (c.1324-1384) an eminent theologian at the University of Oxford, who was also Rector of Lutterworth in Leicestershire and an advisor to Edward III. Basically, the Lollards emphasised the authority of the scriptures over obedience to the clergy, dispensed with the necessity of priests to perform sacramental rites, advocated apostolic poverty, which would involve taxation of ecclesiastical properties, vehemently denied the doctrine of transubstantiation and abhorred the sale of indulgences, grants of absolution for sins. They resented papal authority, made difficult to follow at the start of Henry's reign by the fact that there were three rival Popes: John XXIII of Pisa, Benedict XIII of Avignon and Gregory XII of Rome. Lollards called for the complete reform of the Church: their powerful Protestantism culminated eventually in the English Reformation.

Privately practised, lollard beliefs were considered harmless but publicly expressed their teachings were denounced as 'heretical'. Indeed, 'Lollard Knights' were a close company of courtiers who were tolerated by Richard II since they made little attempt to broadcast their unorthodox opinions. His only real concern was the possible connection between Lollardy and social unrest. By the time Henry IV seized the throne, however, the law was beginning to take a more serious view of the threat Lollardy posed to society in England. The King sanctioned the first burning of a heretic, William Sawtre, who was packed in a barrel that was then set alight early in his reign (2 March 1401). Adherence to the doctrines of Lollards was perceived to jeopardise the delicate balance between priest and people ... church and state .... Heaven and Earth.

Henry V was pressed by the church authorities to protect the established Medieval order but his difficulty was that supporters of Lollardy occupied the highest positions in his realm. One had been Henry's grandfather, John of Gaunt; another was his brother, Thomas, Duke of Clarence. Yet another was his intimate friend, Sir John Oldcastle, immortalised by Shakespeare as 'Falstaff'.[17]

When evidence of his heretical beliefs was revealed, Sir John Oldcastle of Almeley in Herefordshire, who became Baron Cobham by marriage, was brought from Cooling Castle in Kent for trial in London in 1413. He was treated with surprising lenience and he even managed to escape from his prison in the Tower. Possibly this was through Henry's connivance since Sir John had been his close companion-in-arms when he was still Prince of Wales. For a time he was sheltered by a Lollard sympathiser, William Fisher, a parchment maker, at his home in the City. Oldcastle was, according to Holinshed, 'A valient capteine and a hardie gentleman' who stood 'highley in the King's favour'.[18] On 9 January 1414 Oldcastle organised an insurrection at Fickets Field, a lonely spot on the outskirts of London. The plan was to kidnap the King, subvert his brothers, banish the clergy and plunder holy relics. Further, he made an alliance with the Scots to place an impostor, who claimed to be the resurrected Richard II, on the throne instead of Henry V.

This Lollard rebellion had a direct effect on close members of Whittington's family. His brother, Robert, and his nephew, Guy, were ambushed by Lollards, 'armed and attired for war', while riding home with three pages from Hereford to Solers Hope one late autumn day in 1416. Richard Oldcastle, presumably a relative of Sir John, ordered his thirty armed assailants to seize the defenceless pair, bind them and escort them to Dinmore Hill, a steep, wooded mound seven miles distant, where they were relieved of their horses and valuables.

This audacious assault took place at Mordiford where a nine-arched, buttressed stone flood bridge, adjoined by a skewed causeway, still crosses the River Lugg near its junction with the River Wye.[19] This timeless hamlet, four miles east of Hereford, is dominated by the 12th-century Church of the Holy Rood, built on an eminence, and the pleasingly symmetrical white rendered brick 'Bridge House', overlooking the former ford. There was a curious tradition that the Lord of the Manor was liable to present the King of England with a pair of gilt spurs whenever he should cross Mordiford Bridge. It is possible to imagine that if both ends of the narrow bridge were sealed when Robert and Guy were traversing, they and their companions would become easy prey.

After spending one night in a deserted chapel and a second in an ancient mill, where the pair were tortured, Guy was released under parole to procure a ransom of £600. Presumably, the fabulous wealth of Robert's famous brother Richard influenced their decision to make this preposterous demand. Meanwhile, Robert was taken from wood to wood until he was totally disorientated, although he sensed he was nearing the Welsh border.[20] Eventually, father and son, with their servants, were liberated (even though only half of the demand for their release was secured) after swearing on oath not to pursue their captors.

Robert immediately applied to Parliament to free him from his oath and the resources to track down and punish his abductors.[21] The breaking of an oath, even if extracted under duress, was regarded as a mortal sin. The matter received sympathetic attention, however, and was immediately referred to the King in Council who adjudicated in the plaintiff's favour. This was hardly surprising, really, since Robert's brother, Richard, was at that time serving the City for the first and only time as Member of Parliament.[22] It was the duty of the Sheriff to appoint representatives from the City to serve in Parliament although many citizens, especially merchants, avoided serving because it caused great inconvenience and financial loss. This was a pity because this was a time when Parliament was starting to have a real effect on government.

The conclusion of this exciting escapade remains a mystery. Possibly, Robert and Guy were content with the cancellation of the bonds and the official condemnation of their enemies. Even the motive for the kidnapping is puzzling. It may have been purely a local feud or a publicity stunt for the Lollard cause, since the principal assailants came from neighbouring west country families. Indeed, Richard, one of Guy's younger sons, married a relative of one of the assailants, Isabel, daughter of Philip Lyngen.

Sir John Oldcastle was also hunted down, at one stage betrayed by a spy, his large army routed and the tumult crushed. At that time Henry was campaigning in France after appointing his brother, John, Duke of Bedford, as Regent. Despite the offer of huge rewards, the outlawed knight had managed to evade capture for several years but he was finally apprehended in Wales. Retribution was swift and sure. Oldcastle was apparently executed in a manner cruel and unusual, hanged by the neck by an iron chain until consumed by a raging fire, on Christmas Day 1417. Afterwards, Whittington was appointed one of the commissioners to enquire into the lands held by the traitor held either as Sir John Oldcastle or Lord Cobham.[23] The King, although fighting in France at the time, recognised there was now an obvious threat to national security and he authorised the prosecution of fanatical Lollards nationwide. (He was aware of the horrendous fate that now awaited heretics because he had personally witnessed, along with an 'exalted company', that first public burning of a Lollard, Sawtre.)

The Lollard rebellion in the London suburbs at Epiphany 1414 had caused considerable alarm. At the Leicester Parliament which convened three months after the rebellion, a drastic statute was passed which placed all civil power in the country at the disposal of the Church in regard to the detection of Lollards.[24] Further, every secular official, from the Mayor to the Chancellor, was required to swear an oath upon appointment to his term of office to crush every last hint of heresy in the district where he exercised control. These strong measures were intended to enforce law and order in the realm as heresy was now linked to treason. Knights, squires, priests and scholars were arrested alongside craftsmen – hosiers, glovers, fletchers, curriers, brasiers, daubers, spurriers, pelterers, goldsmiths, drapers, weavers, dyers – for intense examination.

Whittington was also among the commissioners appointed to seek out and try suspected Lollards hiding in the City. Their punishment was horrendous. Convicted heretics were hung in chains above smouldering faggots. The halter for the King; the fire for God. Lollards could be pardoned upon recantation and payment of a hefty fine, although those who relapsed were denied further mercy. Mayor Thomas Falconer had executed John Claydon in 1415, a harmless, educated skinner, who was publicly burned along with his offending books, in the King's absence. At that crucial period heretics were regarded as a threat to the realm, particularly during foreign campaigns, since they would bring down the wrath of God upon Henry's vulnerable kingdom.

Persecution of heretics caused a protest among London's wool traders. John Russell, 'wolpakker', spread false rumours in the City about Thomas Fauconer, citizen and Mercer. Russell claimed that Fouconer, when Mayor, was responsible for ordering the burning of Richard Surmyn ('Turmyn' or 'Gurmyn'), a Baker, along with his letters of pardon at Smithfield. Fauconer was duly fined £1,000 and imprisoned in the Tower of London. The former Mayor sought to defend his good name but Russell absented himself when summoned to Court. He was found guilty of slander in his absence. The traditional punishment for this offence was for the convicted liar to stand in the pillory on three separate market days with a whetstone hung around his neck. Russell sought sanctuary in Westminster Abbey but at the end of nine months he appeared voluntarily to face his inevitable humiliation.[25] Russell continued to cause unrest in the City and was later found guilty of treason and hanged at Tyburn.[26]

Whittington stood surety for one imprisoned Lollard. His name was Beauchamp. Probably he was a gentleman of repute. Interestingly, the Beauchamps were neighbours of the Whittingtons since they hailed from Redmarley and Dymock near Pauntley in Gloucestershire. He may even have been Sir Richard Beauchamp, for whom Whittington acted as mainpernor in the previous reign. Mercifully, he was released from the indignity of being chained in a cramped cell and permitted to occupy more comfortable rooms in the precincts of the Tower. His bail was set at 4,000 marks. And within three months he had recovered his full liberty thanks to Whittington's intervention. This was curious, since

Whittington exhibited no empathy with Lollardy. Throughout his lifetime he revealed himself to be a pious and conventionally religious man, even going to the lengths of purchasing a papal licence to choose his own confessor.[27] In this instance, however, Whittington had acted with compassion and generosity and without fear of recrimination from his sovereign. The threat from Lollardy had, in any case, effectively been eradicated, at least temporarily, by the execution of Oldcastle. Once the hour of danger had passed, the time of clemency was allowed to begin. Lollards were generally absolved of their crimes for 'it was no part of Henry's policy to fret a rankling sore'.[28]

After all, King Henry had, by that time, proved his authority and won divine approval in triumphing at the greatest battle of the Medieval world...

Mobilisation of England

Henry V, already a veteran military leader after defeating the Welsh rebel Owen Glendower while he was Prince of Wales, was determined to unify his country in foreign warfare. And cleverly, by patriotic propaganda, he sought to make his royal campaign a national one. There had been few victories within living memory for his subjects to celebrate against the French. Lands conquered by his great-grandfather, Edward III, had slowly, inexorably been whittled away; and previous reigns had even condemned wars of retaliation as savage, immoral and unjust.[29]

Henry resurrected Edward III's claim to vast territories in Normandy surrendered by him at the Treaty of Bretigny in 1360 and later extended this to the throne of France (which Edward had also renounced). Adamantly, he maintained that it was his by right of succession from his great-great-grandmother, Isabella, daughter of Philippe IV.[30] King Edward had won his great victory over the French at Crecy in 1346 while his son, the Black Prince, also defeated them at Poitiers in 1356. Henry contemplated his royal ancestors' achievements with immense pride and was determined to emulate the warlike spirit of 'The Black Prince'.

France was ruled by a schizophrenic King, Charles VI, whose current heir was the impetuous Dauphin Louis.[31] Vicious infighting among the royal dukes further divided the country, which was ripe for invasion. Henry, undoubtedly the aggressor, veiled his terms for peace in honeyed words. He made preposterous demands – including the hand in marriage of Charles' thirteen-year-old daughter, Catherine of Valois, together with one million crowns as dowry – that were met with predictable scorn.[32] His formal approaches were simply a screen couched in chivalrous terms: 'To the most serene prince Charles, our Cousin and adversary of France...' one letter began. It ended: 'By the bowles of Jesus Christ, friend, render what you owe.' The tale of the demented King's insulting response of sending 'a tonne of tenys ballys' in payment of the royal dowry which Henry threatened to 'bandy with gunstones' is apocryphal.[33]

Henry mobilised the entire nation – statesmen, nobility, civilians, clergy – in preparation for his conquest of Normandy. Artfully, he distracted his opponents from examining his tenuous claim to the throne of England by harnessing his subjects in his extravagant claim to the throne of France. 'Henry's army would be drawn from every quarter of the kingdom,' comments Juliet Barker. 'As a consequence of this unprecedented level of national involvement, the campaign inspired an exceptional degree of pride and enthusiasm across the country, all of which centred on the charismatic figure of the King himself.' Shakespeare, more cynically, presents Henry putting into practice his dying father's wise advice to 'busie giddy minds with foreign quarrels' (*Henry IV Part 2* Act IV Scene V).

King Henry meticulously planned his expedition but realised that it would be folly to proceed unless it was properly funded. The actual cost of the campaign was phenomenal, but the defence of the realm in his absence also threatened to bankrupt him. Parliament was summoned and petitioned for finance. Its representatives voted for double taxation which, frustratingly, would be paid in two halves, before and after the campaign. The Exchequer, though, immediately surrendered £2,274. On 10 March, Henry summoned the Mayor, Thomas Fauconer, Aldermen and certain Commoners to the Tower of London – which fortuitously housed the royal arsenal – to inform them that he intended crossing overseas to recover by conquest his lawful inheritance. On 16 June, the City promised the King a phenomenal loan of 10,000 marks to be secured on the customs on wool of the Port of London to be repaid on New Year's Day 1417. Henry, as security, deposited with the Mayor his own exquisite SS gold collar known as the 'Pusan d'Or'.[34]

Henry made personal and direct appeals to towns and cities across his kingdom and their response was generous and impressive. A further appeal was made to the church leaders since this was to be regarded as a religious crusade in order to resist 'the malice, impudence and harassment of England's enemy'. Religious orders throughout the land surrendered almost £9,000. Abbots, priors and deans of cathedral chapters offered modest contributions while wealthier bishops donated an incredible £44,243. Supposedly, all these enforced loans would be repaid with money derived from customs, taxation and various incomes received by the Crown.

High-ranking commissioners were despatched to make additional borrowings from merchants countrywide. They made it obvious that these loans were not entirely optional. Voluntary donations would, however, ensure the King's favour and future preferment. The King prided himself that all these loans would be repaid promptly, but there could be no consolation of interest on ready cash since usury was strictly forbidden by the Church. (Jews, however, were expressly exempt from this prohibition of money lending which gave them an important role in expanding the economy of Europe.) London was already regarded as an international centre for trade and the City's own merchants were extremely affluent. Merchants were foremost in lending their sovereign funds

Above: 1. A glimpse of the scant remains of Medieval Pauntley Court, Richard Whittington's birthplace, that still manages to dominate the remote, tranquil hamlet, ten miles north-west of Gloucester.

Right: 2. The Whittingtons' substantial dovecote is typical of those that existed in the Cotswolds. Doves and pigeons were an important source of winter meat for influential families who were licensed to keep them, since they were notoriously destructive of crops.

3. Richard Whittington would have been baptised as an infant in the neighbouring church of St John the Evangelist. This sturdy Norman church stands high on a knoll lifting it above the Leadon Valley and blends in magnificently with the rolling countryside.

4. A pair of weathered monuments in the church of St Giles, Coberley, depicting Sir Thomas Berkeley, dressed in the armour he wore at the Battle of Crecy (1346) and his wife, Lady Joan. When widowed in 1350, Lady Joan married Sir William Whittington and became the mother of three sons, the youngest being Dick Whittington.

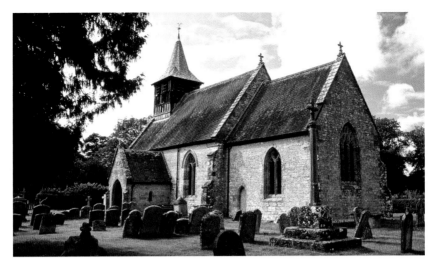

5. Richard's elder brother, Robert, inherited the family manor of Sollers Hope, a remote hamlet nine miles south-east of Hereford. He rebuilt the Saxon church of St Michael, distinguished by its wooden bellcote with its shingled spire topped by a gilded weather vane.

Above left: 6. A series of fifty cast iron milestones with a beribboned string of diminishing bows indicating the distances to the church door of St Mary-le-Bow were placed along the former main road from Eastbourne/Lewes towards the City of London. This one – 40 miles – dates from the mid-18th century and is located at the Lampool Roundabout, Maresfield, East Sussex.

Above right: 7. The magnificent steeple of St Mary-le-Bow church, Cheapside, contains a dozen bells steeped in history. They are arranged in the ringing chamber in a wide circle and graduate from the smallest bell to the heaviest in a clockwise direction where they seem to be paying homage to the Great Bell in the centre. All twelve bells are named and their titles form a delightful anagram: 'D.WHITTINGTON'.

8. Traditionally, the young Dick Whittington runs away from London and falls asleep on Highgate Hill where he is befriended by a stray cat. Today, a stone half way up the hill, once the base of a wayside cross, is surmounted by a granite cat peering through decorative railings. It was commissioned by Donald Bissett, a character actor and children's author, and his circle of friends.

9. Richard Whittington lies buried on the south side of the altar in the church he founded, St Michael Paternoster Royal, which has suffered various disasters over the years. The spectacular east window, created by John Hayward in 1969, features the traditional tale of Whittington and his cat which, alas, was badly damaged during recent riots in the City but repaired.

Above: 10. London's Guildhall was remodelled in Medieval times as part of a campaign of improvements to the City. Whittington's executors contributed greatly towards its modernisation by the addition of glass windows and marble paving. Whittington appears in stained glass there as a tribute to his own important contribution towards its impressive enhancement.

Right: 11. Sir Ivo Fitzwaryn, Whittington's father-in-law, is depicted in a full-length brass on a pillar in the north transept of the Church of Saints Peter and Paul at Wantage, Berkshire. He wears the armour of a military knight, resting his head on a (badly damaged) jousting helm, intended to present him as a defender of the realm. (Photograph: Neil Aston)

Above: 12. The impressive facade of London's Guildhall today presents a conscious assertion of civic pride.

Below left: 13. A Portland stone statue of Richard Whittington by John Carew appears high up on the north wall of the Victorian Royal Exchange at Bank, London. Whittington is presented in proud prosperity wearing his Mayoral chain, his hand resting upon an elaborate mace.

Below right: 14. Richard Whittington funded the start of Henry V's campaign that resulted in his triumph at Agincourt in 1415. The stained glass window of Henry includes the image of Whittington at its base on the north side of the nave in Westminster Abbey, unveiled in 1913. It features his (fictional) cat.

15. The field of Agincourt today in Northern France. English archers held sway and triumphed spectacularly over the numerically superior French forces. Whittington was involved in a heated debate over the exchange of a French prisoner, Hugues (or 'Hugh') Coniers, captured at the decisive battle.

16. The sumptuous grounds of Whittington College, relocated to Felbridge, near East Grinstead, Sussex, in 1965, provide a tranquil haven of peace and beauty for residents, retired professional people from all over the world. The twenty-eight acres of manicured grounds include a raised woodland walk, a rhododendron dell and a lake with waterlilies.

Left: 17. The patchwork lawns and gardens of the modern Whittington College include sundials, fountains and statuary. In one secluded corner of the courtyard stands John Carew's relocated statue of Dick Whittington, a reminder of the generous founder and benefactor.

Below: 18. For Christmas 2012, Fortnum and Mason's, Piccadilly, chose the story of Dick Whittington for their iconic festive windows. The magical displays by Paul Symes include a scene where Dick's ginger tom pursues vermin from the Sultan of Morocco's Palace, the source of his fabled fortune. The window displays were unveiled by the then Lord Mayor, Roger Gifford, attended by the cast of Hackney Empire's 'Dick Whittington'. (Photograph © Fortnum and Mason)

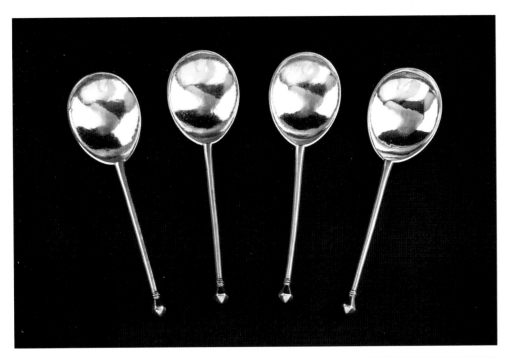

Above: 19. Whittington presented twelve silver spoons with gilt knops – four of which remain with the Mercers' Company – to his College of Priests, portable items of highly redeemable value. They may have been among his personal possessions and reveal that he was an admirer of beautiful things and a connoisseur of fine workmanship.
(© The Mercers' Company)

Right: 20. This illuminated deathbed scene is taken from the 'Ordnances of Whittington's Charity'. Whittington lies emaciated, naked apart from his nightcap in his grand tester bed pointing to his diminishing pulse, while his doctor examines a phial of his urine. He is attended by his executors, John Carpenter, John Coventre, John White and William Grove, and thirteen bedesmen from his future almshouse are headed by their first elected tutor, Robert Chesterfield, who holds a rosary. Below left are Whittington's arms: a chequered horizontal band in gold and blue on a red background with a ring or annulet in the top left corner.
(© The Mercers' Company)

Above left: 21. A Victorian engraving of Mercers' Hall in Cheapside. The Mercers' Company is a trade guild representing the interest of members who export woollen and import silks, velvets and luxury fabrics. Whittington was a prominent member of the early Company when the Mercers held their meetings in a monastery on the site of the birthplace of Thomas Becket. Their first hall, completed in 1524, was built next to the monastery but this was burned in the Great Fire of London. The second hall, built directly on the site of the dissolved monastery, was destroyed by enemy action in 1941. The present hall – the third on the site – was opened in 1958.

Above right: 22. Whittington College and Almshouse on College Hill was founded by his executors in the vicinity of his main residence in the City and the Church he had founded, St Michael Paternoster Royal, the tower of which appears just beyond.

23. The crowded 'Tally-Ho' London to Birmingham stage coach passes the re-sited Whittington College (almshouse and hospital) in Highgate at the foot of Archway Road. (Courtesy of The Tate)

Above: 24. Whittington's executors made a substantial donation to the repair of Rochester Bridge that spans the River Medway in north Kent. This facilitated an important link between London and Sandwich, a premier Cinque Port in Medieval times. Further, the repair of this stone bridge helped pilgrims – on horse or foot – to worship at the shrine of the murdered Thomas Becket at Canterbury Cathedral.

Below left: 25. A rare image of Dick and Alice starring in a First World War pantomime, presumably to entertain British troops at an undisclosed venue. Dick wears a Tommy's khaki service dress tunic and trousers, forage cap, puttees and boots. A Red Cross badge on his sleeve indicates he was a volunteer for the British Red Cross serving as either a stretcher bearer or an orderly in a hospital. Perhaps this was where he met Nurse Alice?

Below right: 26. Miss Ethel Erskine, a beautiful actress noted for her dazzling eyes, appears as a Victorian Alice.

Left: 27. A young, sprightly and enchanting female 'Dick' at the start of the last century.

Below: 28. This rather starchy photograph shows a performance of 'Dick Whittington' in a private house in Victorian times. Young Dick looks strangely garbed in all-weather gear as he cuddles a fairly unconvincing cat. The cook and kitchen maid pose alongside sailor boys –while presumably that is Alice looking on?

Top right: 29. A pottery children's teapot showing young Dick, dressed in Lincoln green, resting during his flight from the Capital City, his spotted haversack at his feet, confronting a beribboned black cat on the lid with the inscription: 'Turn again Whittington, Lord Mayor of London.'

Middle right: 30. The 'Victory' children's jigsaw featuring Dick Whittington dressed in a garish red jerkin, his foot resting upon a square milestone, a spotted blue haversack at his feet, looking wistfully back towards the City of London, a black cat staring hopefully up at his prospective new master.

Below right: 31. A 1950s child's tin money box by Chad Valley revealing young Dick striding purposely through the open countryside where he is joined by a new black and white companion as the pair pass a milestone.

Below: 32. A limited edition Royal Doulton toby jug presenting a triumphant Whittington with feathered cap and chain, a purse of gold coins and city bells, depicted as 'Lord Mayor of London'.

33. This alarming illustration of the young Dick Whittington being scolded by the cook heads the sheet music for piano composed by Charles D'Albert (1809-1886). Charles D'Albert was a German composer and dance instructor who emigrated to England where he spent most of his life composing popular music including 'The Whittington Quadrilles'.

34. An early engraving showing Whittington feeding his startled dressed cat while a bespectacled cook looks on benignly.

35. An authentic representation of a mature, successful Richard Whittington by Renold Elstrack, *c*.1590. The original engraving depicts the prosperous Mercer cum Mayor with his hand placed upon a skull, which was changed to a cat by the 19th-century print seller, Peter Stent, to meet popular demand.

36. A colourful illustration for a Victorian children's story book showing a pensive Dick Whittington having urgently escaped to Highgate Hill, with a distant view of the City he has left far behind.

Above left: 37. An impressive terracotta flatback figure (24 inches high) of a relaxed Whittington wearing a jerkin, cap and belt with a bindle slung over one shoulder, leaning against a milestone, attributed to the London sculptor Charles Bell Birch, 1873.

Above right: 38. A Victorian polychrome Staffordshire figure (17 inches high) depicting a mature Dick Whittington wearing a cloak, tunic and breeches with a purse and bindle, leaning against a milestone, 'IV miles to London'.

Below left: 39. A small mantlepiece figure of a youthful Whittington, with his bindle slung over one shoulder, climbing over a fence and joined by a rather aggressive feline while escaping from the Capital City.

Below right: 40. Madame Tussaud's waxworks hand-painted ceramic figurine of Dick Whittington with his black and white beribboned companion.

for his campaigns since they had accumulated unparalleled wealth. Among their number, John Hende, the richest merchant in London, made the largest single loan and he bankrolled Henry to the tune of £4,666 13s 4d. (This would be worth over four million pounds today.) Whittington, it seems, who had been generous to his sovereign upon his accession, made no further loans at this time, although his recent magnanimity in addition, perhaps, to his age, once more rendered him exempt from military service.

Budgeting for the aggressive expedition was thorough and realistic. The Exchequer scrutinised every single item, from iron horseshoes to arrow feathers,[35] taking into account the massive sums required for weapons, ammunition, transport, wages and provisions. England's craftsmen were 'arrested' (i.e. commissioned) to forge arms and armour for the invasion. Mechanics were ordered to renovate veteran siege engines that worked by torsion, tension and counterpoise and engineers were instructed to overhaul modern cannon. About a dozen were to be brought from the Royal Arsenal in the Tower. For the first time, the itinerant royal arsenal would include 75 gunners supervised by four master gunners, all Dutchmen. Customarily, masters of merchant ships impressed for wartime service were entitled to claim not only for the wages of their crew but also compensation, paid quarterly, for wear and tear of their vessels. Henry was totally involved in these meticulous preparations for the campaign and personally supervised every aspect of the war effort.

England at that time did not possess a standing army, which meant that every soldier had to be recruited individually. The old feudal system whereby a knight swore personal allegiance to his sovereign in return for a parcel of land had long since disappeared, although the King still had a constitutional right to demand military service from his subjects. It had now become the custom for individual magnates to raise companies of archers and men-at-arms under an indenture system for a limited period and a fixed rate of pay. This innovative contractual system involved a scale of wages that varied from the royal dukes at 13s 4d per day to archers, whether mounted or on foot, at 6d. This was a decent wage since they were also entitled to reasonable rations. Further, the King was obliged to pay his troops' transport in both directions, before and after conflict, with allowances for their retinue, horses and baggage.

Henry's army contained 2,000 elite men-at-arms. This term had replaced the obsolete 'knights-in-armour' and referred to every rank from a royal duke to the humblest esquire who fought with either the infantry or cavalry and equipped himself with the required warhorses, armour and weapons – a sword, dagger, lance or mace. Archers amounted to approximately 8,000 and outnumbered the knights by 3 to 1. Even the regular clergy, from precentors to hermits, were recruited from every diocese and armed, according to their status, since this was a Holy War whose purpose was 'the defence of the realm and of our Mother Church of England and the Catholic Faith'. And as a reminder of divine approval for the French campaign, every soldier in the muster was compelled to wear a red St George's cross prominently on his battle tunic.[36] Students at Oxford or Cambridge – even the rowdy ones! – were exempt from conscription.

There were two Admirals at a time in commission: one commanding the fleet of the ports northward and eastward of the Thames (Admiral of the North) and the other the ports northward and westward of the Thames (Admiral of the West). Each had under him a Vice-Admiral. During wartime these fleets were commanded by a High Admiral. His task, in the absence of a Royal Navy, was to commission commercial ships and equip them for warfare. An order was duly issued on 11 April 1415 to impress every ship with a portage of twenty tons and upwards that could be found in any English haven from Bristol round to Newcastle and to have them assembled at London, Sandwich, Winchelsea and Southampton by May.

The Cinque Ports of Kent and Sussex were duty-bound to provide a total of fifty-seven manned warships. According to the 'Black Book of the Admiralty' (1336), a Medieval codification of English maritime laws, the High Admiral, after assembling his feet, was to choose the best ship for the King and the next suitable ship for the steward of his household for the King's hall, wardrobe, larder and kitchen. Good ships were also to be provided for princes who might accompany him. The Admiral was duty-bound to approach the King every evening to take his orders and the royal ship was identified at night by three large lanterns, arranged triangularly. (The Admiral carried two lanterns and the Vice-Admiral one.)[37]

All the ports were sealed for reasons of security, the usual precaution in times of war, and the empty seas around Britain were eerie. Embarkation point for Henry's vast army consisting of 12,000 men and 25,000 horses,[38] all of which had to be winched aboard, was along the coast of Hampshire opposite the Isle of Wight. There, over a period of several months during that scorching summer, men-at-arms had assembled with their attendants, grooms and pages.[39] There were master gunners, gunners and their assistants, plus experts who would operate the cumbersome catapults and siege engines with their strange sounding names – belfries, trebuchets, mangonels and brides. Non-combatants numbered armourers, blacksmiths, carpenters, tentmakers, wheelwrights, fletchers, bowyers, carters, saddlers, tentmakers, masons, butchers, bakers, cooks, surgeons, chaplains[40] and a host of legal experts and clerical staff. (The Royal Household alone numbered about nine hundred.) Additionally, there were minstrels – trumpeters, pipers, fiddlers, drummers – to warn, impress, command and boost morale.

Four great ships, part of the fleet 'in the pool of the Thames', were ordered to be equipped and manned while for miles along the coast every inlet and creek was packed with shipping. A motley assortment of merchant ships – 'coggeships, crayeres, ballingeres, helebotes, busses, farecosts, doggers, lodeships, collets, bargees, picards, spinas, passagers and navis' – commandeered from England and Holland had been assembled. They had been fortified with the addition of forecastles and aftercastles to convert them into floating 'sea castles' to transport the company.[41]

Anchored off Spithead was Henry's flagship, *Trinite Royale* (540 tons) inherited from his father, the largest ship in the Royal Navy. (Henry shared with his father a special affinity with the Holy Trinity and a vessel bearing this name would surely offer him divine protection.) The top castle of the mast sported a burnished copper-gilt crown; on the capstan was a sceptre with a trio of fleur-de-lis and at the deckhead was a carved leopard painted in gold sporting a silver crown. (Her sister ship, *Holy Ghost*, which also required a crew of three hundred sailors, was adorned with the royal insignia of a swan and an antelope.) Flying atop the main masthead, which carried an enormous purple sail, was the ship's banner woven with images of the Holy Trinity and Our Lady plus the arms of England and Saint George. A truly magnificent spectacle.

Countless officials were contracted to attend the King and every part of the Royal Household was represented: the Chamber, the Wardrobe, the Hall, the Kitchen, the Bakehouse, the Poultry, the Pantry, the Larder, the Scullery, the Buttery, the Napiery, the Spicery. Many of these departments required their own ship in the royal fleet. The trumpeters, pipers and fiddlers were also required for religious services. There were three heralds, Leicester, Guienne and Ireland, whose main duties were the conveying of formal messages and challenges. They also supervised rules of precedence and etiquette during truces and after surrender since this campaign would be strictly governed by the laws of chivalry.

Before Henry left London he ordered unspecified wares – probably luxurious fabrics for clothes or drapes in anticipation of victory celebrations on his French campaign – which Whittington, as Mayor of the Staple, delivered to John Spencer, Keeper of the Great Wardrobe. His charge came to a grand total of £667 11s. Henry directed this to be paid by midsummer.[42] Shortly afterwards, Whittington made a complaint which the King personally resolved. As mentioned earlier, in that year Whittington had suffered a disaster in business. One of his ships, laden with wool (packed in 31 sarplers plus 1 pocket) and bound for Calais, was shipwrecked almost immediately it left Chichester Harbour. The cog was cast ashore in a sudden storm and the bales were scattered along the coast near Shoreham in Sussex. The crew managed to salvage the bales and load them onto another ship, which sailed without further incident across the English Channel. Overzealous customs officers John Bartelot and John Bradbrugge billed Whittington a second time for export duty and he was naturally annoyed. He and his partner, John Alleyn, petitioned the King. Fortunately, Henry, grateful for the loyal support Whittington continually gave to the Lancastrian royal family, waived the further fee on the same cargo, declaring that it was unlawful.[43]

Disaster also struck Henry's own expedition almost on the point of departure. A tangled plot was discovered involving a trio of conspirators: the Earl of Cambridge, Sir Thomas Gray and the highly trusted Henry, Lord Scrope of

Masham. These traitors, who were also suspected of being Lollards, planned with the connivance of the French to assassinate the King and replace him with Edmund Mortimer, Earl of March. Ironically, this malleable, young nobleman, who escaped punishment, could demonstrate a far stronger claim than Henry to the crown. He was the great-great-grandson of Edward III through Lionel, his second surviving son, whereas Henry was descended from his third son, John of Gaunt. Executions followed.[44]

These same traitors had caused an earlier, minor affray when Henry, attempting to pacify the North of England during his absence, had negotiated an exchange of prisoners. Hotspur's son, Henry Percy, still held captive in Scotland, was to be released in exchange for the Duke of Albany's son, Murdach, imprisoned in the Tower. This amenable scheme disintegrated when Murdach, while being escorted to the midway point at Newcastle, was kidnapped by the conspirators. Sir Thomas Gray approached the Earl of Cambridge at Conisborough Castle, near Doncaster, with an impractical scheme whereby Percy should be exchanged for either the luckless Murdach or a prominent loyalist. Heading his list was Richard Whittington! The conspirator's misconceived aim was then to make their own exchange – Murdach, or Whittington, or at least somebody, for Percy – and head a rebellion against King Henry. This convoluted plot disintegrated when Murdach was captured once more for the King.[45]

Summer was slipping away...

11

Henry V's French Campaign

The English Armada

On the mid-afternoon of Sunday 11 August – drums beating and trumpets braying – the charismatic figure of Henry V boarded the *Trinite Royale* where he was greeted by her master, Stephen Thomas. After appointing his brother, John Duke of Bedford as Regent, Henry ordered his flagship to weigh anchor and head south. The High Admiral, Thomas Beaufort, Earl of Dorset, escorted the fleet in the van on its clandestine mission. It was a hot day of bright sunshine with a gentle sea breeze that lifted the square banners and forked pennants of Henry's vast armada as it slipped from the shelter of Southampton water into the Solent and sailed 'cheerily to sea' across the English Channel. It was by far the largest fleet ever to have left England.

Henry could not conceal the scale of his preparations but he was determined to keep secret its intended destination in order to steal a military march on the French. Once afloat, he revealed his plan to sail round the north coast of France to first recover his own Duchy 'which is his fully by right since the time of William I, the Conqueror, though now, as of long time past, it has been withheld from him against God and all justice by the violence of the French'.

A two-day voyage took the English invaders along the northern shore of Normandy to the royal town and port of Harfleur. Eventually, they reached a secluded bay cut into the westernmost tip of the great chalk headland lying at the mouth of the River Seine. Above them, across the desolate salt marshes, loomed the high, castellated walls of the greatest fortified town on the banks of the Seine Estuary. And from their rolling ships in the Bay of Biscay it must have appeared even to Henry's experienced sailors and trained soldiers totally impenetrable.

Harfleur was considered one of the most significant ports in France.[46] The prosperity of this ancient abbey town, whose population was about five thousand, arose from a variety of industries including weaving, dyeing, fishing and smuggling. A thriving route had long been established there between the two countries and masters of merchant ships, commandeered as transports, were familiar with the coastline. They would have been able to provide Henry with details of the harbour and its defences. English merchants – such as Whittington – were protecting their own interests by financially supporting Henry's invasion because Harfleur had recently become the base for hostile ships attacking commercial vessels on the southern coast of England.

Henry had purposely selected Harfleur as his point of attack since the town controlled the access to France's most important waterway, the River Seine. Forty miles upriver lay Rouen, where a royal naval boatyard had been established a century before. Eighty miles beyond lay Paris, capital city, royal residence and administrative centre of France. If the English captured Harfleur, they could then gain a stranglehold on military and commercial traffic employing this tidal river to enter the English Channel. Further, the French had deployed troops from Harfleur to support rebels in Scotland and Wales who were constantly harassing the English armies. His invasion, therefore, would serve a dual purpose: to improve the safety of English shpping and establish another military base, like Calais, for any future campaigns in France. Harfleur was, in short, 'The key to the sea of all Normandy'.

Siege of Harfleur

Harfleur's strategic importance had ensured that it had recently been provided with the best protection that Medieval military thinking could devise. Immense stone walls – two and a half miles in circumference – encircled the whole town and its harbour. These walls, thicker at the base than at the top, sloped outwards in order to deflect missiles from catapults and cannon. Punctuating the walls at every angle was a sequence of twenty-four semi-circular watchtowers that served as vantage points and from which flanking fire could be reigned down upon an approaching enemy. There were only three gates guarding the entrances to the town – from Montvilliers to the north, Rouen to the south-east and Leure to the south-west – and these were protected by drawbridges over a deep moat.

All the natural advantages of the site had been fully exploited. The town lay about a mile from the River Seine at the head of the tributary valley of the River Lezarde. The southern approach was protected by the ebb and flow of the tides over treacherous salt marshes. And its great moat encircled more than half the town, from the north-east to the south-west, that defended it against attack from the upper reaches of the river valley. The harbour was even more strongly defended. It had been created by constructing a massive wall around a loop of the river to the south of the town. This was then flooded to form a grand harbour that was both a commercial port and a military arsenal. Protected to the north by the town walls and flanked by its own taller walls surmounted by massive turrets, its seaward approach was guarded by twin towers with chains strung between them to prevent enemy access.

Henry's trained troops stormed the slopes and began to entrench. They closed all the approaches, burned the suburbs and demolished surrounding buildings to make way for an encampment. Pavilioneers erected hundreds of tents – Henry's was surmounted by a gilt crown – to establish a temporary city on the steep hillside. All around was commotion. Heralds, minstrels, chaplains, choristers, carpenters, painters, surgeons, pages, grooms, cooks, butlers, bakers, clerks, watchmen, officials of the wardrobe and counting house moved purposely between the brightly emblazoned marquees. Engineers tinkered with war machines, gunners checked their cannon, soldiers were instructed, drilled and marched. The King encamped on the hillside to the north, the Earl of Suffolk to the west, the Duke of Clarence to the east. To the south, at the mouth of the Seine, the English fleet blockaded the harbour. Harfleur was crushed by a combined landward and seaward blockade.

The French town's fighting force was comparatively small but its defences, already strong by nature, had been rigorously overhauled. And although the inhabitants had missed their chance of opposing the landing, they had not been inactive in preparing their protection. Harfleur's defenders had, therefore, complete confidence that they could resist the invaders until they were relieved by their fellow countrymen. And at the start of hostilities it appeared that their hope might be realised. They felt perfectly justified in refusing Henry's offer of a peaceful surrender. Thus, on 17 August, there commenced a vigorous siege.

Henry personally supervised the assault by 'great engines' and 'cunning instruments' on Harfleur. English gunners trained their cannon upon the gates and towers and working in shifts maintained a devastating bombardment by day and night, aided by an obliging full moon, while Welsh miners, operating under protective cover, meticulously undermined the foundations of the defensive walls. Antiquated war engines – arblasts, bricoles, catapults, mangonels, springalds, robinets and trepgets –were almost as effective in hurling missiles over the walls, wreaking havoc on their intended targets. (Such strange names were given to identify the different types of catapults, which were fitted with a variety of mechanisms for 'tension, torsion and counterpoise' to increase the force of the projectile.)

Generally, catapults had a wider range than most guns, were more reliable, far more manoeuvrable and almost as destructive as the newly invented cannon.[47] A great stack of gunstones needed to be transported to the war zone and when the entire stock had been exhausted millstones needed to be broken up for supply. All these war machines, ancient and modern, relentlessly pounded the masonry of the walls, towers and gates of the hapless town. The earthworks in the bulwarks began to crumble so that huge hunks of stone were knocked out and crashed down into the streets with a 'frightful noise'.

Trapped inside their walled enclosure the courageous inhabitants responded with equal ferocity. They shot flaming arrows, firebrands and incendiaries from the battlements, poured boiling water, oil and fat over the ramparts and sprinkled powdered chalk, sulphur and quicklime from the walls that the wind blew into the invaders' faces, blinding them.

Nevertheless, deprived of sleep and supplies, finding their battlements breached and lacking the expected reinforcements, the townsfolk faced the inevitable. They had constantly appealed to their unstable King and his son, the Dauphin, for military assistance without success. After enduring a final vigorous assault from English 'gounnys, trepgettis and engeneys' on the morning of 18 September, they capitulated to the superior invading force.[48]

At midday on 22 September, Henry was ensconced on his portable throne draped with cloth-of-gold – presumably commissioned from Whittington – inside the royal pavilion attended by his remaining healthy knights and nobles, who posed like myriad stars around the sun. Sir Gilbert Umfraville held aloft the King's tilting helm on a pole while all around the hillside fluttered standards of St George. The dignitaries were led out from their besieged town in humble submission, wearing shirts of penitence with ropes fastened about their necks in imitation of the burgers of Calais who had knelt for mercy before Henry's great-grandfather, Edward III. The King deigned to receive the keys of the town from a veteran knight, Raoul Sire de Gaucourt, who had defied him by leading the armed resistance. Perhaps feeling sympathetic towards their predicament, caused by the procrastination of their own countrymen, Henry felt inclined towards clemency and he settled for this ritual humiliation as punishment. The next day, he made a solemn entry through the main gate where he walked barefoot along the battered streets to the Church of St Martin, where the steeple had toppled and the bells had crashed to the ground, to offer devout thanks for his victory.

The English army had suffered heavy casualties. Desperately short of supplies, although a regular shipment of fresh fish, beef, wheat, wine and ale had arrived, Henry's troops had been tempted to devour the tainted shellfish and drink the infected water from the polluted creeks.[49] Consequently, they succumbed to dysentery, the 'bloody flux', rife during that uncommonly hot summer. It is estimated that more than 2,000 soldiers died on those melancholy flats while perhaps 5,000 men were sent home invalided.[50] The numbers are disputed. Among the noblemen who returned through ill health were Thomas, Duke of Clarence, Edmund Mortimer, Earl of March, and John Mowbray, Earl Marshal of England.[51] Most of the redundant cannon and siege engines were shipped home with them. Henry was disgusted to learn that a large number from his ranks had deserted. He had, in any case, brought over far too large an army necessary for a successful siege. His purpose was foremost to prove the will of God – and risk his own life – in a pitched battle with the French.

Heartlessly, Henry ordered the deportation of all the impoverished inhabitants of Harfleur before he ensured the town was made defensible. Henry's purpose was to populate his town with English citizens who would be encouraged to emigrate after builders and tilers had repaired the blitzed buildings. All the town's records were publicly burned in the marketplace to obliterate claims of previous ownership of property. The conquered port, twinned with Calais, would allow him to command the entrance and control the traffic of the River Seine. Defeated noblemen, however, were pledged to meet him at Calais to organise their ransoms. Leaving his uncle, Thomas Beaufort, Earl of Dorset, in supreme command as Captain of Harfleur, with 300 men-at-arms and 900 archers to garrison the town, Henry resolutely left to march his depleted army through Upper Normandy. His strategy was to remove his army swiftly, drawing the French royal forces away from vulnerable, embattled Harfleur.

Throughout the siege, Henry had constantly attempted to secure additional loans to pay and provision his fighting force. Whittington had no hesitation in lending his sovereign funds at this crucial period of the Hundred Years' War. Henry's official letter openly acknowledged Whittington's generosity and ensured he would receive due recompense, albeit by assignment:

The King sends greetings to all who shall receive this letter. Know ye that our beloved Richard Whityngton, Citizen of London, has lent us 700 marks for and concerning the Siege of the town of Harfleur, and God willing, for the maintenance of the same, they will be transmitted for that purpose.

We wish for a prompt and secure payment of the said 700 marks to the said Richard from us to be effected.

We have granted to the said Richard that he himself may have and recover the said 700 marks from the first of our monies raised from the customs of our wool trade in the port of the City of London and in the ports of the towns of St Botolph and Kingston-upon-Hull therefrom emanating, viz

In the said port of London	200
In the said port of Botolph	200
In the said port of Kingston-upon-Hull	200

To be collected at the hands of the collectors of the said customs according to the form and effect of certain taxes and levied in this regard for the aforesaid Richard.

Witnessed: John, Duke of Bedford, Comptroller of England, at Westminster 2 September 1415.[52]

The very fact that Henry instructed his clerks to pay Whittington promptly from the tallies on wool subsidy in the three ports proves that he remained in high regard, since the King was beginning to feel the pinch with the war effort and was now forced to shuffle money around.

Today, there is little left to indicate that Harfleur was once the most important port of Northern Europe. It has been almost completely overshadowed by nearby Le Havre, founded by Francis I in 1517 after the harbour became inaccessible. The modern elevated town is besieged by cranes and derricks from the commercial docks plus chimneys and cylinders from the ubiquitous oil refineries. Nevertheless, there are vestiges of rebuilt half-timbered dwellings that line the redirected route of the winding River Lezarde and pockets of crumbling fortifications from the Medieval walled city. Rouen Gate alone remains with its conical tower and arched footbridge over the former moat. These ruins are now the object of intensive archaeological excavations.

The crowning glory is the battle-scarred Church of St Martin where Henry worshipped after his totemic victory. The soaring spire, surrounded by buttresses and pinnacles, dominates the heart of the modern town. Its square interior with its massive columns, vaulted ceiling and side chapels is cold, grey and forbidding. St Martin's bells still toll belligerently to summon indolent worshippers to their devotions.

March Towards Calais

After his success at Harfleur, Henry had planned to march upon Paris but with a depleted army that objective was clearly not practical. Instead, he decided upon a 'chevauchee', leading his diminished resources – estimated at 900 men-at-arms and 5,000 archers – across the twice-won Duchy of Normandy. Early in October, he set out resolutely with his three battalions along the meandering coastal road. Most baggage wagons had been abandoned but the royal coffers were transported with prized paraphernalia including the chancery seals, a crown, a sword of state, a gold cross beset with gems and a portion of the True Cross.[53] Henry's revised destination was the English port of Calais.[54]

It was late in the season and the march was calculated to be an eight-day trek. (This was based on the assumption that an army would travel at the rate of nineteen miles per day, which was the accepted standard for travelling overland.) His maimed, battered, starving and demoralised army, trudging through northern France, was compelled to make a major detour to cross the River Somme. They were formed once more into three battles as they had upon landing, with Henry himself leading the main one at the centre. Although the sight of the long straggling lines of troops were sure to strike terror into the hearts of the population, Henry was not intent upon destruction. Nonetheless, the country peasants retreated behind their fortifications as the English marched relentlessly past, northwards, 'by townes grete, and castell hyghe'.[55]

The fall, rather than the defence, of Harfleur mobilised the military leaders of France. King Charles VI and his lazy but loyal young son, the Dauphin, as Captain General of the Fighting Forces, finally assembled at Rouen with a tremendous army but they were dissuaded from aggressive confrontation by the Duke de Berry. Subsequently, Constable Charles d'Albret and Marshal Boucicaut assumed responsibility for the defence of their country although initially they, too, advised appeasement. They were not, in any case, authorised to command the powerful dukes and princes. Younger noblemen, burning to avenge the disgrace of the recent siege, were intent on confrontation but because of their arrogance and presumption they exhibited weak and confusing leadership. Burgundians, Armagnacs, Bretons, Gascons and Poitevins continued bickering right up until the moment of battle. And this discord was reflected in the appalling weather. Storms produced widespread flooding and eventually famine.

As the bedraggled English army made their way across Normandy and entered Picardy, the superior French army shadowed Henry's movements. The French were assembling one of the largest armies of the war composed primarily of knights drawn from the nobility.

Henry, by contrast, had formed his army from all classes of society that he had united in a common cause: the defence of England's honour. Chroniclers, swayed by national pride, estimated that the English faced an opposing army of between 25,000 to 30,000 men. Modern historians Professor Anne Curry and Ian Mortimer adjust these figures significantly and insist that the two opposing armies were far more closely matched than previously credited. The most extreme modern estimate is 15,000 Frenchman against 8,000+ Englishmen, which allows an imbalance of 2:1.[56]

The leaders, realising that Henry was 'determined, resourceful and ruthless', resolved to halt his progress on their soil. They purposely selected the ideal 'champ de bataille' in the newly ploughed open fields between Agincourt and Tramecourt. This wide expanse, they believed, would provide the perfect stage for a fair and honourable fight to be fought free from snares and ambushes. And this strong defensive position was further strengthened by dense woods on either side that would protect their flanks. Fatally, their chosen battlefield funnelled towards the south where it was hemmed in by trees: this particular location inevitably denied the French freedom of movement, essential to the deployment of so large a number of attacking infantry and cavalry.

Henry drew up his own modest army in a field of fresh wheat between the southern sides of the woods, about one mile distant from the enemy, in the direction of Maisoncelle. Dispirited, they prepared to face the inevitable violent assault. The opposing armies were in such close proximity that the English could hear the muffled voices of the French as they constructed their own camps on that moonless night. Henry ordered strict silence to be observed and bonfires extinguished. The French, by contrast, lit watch fires, suspecting that they might catch a glimpse of the invaders as they decamped in panic. It was rumoured they were casting lots for the English lords they would take prisoner on the morrow. Torrential rain, numbing cold, unnatural stillness, fervent prayers and final preparations. Henry, displaying his remarkable mixture of regality and humility, moved among his drenched troops, watching, calculating, surveying, encouraging. Famously, English soldiers, in this manner, experienced his unique personal involvement in their crusade. 'A little touch of Harry in the night.'[57]

Surprisingly, the location of the decisive battle fought by the two most powerful military nations in Europe appears little changed. Three picturesque villages: Tramecourt, hidden among mature trees, lies to the north-east, Agincourt,[58] marked by the steeple of St Nicholas' Church, to the north-west and Maisoncelles, where Henry's troops encamped among orchards, fields and barns, to the south. They form a triangle among remnants of woods. The historic battlefield stretches as an exposed rectangle between all three communities. Through the centre of the gently tilting wheatfields – from south to north – runs a minor road, used mainly by local farm tractors and hay wagons, which leads eventually to Calais. At the south-east corner, a monolith indicates the starting position of the advancing English army, while northwards a calvary concealed in a woodland glade marks one French ossuary. Only the whirling blades of ubiquitous wind turbines rotating above the treetops return the observer to the present...

Battle of Agincourt

At daybreak, as a watery sun rose over the pale autumn sky, the two armies prepared to fight. It was Friday 25 October, the Feast of the Gallic Saints Crispin and Crispinian, a favourable omen for the French. The confident nobles, clad in burnished armour, their surcoats bearing a distinctive white cross, were still jostling for a prime position in the coveted vanguard, certain of the victory, they believed, that would bring them glory. Eventually, they formed the traditional three battle lines, long and deep, consisting of a front row of dismounted men-at-arms with swords and lances, commanded by d'Albret, a second straggling row of unmounted crossbowmen and a rearguard of cavalry who also occupied the wings, along with catapults and cannon.[59]

The dispirited English army, hopelessly outnumbered, did not expect to attack but prepared only to defend their honour. Henry, after attending morning mass, rode on a small white horse among his men, preparing them for battle. Slowly, purposely, they began to form an elongated, shallow line. Henry placed his men-at-arms, who were all dismounted, in the middle and at the two far sides where they would be commanded by either Edward, Duke of York,[60] or Thomas, Lord Camoys.[61] There were, in fact, a dozen aristocrats who fielded companies in the battle. The King's youngest brother, Humphrey, Duke of Gloucester, who generally showed little aptitude for leadership and was more at home in his library, proved he was far from lacking in courage. He commanded the second largest company that comprised 200 men-at-arms plus 600 archers. Among his men-at-arms was Whittington's nephew, Guy, who must also by inference have previously taken part in the Siege of Harfleur, which his uncle had part-funded. Guy brought his own small contingent of archers who are named on the muster roll as John Kynge, John Payne and William Kyngston.[62] (Carelessly, Guy's own name was incorrectly entered as 'Ivo' on the muster roll, but later crossed out.)

Archers formed triangular banks which separated these three divisions or 'battles') although the great majority of them were positioned on the flanks where their formation curved inwards in order to subject the enemy to deadly crossfire. They stood behind sharp stakes sunk into the rain-soaked soil to impale charging horses. Henry donned his dazzling armour and splendid surcoat which displayed the arms of England and France. After receiving the sacrament, he put on his bascinet encircled with a gold crown studded with jewels. His spectacular presence was sure to draw the wrath of the enemy whose prime object was to capture or kill him. He then took command of the central position where he intended to fight alongside his soldiers on foot.

The English archers, whose fearsome reputation had been firmly established at Crecy (1346) and Poitiers (1356), were now refined to form a highly manoeuvrable and devastatingly destructive force. They were marshalled by the aged yet experienced Sir Thomas Erpingham who demonstrated his expert organisational skills in this projectile warfare.[63] Cheshire yeomen, who had learned their skills from the hillmen of Wales during the reign of Edward I, had gained the awesome reputation of being the finest English longbowmen. This deadly weapon seemed perfectly designed for the Anglo-Saxon Englishman's physique, and their extraordinary skill with the longbow, which they preferred to the Continental crossbow, was unassailable. Although technologically advanced, crossbows proved inordinately slow to operate under duress, although Henry, an excellent shot, employed one for hunting.

Acts were passed – Edward III's Acts of 1363 and 1365 were ratified by Richard II in 1388 and reinforced by Henry V in 1410 – to prohibit alternative sports and 'idle games' on High Days and Holy Days in England. Men and boys between 16 and 60, irrespective of rank, were compelled to practise at the butts after attending divine service. (Churchyard yews, however, were sacrosanct and, therefore did not, contrary to popular belief, provide bows for battle.) Butts were laid out on the outskirts of towns and cities and in inclement weather even the long naves were sometimes employed for archery practice in cathedrals. Trained from boyhood by constant practice at the bowmarks that were fixed near every parish church these skilled longbowmen could hit the prick – or 'oyster shell' – in the centre of the butt. For nimbleness in the field they stood unrivalled in the western world. Further legislation in the 1360s made it illegal to export homemade bows and arrows, which guaranteed a plentiful supply even in peacetime. (Though yew would over time have to be imported.) Prized bows were even bequeathed in wills. In this manner, English archers developed their formidable skill, firing with lightning speed and deadly aim, so that their native longbow evolved into the principal weapon of the English army. At that time, it was quite simply the most formidable weapon in the world.

Archery required the skills of two separate craftsmen who eventually formed themselves into two separate Guilds: the Fletchers and the Bowyers.[64] Longbows were five or six feet long and fashioned from yew, although Bowyers sometimes made them of wild elm, ash, or wych-hazel. Their staves were coated with oil or wax to keep them supple and protect them from warping through rain. Bowstrings made of horsehair were drawn back to the ear – the string of the shortbow was drawn back to the chest – and a skilled archer could shoot accurately at distances of up to 300 yards. Veteran longbowmen shot, on average, twenty arrows per minute. The Fletchers supplied two types of arrows employed for military purposes: the first, for long range, was a yard long, made of light wood such as poplar and having a barbed iron tip that lodged in the victim's flesh and was therefore effective against unarmoured horses and riders. But a second arrow had been developed to penetrate plate armour. This had a shorter, heavier shaft, usually made from ash, and a hardened, sharpened, steel point called a 'bodkin'. Flights were formed variously of goose, duck or peacock feathers and even parchment, tightly bound with silk thread. At close ranges these fearsome arrows could pierce through a steel helmet. Three million arrows were ordered to keep up the relentless volleys in France.[65] Henry had learned from the fact that Hotpsur had lost the Battle of Shrewsbury partially from his lack of arrows.

At Agincourt, archers fought on foot. They wore the minimum of protective clothing, a padded deerskin hauberk (or jacket) belted at the waist to hold a sheaf of at least a dozen arrows, often in a quiver, plus a stout wooden club for close fighting. They might fight naked and barefoot. Most, though, wore a conical cap formed of wicker, covered with leather and strengthened at the crown with strips of iron. Barker comments perceptively: 'The archers invariably outnumbered the men-at-arms by three to one, a proportion that was unusually high, unique to England and would decide the day at Agincourt.'[66]

Henry took the initiative. Against all the rules of engagement for an outnumbered army, he gave his soldiers the astonishing order to advance. They pulled up their defensive stakes and moved forward. The territory gained was crucial. Boldly, the archers took up a position two hundred yards further on from their original position and drove their sharpened stakes back into the sodden earth. Henry's ploy was to tempt the stationary French to attack since they were now well within the range of his archers. He knew that longbowmen would be most successful if they could force the enemy to engage them while they were in a static position. This allowed his archers to cut down the mounted knights as they charged towards them. Inevitably, the first fallen ranks would slow up those racing behind while the archers mercilessly cut them down...

Meanwhile, the French unfurled their sacred war banner, the oriflamme, that signalled no prisoners would be taken in this battle.[67]

Around noon, Erpingham barked orders to his thousands of disciplined longbowmen: 'Stretch!' A lethal hail of arrows was let loose into the air, 'so dense, so fast and so furious' that the autumn sky darkened. This provoked the French cavalry on the wings into making a thunderous charge down the saturated field in an attempt to demolish the archers but, blinded by the barrage, the horsemen veered, collided and careered into the stakes where their mounts were either impaled or took flight. The front row of French men-at-arms, preparing to attack with their lances, were forced to disperse as maddened steeds stampeded. Their riders, out of control, turned and trampled their own confused ranks.

The reserve lines of crossbowmen were caught off guard so that their response was hurried and, consequently, their aim wide of the mark. The Frenchmen, fast losing confidence when they witnessed the carnage, were reluctant to reform as the English archers launched a second attack. 'Right as a line they volleyed furiously into the advancing mass,' records Wylie, 'and smote the French through camail and visor forcing them to plunge their heads as they pounded forward in their heavy armour ankle-deep in mire.'

After this initial drive – brilliant and bold – the heavier numbers of the French told and the English momentarily recoiled. The elite French knights, the human tanks of the day, rushed with the full force that their armour allowed in order to knock the English off balance. Again, the archers let fly a volley and when all their arrows were spent they made a frenzied attack on the dismounted men-at-arms with 'snatched swords, hangers, mauls and hatchets'. They assaulted the French with improvised weapons, war hammers, spiked maces, bill hooks and poleaxes normally reserved for killing cattle.

Heartened by their courageous stance, the English men-at-arms pressed this advantage home and attacked the French front line, pushing them back against their own advancing columns. The solid mass of the French formation proved disastrous, for the men-at-arms were crushed in the narrow confines of the battlefield by their own comrades who were struggling to stand upright in the waterlogged ground already churned up by countless warriors and warhorses. The French knights were so tightly congested that they could not raise their arms to wield their weapons and they were slaughtered as they struggled to keep their balance in the suffocating mud. Some drowned in the bloody quagmire.

King Henry, protected by a ring of bodyguards, fought bravely as a path was cleared for him to challenge highborn noblemen. An elite company of French knights had formed themselves into an assassination squad vowed to eliminate the English king. All eighteen were killed in their attempt, although one knight engaged Henry in such close quarters that he struck a mighty blow to his bascinet and snapped off one of the fleurons of his crown.[68] (Both Henry's decoys, identically disguised, were reportedly killed.) English victory seemed certain when after midday there were few Frenchmen left standing in the blood-stained wheatfield. His men-at-arms were distracted from fighting and became absorbed in the more profitable activity of taking prisoners for ransom.

Then came news that the impetuous young Anthony, Duke of Brabant, who had arrived late on the scene, was assembling reinforcements to organise a fresh attack. Henry, ruthlessly, ordered the immediate and indiscriminate slaughter of all prisoners, irrespective of rank, since he feared they might gain their freedom and renew their attack.[69] Thus, the 'cream of French chivalry' was dispatched. The Frenchmen's renewed offensive proved futile and the remaining cavalry wandered ingloriously away. Walls of corpses mounted high and after three hours of bitter conflict, the confused foe, rendered powerless, conceded defeat. The number of Frenchmen killed according to modern estimates was between 7,000 and 10,000[70] compared to fewer than 500 Englishmen. (The leading nobleman to have lost his life was Michael de la Pole, Duke of Suffolk, who had commanded at the Siege of Harfleur.) The French commander d'Albret was slain but Boucicaut survived and was among the noble prisoners who were compelled to serve Henry at his celebratory supper on bended knee at the end of that short, decisive day. Apparently, Henry, after inquiring as to the name of the distant fortress, whose turrets were barely visible through the rain, himself called the blistering battle 'Agincourt'.[71]

This dazzling English victory had been won by Henry's inspirational leadership and his army's professionalism. His tactics contrasted markedly with the lack of leadership, organisation and resolution exhibited by his opponents. The French herald, Montjoie, nimbly picking his way through the carnage, declared that Henry had fought according to the strict rules of chivalry and that he had expressed his moral right to the French throne. Scrupulously, Henry assigned his conquest to God. This was not to be interpreted as a public demonstration of royal humility but an acknowledgement of divine approval of his double inheritance. Even if Henry's claim to the French throne could not be justified in law, he had demonstrated divine approval through his triumphant achievement which, according to Mortimer, was actually born out of 'fear, luck and pride'.[72] Despite being the son of a despised usurper, he could now return to England having proved to the world that God was visibly on his side.[73]

Reaction in London

Rumours, in the absence of specific information, ran riot across London. The authorities had not heard anything positive of the English army since the capture of Harfleur and there were fears of a massive defeat, spreading panic through the City. But in the midst of the citizens' deepest despair, official notification was received of Henry's triumph at Agincourt.

On the Feast of St Edward the Confessor (13 October) the Mayor and Commonalty of the City had assembled at Guildhall Chapel to hear Mass, accompanied with solemn music, in preparation for the election of their new Mayor. Thomas Falconer, the retiring Mayor, accompanied by the Aldermen, the Recorder, two Sheriffs and 'an immense number of the commonalty', then retired to Guildhall where they turned their attention to the choice of a suitable successor. In their wisdom, they chose Nicholas Wotton, a member of the Drapers' Company, known to his opponents as 'Wytteles (Witless) Nick'. On the feast of Saints Simon and Jude (28 October) Mayor Wotton took his oath of allegiance at Guildhall and prepared to repeat his vows on the following day before the Barons of the Exchequer at Westminster. Celebrations were naturally muted and tempered by the uncertainty of the fate of the English expeditionary force...

Then, early next morning, while most were still abed, a messenger arrived posthaste with sealed letters for the new Mayor. They contained intelligence that King Henry and his army had reached Calais. Bishop Beaufort of Winchester, the Lord High Chancellor, read out the thrilling news to the citizens from the steps of St Paul's. Immediately, London's deep depression turned to exhilaration. Men flocked to their own parish church to offer thanksgiving while bells swung jubilantly from every steeple. The procession to Westminster was hastily rearranged so that now it would be taken on foot in humble gratitude to God for the English victory.

Thus, Mayor Wotton headed a grand procession of Aldermen, Sheriffs, citizens, craftsmen and clergy through the swiftly decorated streets to Westminster Abbey. There, the Mayor made his traditional offering at the Shrine of St Edward the Confessor. Whittington[74] walked barefoot among the throng. After High Mass, which gave due acknowledgement to God for this great victory, the incoming Mayor was presented, admitted and sworn before the Barons. The ceremony took place in the presence of Queen Joan, Henry's stepmother, and an immense throng of clergy, lords and peers of the realm. After kneeling before the Confessor's shrine, the pilgrims made their return journey into the City for a Te Deum at St Paul's. This time, though, everyone decided to return in comfort and style, 'riding merrily as they were wont to do before'.

Meanwhile, Henry's exhausted army resumed its slow journey and from Calais, in dribs and drabs, the fatigued soldiers made their own way home in a 'prosperous gale' across the English Channel. Disgracefully, the archers, who had earned world fame in battle, were refused food at Calais and found that their pay had ceased the moment they stepped ashore in Dover. The King endured a hazardous crossing in a blinding snowstorm, but at nightfall his flagship finally reached the safety of Dover harbour. The Barons of the Cinque Ports waded into the freezing water, lifted him from his longboat and carried him high on their shoulders to the foreshore. For the valiant troops, however, it must have seemed an anticlimax since they were greeted 'without flourish or fanfare'.

King Henry assembled his closest companions and commenced his long ride across Kent to London. He paused at Canterbury where he prayed at the shrine of St Thomas Becket and refreshed himself at Eltham Palace. His deliberately meandering route allowed time for his spin doctors to organise a 'joyeuse entree' into the City of London.

At first light on St Clement's Day (23 November) Mayor Wotton and twenty-four Aldermen rode the four miles out from the City as far as Blackheath, the traditional place of greeting for people of importance, to receive 'Goddys Knight'.[75] They wore their warm furred scarlet gowns with striped black and white hoods. Accompanying them was a huge crowd of citizens and craftsmen – Whittington would be prominent among them – sporting their distinctive devices that marked their status as a member of one of the twelve liveried companies. Everyone was dressed alike from hood to hose in scarlet and white, the patriotic colours of England and St George.[76]

About ten o'clock Henry appeared on the horizon accompanied by the modest retinue that had attended him across Kent. After a welcoming speech from the Mayor, Henry prepared to ride into London. Surprisingly, the King had not only discarded his armour and his weapons, but also his crown. And he had chosen to wear sober clothes that expressed his humility, including a plain purple gown – the colour of mourning.[77] He would not even permit his battered helmet nor his dented sword to be carried before him along the highway. By contrast to his lack of ostentation, his captives were accorded the dignity of riding in splendour with their banners held high by their heralds sporting the emblems of France. Marshal Boucicaut was paraded prominently among the prisoners; his enviable fate was to live in luxury at England's expense for the remainder of his life.[78]

A Prisoner Exchange Rate

Whittington was later involved in a heated quarrel over the exchange of a French prisoner, Hugues (or Hugh) Coniers, captured at Agincourt.[79] Whittington claimed a share in his ransom, which he later sold onto Stephen Turnebonis, an Italian merchant, on 10 July 1420. Coniers was brought to England where he would have been lodged at Whittington's expense at his mansion until a favourable deal was struck between the two merchants. Such was the mercenary character of Medieval warfare, where a prime incentive was the possibility of capturing highborn prisoners from and for whom heavy ransoms might be extracted.

Although Turnebonis was committed to repurchasing the prisoner there was a bitter dispute over the payment: £296. Ultimately, Whittington brought the case before the courts, which found in his favour and awarded him costs.[80] The misfortune of the French prisoner, who changed hands twice during his long captivity, may have been due to an inability to pay his ransom. There is a hint that Turnebonis was part of a syndicate of Italians formed to buy up noble prisoners as an investment. This episode reveals a harsh, tenacious, mercenary side to Whittington – akin to trading in human misery – which to modern minds is distasteful. But it is also reminiscent of recent worldwide financial dealings involving the sale of bad debts...

Victory Celebrations

Henry V's victory cavalcade rode towards Southwark. And as this great Riding neared London Bridge, where the battlements were garlanded, fanfares announced its approach. The bridge chapel bells rang and virgins eulogised: 'Welcome Henry ye fifte, Kinge of Englond and Fraunce'. London, then as now, excelled in celebrations. Parades through the cobbled streets, heraldic displays on civic buildings, church bells pealing, water conduits spilling wine... Banners and standards fluttered from turrets while clarions and trumpets resounded. Every public building along Leadenhal, Cornhill, Poultry and Cheapside was decorated with tapestries, standards, escutcheons, shields, arches of halberds, military tents, model forts, miniature castles and ubiquitous figures of St George. All the time, the King maintained a cold, stern expression as he passed through the excited crowds. Festivities drew to a sedate close with inevitable services at St Paul's Cathedral, where Henry paid homage at the shrine of St Erkenwald[81] and Westminster Abbey, where he made offerings to the tomb of St Edward the Confessor, before returning to the comparative privacy of Westminster Palace.

A carol for three voices, 'Deo Gracias Anglia', was commissioned to laud Henry's praises. Popularly known as 'The Agincourt Carol', it was probably a production of the King's royal chapel. The original notation of the song was penned in black diamond-headed notes onto a roll of vellum. Handwritten copies are preserved in the Bodleian Library, Oxford, and Trinity College, Cambridge:

Our King went forth to Normandy
With grace and might of chivalry,
There God for him wrought marvellously,
Wherefore England may call and cry ~

Deo gratias Anglia
Redde pro victoria.

He set a siege, for sooth to say,
To Harfleur town with royal array,
That town he won and made a fray
That France shall rue till doomsday ~

Deo gratias Anglia

Redde pro victoria.

Then went him forth our King comely,
In Agincourt field he fought manly,
Through grace of God most marvellously
He had the field and victory ~

Deo gratias Anglia
Redde pro victoria.[82]

Obsequiously, Parliament granted Henry customs duties on all imports and exports of wine, wool and hides for the duration of his reign. This was an extraordinary demonstration of confidence in his kingship. The right to grant taxes was a privilege that Members of Parliament jealously guarded as their principal bargaining power for obtaining concessions from their sovereign. (There had been only one precedent for a lifetime grant of a levy on wool and that had been extracted under duress by the autocratic Richard II.) Henry interpreted their generous gesture as a positive vote for the continuation of his French campaign.

Another resolution was that a special honour should be awarded to St George as England's patron. In future, on his feast day (23 April) all work must cease in order that people could attend church to glorify his memory. Two further acknowledgements were to be made to Saints Crispin and Crispinian in recognition of their supernatural aid during the campaign.

These cobblers from Soissons who had been martyred for their beliefs in the third century had obligingly changed their allegiance from France to England. Their feast day had coincided with the battle and so, from now onwards, it was to be strictly observed on the anniversary of Agincourt.

12

Fourth Time Mayor
of London

RICHARD WHITTINGTON had been elected three times Master of the Mercers' Company: 1395-6, 1401-2 and 1408-9. After that time his interests were deflected from dealing in mercery into high finance and his name no longer features regularly in the company accounts. He did, however, remember the Mercers in his will and bequeathed them the comparatively modest sum of £13 6s 8d. His trading in luxury cloths, which began to decline in the reign of Henry IV, was drastically reduced under Henry V but did not cease entirely.

In 1413, Whittington had been tempted to purchase Spanish merchandise that had been forfeited to the King and in that same year he imported 'reynes', 'naperie' and 'towell' (valued at £57 16s 8d) into Sandwich, Kent. Two years later he was owed over £600 for materials supplied to the Great Wardrobe that had been authorised by John Spencer, appointed Keeper at the beginning of the new reign. There is, however, no record of any further purchases from him in the two extant account books (1419-20 and 1422-3) for the remainder of Whittington's lifetime. And this dwindling interest in trade is confirmed by the absence of any further record of him enrolling apprentices in the Wardens' Accounts of the Mercers' Company.[83]

In 1418, a regrettable incident occurred when a woman publicly slandered Whittington. This is a rare hint of scandal over his long career. Johanna Hert, jeweller, published abroad that Whittington owed her large sums of money and in addition was in possession of some of her jewellery, worth several hundred pounds. Swift to clear his name, Whittington, on 21 June, brought her before the Mayor's Court to test the truth of the story.

Obliged to swear on the Gospels, Johanna admitted that, in truth, she owed him far more than he owed her. The woman had plainly done her sums wrong. After openly acknowledging her fault, Johanna begged forgiveness. The prescribed punishment for defamation was for the perpetrator to stand with a whetstone about their neck in the 'thew' (a pillory reserved for women) at the marketplace. Whittington, to his credit, accepted Johanna's apology and, since he was no longer vilified, exercised clemency towards the apparently deluded woman.[84] This incident is a confirmation that Whittington occasionally dealt in jewels.

Richard Whittington was elected Mayor of London for the fourth and final time in October 1419.[85] This was a tremendous achievement for a man who must have been approaching eighty! His Sheriffs were named as Robert Whityngham, Draper, and John Botiler, Boteler or Butler, Mercer. As before, his election had followed the 'mass of Holy Spirit devoutly and becomingly celebrated with solemn music' in Guildhall Chapel. Correct procedure for the election had been followed. The Mayor, Sheriffs, Aldermen and Common Councillors had been summoned to Guildhall where they assembled in the Lower Chamber, normally reserved for meetings of the 'Full Husting'. The Commoners retired to one end of the room where they nominated two Aldermen, each of whom had previously served as Sheriffs, which they presented as their candidates as Mayor. The Mayor and Aldermen then ascended to the Upper Chamber where they elected, by plurality of votes, under the scrutiny of the Common Clerk and supervision of the Recorder, the Mayor for the ensuing year.

The following day, Whittington was presented to the King before the Barons of the Exchequer at Westminster Palace.[86] In the 15th century, it was impossible for a citizen to hold office – Mayor, Sheriff or Alderman – unless in the livery of one of the City Companies. Invariably, London Mayors were elected from members of the six principal Companies – Mercers, Grocers, Drapers, Goldsmiths, Skinners and Fishmongers[87] – but by far the majority of citizens who held that office were drawn from the first and foremost Company, the Mercers. Unsurprisingly, the Mercers' Company members were extremely proud of their former Master and recorded the scene in their Minute Book: 'The Company attended the cavalcade of Whittington chosen mayor for the fourth time with eight new banners, eight trumpeters, four pipers, seven nakerers'.[88] Certainly, the Mercers were determined to proclaim abroad the extraordinary success of their most prominent and esteemed member.[89] Indisputably, they recognised that Whittington's reputation had enhanced their company's reputation.[90] Indeed, Whittington's quadruple election to the Mayoralty confirms the adage that the 15th century was the 'golden age' for Mercers.[91]

The actual procedure of Whittington's election was slightly altered from former times. Five years earlier, a rabble of apprentices, workmen and strangers had disrupted an election causing 'riots and tumults' at Guildhall. It was decided that in future admittance should be restricted to members of the Common Council. Following a further disturbance with clamorous shouting in 1442, a royal writ was obtained forbidding anyone to attend 'unless specially summoned thereto' and even they were required to wait until called by name at the door.

Today, the Lord Mayor is elected annually on the second Friday in November when a small and select gathering of high officials is invited into a private chamber in Guildhall. What follows is known as 'The Silent Ceremony', when with 'swish of robes, click of heels and scratch of quill', the new Lord Mayor is confirmed. During the course of the dignified ceremony an ornamental mace is formally passed from the outgoing to the incoming Lord Mayor as a symbol of his authority. This hallowed object is called the 'crystal sceptre' or 'the sceptre of the City of London'. Its origins are steeped in mystery but it is believed to date from Saxon times. The exquisite mace is composed of a rock crystal shaft approximately 17 inches long entwined with barley sugar threads of gold and decorated with large crystal knops mounted in pure gold. The head, considered to be a 15th-century embellishment, is encircled with a bold coronet of miniature golden St George's crosses and fleur-de-lis, while beneath is a circlet of sapphires and amethysts interspersed with droplets of pearls. Painted on vellum and encased under a crystal plate at the top are the arms of England quartered with those of France. For this reason, it is assumed that this sceptre is the same mace carried by the Mayor at the coronation of Catherine de Valois after her marriage to Henry V in 1421. Traditionally, the precious mace, retained by the Chamberlain, is carried by the Lord Mayor at coronations. Mayor Whittington, it can be assumed, would have carried this precious sceptre in its original form, before his sovereign on solemn occasions when escorting him through the City.[92]

Mayor Whittington's seat of office was, of course, Guildhall. This, according to Fabyan's 'Chronicle', had been 'edyfied' in 1411 transforming 'an olde and lytell cotage' into 'a fayre and goodley house'. Apparently, the early 15th-century building was an enlarged version of the 12th-century one, the main alteration being the insertion of internal vaulting to form an undercroft with an upper ground floor to create a chamber with probably five bays. The remodelled Guildhall then consisted of three rooms for administrative and legal purposes. The large undercroft, which was then entered from the west end, contained a dais at the east end for the Court of Hustings. On the upper floor there would have been an entrance lobby at the east end, entered via steps from Guildhall Yard, leading to a substantial courtroom four bays long. This room would have comfortably accommodated two hundred councillors seated on long benches, although attendance in greater numbers necessitated a 'standing' meeting in the larger five-bay chamber below. The adjoining 'interior chamber' would have been situated in the north-east corner of the building, the space allowing for perhaps twenty people to meet, seated around a table, to form the Mayor's Court.

Whittington's Christmas celebrations that year must have been a subdued occasion. The previous Mayor, Richard Merlew, passed a resolution banning mumming or masquerades over the seasonal festivities in 1417. The next Mayor, William Sevenoke, ratified this regulation the following year:

The Mair and Aldermen chargen on ye Kynges byhalf, and his Cite, that no manere persone, of what astate, degre, or condicioun that euere he be, during this holy tyme of Cristemes be so hardy in eny wyse to walk by nyght in eny manere mommyng, pleyes, enterludes, or eny other disgisynges with eny feynd berdis, peyntid visers, diffourmyd or colourid visages in eny wyse, up peyne of enprisonement.

Citizens were exhorted to be 'honestly mery as he can, with in his owne hous dwellyng'. Further, every householder was obliged, by law, 'to hang out of her hous eche night, during this solempne Feste, a lanterne with a candell ther in, to brenne as long as hit may endure' or to pay a fine of four pence 'eche tyme yat hit faillith'. It is a surprise to learn that Whittington, the hero of pantomime, could be such a spoilsport at Christmastime [93]

The banning of mumming at this time is puzzling although roaming the streets with frightening disguises presumably risked intimidation and extortion. The Watch on each ward was instructed to arrest anyone concealing their face since this implied they were involved in criminal activity.[94] Christmas was a religious festival honoured rather than celebrated. Biblical stories, when acted by low comedians, were 'disfigured with gross indecencies'.[95] They involved ridicule or ribaldry and were an excuse for satire. This might explain the authorities' motives in controlling mummers' mocking performances. Epiphany was regarded as a season more suited to frivolities. Henry V attended a special mass where a gold star of Bethlehem was suspended in the body of the chapel at Westminster Abbey. Afterwards, he feasted in state and watched 'disguising games' in Westminster Palace. This midwinter festival was an opportunity to demonstrate his sovereignty. Christmas and Epiphany were two of the three special days appointed for the King to wear his crown.[96]

Whittington, inevitably, soon settled down to the day-to-day business of presiding over either the Mayor's Court or the Court of Common Council. From the scanty evidence that survives, it appears that Whittington managed to attend around half of the meetings, an indication that he retained his impressive stamina. He signed 'writs of protection' formally exempting a person from arrest while on the King's service abroad; he exonerated apprentices from completing their apprenticeship after their master had defaulted on the terms of his contract, and witnessed leases for city shops and houses, one of which stood in 'Fletestrete in the parish of St Bride, bounded on the east by a tenement called Hell'. There were several cases concerning debts: money was claimed by owners for silverware, jewellery, materials and a framed altar picture. He authenticated the legal authority of a coroner, Richard Alfeld, in London; he intervened in the return of a widow's possessions and accepted surety for William Holcroft, Goldsmith, 'who was reputed among his neighbours to be a nightwalker'.

Far more serious offences were brought before Whittington, acting as Chief Justice of the Bench. John Barkefold, wiredrawer, 'dwelling in the parish of 'St Bennet Shorhogge', was accused of slandering the King by claiming that he had tortured and murdered victims who refused to pay his exorbitant taxes.

The case was dismissed not only through lack of evidence but because the jurors were convinced that the defendant was a man of exemplary character. Mayor Whittington was far more actively involved when disturbances erupted in several City wards during the summer of 1420. Irate residents violently resisted constables and collectors sent to collect their authorised share of 2,000 marks granted by the Common Council to fund Henry's third expedition into France. Whittington accompanied by his Aldermen marched upon Sheriff Robert Widyngton's rebellious ward and ordered the arrest of the demonstrators who had rescued their leader, Nicholas Stanour, after he had been taken into custody by one of the sergeants-at-mace, Thomas Warner. The ringleaders were imprisoned in Newgate until the whole of their allocated sum was safely banked.[97]

Whittington next turned his attention to the plight of prisoners. William Sevenoke, when Mayor, had made the disastrous decision to close Ludgate Gaol for the simple reason that he considered it had become too comfortable for its inmates. Alas, a great number of the prisoners who had been transferred to Newgate had since died because of its 'fetid and corrupt atmosphere'. This struck Whittington's conscience. Always sympathetic towards prisoners, particularly debtors, he ordered that Ludgate be immediately opened to receive 'respectable' prisoners and took steps to ensure that it was properly regulated by its Warders.[98]

Dispute with the Brewers' Company

During his third mayoralty, Whittington was involved in an acrimonious dispute with the Brewers' Company. The Mayor was authorised to judge serious trading offences and the severity of the punishment of the guilty parties varied with his temperament. The City was renowned for its ale – wine already becoming expensive – which was brewed in vast quantities. Even the King obtained ale for the royal household, especially when entertaining important visitors or preparing for a campaign, by either purchasing or requisitioning it from London brewers. Ale was brewed at the plentiful taverns where it was sold and a check was kept on its quality by 'connors' appointed to every ward. Brewing was a common occupation for women, especially widows, who also kept alehouses where they were notorious for being both flirtatious and fraudulent with their customers.[99] One of the responsibilities of the Mayor was checking the quality and regulating the prices of ale brewed in the City.

There was a long history of antagonism between the victual and non-victualing companies, particularly the Mercers and the Brewers, and their lamentable rancour was exacerbated upon Whittington's assumption of mayoralty. The Mayor, Sheriffs and Aldermen were expressly forbidden to keep either a brewery or tavern, according to 'Liber Albus'. William Portland's 'Memorandum Book' and the Brewers Company Extract of Minutes

(1418-1440) together record the prolonged quarrel.[100] A supposed slight that Whittington took personally centred upon the fact that the Brewers had served 'fat swans' at the recent feast to welcome their new master, Thomas Grene. The Brewers' Company were gastronomically ambitious and were renowned for their extravagant entertainments, which often included swan roasts.[101] Presumably, they thought Whittington was irritated by the fact that the poultry they offered was far superior to any that he could obtain for his guests at Guildhall.[102] Perhaps he was!

Whittington's personal animosity towards the Brewers seems to have been motivated by petty jealousy and clearly he ought to have avoided direct confrontation with a company whose services were so indispensable to the Crown. The Brewers, for instance, provided ale for the celebrations to welcome King Henry back from France and for the subsequent coronation banquet of Queen Catherine. The Mayor's attitude towards them was in no way softened by their generous provision of two pipes of red wine, which they presented to his butler at considerable expense: £7 3s 4d.

Obviously, it was of paramount importance that a plentiful supply of wholesome beer and ale was available – water often being undrinkable through pollution – at reasonable prices to the citizens of London. And it was the responsibility of the Mayor to set the retail price for standard grades since this would check the tendency for brewers to profiteer when supplies fell short. Further, the Mayor was required to check the quality of commodities – bread, meat, fish, coals and beer – and mete out humiliating punishments for shopkeepers who sold inferior goods.[103] Whittington ordered one fraudster, William Horold, who had doctored his casks with gums and spices before filling them with inferior Spanish wine, 'to have a lykly manere taste and smell to the drynkyng of Romeny' (Malmsey), to stand in the pillory.[104]

Whittington's first measure against the Brewers was to standardize the vessels in which beer and ale were sold in the City. The Mayor was adamant that all the coopers should register their marks for beer barrels and kilderkins before the following Easter at Guildhall. Moreover, he imposed an impractical penalty of 40 shillings upon every barrel that left the workshop without an official cooper's mark. Furore erupted after he stipulated their prices for beer and ale: 3s 6d was the highest that might be demanded for a barrel of beer sold outside a brewer's own house. The Brewers complained that the price of beer was outside their control because it depended upon the fluctuating price of malt. Their resentment of his interference is recorded minutely in an entry in their Letter Book headed: 'A long narrative of a second most violent and tyrannical attempt by Whityngton to oppress and extort money from the Brewers of London'.

The facts, at least according to the Brewers' Records, are these. In July 1421 Whittington summoned all the female 'Huksteres' selling beer and ale in the City[105] to appear before him at Guildhall. There he demanded of them upon oath the prices at which they sold their beer and the names of their suppliers, which were duly recorded in the Chamberlain's book. On 22 August, the Brewers named were summoned and they, too, were closely examined. To his disbelief, their prices tallied with the women's statements – '... but the Mayor declared them false and grievous transgressions.' He pronounced, without hard evidence, that the Brewers had breached a bond made with the Court and thus had incurred the penalty of £20.

The Brewers attempted in vain to justify themselves and their bold spokesman, Thomas Dryffeld, 'dared to venture his life' that they had spoken the truth. Whittington responded by ordering them, 'with great insolence and severity', to appear before him again on the following Tuesday. After great deliberation at Brewers' Hall, the masters duly returned. They pleaded ignorance of the bond and asked to see a copy but were refused. Reluctantly, upon their insistence, the bond was eventually produced. They disputed its terms and refused to attend to the Mayor 'who continually urged them to pay the sum, with violent threats'. Whittington passed an impractical resolution in the Common Council that if they did not submit to his will, 'the whole company should be undone and dissolved.'

When the Court reconvened on 1 October, Whittington changed tactics and calmly addressed the brewers with 'flattering promises'. Thomas Grene, their newly elected Master, attended in person but he was curtly informed that the fine of £20 must be paid in full before the end of the month 'otherwise the same should be increased to £100'. The Brewers attempted further delaying tactics – they realised it was almost the end of Whittington's term of office – but the Mayor, his temper frayed, lost patience and ordered the Chamberlain to collect the £20, 'or else to shut and fasten their doors'.[106]

The Brewers were swift to protest at what they deemed to be unfair treatment: 'A record that in the grievances of great charges imposed on the company by Rich. Whityngstone all the year of his mayoralty the Brewers declined to make Feasts or Breakfasts or to provide their yearly Livery.'[107] Artfully, the Company managed to postpone payment of the unjustly imposed fine until the termination of Whittington's term of office. Happily, there was an entirely different response when on 6 November, the Chamberlain duly repeated his demand for payment of the fine. The new Mayor, William Cambrigge (or 'Cambridge'), dealt with the Brewers far more leniently and readdressed their plight by allowing them to pay the fine with a deposit of £10 and the rest in installments. It seems unlikely that a prominent City Company should be so strapped for cash and their deferred payment must surely have been a matter of principle.

Alas, the quarrel outlasted Whittington's mayoralty. When Sir Robert Chichele[108] became Mayor, Whittington himself brought a complaint before his court on 30 July 1422. He accused the Brewers of still selling beer and ale more expensively than was allowed by law and declared they had deliberately 'ridden into the country and forestalled the malt to raise its price' before it arrived in London. Cunningly, this drastically escalated their prices!

On this occasion the Court found the Brewers guilty of deliberately inflating prices – selling ale at 5d a barrel – and they were therefore condemned to forfeit the bond which they had reluctantly surrendered to Whittington during his late mayoralty. Four masters of the company, Robert Smyth, William Crane, Hugh Neel and John Philippe, were consigned to prison until the full amount was received for the new work at 'Gyldhall'.

The Brewers were later placated by the diplomacy of the common clerk, John Carpenter, who took them to one side and privately offered them consolation. He assured them that their masters would not be imprisoned nor the company forced to pay the fine. Confidentially, he whispered in their ear: 'for wel yei wysten and knewen that alle ye forsaid Juggement of ye Mair and Aldremen was not don at yat tyme bot for to plese Richard Whityngton, for he was the cause of all the forsaid Judgement.'[109]

This was a damning admission by one of Whittington's closest confidants. (Carpenter would not, of course, have been influenced by the Brewers' handsome gesture of 20s for his council.) Whittington alone received the condemnation of the Company, who offered fulsome praise towards both his successors, Cambridge (1420) and Chichele (1422). All the Aldermen – younger men, perhaps, who recognised the economic factors that increased the price of beer – were far more amenable towards the Brewers' business activities. Tellingly, after Whittington's demise there were no further attempts for a dozen years to control the price of beer and ale sold in the City.[110]

This prolonged dispute between the Mayor's court and the Brewers' Company does not present Whittington in the best light. Admittedly, Whittington was simply enforcing a previous statute: an ordinance of 1408 directed that no brewer should sell a gallon of best beer within his house for more than 2d by marked measure and outside his house for a halfpence less. The statute had been passed with the full approval of Henry's Council. The Act was designed to check the practices of false brewers and corrupt ale sellers, which actually would have been in the interests of Company members.

Details of the Company's affairs were meticulously recorded in perfect longhand in their original Record Book preserved at Guildhall. Later, relevant entries in Latin were roughly transcribed – with plentiful scribblings and crossings out – by a company clerk who was not hesitant in his condemnation of Mayor Whittington as malicious and vindictive towards its masters and members.[111] Sadly, this biased record, which at times quotes him verbatim, is the closest one can get to Whittington at the end of his long life. This glimpse of his character and personality certainly reveals him to be not only authoritative but a formidable opponent, who acted scrupulously within the law. But he also appears stern, officious, petulant and cantankerous in his rectitude concerning matters of trade. Perhaps by this time he was showing signs of old age, weariness, even senility? The fact cannot be avoided that Whittington's fourth and final term of office was, at times, disastrous.

At the time of Carpenter's intervention there was a definite concern that the office of Mayor was an arduous one involving time and money. In 1389, the Aldermen reached a decision that no one was allowed to serve as Mayor for more than one year at a time and no one might be reelected to the office until five years had passed. This acknowledged that the role was a costly affair and that the burden should be shared equally among the Aldermen. One may also detect a strong desire to limit the control of government by certain powerful City Companies. In the 14th century, the Fishmongers held sway but this new ruling ensured that the choice of Mayor was distributed more fairly among the other leading Companies. During the 15th century the majority of Aldermen who became Mayor were Mercers, Drapers or Grocers, although there were several Goldsmiths, Skinners and Fishmongers. These were, after all, the six principal City companies and no one who did not belong to one of the twelve greater Companies ever held office as Mayor.[112] In 1426, it was ordained that a man should not be eligible for reelection as Mayor until seven years after his past term of office; and nine years later that no one should be called upon to serve a third term. There is here more than a hint that it was thought wise to prevent men from holding office for too long a period. This last decision, taken shortly after his demise, may have been provoked by Richard Whittington's fairly calamitous fourth term of office.

Arrest of Queen Joan

Mayor Whittington was now presented with an unenviable task by Henry V. He was ordered to apprehend the dowager Queen Joan. At the time of her arrest on 27 September 1419, the King was again absent, fighting in France. He was convinced that his stepmother had attempted to poison him through witchcraft. According to the *Brut* Chronicle: 'And in that same yere Quene Iahan was a-rested and brought to Retherhyde.'[113]

The English people had never accepted Joan and they resented her foreign attendants. Initially, Joan had displayed affection for her husband's children but she became a thorn in the flesh of his eldest son once he became King. Henry exploited the occasion. He sequestered her lands. This substantial revenue funded his later wars. Nevertheless, Queen Joan was kindly treated and she even lived in comparative luxury at Rotherhithe Manor. Her confinement there ceased only after Henry's demise.[114] Perhaps this incident reinforces the idea of Whittington's chameleon character that ensured not only his success but his survival?

Compilation of 'Liber Albis'

During his final term, Whittington instigated the compilation of the celebrated 'Liber Albis' ('White Book') by the new Common Clerk, John Carpenter. The purpose of this 'Repository' was to record for posterity the City's laws, privileges, rights and customs. It is, according to Besant and Rice, 'the most valuable and important work ever undertaken for any city'. The project may have been prompted in the first instance by Richard II's repeated infringement of the citizens of London's long-established rights. It demonstrates Whittington's legalistic mind. Undeniably, it was an arduous task. In the course of its preparation Whittington became friendly with Carpenter and, indeed, held him in such high regard that he later appointed him executor of his will.

The manuscript reflected the life of the City in all its aspects and dealt with the customs, laws, trade, social conditions and general conduct of its government. Laws appertaining to the City covered every aspect of communal life: Brothels were forbidden within the walls; innkeepers must close their doors to customers after curfew; boats were not to be left unattended overnight unless moored along the banks to avoid their misuse by miscreants; swords or knives should be handed over by guests to their hostelier and certainly not be unsheathed while proceeding across London.

There was a strict regard to health and safety. Butchers were to be careful with their disposal of entrails; market stalls should not impede the passage over the bridge; carters were forbidden to speed through the streets with their light, empty carts; barber-surgeons were to drain bowls of their patients' blood in the Thames; swine were not to be left to roam the streets at night, except those belonging to Saint Anthony's Hospital (identified by a bell hung about their neck).

There were strict regulations regarding the sale of food and drink in order to protect the welfare of customers. Butchers were not allowed to sell their meat 'by light of candle'; Brewers were forbidden to corrupt their wine by mixing new with old; the consistency of bread called 'puffe' (or 'pouf') was stipulated while shellfish should not be offered for sale 'beyond two ebbs and a flood (tide).' The impression is given that the City of London was well organised and fairly governed in order to ensure that its citizens inhabited a safe and to some extent caring community.

The original 'Liber Albus' is now preserved at the London Metropolitan Archives. Its vellum pages are much thumbed and repaired through sewing. When the binding decayed, it was rebound with old oak boards and brass fittings early in the twentieth century. Carpenter's name appears on the verso of the flyleaf with a great flourish. In his introduction, he explains that his laudable purpose in combing through the unclassified books, rolls and charters of the City of London was due to 'the fallibility of human memory and brevity of human life'.

Evidently, the book was written by more than one person since it displays several different styles of handwriting. It was probably penned by minor clerks under Carpenter's direction. One scribe, however, decided to enliven the margins of the carefully ruled pages with doodles of beasts, monsters and human faces in profile. The Four Books into which the tome is divided incorporate beautifully decorated prefaces while gold leaf capitals mark each question and answer. 'Liber Albus' is a meticulous record of the precise formalities regarding the election and duties of the Mayor, Sheriffs, Aldermen and Officials of the City of London from 1275 to 1509.

Marriage and Coronation of Catherine De Valois

Henry's victory at Agincourt laid the foundations for the resurrection of an English empire in France. During the conflict, the slaughter of the noblemen and the decimation of their armies paved the way for two further expeditions into Normandy. The second campaign, whereby Rouen was besieged and Paris surrounded, culminated in the Treaty of Troyes (1420) whereby Charles VI disinherited his indolent son, the Dauphin Charles, and instead recognised Henry as his lawful regent and heir. To seal the union between the two countries, Henry married Charles's daughter, Catherine, on 2 June 1420. A contemporary painting held by the British Museum depicts the solemn moment when the Archbishop joins the royal couple's hands in marriage. The pair are wearing cloth-of-gold gowns and golden crowns. Catherine displays the long hair of a maiden and adopts the provocative 'whiplash' stance, considered a most fashionable pose.

Early the following year, Catherine was brought over to England. Henry proudly escorted her from Eltham Palace to the Tower of London. This was a joyous occasion with the Mayor, Aldermen and Commonalty arrayed in 'white garmentis and rede hodis or rede kappis' while each company sported its own livery as they paraded through the City of London. On 23 February 1421, Catherine was crowned his consort at St Peter's Church, Westminster. Dressed in pure white, she rode in a gorgeous coach through the decorated streets from the Tower of London to Westminster Abbey. The scene was truly spectacular, with 'euryry strete hongid rychely with riche clothis of gold and silke, and of velewettis and clothis of araas,' marvelled the author of the *Brut*, 'the beste that myght be gotyn.' These sumptuous furnishings bear the hallmarks of Mercer Whittington.

Afterwards, Queen Catherine was escorted across to the Palace of Westminster for her coronation banquet, a slightly muted affair because it fell in Lent. All the same, the royal cooks devised an imaginative bill of fare even though it consisted almost entirely of fish. The menu for 'ye Coronacion of Kateryne, ye Quene of Englond' included 'Pyke, Troute, Codlyng, Breme, Soles, Roche, Turbutt, Perche, Smelt, Elys, Lamprey poudered, Merlyng ffryed, Porpas rosted, Lopsters,

Welkys, Grete Crabys, Crevis and Scrymppys'.[115] It would have been contrary to etiquette for Henry to attend since all the honours were to be bestowed upon Catherine.

Queen Catherine sat on a dais under a rich canopy of state with the Archbishop of Canterbury on her right hand and on her left the 'Kynge of Scottys'. Her Majesty was attended by the Earl of March, kneeling and holding a sceptre, upon her right side and the Earl of March, in like manner, upon her left while she was served countless covered dishes. Sir Richard Newel was carver; the Earl of Suffolk's brother was cupbearer and these important little ceremonies were overseen by Humphrey, Duke of Gloucester, who stood bareheaded before the Queen. The Earl of Worcester, Lord High Marshal, rode about on a heavy charger, wielding his tipstaves to clear a pathway through the Great Hall. Below the Queen, the Barons of the Cinque Ports were closest on the table upon the right hand before St Stephen's Chapel, while next to the cupboard displaying the royal plate sat the 'mayre of London', a privileged guest among his brethren the Aldermen.[116] Richard Whittington does not appear among the guest list but it is hard to imagine that such a prominent figure would have been absent during these festivities.[117]

Burning the Bonds

A persistent story concerns Whittington's magnanimous generosity to his sovereign. He entertained King Henry and Queen Catherine to a banquet at his own mansion[118] as a belated celebration for the English victory at Agincourt. At this time, we are told, the King's war bonds to the London citizens amounted to a phenomenal £60,000. Lysons relates intimate details of the celebrated incident when Henry stood warming himself by the open fire 'in which were burnt several sorts of woods, mixed with cinnamon and other spices'.[119] Besant and Rice itemise these bonds: 10,000 marks due to the Mercers' Company; 1,500 marks due to the Chamber of London; 2,000 marks due to the Grocers in addition to Whittington's private loans and advances.[120]

Whittington produced the bonds and burnt them, instantly freeing Henry from his mountainous debts. Amazed at his gesture, Henry exclaimed, 'Never had a Prince such a subject,' to which Whittington, predictably, responded, 'Never had a subject such a Prince.' As a reward Henry knighted Whittington at the height of the festivities. Alas, there can be no substance to this tale of cash for honours. Documents prove that Whittington was regularly rewarded for his royal loans while the amount mentioned as a loan from the Mercers' Company would then have been far beyond their resources.[121] Whittington constantly avoided the general distraints for knighthood under successive reigns but preferred instead to pay the requisite fines. Nor was Henry so lightly freed from his war debts. Alas, this story, unlike the celebrated battle, bore no truth as it passed into legend...

Catherine gave birth to a son named Henry in his father and grandfather's honour, on 6 December 1421 at Windsor. Henry received the news abroad and celebrated by besieging and battering the riverside town of Meaux with 'Gounnys, Tregettis and Engenys'. In London, the bells were pealed and a Te Deum sung at St Paul's in the presence of the Chancellor, the Mayor, Aldermen, guildsmen and bishops. After spending a brief period in England to raise funds for his renewed war efforts, Henry returned once more to vex France and repel the Dauphin.[122]

Henry caught dysentery after the siege of Meaux and died at the age of thirty-four at Vincennes on 31 August 1422. His bones were brought home and enshrined at Westminster Abbey. Thousands lined the route across Kent and into London to pay their last respects to this mighty Medieval war hero, 'off whose Soulle Jhesu have mercy'. Whittington would have closely observed the magnificent funeral procession. Accoutrements of war were displayed alongside Henry's elevated tomb, revered relics of his military achievements: his saddle, his shield, his 'bruised helmet and his bended sword'.[123] Henry failed to achieve his lifelong ambition to rule two Kingdoms – England and France – both of which were ostensibly inherited by his infant son who reigned as Henry VI.[124]

Lamentations for the premature death of Henry V were tempered by his tremendous victory in France. Whittington, approaching his own mortality, continued to serve in civic government while his last months, which reached briefly into the new reign, were taken up with preparations for the distribution of his vast wealth for the lasting benefit of his beloved City of London.

THE REIGN OF
HENRY VI

13

Whittington's Properties and Investments

HENRY VI, at the age of twelve months, was King of England and France. Custody of his realms during his minority fell to his uncles, John, Duke of Bedford, and Humphrey, Duke of Gloucester. They vied for power with their relative, Henry Beaufort, who became a cardinal in 1426. All three fought over Henry V's legacy. His adult life was marked by a succession of military disasters: Harfleur was recaptured in 1435, Rouen fell in 1449 and the Duchy of Gascony was lost in 1453, leaving Calais as the only possession in France.[1] The new reign of Henry VI, with powerful guardians exercising strict control over him and an idolised father passing swiftly into legend, was doomed to failure from the start.[2]

Henry V was laid to rest in a vast tomb behind the High Altar at Westminster Abbey. Today, it appears stripped of its ornate decoration, a musty memorial to his spectacular military achievements. His effigy, through time, lost a head but this was replaced by a polyester resin replica towards the end of the twentieth century. Even this is raised beyond casual public view. Henry's shield, saddle and tilting helm from Agincourt are displayed in the Abbey Museum. The body of his consort, Catherine of Valois, was embalmed and lay in an open tomb for three hundred years. Pepys unforgettably records in his diary on 23 February 1669 how he was favoured with a viewing of her corpse on his 36th birthday. 'I had the upper part of her body in my arms, and I did kiss her mouth, reflecting upon it that I did kiss a Queen.'

Fanned clockwise around the shrine of Edward the Confessor behind the High Altar are the exalted tombs of Medieval kings, queens and their royal families. The Confessors' shrine was once a magnificent structure, encased in gold and ornately bejewelled, but this is now concealed from public gaze. Edward III's tomb by Henry Yvele retains a row of six figures, recently regilded, and a carved canopy. Nearby are the tombs of his consort, Philippa of Hainault, and their youngest son, Thomas, Duke of Gloucester. Richard II and his adored wife, Anne of Bohemia, lie together in a single tomb. Touchingly, their effigies were meant to convey their deep love by depicting them holding hands for eternity. Alas, their arms are broken off.

It is astonishing to consider that Richard Whittington, from humble beginnings in a remote hamlet in the countryside of Gloucestershire, knew several of these royal figures intimately. He served, advised, befriended and sumptuously clothed them and their immediate circle. And since his eventful life stretched only as far as the beginning of the long minority of Henry VI, it is enlightening to reflect on that other nobleman's family who played such an important part in his rise to prosperity and also his own personal life.

Sir Ivo Fitzwaryn

Richard Whittington, following the trend among professional men, married late in life. It was an accepted fact that a merchant might deliberately defer his marriage until his business flourished and his prospects were secure. Then he could assume a far more advantageous bargaining power in the matter of dowries. It was a means of obtaining capital to extend business and it was considered a great personal triumph.[3]

Whittington had chosen as his wife, Alice, the youngest daughter of Sir Ivo (or 'Yvon') Fitzwaryn,[4] who was his social equal since both were born to gentlefolk. Sir Ivo was, however, foremost a military man who had led a fairly distinguished career. Muster rolls exist that show he served under several great men including the Earl of Hereford (1371); the Earl of Warwick (1373-4); Sir John Darundell (1378) and the Earl of Arundell (1387). Further, there is evidence of his intention to serve both with the Black Prince (1369) and Thomas of Woodstock, Earl of Buckingham and later Duke of Gloucester (1380).[5] Muster rolls are incomplete for the Duke's campaign in France but Sir Ivo may, by inference, have been present with his banner and pennon at the Siege of Nantes in 1380.

Perhaps this provided the actual occasion for the Duke of Gloucester to introduce Whittington to Fitzwaryn at a royal function – sometime in the later reign of Richard II or the early one of Henry IV – which resulted in the marriage.[6] Country gentry, sensitive to the prestige of birth and position, were often reluctant to match their daughters to merchant families unless they owned lands or were related to gentry. Whittington, the son of a knight, his disgrace conveniently forgotten, and a prosperous merchant, fitted the bill perfectly and so their union was not remarkable.[7] There is, of course, just the slight chance that this marriage was a love match, but it is unlikely.

Fitzwaryn Memorials in Wantage Church

The magnificent Church of Saints Peter and Paul stands at the western end of the Market Place in Wantage, Oxfordshire.[8] Cruciform in design, the church dates from the early 13th century but may have replaced an even earlier timber construction mentioned in Domesday Book. The existing building has been greatly enlarged over the centuries, probably through the generosity of the later Fitzwaryns. Central is the honey-coloured limestone tower with its decorative crenellations and gilded weathervanes. The raised churchyard is enriched by an avenue of young trees through which a flint and flagstone pathway leads to the substantial porch. Jackdaws hop across the weathered tombstones while butterflies flit among the buttercups on the narrow lawn. A former parishioner, Sir John Betjemen, waxed even more lyrical about the church interior in his foreword to a guide book.

Inside, there is evidence of the 'lapse and wear of centuries'. The north transept has a fine clustered shaft with cap and base (*c*.1250) and a font whose mouldings are enriched by tooth ornamentation characteristic of the Normans. The south chapel dates from about 1450; the north chapel either late 15th or early 16th century. The north and south aisles of the nave belong to the 15th century and, indeed, the timber roof is a splendid specimen of contemporary carpentry. At the termination of the hammer beams one carved shield bears the arms of the Fitzwaryns. The chancel with its carved screens separating the side chapels and the misericords in the stalls demonstrate further intricate 15th-century workmanship.

Tucked against the north wall is the altar tomb depicting alabaster figures of Sir William Fitzwaryn K.G. (dated 1361) and his wife, known variously as Amice, Amica, Annie or simply Ann. Their canopy, which originally would have been brilliantly painted and tricked out with gold, has sadly disintegrated. Buried next to his father on the north side of the chancel is their son, Ivo, who died at Wantynge Brian, Berkshire on 6 September 1414.[9] He is commemorated in the church by an exquisite full-length pictorial memorial brass.[10] It was removed, without its canopy, from a recumbent position on the floor of the nearby chantry chapel that Sir Ivo founded to a pillar in the north transept.

Captain Symonds made a detailed sketch of the brass which at that time lay 'upon a flat stone in the north part of the said cross aisle'. This finely detailed brass, possibly wrought in London, depicts Sir Ivo as a military knight, resting his head on a jousting helm, now badly damaged. Ironically, he is sporting the full suit of plate armour that he would have worn in battle had he lived to take part in Henry V's French Campaign, which culminated at Agincourt. It was never intended to be a naturalistic portrait – although his moustache is a distinctive feature – but, instead, presented Sir Ivo in his role a defender of the realm.

Great changes had occurred in the development of armour since his father, Sir William, had fought in the French Wars of Edward III. Sir Ivo's memorial demonstrates these improvements. The feudal system of service had long since disappeared and this was replaced with recruitment by indenture so that inevitably soldiers invested wisely in their own personal protection. Chain mail, although easy to manage, was excessively heavy and risked being knocked into the wearer's flesh by heavy blows from a poleaxe. Gradually, it had been superseded by less cumbersome and more resilient plate armour, which allowed the wearer both strength and agility. Plate armour, because of its polished steel finish, was referred to as 'white harness'.[11]

Sir Ivo was knighted and bore the FitzWaryn arms. In addition, he chose as his personal crest a swan naiant between ostrich feathers. Beltz believed this derived from the time he attended Thomas of Woodstock, Duke of Gloucester, at the Siege of Nantes. Gloucester himself had inherited the swan emblem from the Bohuns and the Mandevilles, who claimed descent from the mythical 'Chivalier a Cigne'. Sir Ivo's seal features a twin bush springing from a mound in front of which is a shield bearing his coat-of-arms supported by the beaks of two swans.[12] At the base of the brass is a Latin inscription that translates: 'In the grace and mercy of God. Here lies Ivo Fitzwaryn knight who died on the sixth day of the month of September in the year of Our Lord 1414, on whose soul may God have mercy.'

Sir Ivo's Will

Sir Ivo made his will on 6 November 1412.[13] It reveals him to be a compassionate landlord and a pious parishioner. Medieval wills, often dictated to a parish priest, were concerned with both spiritual and material bequests. But he made sure that his executors should concentrate on caring for the poor and feeding his neighbours rather than incurring great expense at his funeral.

His father, William, and his mother, Ann, had predeceased him as had his wife, Matilda, (also called Dame Maud, Molde or Maulde) and his daughter, Alice. He therefore ordered that most of his estates should pass to his eldest daughter, Eleanor.[14] Surprisingly, there is very little of a personal note. He left his sister, Philippa, a nun, his 'best furred gown', which would ensure she was kept warm in her draughty cell in the convent at Wilton. She would, of course, have been in contravention of her vows by wearing such ostentatious apparel and this flaunting of the rules of a religious order often provoked censure.[15] Sir Ivo's son-in-law, John Chideok, of Dorset,[16] who had married Eleanor, acquired his 'best bed with all its appurtenances'.

His more famous son-in-law fared far better. To Richard Whittington, he bequeathed 'one silver gilt chalice with a cover of the same make, and a pair of rosaries of pure gold, enamelled with clear red, with jewels of pure gold, enamelled with white, in the form of the head of St John the Baptist'. Sir Ivo appointed Richard Whittington as his chief executor, for which service he was to receive the handsome fee of one hundred shillings. Whittington forever afterwards remembered his father-in-law in his personal prayers.

Whittington's Investment Choices

Remarkably, Whittington, unlike most Medieval merchants, does not appear to have invested any considerable proportion of his own wealth in acquiring land in the country. His father had died possessed of Pauntley, Gloucestershire, and

Sollershope, Herefordshire. These were inherited first by his eldest son, William, who died without heirs, and then by his brother, Robert, who bequeathed them to his own son, Guy. Whittington, curiously, made no claims on these minor family estates. He did, however, lay claim to another manor, Over Lyppiatt, in Gloucestershire, which he acquired from his unreliable maternal uncle, Philip Maunsell, in lieu of a debt of £500, in 1395.

Uncle Philip also owned property in Berkshire and Oxfordshire that may have been acquired through speculation. It appears he died a pauper and in prison, leaving neither heir nor will. Lypiatt Manor was successfully claimed through litigation by his brother, Robert, and his nephew, Guy, after his demise. There is a suggestion that Whittington made a nuncupative will — one made verbally in the presence of witnesses – in Robert's favour.[17] Inexplicably, these close relatives were hampered in their reasonable claim by Whittington's former apprentice, Thomas Roos. They resorted to the Court of Chancery where they established that the manor was their lawful inheritance, according to the 'right and reason to the intent and will of the said Richard Whittington'.[18]

Barron points out that Whittington at one time also part-owned Sir Ivo Fitzwaryn's manor of Poorstock in Dorset. Whittington is recorded as holding lands at Melbury Osmond, Fifehead Neville, Blackland, Ramsbury and Mappowder. Possibly, these formed part of that depressingly named estate of Poorstock held as security on a loan to his father-in-law for a short period until a debt was fully repaid.

Evidently, Whittington did not show any real interest in property outside London. For a time, however, he gained a part share in the manor of Sandhurst in Berkshire and lands at Ulcombe in Kent. He appears to have acquired a temporary interest with fellow citizens and Mercers in scattered properties: the manors of Broxham, near Edenbridge, Kent,[19] North Mimms, Hertfordshire, Grantchester and Barton, Cambridgeshire. He also held lands jointly at Southend, Chichester and Bermondsey. (The latter led down to the River Thames and formed part of the London Bridge House Estate.)

He enjoyed a share in the income from properties in Devon, Dorset and Somerset through his friend John White, the reversion of an estate in Coventry which he shared with Thomas Fauconer and John Shadworth,[20] and he held the fief – an estate of land held on condition of feudal service – of Thorley, Hertfordshire (worth £7 per annum), from Thomas, Duke of Gloucester.[21] Whittington's interest in these lands and properties was mainly transitory, they were often subsequently leased and any related transactions were purely financial. 'They do not indicate,' Barron believes, 'that Whittington's purpose in acquiring them was to build up a substantial country estate.'

Whittington's Mansion

Numerous houses in the City of London have been definitely attributed to the ownership of Richard Whittington. He inhabited for certain a grand mansion in a most desirable location a short distance from the bustling river front. He acquired it shortly before his intended marriage to Alice Fitzwaryn. It was situated half way along the steep College Hill just to the north of his parish church of St Michael Paternoster Royal. Alternative names for College Hill were Royal Street or Tower Royal. ('Royal' derives from the resident wine merchants who originated from La Reole, a region of Bordeaux.) He acquired this property from Sir Baldwin Berford, Kt., on 22 February 1401. (Previously, it had belonged to Sir Nicholas Brembre, who had been Mayor of London in 1377 and 1383-5.) Associated with the conveyance were William Hedyngton, Thomas Fauconer, Thomas Roos and Henry London. These were all his former apprentices who had become successful Mercers. Indeed, Hedyngton was Chaplain to the Mercers' Company.

Whittington's House was perfectly situated for access to the City. St Paul's and Guildhall were within walking distance; it was handy for the markets of Cheapside and Gracechurch Street but most importantly, Lombard Street, where he could make use of the Italian banks to transfer credit across the Channel for his increasing overseas trade. And it was a stone's throw from the commercial quays where he could conveniently entertain important customers arriving by ship. London was then a city proud of its sense of community where loneliness was not yet a social problem, nor was there then much evidence of the segregation of classes and occupations. Whittington, on his daily travels, would have been known to and known by everyone.

This house, after all, would not only serve as a home for himself, his wife and his team of apprentices, but all his mercantile affairs would be conducted either there or in his 'ware-chamber'. It would also be the place where he secured his chest of cash and valuables.[22] Whittington might regularly pay host to his Italian counterparts who would expect to lodge there while business was transacted, amicably and advantageously to both parties.[23] The house doubled on occasions as his official Mayor and Wardens' residence – the Mercers' Company may even have rented part of it – where Whittington might conceivably have entertained royalty. 'It was characteristic of a merchant to be appreciative of food and drink,' declares Thrupp, 'and to have a fine sense of hospitality.' Stow adds that it was the custom at All Saints' festivals in summer for wealthy citizens to light bonfires in the streets and set out tables loaded with food and drink 'whereunto they would invite their neighbours and passengers (passersby) also to sit and be merrie with them in great familiarities, praysing God for his benefites bestowed on them.'

The population density in the City was already compelling merchants to build in a more compact way on smaller sites.[24] This may have been the reason why Whittington chose to purchase an older property which he deemed suitable for his threefold purpose of trading, living and entertaining. He could expand or alter it to suit his own requirements. It is reasonable to assume, granted his phenomenal success in business, that Whittington's house was still far grander than the typical merchants' town houses. This consisted of three storeys with a shop and warehouse, wardrobe or storeroom on the ground floor; a hall, parlour or solar with pantry, larder and buttery on the first floor and bedchambers in the top floor attic. The kitchen, for reasons of hazard, would be situated in the back yard along with extensive stables and entrance to a cellar. Maybe there was even a private chapel. There was at that time little notion of privacy.

Whittington's house must surely have been one of the most impressive private residences in the entire City. After all, this was the place where 'many of the most beautiful cloths and foreign goods must have passed through his hands'.[25] Medieval houses displayed a dearth of furniture, generally restricted to benches, tables and beds, but visitors would have been greatly impressed by the woven tapestries and woollen hangings, which added to the comfort and warmth of the interior. Whitewashed plaster walls were transformed into a blaze of clashing colours – crimson, emerald, blue, purple, orange, yellow and black – from the cushions and drapes, patterned in dots, checks and stripes.

Prominent in the hall, on special occasions, cupboards and sideboards displayed silver cups, ewers, plates and mazers, which sparkled in the light from the wax candles in the wall sconces and heavy chandeliers at night. Everything purposefully proclaimed the owner's status and wealth. Whittington's house would compare favourably to a modern show home.

Despite all these vivid descriptions conjuring up a luxurious residence alive with display, colour, entertainment and merriment, it must be remembered that this particular property was acquired with the attention of it being Whittington's family home. After a short period of marriage, Alice died, leaving him a successful merchant but a desolate widower. Barron pictures Whittington poignantly, living alone in his declining years in this rambling house, which 'with its shops and solars and gardens, extended to La Riole in the west and to Walbrook in the east, to the site of the later Cutlers' Hall in the north and to the church of St Michael Paternoster in the south'. Lacking close relatives but with a few loyal friends, he was 'surrounded by his household of servants and by the many objects of beauty, luxury and value which he had collected during a lifetime of trade'.

When Whittington died, his 'great tenement' was transferred by Thomas Fauconer and Thomas Roos to his executors on 3 January 1423/4. It was then sold, in accordance with the directions in his will, and conveyed to Thomas Wandesford on 4 November 1425. This was the only property that Whittington had owned in the City that did not eventually form part of the endowment of the new College and Almshouse. There was an abortive attempt by the Mercers' Company to acquire the valuable house later in the 15th century but either the price was too high, above £200, or they could not get the exclusive title to the property that they required, as nothing more was heard of the proposal.[26]

Whittington's Cellars

Whittington's House on College Hill was razed in the Great Fire of London. The imposing building which then occupied the site was constructed by

Sir Christopher Wren in 1686. Its rusticated facade incorporates a pair of ornate oval windows over pedimented stone gateways with stout timber doors opening onto a modest paved courtyard.[27] They may have led to the stables of Buckingham House, home of the Second Duke of Buckingham, which stood opposite on College Hill. An entrance between them has a stairway leading down to a warren of brick passages with low, narrow, barrel-vaulted ceilings. The extensive cavern – now an Indian Restaurant but formerly promoted as 'Whittington's Wine Bar' – appears, disappointingly, to date only from the mid-16th century.[28]

Whittington's supposed cellars were inspected by Ian Betts, expert in building materials from the Archaeology Department of the Museum of London. He informs us that the red colour of the bricks, regrettably now whitewashed, confirms that they were made locally in London. Their size and construction – clamp rather than kiln – indicates that they date from the Tudor period. Medieval cellars were generally formed of stone or chalk blocks, according to Betts, whereas brick was not employed universally for domestic buildings, chimneys and cellars until later Tudor, Stuart and most commonly Georgian times.[29]

The Department of Urban Archaeology from the Museum of London carried out an excavation in the yard behind Nos. 19-20 College Hill, immediately to the south of No 21, Whittington's House, in 1981. The archive reports reveal that wall foundations were found which probably belonged to Whittington's Almshouses built in 1426. They were the sandstone, ragstone and chalk walls of a cellar faced with ashlar blocks. Probably the cellars below Whittington's mansion, although already built when he purchased it, were of that very same construction.[30] Moreover, there is a strong possibility, because of its antiquity when it was acquired, that Whittington's house was timber framed and this would account for its complete devastation in the Great Fire.

City Properties

Whittington owned further properties scattered across the City. He began to acquire shops and tenements in three parishes: St Gregory in Castle Baynard in July 1384, lands and tenements in St Michael Bassishaw (Bassinghall) around December 1400, and shops and tenements in St Botolph-without-Billingsgate (date unknown).[31] Evidently, all three sites were included in a deed, now lost, dated 3 August 1402, which conveyed them through his close circle of trusted friends and Mercers to Richard and Alice Whittington.[32] Presumably, the purpose of their acquisition was solely for rental. All the properties subsequently mentioned in Whittington's will had already been acquired before 1402. These formed the nucleus of his London estate. Properties purchased after this date were mainly sold before his death, which explains in some measure the considerable amount of ready cash he left at the disposal of his executors.[33]

He also purchased three properties adjacent to his mansion. John Cok's Cartulary records that Whittington purchased a large tenement with two more annexed to it on the north side, that formerly belonged to the Countess of Oxford, in the Royal.[34] (This property incurred an expensive quit rent, which was recalled after his demise by the Master of St Bartholomew's Hospital.) He also bought a parcel of land from William Weston, a Draper, in 1409 and a tenement known as 'The Tabbard on the Hoop'[35] from Richard Broun, Baker, along with a row of shops adjoining the north side of the church, about 1411. These latter properties were acquired, together with a vacant piece of land donated by the Mayor, Thomas Knoles, Grocer, and the Commonalty of London, with the intention of replacing them with a college and an almshouse.[36]

First, Whittington set about rebuilding his modest parish church...

St Michael Paternoster Royal

Whittington, like all Medieval men, was deeply concerned that his soul should benefit from the prayers of the living to assist it through the 'purging fires of purgatory'. Prayers by the poor, he knew, would be the most efficacious and therefore he began to rebuild his parish church, just south of his place, to which he later attached an almshouse whose inhabitants would pray ceaselessly for the welfare of his soul. The rebuilding of St Michael Paternoster Royal, the internal decoration of which may have glorified the traditional Nine Orders of Angels (most prominent among them the Archangel Michael) is the earliest recorded instance of Whittington's public generosity.

During the 14th century the merchant class had turned the attention of their charitable works towards their parish churches and craft halls. London citizens were now generous to their churches on an unprecedented scale: extensions to the fabric, donations of vestments or relics, establishing chantries where priests could chant masses for their souls and those of their families... Prominent citizens and wealthy merchants could well afford to be remembered in spectacular fashion.

The date that the work commenced on his parish church may be significant – 1409 – for it would appear that around this time his wife died leaving him without an heir.[37] He would have needed to prepare a suitable resting place for both Alice and, eventually, himself. The building of such a fine holy place was an insurance for their welfare in the life to come. Whittington would therefore take a keen interest in its construction and would regularly visit the nearby building site to watch the stone walls rise. Eventually, he hoped to emulate his fellow merchants who would occupy a prominent private pew, often with its own lock and key, in their parish church, where they could look down from their lofty vantage point upon the congregation.[38]

Whittington's original 'Paternosterchirche' actually dated from the late 13th century. Early records relate to the appointment of rectors – the first noted was Hugh le Derby in 1283 – and to the establishment of chantries including those founded by Laurence Duckett in 1290 and Richard Chaucer, an ancestor of Geoffrey Chaucer, in 1349. Its name combines two ancient thoroughfares: Paternoster Lane and Le Ryole. Whittington lived just north of the church on what is presently known as College Hill but in his lifetime this street was called Paternoster Lane after the vendors of 'paternosters' (or rosaries) who worked there. As previously noted, Royal derives from a neighbouring street, Le Ryole, an anglicised form of La Reole, an important wine centre near Bordeaux with which the vintners of the City traded.[39] The church is in fact situated in Vintry Ward – the name derives from 'vintarii', meaning wine importers – that stretched between Dowgate and Queenhithe by the Thames.[40]

Over time, St Michael's had become dilapidated and it was obviously far too small to honour such a distinguished resident in the parish as a former Mayor of London. He had purposely acquired, together with Henry London, his apprentice, and John Chamberleyne, his chaplain, from William Weston, a Draper, and his wife, Johanna, a parcel of land adjoining the modest churchyard on 18 April 1409. These responsible worthies obtained a royal licence on 20 December that year to grant the land to John White, Rector, in perpetuity for the rebuilding of the church, which had become 'small, frail and ruinous'. This grant became effective on 13 April 1411. The rebuilding programme soon began in earnest, continued throughout Whittington's remaining lifetime and was completed by executors after his death.[41]

College of Priests

Wisely, Whittington had given directions for the foundation of a College of Priests to staff his new church. He had thoughtfully purchased suitable land for this extensive building and his executors dutifully applied for permission for the College of St Michael Paternoster Royal from the Archbishop of Canterbury. (Previously, the church had been an archiepiscopal peculiar.) His executors obtained a Charter of Foundation and Regulations from Henry VI on 17 December for the College. It was dedicated to 'St Spirit and St Mary' and placed under the general supervision of the Mercers' Company.

The Master of the College was Rector of the Church. He was responsible for four subordinate secular priests or chaplains charged with the specific duty of praying for the souls of Richard Whittington, his wife, his relatives, his beloved sovereign, Richard II, who had been his special patron and, curiously, the murdered Duke of Gloucester. These chaplains lived in a purpose-built dormitory at the east end of the church beyond the churchyard. Generously, Whittington had ordered the payment of wages for all the staff – Fellows,

Clerks, Conducts and Choristers – which amounted to thirty people. Further, he provided funds for the perpetual maintenance of his restored church.

Among the clerics who held the dual role of Master-cum-Rector were two academics with completely opposing religious views: Reynold Pecock (1431-1444), afterwards Bishop of St Asaph and of Chichester, a Lollard scholar and author who was forced to abjure his beliefs at St Paul's Cross prior to his imprisonment;[42] and Richard Smith (1537-1550 and 1553-1559), 'the greatest pillar of the Roman cause' who was compelled to surrender the Rectory during the reign of Edward VI. He was returned to the living by Mary I but lost all his preferments upon the accession of Elizabeth I. According to an entry in the Wardens' account, it must have been the tradition that the new Master was presented by the Mercers' Company to the Prior and Chapter of Christchurch, Canterbury, at Lambeth: 'Item. Ils demandment allowance pour Botehire vers Lembhith pour le presentacion de Maister Reynolde Pecock: xxd'.[43]

Whittington's College of Priests was dissolved in 1548. The confiscated buildings were sold – plus all the contents but minus any jewels and gold or silver vessels – to Armigale Wade, a clerk of the Privy Council. The property was described at the sale as 'the capital house and site of Whittington College with a porch and entry leading from the highway called The Royal and two chambers above the porch, a small garden abutting on the east end of the entry and a hall, a parlour, and a small garden adjacent to the hall'. Having paid a small fortune for the grant – £92 2s 7d – Wade promptly sold it on at a profit. There were several more owners until the devastated land was acquired by the Skinners' Company after the Great Fire. Today, Skinners' Hall occupies part of the site of Whittington's College. The name, College Hill, is, of course, a remembrance.

After the dissolution of the College, the church reverted to a rectory and its living became a gift of the Dean and Chapter of Canterbury. The Mercers' Company, which had been appointed overseer of the College by its founder, claimed the right of presentation to the mastership even after the Reformation. Their final attempt to make their own choice of Rector was upon the death of Richard Worme in 1636, but they were opposed by the formidable Archbishop Laud and it was his nominee, Luke Proctor, who was appointed to the living of St Michael Paternoster Royal.

Contemporary Views of St Michael's Church

A glimpse of Whittington's Church is gained from a study of the 'Copperplate Map' *c.*1559.

This is believed to have consist of fifteen copper plates, although only three survive, two displayed in the Museum of London and a third, focusing on Old St Paul's Cathedral, at Dessau Art Gallery, Germany. Fortuitously, these three plates are contiguous and cover a north-south section of the City from

Shoreditch to London Bridge and westwards to a little way beyond the River Fleet. There are no known original prints of this first surviving view of London but modern reproductions from the two consecutive reversed plates show a section of the eastern area of the City from Shoreditch in the north to London Bridge in the south.

St Michael Paternoster Royal is readily discernible among the jumble of buildings along 'Wittyn. College' (College Hill) leading to 'Tamys Strete' (Thames Street). The engraver's image shows the church to have an embattled tower surmounted by a large cross, a great arched doorway and a steep pitched tiled roof over a serried row of windows, although whether this was intended to be an exact likeness is debatable.

The 'Copperplate Map' was probably commissioned by Mary I (1553-8), possibly at the instigation of her husband, Philip of Spain. High authority, indeed, would have been necessary for such a costly and painstaking undertaking as surveying the Cities of Westminster and London. Almost certainly, it was engraved and printed in the Netherlands, then under Spanish control.[44]

Modern images are obtained by reverse photography. Precise topographical details are revealed by the cartographer employing primitive surveying equipment in Tudor times. Recognisable buildings number the splendid 'Guilde hall', 'Gray freres', 'ledden hall' – where even the scales are delineated – and Mercers' Hall, which retains its name, 'St Thomas' (of Acon). The map also includes such insignificant features as garden wells, wine barrels, dog kennels, laundry baskets, public gallows, rowing boats, musketry practice and archery butts. There are rivers, wharfs, post mills, city gates and even the royal barge being towed along the Thames. The City churches have been individualised with relevant details – stair turrets, weather vanes and louvred windows – which makes it tempting to assume that these features reflect the true appearance of these ecclesiastical buildings. Whittington's mansion may be depicted among the jumble of domestic dwellings behind the tower of St Michael's Church.[45]

By 1630, St Michael's Church was in need of repair and this was carried out for the grand sum of £120 9s 0d. After all that effort, the beautiful church was destroyed in London's Great Fire. The church was rebuilt between 1685 and 1694 by Edward Strong, Sir Christopher Wren's master mason, but by then the cost had risen astronomically to £7,455 7s 9d. In fact, it was one of the last of the City churches to be reconstructed after the conflagration and it was intended to serve four consolidated benefices: St Michael Paternoster Royal, St Martin Vintry, All Hallows the Great and all Hallows the Less.

The walls were newly constructed of red brick faced with Portland stone dressings but the bell tower was not added until 1713. Towards the end of the Second World War, a VI flying bomb caused the roof to crash and wreck the historic interior. Only the tower and four walls remained standing, but these were left in such a badly scarred condition it was heatedly debated whether it was worth repairing. Fortunately, after much deliberation, Wren's fine church with its elegant three-tiered spire was restored by the Church Commissioners after a petition to Parliament by the City Corporation.

The London Blitz that devastated Whittington's tomb also uncovered the strangest object: a mummified body of a domestic cat concealed behind a cornice in the tower.[46] It had remarkably long legs and retained distinctive brown fur. Attwood asserts: 'There was no doubt in the minds of those workmen who had been sent to repair the church that the cat had been originally in the same tomb as the remains of Dick Whittington.' It was assumed the cat had been placed in the tomb after Whittington was reinterred following the Great Fire of 1666. Perhaps those superstitious workmen were reviving the pagan practice of placing a living sacrifice in the walls of a new building to ensure its protection from the malevolent gods.

The Church Today

St Michael Paternoster Royal is a prominent building facing the aptly named Elbow Lane adjacent to Cannon Street Railway Station. It is an imposing structure with a series of arched windows, watched over by chubby cherubs piercing the white stone south facade. The prominent north and east fronts are faced with brick and the roof is attractively balustraded. The tower, which rivals that of the nearby St James Garlickhithe, is notable for its stone spire designed by Nicholas Hawksmoor. It consists of a three-stage octagonal lantern supported by columns topped with urns and a dome surmounted by a pennant weather vane.

The interior is square, light and spacious. All the panelling, pews and windows are new, but the church does preserve some original features. The wall plaques and monuments have been cleaned, the ironwork has been repainted, the font repositioned and the organ re-sited on the west gallery. The wineglass pulpit. with its hexagonal sounding board, was carved with swags of fruit and flowers by Grinling Gibbons, the reredos and lectern have been returned to their original position after restoration. The magnificent 17th-century brass chandelier which hangs over the centre aisle was rescued from all Hallows the Great.

Chief glory are the modern stained glass windows by John Hayward. Light filters through them to illuminate the interior with a veritable kaleidoscope of colour. The striking east window depicts the church's patron, Saint Michael, the archangel, triumphant after defeating Satan. This is flanked by the gold figure of the Virgin Mary protecting the infant Christ from a red seven-headed dragon and a green-winged Saint Gabriel expelling Adam and Eve from the Garden of Eden. The artist has skillfully drawn all these images from the Book of Revelations.

The westernmost window on the south side, through which the sun streams at midday, depicts the legendary Dick Whittington. Our pantomime hero is shown wearing a long, buttoned coat with a flat cloth cap and a spotted knapsack thrown over his shoulder. Behind him rise the myriad spires and turrets of the Medieval City churches and beneath his feet the streets are famously paved with gold. A blazing vermillion sky incorporates both the heraldry and seal of the Mayor as a reminder of the historical Whittington's very real fame and fortune. Also incorporated are the Mercers' Maiden and Whittington's crest. At his heels strolls a startled tabby cat – tail erect, eyes aglow. Speckled lights from these delightful windows falls playfully over a modern floor plaque which marks the supposed last resting place of the church's founder.[47]

The Church Commissioners made it a condition of their postwar refurbishment of St Michael Paternoster Royal that part of the new church must accommodate a charitable organisation. Thus, in 1968, the restored building was re-hallowed as a place of worship in the presence of Prince Philip, Duke of Edinburgh, who also officially opened the building as the Headquarters of the Missions to Seamen (now renamed 'Missions to Seafarers').[48] This voluntary maritime society associated with the Anglican Church is responsible for the practical and spiritual welfare of sailors of all faiths and nations worldwide. The emblem of the society – the flying angel – appears prominently on banners hanging from the balcony and the altar cloth inside the church.

St Michael Paternoster Royal was made a Guild Church in 1954. Ten years later, however, this status was rescinded and the church was demoted to a chapel in the parish of St James Garlickhythe. An exchange of land to the south of the church resulted in a pleasant open space, complete with modern sculptures and a fountain, created and maintained by the City Corporation, known as 'Whittington Gardens'.

14

Whittington's Final Years

Usury Trials

Even towards the end of his life, Whittington remained diligent in his civic duties, attending half the meetings at the Court of Common Council between 1416 and 1423. (He attended sixty-three out of the sixty-five meetings between 1419 and 20.) Further, he was present for half of the meetings of the Court of Aldermen between 1416 and his death and all but two of its meetings when he was Mayor for that last time in 1419 and 20.[49] Truly, this was committed service.

Just a couple of years before his demise, Whittington was present as one of the judges at the Usury Trials held at the Mayor's Court in London between June and August, 1421. These trials attracted a great deal of interest and they were well attended. Usury, which then meant charging an interest rate above ten per cent, was considered to compromise the City's commercial reputation because it was expressly forbidden by the Church. Two dozen cases were presented – all involved comparatively large loans with high rates of interest – and thirteen defendants were unanimously found guilty and imprisoned.[50] The authorities were determined to give the rogue businessmen a short, sharp, shock. The elderly Whittington, who had just completed his third and final term of office as Mayor, managed with a supreme effort to attend all these prolonged show trials. This presupposes that he was closely involved in the proceedings and condemned the dealings of the avaricious bankers. After all, he had personally proved that it was possible to amass a fortune without charging an usurious rate of interest and resorting to chicanery.[51]

Whittington's Will

Producing a male heir was considered crucial for knightly and gentry families. This would ensure the continuation of family identity with its attendant name, estates and coat-of-arms. Alice predeceased her husband who never remarried and so Whittington was left without a direct heir. The alternative was to fund chantries and commission effigies in churches to perpetuate a family name. Instead, Richard Whittington determined to found numerous public charities and this proved to be a most durable monument.

It was the custom to formulate a will towards the end of one's life.[52] This was perfectly sensible in view of the fact that fortunes might fluctuate, especially among merchants. Exceptions might be made if the testator was terminally ill, anticipating demise or embarking on a military campaign. Whittington, knowing he was dying, summoned his colleagues and confidants to his bedside. In their presence, he made arrangements for the settlement of his debts, the disposal of his wealth and the fine details for the establishments of his charities. His will was largely impersonal, making bequests to the standard charities, and it was 'designed to control his executors but not trammel them'.[53]

Richard Whittington, Alderman and Citizen of London, made his will on 5 September 1421. This was proved on 8 March 1423 and enrolled in the Court of Hustings.[54] After commending his soul to Almighty God and the Blessed Virgin Mary and All Saints, he willed that his body be interred on the north side of the high altar of his own church, St Michael Paternoster Royal. He left a generous amount for his funeral expenses – one hundred pounds[55] – and for the recitation every evening after his death for the duration of one month a requiem mass to pray for the souls of himself, his wife, his parents and relatives. For this he left 6s 8d to the chaplains; 40 shillings to the clerk (named Thomas), 40 shillings to the late recorder (also called Thomas), plus 100 shillings to be distributed among poor parishioners. And on the day of his funeral he directed that every poor man, woman and child should receive one penny each from his executors. It was a common custom for coins to be give away at the graveside.[56]

He named his executors as John Carpenter, John Coventre, William Grove and John White with Sir William Babyngton acting as their supervisor. Babyngton was Chief Justice of the Common bench who was made a Knight of the Bath upon the coronation of Henry VI.[57] He had selected these men with much deliberation and care. Imray affirms that 'Whittington could not have chosen four men whose combined knowledge and experience were better suited to the task they had to perform'. They were, after all, to be invested with liberal discretionary powers by their phenomenally rich and influential testator.

John Carpenter (*c.*1372-1442) was the highest ranking legal expert that Whittington could possibly have engaged in his services. Whittington held him in the highest regard. Carpenter ('Carpinter' or 'Carpynter') was born in Hereford about 1372 although he was not Christened in the Cathedral until 1378. He prospered in London and he served as 'common Clearke to the Citty'[58] from 1417 until 1438. He would have been appointed by the Common Council and paid a salary of ten pounds per annum. He is remembered as the author of 'Liber Albus', the 'White Book', regarded as the first book of English Common

Law. The purpose of the volume, stated clearly in the prologue, was to record the written and unwritten customs of the City of London. He began the work during the third mayoralty of Whittington and, indeed, it may have been written at his instigation. He was twice a Member of Parliament for London in 1436 and 1439. Carpenter obtained a letter patent from Henry VI (3 December 1418) exempting him 'for the whole of his life from all military and civil duties' and also absolving him from receiving the onerous honour of knighthood. Precisely what service he rendered to the Crown is unknown...

He is recognised as the founder of the City of London School for Boys. Stow records his bequest: 'He gave tenements to the Citye for the finding and bringing up of foure poore men's children with meate, drinke, apparell, learning at the schools in the universities, &c., until they be preferred, and then others in their place fore ever.' 'Carpenter's Children' were required to assist at divine service on festive days in the choir of the Guildhall chapel.

An Act of Parliament in 1834 permitted the combining of several accounts to establish the City of London Boys' School, which moved to the east end of John Carpenter Street and Queen Victoria Street in 1986. His statue, which shows him holding his famous law book, stands prominently on a plinth high up on the wall of the atrium attached to the Great Hall of the present City of London School situated on the riverside opposite the 'wobbly' Millenium Bridge.

Carpenter's intense legal training, involving a familiarity with the interpretation of complicated documents written in Latin coupled with his administrative professionalism, brought him high renown. It was common for family lawyers to act as executors for prominent merchants and often this service was reciprocal. He penned a humorous description of Henry IV's entry into the City of London in February 1432, which he signed under his pseudonym, 'Woodwright'. Carpenter became fabulously wealthy by his services and lived in luxury. He owned over 300 tenements and his own house boasted an unusual feature, a state-of-the-art fish pond that doubled as a reservoir, on its roof. Apparently, he bequeathed a great part of these lands and tenements to the City, although his will is now lost. When he died in about 1441, he was buried in St Peter upon Cornhill[59] and later, his Dutch wife Katherine was laid to rest alongside her illustrious husband.[60] Wisely, Whittington appointed him his Chief Executor.

John Coventre, as Mercer, Alderman and former Sheriff, would prove invaluable as an intermediary between the Mercers' Company and the City Corporation. (He was Master of the Mercers in 1417 and 1423; Sheriff in 1416/7 and Mayor in 1425/6.)

John White was a loyal and trusted friend. First Rector of St Michael Paternoster Royal, he had surrendered this lucrative living to take up the appointment as Master of St Bartholomew's Hospital in 1417. This indicates his total commitment to the task and genuine concern for the care of the sick and infirm of the City. White resigned from this eminent office to concentrate on his deceased friend's charitable affairs on 18 February 1422/3. He moved into

Whittington's house with the intention of remaining there until it was sold and for his loyalty he was rewarded with a bequest of one hundred shillings. He did not live long enough to enjoy this deserved windfall, however, because he died soon afterwards in January 1423/4.

William Grove, described as 'scrivener' (a clerk or scribe) could be relied upon to make an accurate copy of all their transactions.

These trusted executors were responsible for the distribution of a fabulous amount of money from Whittington's estate among numerous deserving causes in London and the country. Recipients who benefitted from his bounty encompassed the whole spectrum of Medieval charity recipients: paupers, patients, prisoners, parishioners and priests. There were bequests to London churches, hospitals, prisons, libraries and religious foundations. His only secular concerns, important for a merchant, were for the repair of highways and a road bridge.

Although many of these bequests were merely temporary, the executors ensured that the majority of Whittington's estate was disposed 'in works of charity for the good of his soul'. Indeed, almost half of the thirty bequests listed in his will state a condition that the beneficiary should pray constantly for himself, his wife and his ancestors long after his demise. Medieval piety was structured around the belief in purgatory, described by Eamon Duffy as 'the defining doctrine of late medieval Catholicism'.[61] And the most powerful release from purgatory was, according to the Roman Catholic church, the number of masses offered for the souls of the departed. Whittington ensured that several religious foundations would receive ample donations specifically for that purpose, which would not only fund their adornment and repair but ensure the speedy transition of his soul through purgatory into Heaven.

Five City churches were main beneficiaries. They were all parish rather than private churches. All Hallows in Honey Lane, where the beekeepers worked busily to make wax candles for churches, received 40 shillings, St Margaret Lothbury, where the coppersmiths cast candlesticks, 100 shillings. (A former priest of the latter may have been a personal friend because this additional award was 'to pray for the soul of Roger the sometime rector there'.) St Pancras in Soper (or 'Shopkeeper's) Lane – created in the 13th century as a short cut through the Mercery – was where a multitude of small shops lined the narrow street, although it was regarded as a poor parish and so it was left 53s 4d. St Mary Staining in Staining Lane and St Alphege by London Wall each received 40 shillings. Most of these churches were destroyed in the 'dismale fire'. St Margaret Lothbury alone survives, having been rebuilt between 1683 and 1692 to Wren's design. Distinguished by its white stone tower with its projecting clock and needle spire, this imposing church stands in the shadow of the Bank of England. The interior is irregular, oppressive and crowded with exquisitely carved woodwork rescued from other churches.[62]

Impoverished parishioners were liberally provided for: 40 shillings were allocated to the poor and needy of St Stephen in Coleman Street and the same amount to those of St Michael Bassishaw in Bassinghall Street, while half that amount was to be shared among the deprived parishioners of St Alphege living under the shelter of London Wall.

There was a general bequest of forty shillings to be distributed at his executors' discretion among several of the orders of monks in the City. There was the unimpressive sum of 8d for the stipendiary chaplains in London and the country. Ten pounds were to be set aside for the care of the residents of three hospitals, St Mary without Bishopsgate, St Mary of Bethlehem and St Thomas of Southwark,[63] and two leper colonies, St Luke Hackney and St G (indeciphera ble)-without-Holborn.[64] The inmates of the Hospital of St Bartholomew in West Smithfield fared even better: they received 100 shillings.

Abundant funds were available to be shared among the country's religious houses. The Augustinian canons who ministered to the blind residents of the Priory Hospital of St Mary within Cripplegate were to receive 20 shillings.[65] The nuns of Cheshunt and Rowney, near Ware, Hertfordshire, and Broomhall Priory near Windsor, Berkshire, were awarded 40 shillings, but the nuns of Burnham, Buckinghamshire, were bequeathed 100 shillings. One hundred shillings was also willed to the Carthusian Monastery, known as 'Charterhouse', beyond Smithfield.

By far the greatest monetary bequests in Whittington's will related to prisons. He left instructions for his executors to distribute forty shillings each week among the destitute prisoners of Newgate, Ludgate, Fleet and Marshalsea Prisons and those of the King's Bench until the enormous fund of five hundred pounds had expired. 'Concern for prisoners incarcerated for debt was fairly common among merchants who were only too aware how fortunes could fluctuate,' notes Imray. For this reason, one of the executors, John Coventre, also bequeathed money to assist debtors languishing in gaols.

There was a touching gift of one hundred pounds to be divided among new brides of his parish (in the spirit of modern pantomime) and another one hundred pounds was allocated for the repair of roads (although this was not nearly enough for them to be paved with gold). Whittington's will demonstrates that in Medieval times pastoral care was provided by both the living and the dead.

Whittington had ensured that there were funds aplenty for his generous bequests. In addition to hard cash there were those 'buy to let' properties with adjoining lands and tenements in the parishes of St Andrew by the Wardrobe, St Michael Bassinghall and St Botolph Bishopsgate, plus his own mansion and adjacent tenements in the parish of St Michael Paternoster Royal available for disposal. John White, however, moved into Whittington's own house so that he could supervise the construction of the Hospital and Almshouse, projects which were closest to Whittington's heart.

Whittington directed that after paying his debts and honouring his legacies, all further assets should be turned into cash and disposed of in charitable works to please God and for the benefit of his soul. He emphasised that no executor should act alone but any decision regarding future bequests ought to be taken when at least three out of the four men were present – and one of these must always be John Carpenter. Wisely, he insisted that a stout chest with three locks should contain his bounty and that each of his executors hold only one key. Thus he ensured that nothing might be removed from it without the presence and consent of his executors. At the end of this rambling legal document Whittington gave his approval by affixing his familiar personal seal. This featured a raised profile of a young man on a rectangular panel. It was inscribed 'RICARDI WHITYNGTON' and at the top centre appeared a fleur-de-lis with the letter S which stood for 'Signillum' (seal).

A Collar of Esses

Curiously, there is no mention of any relatives in the will. Richard's elder brother, Robert, was already in possession of the family estates and his nephew, Guy, would in time automatically succeed to them. Intriguingly, Lysons, apparently drawing on private information, asserts that Whittington had already made a handsome presentation to his brother. This was a Lancastrian collar of interlinked metal esses (SS). which would indicate that Whittington was in the service of, and stood in high favour with, Henry IV and Henry V. 'Robert Lord of Pauntley and his heires a Collour of SS, three dosn, of Sylver Cupps with Covers: the on dos. gilt, the other pcell gilt, the third whyte. Three basons and Ewres, 3 nests of Bowles, three flagons and three Lyverye potts all of the same sorte'. The presentation of collars as a mark of extreme favour had begun at the court of France and was adopted by the English aristocracy. The Victorian biographer makes the observation that, since these keepsakes comprised his badge of office and service of plate, they can only have been handed over towards the end of his life.[66]

Caroline Barron draws several intriguing inferences from this mysterious collar of esses. She rehearses a complex story about a collar which Whittington had at one time in his possession. On 12 June 1400, Whittington lent £666 13s 4d for expenses to the Royal Household and in return he received a number of jewels as security. By March 1402, the money had not been repaid but Whittington returned these jewels and instead received an assignment on wool subsidy in London, for which he was already Collector. Meanwhile, Whittington had mislaid an SS collar which he was duty bound to return to the King. Embarrassed, he was obliged to pay £8, which represented its intrinsic value, to the Exchequer in May 1402. It is tempting to conjecture that this was the very same collar that had found its way into the possession of his brother, Robert.

A tremendous number of laudable works for which Whittington is remembered were undertaken by his executors in accordance with his privately expressed wishes. They were responsible, under residuary clauses of the will for the founding of the College of Priests and the Almshouse, the rebuilding of Newgate gaol, the building of the South Gate of St Bartholomew's Hospital and the furnishing of the Libraries of Greyfriars and Guildhall. Beyond the City of London there were further donations to the renovation of the Bridge Chapel at Rochester in Kent and possibly the restoration of Gloucester Cathedral.

Richard Grafton wrote a puzzling note in his 'Chronicle' (1569) in which he stated that he had seen an addendum to the will, perhaps a witnessed codicil, in Whittington's own hand. The note, naturally, has not survived but he meticulously records its content:

> ... besyde many other (charitable deeds) I will shewe unto you one very notable, which I receyved credibly by a writing of his awne hande, which also he willed to be fixed as a schedule to his last will and testament, the contentes whereof was that he willed and commaunded his executors as they would aunswere before God at the day of the resurrection of all fleshe, that if they founded any debtor of his that ought to him any money, that if he were not in their consciences well worth three tymes as much, and also out of the debt of other men, and well able to pay, that then they should put no man in sute for any debt due to him.

Whittington's will is a conventional legal document, 'cold and formal'.[67] There is an absence of formal bequests and, apart from Roger, the elusive parish priest, only the four executors of the will and the overseer are named individually. There is no mention of family, friends, relatives, a loyal apprentice or a member of his household, with a personal testimony to affection or care. (Provision, however, was made for the sustenance of his household for a year after his death.)

Later chroniclers John Stow and Richard Grafton applauded the generosity of London's thrice Mayor and ensured that he was remembered and celebrated by future generations. 'This worshipful man so bestowed his goodes and substuance to the honor of God, to the reliefe of the pore and the benefite of the common weal,' wrote Grafton, 'that he hath right well deserved to be registered in the boke of fame.' And after enumerating Whittington's benefactions, they concluded: 'Look upon this ye aldermen, for it is a glorious glass.'[68]

Deathbed Scene

An illumination from the English Translation of the 'Ordinances of Whittington's Charity', probably made for the Mercers' Company when they took over the administration of the Almshouse in 1442, portrays a pathetic scene of Richard

Whittington on his deathbed.[69] It is, in fact, a fine pen drawing (the ink has turned brown with age) delicately tinted, probably executed by the celebrated London 'lymner', William Abell.[70] His distinctive style is reflected in the angular modelling of the faces, with a clear preference for three-quarter profiles, and the finely modelled eyes, with white catchments next to dark, unmodelled irises.[71]

Whittington lies naked, apart from his nightcap, lean, consumed and emaciated. His face is long, thin, grey and clean-shaven. He is propped up on a pillow placed over a bolster in a testor bedstead.[72] The striped curtains hanging from the fringed canopy are drawn aside to allow his close companions to attend him and take careful note of his final wishes. The richness of the chamber – it would have been on an upper floor – is emphasised by the elaborate furnishings consisting of floral tapestries on the walls, diagonal patterned terracotta floor tiles and a woollen bedspread with an embroidered border covering the thick feather mattress. These are all the trappings of a wealthy Medieval merchant.

Whittington points to his diminishing pulse. This adds poignancy to the scene where he has urgently summoned his four executors to his bedside. They are identified by their names written vertically on their costume in the illustration: John Carpenter, John Coventre, John White and William Grove. Carpenter, Town Clerk of London, is pictured standing on the near side of the bed appearing to address the assembled company of loyal and intimate friends.[73] He is depicted as small of stature, which bears out his soubriquet, 'Jenkin' or 'Jenken' ('Little John'). His legal training and experience meant that he was much in demand as an executor and he provided this service for at least three acquaintances. He drew up wills for John Marchaunt (his predecessor as Town Clerk) in 1421, William Est, citizen of London, in 1421 and Hugh Kynder, citizen and tailor, in 1441. Carpenter was one of the first Town Clerks to regularly employ English in his composition of official documents.

Carpenter, it will be remembered, was later instrumental in obtaining a charter from Henry VI, confirming an earlier grant of Richard II, whereby London's Mercers were created a brotherhood, which ensured that its members were suitably protected should they suffer misfortune while trading at sea. The effect of this charter was to make the ancient 'misterie' a corporate body with certain legal rights and a common seal. Subsequently, Carpenter was invited to become an honorary member of this new corporation and he was thereafter described as 'Mercer'. Moreover, he was twice elected, in 1436 and 1439, as a Member of Parliament to represent the City of London.

Henry VI rewarded Carpenter's long service to the City, which dated from 'the time of his youth', by granting him and his wife, Katherine, a splendid tenement in the parish of St Peter upon Cornhill. Their annual lease was charmingly a single red rose. The site of these premises is now enveloped in Leadenhall Market. The King later exchanged this property for a country manor, 'Theobalds', at Cheshunt, Hertfordshire where the yearly rent was increased to one bow and one barbed arrow! Carpenter outlived all the other executors and when he finally died on 12 May 1442, he was buried near the pulpit in St Peter's Cornhill.

Coventre was Sheriff of London in 1417 and Mayor in 1425. He died on Easter Monday (13 April) 1429 and was buried in St Mary-le-Bow, Cheapside, where a monument was erected to his memory. His executor, Henry Frowyk, a fellow Mercer, established a substantial chantry there under the terms of Coventre's will.[74] In the illustration, he stands at the right-hand side of the bedhead and leans forward to capture every whispered last word of Whittington. John White was the first Rector of the restored church of St Michael Paternoster Royal and he was also appointed Master of St Bartholomew's Hospital in January 1418. He died about 1424. White's name alone is absent, but he is readily identified by his clerical robe and tonsure. Grove is depicted as a man of considerable stature with a long grey beard, his expression grave, his hand raised in assurance of the dying man's wishes. Since the illustration appeared only a couple of decades after his demise, these four figures might be primitive portraits.

All these dignitaries are dressed in garments characteristic of the early 15th century. They each wear the long formal gown with high neck and full sleeves called a 'houppelande'. These were expensive because they were woven in wool, dyed in rich colours and trimmed with fur. Draped over their shoulders are the fashionable variation of the hood known as 'chaperones'. This reveals their hair, cropped short above the ears.[75]

This composite illustration allows for all thirteen bedesmen from Whittington's future almshouse, eventual recipients of this pious man's charities, to pay homage to their patron at the foot of his bed.[76] They, too, wear gowns, but not as full as those of his wealthy executors. These would have been woven from rough, undyed wool. They also wear caped hoods of cheaper material, worn in the traditional manner, over their heads. The most senior bedesmen was known as the Tutor. The first elected Tutor was Robert Chesterfield who is depicted rosy-cheeked but grey-haired and sorrowful. He carries a staff in his left hand and a rosary in his right to indicate his intercessory office.

Whittington's doctor is in the background.[77] Whittington retained a family doctor, Master Sampson, but whether this rosy-cheeked, middle-aged man is intended to be an actual portrait is debatable. He holds a glass phial containing the patient's urine. Great store was set in Medieval times by testing urine and, indeed, a urinal was the accepted symbol of a physician. Doctors examined its colour, smell and taste. Its colour was compared to a graduated chart depicting every hue from white to red, but mainly green. One textbook related twenty different shades of urine to the same number of diseases. Practitioners in later years who professed to diagnose all disorders from samples of their patient's urine were dismissed as 'piss prophets'. Today, doctors will routinely study their patient's urine. A strong smell or a cloudy sample will indicate an infection and, although they are understandably reluctant to taste urine, formerly a sweet taste would have indicated the presence of sugar caused by diabetes. (More sophisticated testing of urine samples will reveal a number of diseases, infections and also pregnancy.)[78] Ominously, Whittington's urine is jet black.

Ultimately, the scene depicted, lacking wife or nurse, is of Whittington's male-dominated world. Inadvertently, it preserves the impression of the complete lack of privacy in a businessman's bedroom. It may even have depicted an actual event, although the purpose of this contemporary illumination which prefaces the Ordinances must surely have been to confirm that Whittington's executors acted on his full authority because he is shown clearly coherent while expounding to them his instructions. Indeed, the approved foundation charter for the Almshouse, penned in Latin, lies before him, rolled along his bed. Further, it is a visual confirmation that, in the absence of relatives, there are a host of reliable witnesses to his verbal requests. Below the illumination, the first initial 'T' of the text is decorated with Whittington's arms but a later English version of the Ordinances, which lacks an illumination, impales these arms with those of Fitzwaryn.[79] The purpose is to emphasise that the Almshouse was a joint venture of Richard and Alice and that its intention was to perpetuate their marital union.[80]

Demise and Burial

Whittington died, having survived wars and pestilence, riots and revolutions, in late March 1423. Surprisingly, his death was not widely chronicled. He is accorded scant notice in the *Brut*: 'Also Richard Whyttyngton, mercer, died, ye xiiij day of Marche: on whos saule Almyghtti God haue mercy! Amen'.[81] The exact date of his death is unknown but the 'Charter of Foundation' for his Hospital directed that the 23rd or 24th day of that month should be the time of the obit to celebrate his life. This same charter also ensured that his wife, Alice, should be remembered on the last, or last day but one, of July, which gives a vital clue about when she died. There was a scale of fees for the celebrants – master 20d, chaplains 12d, clerk 6d, chorister 3d – and of course, sufficient funds were provided by Whittington himself.

Traditionally, throughout Edward VI's reign the Mercers' Company held a memorial feast on the anniversary of his death. Guests dined well.

Paide yerely for the obitte of Master Whittinton, for spicest brede, with the spices, and whyte bunes and butter, with other things thereto appertyning, xlis viiid. For perres, apples, pyskettes, chese, ale, and wyne, and the butteler's fee, with other things, xxviiis viiid. For waxe and ringing of bells, iis. To the poor men for to offer xiiid. To the Lord Maior of London vjs viiid. To the three Wardens of the Mercers, iijli, and to the Rent warden, xls. To the Clark of the Mercer vis viiid. And as for the Prestes and Clarkes, we never paid none – ixli vjs. Ijd.'[82]

Richard Whittington's long and eventful life had touched five reigns – Edward III, Richard II, Henry IV, Henry V and Henry VI – and he had managed to keep in firm favour with three of these sovereigns. He was buried, in the orthodox way, in the church 'where he was parisshene' (meaning St Michael's) '... right there should he be graven.'[83] His elaborate funeral, attended by 'great mourning and much lamentation',[84] was stage-managed by his close friend, John Carpenter, who was a stickler for legality. Such 15th-century funerals were grand and expensive affairs that invariably took place at night.[85] They involved organising torchlight processions, displaying shields of arms, providing mourning gowns and hiring a horse-drawn hearse in addition to ensuring lavish victuals for guests afterwards.[86] It was also customary for the passing bell to be rung once for every year the departed soul had spent on earth, although, in Whittington's case, his age appears to have remained a mystery to everyone. A Requiem Mass followed a prescribed pattern, but for City dignitaries there would have been additional prayers, hymns, psalms and litanies, some of which are recognised as being among the most beautiful compositions in Medieval literature.

Whittington's interment would have been a dignified affair, correctly observed, attended by the Mayor, Sheriffs and Aldermen, the Master and almsmen from his College, and leading members of the Mercers' Company.[87] Liverymen were expected to carry the coffin, solemnly draped in a richly embroidered funeral pall,[88] for this would have been the last service they could render to their deceased fellow. He would have been wrapped in a luxurious shroud, which since he had been a wool merchant may have consisted of layers of sheep pelts, and laid in a costly coffin. He was buried alongside his wife in accordance with his will in a 'goodly plain tomb in the chancel, with new banners to adorn it, very lately hung up',[89] which would have been ablaze with 'corpse candles' on the south side of the altar of St Michael Paternoster Royal. His friends and colleagues would gather around this tomb each year on the anniversary of his death to remember him in the tradition of the earliest Christians.

Epitaph

Strype preserves the inscription in Latin[90] incised on the base of Whittington's fine marble tomb, bedecked with banners, that lay to the north of the chancel of the original church.[91] Lysons offers this translation:

Sweet as the spikenard's odours rise
In fragrant columns to the skies,
So sweet and fragrantly we see
Ascend this Richard's memory.
He loved that City to adorn
Whose dignities he'd noble worn:
A model merchant prince was he,

Of high souled liberality.
Full much may his example teach.
Minding the Scriptures' high command,
All sordid selfishness he spurned;
Spent fortunes gen'rously to raise
St Michael's Church for prayer and praise.
One bitter day of March cut down
This true supporter of the crown,
This City's Mayor, the poor man's stay,
Was snatched from earth in one short day.
His family his earthly years shall count,
His soul to God's high host above shall mount.
Richard, on all, they bounties thou dids't pour,
Christ be thy spirit's rest for evermore.
Amen.

From this epitaph it would appear that Whittington's illness was sudden and of a short duration.[92] Probably, he succumbed to the extreme cold weather and may have died of hypothermia or he may have caught the severe form of influenza that was prevalent during the bitter winters and springs of that decade.[93] There is another less plausible suggestion that because of his active concern for prisoners, as expressed in his will, he contacted gaol fever. A later Lord Mayor, Sir Samuel Pennant, who is buried nearby, died after contracting gaol fever from prisoners in the dock. Another inference is that the executors, who were also his colleagues and companions, had no idea of his true age when they commissioned his monument.[94] His pampered life perhaps guaranteed longevity, although his actual age remains an enigma.

Sadly, Whittington did not rest in peace. Stow also presents the extraordinary story of how he was thrice buried:

...first by his Executors under a fayre monument; then, in the raigne of Edward VI, the Parson of the Churche, thinking some great riches, as he said, to bee buried with him, caused his monument to bee broken, his body to be spoyled of his Leaden sheet, and againe the second time to bee buried; and in the raigne of Queen Mary the parishioners were forced to take him up, to lap in lead, as afore, to bury him the thirde time, and to place his monument, or the like over him again, which remayneth and so hee resteth.[95]

The avaricious priest mentioned was Thomas Mountague. After rifling the tomb, he was so disappointed by its lack of valuable contents that he purloined the lead sheets in which the body had been lapped. Mountague was a staunch Protestant who boldly continued to read the service from the Prayer Book of Edward VI in defiance of Catholic Mary. He penned his 'Autobiography' which declares his abhorrence of her new religious regime while Rector of 'Sent Myhells in the Towere ryall'.[96]

The third burial was witnessed by Henry Machyn, a Merchant Taylor, described in his 'Chronicle'. Machyn betrays a deep fascination with burials in his writings, which leads scholars to think that he was, in fact, an undertaker: '1557: the VX day of July was nuw coffend again and ... master Wyttyntun and my lade ys wyff at Wyttyntun colege, and had durge over nyght, and the morrow masse, the wyche was the founder of the same colege, and beldyd Nugatt and other places, and was mere of London'.[97]

The Mercers' Company were involved in the regular repair of the elaborate tomb and its banners although, unfortunately, they were completely destroyed in London's Great Fire. Leverich Forster, the Mercers' Clerk between 1541 and 1567, had the forethought to copy the epitaph onto a flyleaf of the Company's first register of benefactors' wills. He indicated that the verse was engraved in brass although he offers a slightly different version from Strype's.[98]

The devastation caused by a flying bomb during the final years of the Second World War which wrecked the church interior[99] allowed an opportunity to investigate the vaults nearest the chancel. This was the probable site of Whittington's tomb but, alas, no trace was discovered of his illustrious remains when the site was excavated in the immediate postwar period.[100] Devastation was absolute. None of the human remains could be identified and so they were ingloriously cemented in a common grave underneath the concrete floor.[101] Only gullible folk will believe that the mummified cat discovered in the roof, displayed in a glass case inside the church, was actually Mayor Whittington's beloved companion.

Whittington's combined estate at the time of his death was valued at between £6,500 and £7,000, which makes him the equivalent today of a multi multi-millionaire. And since his wife had predeceased him and left him without an heir, Whittington was free to leave his money and properties to benefit charitable institutions. He left firm instructions with his executors, who were all loyal companions, as to how they were to dispose of his unimaginable wealth.[102] After their own demise, this fortune was to pass into the hands of his own Company, the first and foremost of London's liveried guilds, the Mercers.[103] Thus, his executors and his Company combined to ensure that his expressed wishes were carried out to the letter for the welfare of the wider community.

Obituary

Twelve years after his demise, by which time his munificent bequests had already made their mark on the City of London, an anonymous versifier penned this glowing tribute:

And in worship now I think on the sun
Of merchandy, Richard Whittington,

That lode star and chief chosen flower.
What hath by him our England of honour,
And what profit hath been of his riches,
And yet lasteth daily in worthiness,
That men and paper may not me suffice
Him to describe, so high he was of price,
Above merchants to set him on the best!
I can no more, but God have him in rest.[104]

Richard Whittington, the son of a disgraced knight from Gloucestershire, had removed to London as a youth to seek his fame and fortune as an apprentice Mercer. Through his industry, tenacity and adaptability, he had become a successful businessman securing the custom of the prominent noblemen of Medieval England. He had attracted the custom of three related but contrasting Plantagenet Kings who had all become in some measure his friend and companion. He had been elected Warden of his own Mercers' Company three times and risen from Alderman, to Sheriff, and eventually four times Mayor of London. He had made his home in the City and was generally respected – even feared – by high-ranking Londoners who he had served in civic government over four decades. He had suffered private tragedies – his friends had been killed, his two wealthiest patrons murdered and his young wife had died prematurely – yet he persevered and survived to leave his amassed fortune for the benefit of his beloved City, where he is remembered even to the present day.

BENEFACTIONS

15

Benefactions to the City of London

DURING HIS LONG London career, Whittington – 'through political upheaval, dynastic change, foreign war and internal rebellion'[1] – accumulated a considerable fortune. He amassed a veritable 'cascade of money'[2] by investing in three distinct spheres: as a Mercer, a royal financier and a wool exporter. Unlike his fellow merchants, he declined to invest heavily in land or property although he also resisted the temptation simply to hoard his money. Wisely, he kept it 'on the move'.

Traditionally, Whittington has been hailed as one of London's wealthiest citizens. Imray assess that he amassed a fortune of between £6,500 and £7,000.[3] A small part of this estimated figure consisted of property in the City of London, including his 'great tenement' in The Royal,[4] but the remainder took the form of liquid assets in cash, bonds, plate, furniture, jewels[5] and cloth. Although, perhaps, he was not as rich as the legend suggests – a number of his contemporaries appear to have enjoyed far greater wealth – he was, nevertheless, a fabulously wealthy Medieval merchant.

The purpose of a Mercer acquiring a great mercantile fortune was, first and foremost, to benefit himself and his family and to ensure that a son would become, at least, a country squire or knight to continue the family name for generations.[6] Traditionally, a citizen was obliged to leave his wife a third of his movable property, another third being divided among his children and the remainder being invested for the good of his soul.[7] Whittington's wife, Alice, who was childless, had predeceased her father. Consequently, Sir Ivo Fitzwaryn's extensive estates passed into the hands of his second daughter, Alianor, and not, as might be expected, into the Whittington family by marriage. As a widower late in life, spurning a vast estate in the country, Richard Whittington turned his attention to establishing charities and benefactions which, in the absence of an heir, would ensure his everlasting fame in the place that he regarded as his home: the City of London.

Whittington, in his lifetime, had been his own almoner. His Ordinances, prepared perhaps by Carpenter or Pecock, proclaim that 'while he lived (he) had right lyberalle and large handes to ye nedy'. He organised a hostel for unmarried mothers and instigated the first public lavatory in the City. He instructed his executors to rebuild Newgate Gaol, not out of concern for increased security but for compassion towards its prisoners, and to construct a gatehouse at St Bartholomew's Hospital, where his friend, John White, was Master. He demonstrated empathy with educationalists by funding libraries at Greyfriars' Monastery and London's Guildhall.

Towards the end of his life, he made detailed arrangements for greater, grander projects – the foundation of a College of Priests and an Almshouse adjacent to the magnificent church, rebuilt under his direct supervision, St Michael Paternoster Royal. True, he made a number of conventional bequests – for the repair of roads, the relief of the poor and dowries for virgins – but all his instructions to his executors, practical or religious, were of immediate benefit to the wide community. These conspicuous signs of his great benevolence, which enhanced his reputation as a humanitarian, were familiar to all Londoners until they were swept away by the Great Fire of 1666.

Whittington realised that according to fundamental religious doctrines, he was accepting temporary stewardship of his fortune. He accepted it as a sacred trust from God. He complied wholeheartedly with church teaching on charity and responded with generosity of spirit. He obeyed Christ's commands by providing food and drink for the hungry and thirsty, clothes for the naked, comfort for the prisoner, shelter for the homeless and hospitality to the traveller. Richard Whittington was actively involved in all these humane concerns because he profoundly believed that charitable works were his passport to Heaven.[8]

This was the reason why his executors, who were his close confidants, complied with all his instructions and carried out his works with commendable speed.

Municipal Relief

London streets abounded with filth – butcher's offal, horse dung, kitchen refuse, trade waste, open sewers and human excrement – so that the daily spoil blocked narrow channels that ran down both sides of the City thoroughfares. Some pigs were allowed to snuffle around freely at night by law[9] and the killing of carrion eaters, kites and ravens, was strictly forbidden since they were natural consumers of City rubbish.

The stench in hot weather was so appalling that rich folk hung bunches of herbs inside their houses and held perfumed pomanders to their noses whenever they set foot outside their own homes. Visitors wearing fine clothes were advised to walk under the jetties of buildings as they passed through the streets. This offered a modicum of shelter from residents emptying the contents of their chamber pots from upstairs windows with the warning cry: 'Gardy loo!'

Gradually, public latrines were introduced into every City Ward. These might be emptied into the City ditch (Ludgate) or into the Walbrook (Moorgate) but common privies were generally drained into the River Thames. In 1419, Richard Whittington provided at his own expense a grand 'House of Easement'. Located at the south end of Friar or Greenwich Lane, it was intended to serve Vintry Ward, where he resided.

His privy took the form of a short pier which, perhaps intentionally, carried offensive smells away from the river bank. There was no privacy for the public who used it, however, for it boasted a double row of seats, sixty for men, the same for women. These seats overhung a long gully that discharged into the River Thames more or less purged twice daily by the tide. Above this handy facility, five rooms or apartments were constructed for the poor of the parish of St Martin Vintry.[10]

Unfortunately, both privy and almshouse were obliterated by the Great Fire. Afterwards, the site was tentatively staked out for reconstruction, but in 1690 irate parishioners reminded the City Corporation of their benefactor's generosity in providing this public amenity.[11] Grudgingly, the Corporation responded by allocating one hundred marks for rebuilding 'Whittington's Longhouse'.[12] But the citizens were caught short of their target since this relatively small grant could only extend to providing seating capacity for six men and women – and without those 'des. res.' almshouse rooms situated above.

Whittington's 'Longhouse', which was sited at the northern end of the present Southwark Bridge, is now occupied by the offices of the Corporation of London's Public Cleansing Department.

Water

London's water supply was a major achievement of the Medieval age. The City's increasing population became too great for the brooks and streams, springs and wells located within or without its walls to suffice. Rivers that might have been an obvious source were often choked with refuse and became dangerously polluted.[13]

Public-spirited merchants generously often paid for conduits, which enabled ordinary folk to obtain a ready supply of fresh water for drinking and cooking. They arranged for water to be channeled through hollowed elm[14] or lead pipes from springs in the surrounding countryside. In this manner, fresh water was obtained from Tyburn Springs[15] and relayed to an open conduit 'castellated with stone and cisterned in lead' at Cheapside in about 1237. In fact, a pair of conduits – the 'Great Conduit' and the 'Little Conduit' – were eventually located at opposite ends of the Cheap.

This innovative municipal water system was selfishly requisitioned frequently for industry – the Brewers, Dyers and Fishmongers made heavy demands on it – to the detriment of ordinary citizens. There was insufficient supply to allow subsidiary piping to individual houses.[16] Private supplies through narrow pipes called 'quills' were permitted only to prominent citizens for a high fee, but access to the public conduits remained free to anyone but traders.[17] Water carriers who regularly delivered water to homes were another option, but their services were expensive.[18] Alternatively, Londoner's water supply was still available from trapped rainwater, springs or pools.[19]

Close by the churchyard of St Giles-without-Cripplegate[20] was a large pool in which a young maiden, Anne of Lodburie, had tragically drowned in 1244. This pool had been partially drained as a precaution against further accidents, but the spring which supplied it was preserved. Whittington's executors, mindful of health and safety, encased the spring with hard stone and added steps, allowing access to it from the banks of the town ditch.[21] This ditch, which was excavated by the Romans, stretched from the Tower of London to the River Fleet, and according to Stow it was called 'Houndsditch' ('Hondesdich' or 'Hundsditch') because it was contaminated by 'dead Dogges' whose carcasses were discarded there by indifferent citizens. The City kennels, which housed hounds for hunting, were nearby.[22]

Whittington, when he was alive, had already improved access to this ready supply of fresh water in the City. He installed a 'bosse' (or tap) in the churchyard wall of St Giles' 'Creplesgate'. His charitable act enabled poor folk to obtain free, accessible, unpolluted drinking water. Effectively, this was an early public drinking fountain. Stow asserts that Whittington's executors additionally installed a 'Bosse of spring water continually running' in the appropriately named Bosse Alley, north of the Church of St Botolph, Billingsgate.

Refuge

According to William Gregory, a member of the Skinners' Company who was later Mayor of London,[23] Whittington' founded a hostel or 'chamber' at Thomas Spital. It was furnished with 'viij beddys for yong weme(n) that hadde done a-mysse' and this 'ospytalyte' was provided 'in truste of a good mendement'. Whittington, with great sensitivity, stipulated that 'alle the thyngs that ben don in that chambyr shulde be kepte secrete ... for he wolde not shame no yonge women in noo wyse, fro hyt myght be cause of hyr lettying of hyr maryage'.[24] Whittington was far ahead of his time in providing this Medieval maternity ward; a secret, safe and secure refuge for unmarried mothers. Certainly, his discretion was exemplary. Mayor Gregory considered the location of Whittington's innovative single parent wing to be in Southwark.

Greyfriars' Library

A small band of Franciscans or 'Greyfriars' arrived in London in 1224. At first, they lodged in a house on Cornhill belonging to John Travers, Sheriff of London.[25] The following summer they were presented with a parcel of land by John Twyn, Mercer, close to the City abattoir in the Shambles, just within Newgate. These mendicant friars built for themselves a modest church, which was demolished in 1306 and replaced with a new one in 1325.

The number of these penniless preaching friars steadily rose and they soon gained the respect of most citizens. 'Their austerity, their poverty, their earnestness, their eloquence, drew all hearts to them,' trilled Walter Besant.[26] Indeed, nobility, and even royalty, heartened by their lack of worldliness, soon showered costly gifts upon the friars. After the Black Death, when they were bequeathed a vast amount of property, they became one of the richest landlords in the City.[27]

Their splendid church boasted three dozen glazed windows, stout roof timbers, marble columns and pavements. Ironically, the church that the friars built alongside their austere Monastery became so magnificent that five English queens were buried there, wrapped in humble woollen shrouds to help secure their swift passage to Heaven. They included Margaret, Edward I's second wife, Isabella, the much-maligned consort of Edward II known as the 'She-Wolf of France', and Philippa, Edward III's devoted consort.[28] These elaborate royal tombs became part of the attraction of the church.[29]

Richard Whittington, impressed by Greyfriars' teaching, established a library there at his own expense and furnished it with £400 worth of books.[30] These books, of course, would have been in manuscript form. They were chained to their shelves. This shows a great enlightenment on his part since Mercers tended to class books, which were mainly imported, as 'tryfylles', even as late as the 16th century.[31] The number of books that merchants owned was actually meagre, although it is probable that the range of reading among them was increased through borrowing.[32]

Whittington's charity indicates that he was a man of taste, but it does not confirm that he was a man of great learning. It is possible that he could read and write – his apprenticeship as a Mercer would have ensured he was taught basic literacy – but there is no evidence that he owned any books. There are none mentioned in his will not even a Bible or a missal, let alone Chaucer's works or French romances. Caroline Barron points out that 'this lack of interest in intellectual matters does not separate Whittington from the bulk of the merchant class of London'.[33]

Building work for the library began in 1421. Perhaps it is too fanciful to suggest that Whittington laid the foundation stone? When Lysons explored it more than four hundred years later, when the monastic buildings had been converted into Christ's Hospital, he reported that it was in a state of 'tolerable preservation' and formed 'the north side of the great cloister having, in two places, an escutcheon with the arms of Whittington'.[34]

Besant also examined the Library, which had survived until the end of the 19th century: 'It is 129 feet long and 31 feet broad; it was circled with wainscot, had twenty-eight desks and eight double settles of wood.'[35] In these measurements, both scholars were confirming details preciously supplied by Stow. Whittington's Library appears to have escaped the Great Fire of London but what happened to the actual books can only be surmised; probably they had already been dispersed at the Dissolution of the Monasteries.[37]

St Bart's Library

London's oldest surviving church is St Bartholomew the Great in West Smithfield.[38] Annually, a cloth fair was held in its churchyard attended by clothiers from all over England at St Bartholomewtide on 24 August. Originally, the church formed part of an Augustinian Priory founded in 1123 by Rahere, court jester to Henry I.[39] King Henry, a son of William the Conqueror, was devastated by the news that his only legitimate son and heir, William, had drowned when the 'White Ship' sank during a winter storm in the English Channel in 1120. The court went into mourning and all mirth ceased.

Rahere, whose joviality was now out of place in the royal household, went on a pilgrimage to Italy. There he contracted malaria. He was nursed by brothers of St John of God at the Hospital of St Giovanni di Dio, whose church purported to contain relics of Bartholomew, on Tiber Island, Rome. He became delirious and dreamed he was rescued from a dragon by the apostle. While convalescent, he made a vow that, should he recover from his fever and return safely home, he would found a Priory with a Hospital dedicated to Saint Bartholomew in London.

King Henry encouraged Rahere in this laudable project and provided him with a parcel of flat, marshy land just outside the City walls. Later, he presented the new Priory for Augustinians (or 'Austin Canons') whose order included both men and women, with a comprehensive Charter of Privileges.[40] These included the granting of the right to hold and gather tolls from the nearby Barthomolew Fair.[41] When Rahere died in 1143, he was buried near the High Altar of his Priory Church, although the vaulted canopy and recumbent figure over his ornate tomb actually date from the 16th century. Rahere is depicted wearing a black habit of the Austin Canons, his hands clasped in prayer and his tonsured head turned heavenwards.[42] Unfortunately, the choir alone remains of the original Norman foundation.[43] Nevertheless, the Priory Church of St Bartholomew – solemn and inspiring – remains the best preserved Medieval interior of all the City churches.[44]

Rahere also founded St Bartholomew's Hospital. At first, it was governed by a master, eight brethren (priests) and four sisters. They vowed to attend continuously in the Infirmary and 'to wait upon the sick with diligence and care in all gentleness'. The homeless, orphans, elderly, infirm, sick and poor of the district were looked after, as well as pilgrims and travellers. Whittington's executors recognised the tremendous benefit this 'hospitality' had upon the community. Everyone in need of care was included, from London's pregnant women to babies born at Newgate Gaol. They founded a library there that presumably consisted of primitive medical textbooks for the canons to consult when dealing with their patients.

John Cok, a vintner, prepared a 'Cartulary', a compilation of all the legal documents, deeds and charters of the Hospital, which lists the books in the possession of the Masters. John Wakering or 'Blakberd', the longest serving Master of the Hospital (1422-1466) was revered for his discretion and wisdom. His black and white shield was adopted as the arms of the Hospital. He lawfully recovered the estate of John White, a previous Master and former Rector of St Michael Paternoster Royal, that included a valuable library of religious books. These books included

...a great Antiphony, with musical notation, lying in the choir, worth £8: also a great Breviary for the master's room, worth £10; also another great Breviary with musical notation, containing the lessons, to wit a couchour, worth £13 6s 8d: also a new and great legend de sanctis and de tempore in one volume, worth £12: also a great Bible complete with a Psalter, worth £16: also a Manual worth thirteen shillings and four pence.[45]

One wonders whether the source of any of these books was Whittington himself since White, who had been one of his executors, had taken up residence in Whittington's own house shortly after his friend's death.

Whittington's executors also financed the building of a magnificent South Gate. They undertook this substantial construction work in compensation for an annual quit rent of twenty shillings on Whittington's House in La Riole due to the Hospital. Payment had been overlooked for several years and was greatly in arrears. The grand gateway, when completed, included a vault or arch in the wall adjoining the Chapel of St Nicholas, a stained-glass window with its tracery representing the 'seven corporal works of Mercery' (feeding the hungry, offering drink to the thirsty, receiving the guest, clothing the naked, visiting the sick and the imprisoned, redeeming the slave and burying the dead). A stone column displayed the carved arms of Richard Whittington. The cost of this ornate gateway – the mason's fee alone amounted to £64 out of a total cost of £174 14s 4d – far exceeded the value of the quit rent. This liberality by the executors might be explained by the fact that Rev. John White had also been a valued Master of the Hospital.

The Hospital survived – although practically penniless – the Dissolution of the Monasteries and it was even refounded under Henry VIII. The presence of medical students there is first recorded in 1662, although it is probable that there were students long before that date, and from that time onwards St Bartholomew's built assuredly upon its reputation as a teaching hospital. James Gibbs stylishly rebuilt the Hospital in four blocks around a courtyard in the mid-18th century. In the mid-20th century, the George V block replaced the south block of Gibbs' Hospital and all traces of Whittington's extensions were obliterated. Indeed, the only Medieval structure to survive is the cramped tower of St Bartholomew the Less. The little church's links with the Hospital are proclaimed by an early 20th-century stained-glass window depicting a nurse, the gift of the Worshipful Company of Glaziers.

St Bartholomew's Hospital was incorporated into the National Health Service in 1948 and, following re-organisation in 1974, it became the teaching hospital for the newly formed City and Hackney Health District.[46] In 1992, the Hospital was no longer considered viable and it was threatened with closure but an intense public campaign secured its future. It now forms part of the London NHS Trust together with the Royal London Hospital and the London Chest Hospital. Today, 'Bart's' remains London's oldest hospital.[47]

Newgate Gaol

Whittington, as Mayor, was also Justiciar responsible for Newgate Gaol. All his life, he had a special interest in the welfare of prisoners, especially those who were incarcerated simply because they owed money. He earned a deserved reputation as a prison reformer.

Newgate, although neither the largest nor the oldest gaol, was indisputably the most notorious penal institution in England. Its inhuman conditions offended the sensibilities of a host of writers, artists and reformers and over the centuries it inspired more poems, plays and novels than any other building in London. The authorities considered it imprudent to spend citizens' hard earned cash on providing comfortable confinement. By Whittington's time, Newgate Gaol had assumed legendary proportions since it doubled as both the gateway to the City and for condemned prisoners –the entrance to eternity.

The Mayor of London and the Court of Common Council were made responsible for appointing two Sheriffs who would supervise Newgate Gaol. Refusal to accept this position incurred severe penalties, either a heavy fine or long imprisonment. Their inauguration ceremony was dictated in the 'Liber Albus'. They received their responsibility for the custody of the prisoners by indenture from the retiring – and relieved — Sheriff.[48] This took place annually on the Eve of St Michael (28 February) and followed a lavish banquet – in contrast to the prisoners' meagre fare – at the Guildhall. The ceremony itself was a dignified affair presided over by the Mayor, who presented the Sheriffs with a bunch of heavy iron keys and the official seal of Newgate.

Afterwards, in violation of the city ordinances, the Sheriffs proceeded to sell the keepership of the gaol to the highest bidder. Naturally, this led to abuses. In order to recover their substantial investment, the new owners charged their prisoners exorbitantly for commodities. Everything had its price: food, water, spirits, candles, bedding, furniture...

This was in defiance of the law, which stated categorically that a prisoner committed to either Newgate or Ludgate should not be charged for lamps nor beds although, curiously, they were required to pay a fee of four pence to the gaoler upon their release.[49]

The prison became a place of extremities. Ordinary inmates were confined in the most appalling conditions and suffered severe depredations while affluent prisoners might purchase simple luxuries and ensure a modicum of privacy. They could obtain release from their shackles, approach the coal fire and even borrow books. Nevertheless, everyone involved in the prison service, from gaoler to gaolbird,[50] incurred unparalleled risks.[51] The noise, stench and disease were legendary. Henry Fielding, novelist and magistrate, condemned Newgate Gaol as 'a prototype of Hell'.

By comparison, Ludgate prison, on the hill leading to St Paul's, was considered too cosy for prisoners guilty of minor misdemeanours. Privileges of that prison were openly abused by freemen 'more willing to take up their abode there ... than pay their debts'.[52] In June 1419, the Mayor, William Sevenoke, decided to close it and transfer the inmates to Newgate. It was literally a fatal error. A vast number of prisoners soon died of gaol fever, a virulent form of typhus. When Richard Whittington was elected to his third Mayoralty on 13 October 1419, he reversed his predecessor's decision and returned the depleted batch of prisoners to the comparative safety of Ludgate.[53]

The harsh treatment of the Newgate prisoners must have played on his mind. He was deeply concerned about 'the fetid and corrupt atmosphere that is in the hateful gaol'. And, being a compassionate citizen and a committed Christian, Whittington was determined to take positive action and alleviate the plight of the prisoners. The ageing philanthropist therefore instructed his executors to 'reedifie the Gaile of Newgate'.[54]

Henry VI granted a licence to Whittington's executors on 12 May 1423 to demolish, rebuild and extend Newgate Gaol and its gatehouse.[55] Work began immediately. While this 'heynous' gaol was being demolished and the new one constructed, the prisoners were removed to the security of the Sheriff's lock-ups, called 'compters'. The modern pentagonal prison that swiftly arose occupied a relatively small site, 80 feet by 50 feet, but it loomed five storeys high. And it spanned the entrance to Newgate Street from Giltspur Street and the steep incline of Snow Hill.

Distinctions were made among the prisoners: freemen were lodged in cells to the north while freewomen were housed to the south. (This distinction between the sexes may well have been an innovation by Whittington.)[56] Further novel features included a chapel and a dining hall.[57] But there was also a purpose built 'pressing room' where prisoners were subjected to weights being placed upon their suspended body until they confessed in terror to their suspected crimes. Or at least they were persuaded to offer a plea.[58] Water, which was not necessarily fresh, was drawn from a fountain on the north side of the new complex.[59]

'Whittington's Palace', as the building was termed colloquially, lasted until the Great Fire when the entire structure was eradicated. Yet even after its subsequent rebuilding, it was still referred to colloquially as 'The Whit'.

As a tribute to the Mayor's munificence a sculpture of his cat adorned a niche in the west wall and this, apparently, survived the conflagration. Intriguingly, this is the first instance of Whittington being historically linked with that legendary cat. Henry Chamberlain in his 'History and Survey of the Cities of London and Westminster' (1770) recorded that the new gaol had four niches, each containing a lifesize statue. Three of these niches were occupied by allegorical figures representing Peace, Security and Plenty. He described the fourth in detail In one niche

...is a figure, representing Liberty, having the word LIBERTAS inscribed on her cap; and at her feet lies a cat, in allusion to the story of Sir Richard Whittington, a former founder, who is said to have made the first step to his good fortune by a cat.

A similar account appears in Maitland.[60] Both their reports are confirmed by the antiquarian Thomas Pennant, who claimed that the cat was a replacement for the one that had formerly graced the facade prior to the Great Fire.[61]

Guildhall

London's Guildhall,[62] Aldermanbury, is the building 'that most embodied and projected civic pride'[63] and has been for eight hundred years the centre of civic government of the City of London. Contemporary documents suggests that a grand hall existed in the vicinity from the early 12th century onwards. Key evidence is a list of rentals from properties belonging to St Paul's Cathedral *c.*1120-30, including the 'terra Gialle', identified as Guildhall, apparently situated in Bassishaw ('Brichmar') Ward. Perhaps the Court of Hustings met, while their Guildhall was being constructed, in Alfwin's House which may have been 'the fortified residence of an Alderman', that gave its name to the nearby street, 'Aldermanbury'.[64]

This first Guildhall was not only the meeting place for legal business, it was also a convenient repository for accounts and a secure place for cash (although Henry III used it as a store for his military tents.) Robert Fabyan, Draper and Alderman, in his 'Chronicle', dismissed it as 'an old and litell cottage', which in the early 15th century was transformed into 'a fair and goodly house'. Documents, however, mention assemblies of the Common Council in an 'Upper Chamber', which would indicate a more substantial structure.

After its completion, it became the largest building in the City after St Paul's Cathedral and the largest hall in the country with the exception of Westminster Hall. It was hailed as one of the grandest secular buildings in England.

Traditionally, it became the place where the Court of Common Council assembled to elect the Sheriffs and the Mayor. Local government evolved there over the centuries, so that today Guildhall is the home of the City of London Corporation that provides municipal services to the Square Mile.

Guildhall was remodelled in later Medieval times.[65] It was part of a comprehensive campaign of City improvements that included repairs to London Bridge, the creation of Blackwell Hall and the expansion of Leadenhall Market. This programme coincided with a time of reconciliation for the citizens following a long period of tension between King and Parliament that had erupted in the latter part of the reign of Richard II.[66] This grand scheme of rebuilding was a conscious assertion of civic pride supervised partially by the charismatic Whittington, who was beginning to be recognised, tentatively, as a patron of architecture.

Guildhall Yard, which was established during the 13th century, was a narrow, gated community, comprising an important complex of civic buildings.[67] Along the western side was the Church of St Lawrence Jewry with its vicarage and cemetery. Opposite, on the eastern side, lay Guildhall Chapel, founded in the 13th century but later rebuilt with an associated Chantry College.[68] Dominating the northern end of this crowded Yard was the spectacular Guildhall, rebuilt in the early 15th century by Master Mason John Croxton, who had trained under Henry Yvele, architect of Westminster Hall. All these impressive buildings exemplified 'the often seamless way in which Christian religion, civil power, cultural life and economic activity were fused together in the late Medieval world'.[69]

Guildhall Chapel assumed a tremendous importance to the City of London in 1405 when it became the setting of the mass preceding Mayoral elections at Guildhall. Henry V permitted the continued rebuilding of Guildhall and declared hired boatmen and carters free from impressment throughout the Agincourt campaign. It is surprising to learn, then, that this prestigious building was referred to as 'small and ruinous' in 1430. This derogatory description might, however, reflect the state of the building while work was in progress for Croxton's improvements. The beautiful facade survived both the Dissolution and the Great Fire but, sadly, the Chapel was subsequently employed for secular purposes until its demolition in order to build new Law Courts in 1822.

Guildhall itself remains a magnificent building. It was remodelled by George Dance in 1789 in his bizarre but beautiful Mogul style. It is entered via a Gothic Medieval porch which bears the City arms in stone and the City motto, 'Domine Dirige Nos' ('Lord direct us'). Croxton's Great Hall was one vast open space, no aisles or arcades, with a double layer of windows along its side walls, two great windows at either end and a roof supported on stone transverse arches.[70]

Completed in 1424, it was intended as the centre of government where the Mayor, Aldermen and Sheriffs held their own separate courts of justice. Its east end was dominated by a dais for the Court of Husting (still the main judicial court although lacking its former governmental or administrative role) while the east end had a similar raised stage for the Sheriffs' Court, which dealt with civil or minor cases. Over the decades the magnificent Hall, which was gaily decorated, assumed even more magnificence with the addition of panelling, tapestries and paintings.[71]

Whittington's executors realised the relevance of this great municipal building to his triple Mayoralty and accordingly contributed funds from his estate towards the modernisation of the Guildhall. Stow says that they presented a total of thirty-five pounds specifically for improving the Mayor's Court and Great Hall, where Mayoral elections were held. This involved covering the rush-strewn beaten earth floor with expensive limestone marble paving[72] and replacing the draughty barred shutters, composed of thin strips of translucent horn, with imported opaque glass windows.[73] There they could insert the vibrant coat-of-arms of their illustrious donor. All this added vastly to the building's grandeur.[74]

Whittington's Library

Whittington's executors also created an extensive library attached to Guildhall Chapel which was administered by the College. According to Stow: 'Adjoyning to the chappell on the south side was sometime a fayre and large library, furnished with books, pertayning to the Guildhall and colledge... This library was builded by Executors of R. Whittington, and by William Burie.' Bury was a fellow Mercer but curiously his will (15 February 1422/3) does not specify a bequest to form a library and so it is assumed that either he expressed his wishes privately to his executors (as Whittington may have done) or there was a later will, now lost.[75]

Whittington's executors made an exchange of land in Bassieshaw for a parcel of common soil measuring 44 feet long, especially for this new library which was completed by the autumn of 1425. Although the site and size of the 'liberary atte Guyldhalle' can only be conjectured, it was obviously an impressive building in Guildhall Yard. Stow reveals it consisted of three chambers at ground level, above which was a long, light, single room in which the books were stored. The library was built of stone with a slate roof, a floor of Purbeck marble and glazed windows on the south side. Inside, the library was furnished with twenty-eight desks to which the precious books were chained. Their spines would have faced the wall with their titles written neatly on the tightly closed leaves. Emblazoned above the doorway were William Bury's initials and Richard Whittington's arms.

The library is described in an inventory of Guildhall College (24 July 1549):

...a certen hous next unto the sam Chapel, called the library, all waies res'ved for students to resort unto, wt three chambres under nithe the

saide library, which library being coverd wt slate is valued together wt the
chambres at xiijs iiijd yearly... The saide library is a house appointed...
for... resorte of all students for their education in Divine Scriptures.

Guildhall Library primarily stored Christian literature since it was attached to a
College, but it also collated important documents relating to the City of London.
It became in fact, the first building to preserve a comprehensive collection of
municipal records. Foremost volume was the celebrated 'Liber Albus', called
after its original pristine white vellum binding, in which were entered 'laudable
customs not written, wont to be observed in the City, and other notable things
worthy of remembrance here and there scattered' in Latin and French. As
noted earlier, Strype says the book was compiled by John Carpenter, the City's
Common Clerk between 1417 and 1438. It is dated 4 November 1419 and
since this was during the mayoralty of Richard Whittington, there is a strong
probability that the book was compiled at his suggestion, possibly because
the memory of these statutes was constantly threatened by recurrences of the
plague.[76]

Today, Guildhall possesses only one book known to have belonged to the
original library. This is 'Biblia Sacra', an early 13th-century metrical version
of a selection of books from the Old Testament and Apocrypha in Latin. The
manuscript is penned in tiny Gothic characters in red and black and the author's
name is revealed in the opening couplet: Petrus de Riga. On the first few pages
the initial letter of each line has a purple wash over it and the flyleaf has a later
inscription in a 15th-century hand. The book was rebound in the 20th century
but the original morocco gilt cover with its delicate leaf pattern is preserved
separately round a dummy.

Guildhall is admired in modern times for 'its impressive frontage and its
soaring limestone vaulting'[77] dominating the Venetian piazza. A new library
was built there in 1974 to house surviving books transferred from a former
Victorian library. This is one of the largest public reference libraries in the City
containing an unrivalled collection of books on London's history, topography
and genealogy. The most valuable works are kept securely in the 'Whittington
Room'. There they are watched over by a mature figure of Richard Whittington,
a powerful reminder that he was the first benefactor of what is regarded as the
first public library in England.[78]

A further acknowledgement of the Mayor's munificence is a whimsical
sculpture of 'Dick Whittington and his Cat' by Christian artist, Lawrence
Tindall. This exquisitely carved Portland stone figure depicts a plump young
apprentice – his fashionable attire showing signs of wear – leaning against a
milestone and musing upon his future. His bright-eyed, bushy-tailed moggy rubs
against his torn stockings while from under the fold of his cloak peers a defiant
rat. The engaging statue was commissioned to grace the loggia of the modern
Guildhall Art Gallery opened by Queen Elizabeth II in 1999.

Whittington College
and Almshouses

Leadenhall

Leadenhall Market on Cornhill is built on the site of the Roman Forum. It takes its name from a lead-roofed mansion[79] that belonged to the influential Neville family in the 14th century. The manor of Leden Hall or 'Ledynhall' had a series of owners in a short time. This great hall passed from Alice Neville, widow of Sir John Neville, to Thomas Cogshall[80] and then from Humfrey de Bohun, Earl of Hertford, to Robert and Margaret Rikeden from Essex. In 1408, Rikeden conferred the manor together with its endowments that encompassed St Peter's, Cornhill, and St Margaret Pattens to several London citizens, including Richard Whittington.[81]

In 1411, Whittington, with typical generosity, presented 'a manor called Le Leadenhalle' to the Mayor and Commonalty.[82] Once in the possession of the City of London, the building began to be developed into Leadenhall Market. This occurred long after Whittington's demise, however, although its seems that a street market may have been established there in his lifetime. Certainly, the area had, since the beginning of the 14th century been regarded as a 'foreign' market, used mainly by country poulterers.

By 1377, foreigners (people from outside London) were allowed to sell dairy products – eggs, cheese and butter – in the City. In 1442, John Croxton, currently constructing Guildhall, was diverted to build a 'garner', which became a general market for poultry, grain and dairy products. Later, wool and leather were also included in the licence for sales. The new granaries or storehouses were two-storeyed affairs with open arcading on the ground floor. The Common Council ordered that the market for poultry, victuals, grain, eggs, butter and cheese should be transferred to within the new granary, which was the inspiration of Simon Eyre, Mayor and Draper.[83] Leadenhall Market was thus firmly established.

The Great Fire devoured Leadenhall Market. By then, however, the market had dwindled and the building was used mainly for the storage of wool sacks, the City armoury and the stacking of props and scenery for street pageants, particularly those presented by the Mercers' Company.[84] Nevertheless, it was cleverly rebuilt as a market around three courtyards. Each yard specialised in different commodities. The first yard was the beef market. On certain days leather, wool and hides were also sold there. The second yard was for mutton, lamb and veal but fishmongers, poulterers and cheesemongers also had their stalls there. The third yard was the herb market, which concentrated on fruit and vegetables.[85]

In 1881, Sir Horace Jones, who had been the architect responsible for Smithfield (1866) and Billingsgate (1875), replaced these scattered structures with the present buildings which form Leadenhall Market, reached via Whittington Avenue. The ornate covered precinct now has shops and stalls specialising in high-quality foods. The market's traditional strengths of poultry and game have been maintained so that mallard, teal, partridge and woodcock are all available in season. In addition, there are mouth-watering displays of seafood, particularly oysters, while delicatessens sell everything from cheese to chocolate.

London Bridge

The Wardens or 'Bridgemasters' applied to Whittington's executors for funds for the repair of London Bridge. This ancient structure was still the only road crossing over the River Thames in its lower reaches linking the City with Kent. London was a walled City that could be entered only by its fortified gateways in the 'unsettled and warlike' Middle Ages.[86] The bridge remained the sole entrance from the south, which meant that it was imperative to defend it at all times. A Great Stone Gate, with a portcullis, stood on a pier just two arches away from the southern shore, while an ancient timber Drawbridge Gate was located five arches further along to the north. This drawbridge was protected by a pair of towers and proved a formidable obstacle when raised to prevent access by marauders from Southwark. A toll of sixpence was charged each time the drawbridge was raised in peacetime to allow the tall masts of ships to pass through and sail along the Thames Estuary towards Queenhithe on the Isle of Sheppey.

Peter de Colechurch of Cheapside was responsible for constructing this first stone bridge with its nineteen arches, that was completed in 1209.[87] Henry II assisted in the funding of this essential project by granting a tax on wool while his son, John, authorised rents and profits from houses built on the bridge to be used for its repair and maintenance.[88] About halfway across the bridge on the downstream side stood a handsome chapel dedicated to Saint Thomas Becket. There were, in fact, two chapels: the main one was entered at street level while the lower chapel (or undercroft) was convenient for watermen who landed at great risk, because of the fast flow of water, at the large stone pier. Becket had been christened at St Mary Colechurch, standing at the corner of Poultry and Old Jewry, where the bridge founder had been priest.[89] Pilgrims setting out southwards for Canterbury Cathedral to worship at Becket's shrine would step inside the chapel to seek a blessing ahead of their journey. (A recent initiative is an annual service held at the centre of the bridge attended by the clergy and congregation of Southwark Cathedral and St Magnus Martyr,[90] whose parish boundaries meet halfway on the modern structure, to pray for a blessing of the River Thames.)

A grand Bridge House with its private wharf stood at the far southern end of the bridge at 'Suthwerk'. No expense was spared on its furnishings to welcome its constant stream of official visitors. Its chambers were enriched with stained glass, carpets, tapestries and murals while its gardens were enlivened with an arbour, vines, ponds and fountains. London's Mayor, Aldermen and Recorder were entertained to a lavish breakfast when, once a year, they paraded over, ostensibly to inspect the stores and receive the audited accounts.

In early September, the Southwark Fair was a cause for greater merriment. This was the perfect excuse for a return visit by the Mayor, Sheriffs and Aldermen. The company assembled at the northern approach in the precincts of St Magnus by the Bridge, which because of its prime location was one of the wealthiest of the City churches. They then rode over in procession across the bridge and passed through the crowded rows of tempting stalls before enjoying a second celebratory banquet at Bridge House.[91] Mayor Whittington must have relished these joyous occasions: the boisterous fair and the audit feast.

Funds for the regular maintenance of London Bridge were collected from various sources: rents, tolls, gifts, bequests and petty fines, including 'unlawfully fishing from the Bridge'. Over a long period of time, however, the constant crossing of heavy carts with their iron wheels over this thoroughfare crowded with houses, shops and the wayfarers' chapel, caused inevitable damage. This was also the venue for jousts that attracted great crowds and caused constant repairs to the structure. When one of the arches cracked in 1424, a frightful view of the fast flowing tidal waters below caused alarm. Traffic was suspended, apart from horses and pedestrians, to halt the offending vibrations.[92]

The Bridgemasters made a sensible decision to replace the decaying timber Drawbridge Gate at the southern approach with a far sturdier stone tower. They organised a lavish breakfast to raise funds to launch this laudable project at Bridge House, on the riverbank downstream, at Southwark. This was a sturdy building where the bridge boatkeeper was stationed with 'the Bridghouse dogges'. Wealthy citizens were invited to attend the occasion to drum up support for the proposed work and Whittington's executors were most likely to have been among the invited guests.[93] Whittington, after all, once had a shop in a prominent position on London Bridge. Application for funds was certainly successful because the gate 'was newe begun to be builded in the Yeare 1426'.

London Bridge became a focus of Jack Cade's rebellion in 1450. His troops scaled the drawbridge and attacked the ropes which were then 'hewn asunder'. The Medieval drawbridge famously displayed the skulls of executed traitors 'lokyng into Kent warde' as a grim warning to people approaching the City of London.[94] This gruesome custom lasted until 1577 when 'Le Drawebrugge' was demolished and the display of heads was transferred to the Great Stone Gate.[95]

Rochester Bridge

Whittington's executors also made a substantial donation towards the repair of Rochester Bridge, spanning the River Medway in North Kent.[96] The Romans had built a first bridge of stone and timber there soon after their occupation of Britain under Claudius in 43 AD. This bridge completed the line of Watling Street, which was the Roman road leading from London to Richborough, near Dover and Sandwich on the Kent coast.

King John had grudgingly granted the citizens of London jurisdiction over the Rivers Thames and Medway.[97] Periodically, both these rivers completely froze. In 1381, there was a particularly cold winter when the flood waters of the subsequent thaw carried away 'the great part of the bridge' at Rochester.[98] Whittington's executors were contributing towards keeping open this ancient road link between London and Sandwich, a premier Cinque Port.

This route was famously known as the Pilgrim's Way leading from London to Canterbury, immortalised by Geoffrey Chaucer in 'The Canterbury Tales'.[99] (In the Monk's Prologue, the company reaches half-way point of their pilgrimage since an aside reveals, 'Loe Rouchester stant heer fast bye...') Whittington, along with fellow merchants, would have been most concerned to preserve this ancient trackway across the Kent countryside – 'Dertford, Graveshend, Rowchester, Sithinborn, Ospring, Fevarsham and Cantuar' – to facilitate the worship at Thomas Becket's shrine at Canterbury Cathedral. His executor's actions would have been perfectly in accordance with his wishes, remembering that the headquarters of the Mercers' Company occupied Becket's birthplace in Cheapside.

Life in Medieval times was viewed as a journey between Earth and Heaven. The poet Langland commanded his readers to take responsibility for the repair of 'bruges broken by the heye wayes' in order that they might 'abide in (Heaven's) bliss, body and soul for ever'. The church constantly promoted charitable donations towards the upkeep of roads and bridges. It preached that generous gifts would smooth the passage of the donor in his own spiritual journey to salvation. The plentiful bequests by merchants and traders responding to this plea improved the ease of movement, creating access to pilgrim sites that benefitted men's souls. More practically, accessible roads promoted mobility, facilitated trade, inconvenienced robbers, and prevented accidents.[100]

Two influential noblemen, Sir Robert Knolles and Sir John de Cobham, generously paid for the rebuilding of Rochester Bridge in the reign of Richard II. The substantial replacement was 560 feet long and comprised ten stone arches with a wooden drawbridge towards its western end for purposes of defence that could be raised to allow tall ships to pass. The bridge was endowed with lands in London, Kent and Essex and was, therefore, opened free of charge to the public. Hence the motto: 'publica privatis' (1391).

At the east end of the Medieval bridge stood a chantry chapel built by Sir John de Cobham in 1393.[101] Since time immemorial there has been a spiritual connection between a permanent crossing and a tidal river.[102] Interestingly, London's Millenium Bridge points directly towards St Paul's Cathedral. At Rochester, 'All-Soulen Chapel' provided a refuge for weary travellers and a place of solitude and repose.[103] Pilgrims journeying the sixty miles from Southwark to Canterbury, with one overnight stay, would have prayed hard for their safety at the bridge chapel.

Three chantry priests were employed to celebrate regular masses of intercession for the benefit of wayfarers at three separate altars dedicated to the Holy Trinity, Virgin Mary and All Saints. This bridge-foot chapel was suppressed at the Reformation and thereafter used for secular purposes until its restoration in 1937. The interior of this prim ragstone chapel is lit by modern plain glass windows but the carved gallery remains at the west end, which formerly linked the bridge chamber with the clock tower. An annual service is held on All Souls Day (2 November) to commemorate the founders and benefactors of Rochester Bridge.[104]

William Sevenoake, a former Mayor whose meteoric career mirrored Whittington's own, was consulted when Rochester Bridge demonstrated obvious signs of decay in the first quarter of the 15th century. A former Warden of London Bridge, Sevenoake was deemed an expert in structural engineering and he was invited to personally inspect the bridge and advise on its repair.[105] Time and weather took their toll of both bridge and chapel and affluent citizens were frequently prevailed upon to donate funds for their maintenance.[106] An entry appears under the list of gifts and legacies in the Account Roll of Bridge Wardens for the period from Michaelmas 1422 to Michaelmas 1423: 'Et de xl li de Executoribus Ricardi Whytynton per manus eiusdem Willelmi Sevenoke.' This is qualified shortly afterwards: 'Et de vijs. viijd. perditis in xl li Receptis pe Willelmi Sevenoke de Ricardo Whytyngton … Pro defectu ponderis.'[107]

Apparently, the executors of Richard Whittington presented William Sevenoake with a donation of forty pounds for the repair of Rochester Bridge. Afterwards, it was discovered that the gold coins were underweight. It is not known, owing to a mere fragmentary account the following year, whether the wardens ever collected the deficit (7s 6d) or simply wrote off the loss as an irrecoverable debt.

The Medieval bridge continued to provide the only crossing of the River Medway at Rochester for almost five hundred years. During this time road and river traffic steadily increased and the stone bridge was replaced by a cast-iron one in the mid-19th century. This substantial structure, built slightly further north downstream, consisted of three shallow arches plus a separate swing bridge at the western approach to allow the passage of sailing ships.

In 1910, the Victorian bridge was reconstructed by raising the roadway and suspending it from arches above to carry vehicular traffic and also trams. Rochester Bridge was supplemented by a second roadway bridge whereby westbound traffic was routed over the old bridge and eastbound traffic over the new bridge in 1970. Today, both Bridge and Chapel are administered by the Rochester Bridge Trust, which has contributed toward the cost of several bridges over the Medway and also owns the Medway Tunnel, which, at present, is leased to Medway Council.

Gloucester Cathedral

Lysons asserts that Whittington made a substantial financial contribution to the repair of the fabric of Gloucester Cathedral. Apparently, the focus of his charity was the High Altar. Alas, the original altar and reredos of the Abbey Church were mutilated by reformers during the reign of Edward VI. The spectacular original stained glass east window, known as the Crecy Window, alone survives and this dates from the 1350s. At that time it was the largest window in the world and it is often referred to as 'England's first war memorial'. Nothing can be traced in the Cathedral archives, however, to confirm Whittington's supposed involvement.

There is, however, a curious feature in the north-east ambulatory Chapel of SS. Edmund and Edward, formerly known as Abbot Boteler's Chapel (now the War Memorial Chapel). There, the weathered carved stone altar bears a series of miniature coats-of-arms, including those of Whittington and Fitzwaryn. Recently restored, they are emblazoned in stone along its ornate top rail although rarely noticed by visitors. The circumstance of their appearance would presuppose that Whittington might, indeed, have contributed in some measure towards the fabric of the Cathedral.

Whittington's College and Almshouse

Whittington's executors, who determined the shape and extent of the foundations by which he was to be remembered, were clearly following detailed instructions he had personally conveyed to them late in his lifetime. His dearest wish was to found both a college and an amshouse in the immediate vicinity of his main residence and the church that he established in La Riole. His purpose, identical to all contemporary founders of similar institutions, was for temporal honour in this life and the smooth passage of his soul in the afterlife.

This is confirmed by the testimony of John Carpenter: 'the foresayde worthy and notable merchaunt, Richard Whitington, the which while he leued had ryght liberal and large hands to the needy and poor people, charged streitly on his death bed us his foresayde executors to ordeyne a house of almes, after his death... and thereupon fully he declared his will unto us.'[108]

Curiously, since the purpose of these foundations was spiritual, government of both the College and Almshouse was entrusted not to a religious institution but to a secular one: the Mercers' Company. At that time the wealthy companies were beginning to concern themselves with impoverished folk, especially with their own members who, through no fault of their own, had fallen upon hard times. Whittington's charity was certainly innovative in that he handed over the administration of this – his last, greatest and most personal venture – to his professional colleagues. This direction anticipated the style of future trusts founded by prominent London tradesmen who tended to appoint the City Guilds as guardians of their own charitable foundations.[109] 'Whittington,' says Imray, 'became their exemplar.'[110]

His executors, true to their word, faithfully devoted their time and energy into putting his desires into practice. The licence for Whittington's foundation had been granted by Henry IV in the eleventh year of his reign (1410) and in the next a vacant plot of land was made available to him by the Mayor, Thomas Knoles, grocer, and the Commonalty. This was an extensive site on the east side of St Michael's Church for the executors to build the College dedicated to the Holy Ghost and Virgin Mary. (It was also known as 'St Spirit and St Mary'.)

It was a small religious fraternity comprising five secular priests, a Master and four fellows, who were to be all Master of Arts considered 'learned and virtuous men without benefice'. They were to be assisted by two clerks and four choristers. They were all to inhabit a 'messuage' newly erected at the east end of the church which must have been large enough to accommodate a common hall since these brethren were instructed to take their meals together. Little more is known of the actual building, which was swiftly completed and opened in the winter of 1424-5.

The executors were presented with the bulk of Whittington's estate, including his mansion, with which to fund his charity. This numbered four shops and the tenement called 'The Tabbard on the Hoop' adjoining the north side of the church. These were conveyed to the executors by Robert Chichele on 1 February 1423/4 because this combined small estate was to be the site of the new almshouses. These were constructed along one side of an internal yard, with an undisclosed number of cells or rooms plus a communal dining hall.

The Almshouse ('Hospital' or 'God's House') was located between the Church of St Michael, abutting the College of Priests, and Whittington's own great mansion on College Hill. It sheltered thirteen poor folk,[111] either men or married couples, one of whom was to act as their leader. Each resident was to be provided with their own residence, consisting of a cell or tiny house with a chimney, to ensure comfort and privacy. There he might spend his time in contemplation of God, according to the Ordinances, 'if he wills'. Their leader or 'Tutor' inhabited 'a little house (with) essentials to himself in which to lie and rest'.

Admittance was restricted to impoverished London citizens, especially those of the Mercers' Company, but excluding liverymen since it was assumed they were already well provided for by their own company. Candidates must be known to be meek of spirit, destitute of worldly goods, chaste of body and of good conversation. Allocation of places for almsfolk were shared equally by the Mercers' Company and the Master of the College of Priests, who was allowed to claim the seventh nomination. Should they fail to agree on a candidate for any vacancy then the decision was left to the discretion of the then Mayor.

The Almshouse must have possessed a common hall or parlour since the residents were instructed to eat together as members of a community. Later, the Tutor and residents were allocated a vacant plot of land with an open shelter adjoining the west side of the Almshouse for their recreation. An alley following the north wall of the church led through the burial ground from the Royal to the almshouse and this was retained by the executors as a right of way for the parish.[112] Regrettably, there were disputes between the almsmen and the parishioners regarding the right to burial in this coveted plot of land.

Building proceeded at a rapid pace and the College and the Almshouse were soon habitable. Whittington College was conveyed to William Brooke, Master, the Rector of St Michael's Church, and the four minor chaplains, while the Almshouse was transferred to John Chesterton, Tutor, and twelve residents in the winter of 1424.[113]

One firm instruction Whittington gave to his executors was to sell all his London properties[113] in order to fund his various charities and this they proceeded to do. Wisely, they bought everything back again – excluding his own house – in order to provide the main endowment of both College and Almshouse. Revenues from City properties – shops and tenements in St Andrew by the Wardrobe; lands and tenements in St Michael Bassieshaw; shops and tenements in St Botolphs without Bishopsgate[114] – proved that their purchase was an excellent investment.

The executors acquired further properties in the City. These included lands, tenements and rents in St Laurence Jewry, St Mary Magdalen in Milk Street and All Hallows Barking; two tenements with four shops in St Dunstan in the East; lands, tenements and rents in St Stephen Coleman St.; 'Le Greyhound' and adjoining mansions in St Leonard Eastcheap and three shops in St Margaret Bridge St.[115] All these purchases were made under the able direction of John Carpenter who accumulated further valuable properties – lands and tenements in St Bartholomew the Less, St Benet Fink, St Michael Cornhill and St Lawrence Pountney – the rents from which amply secured adequate annual incomes to the College (£63) and Almshouse (£40).[116]

After the death of Whittington's executors all these properties were conveyed to the Mercers' Company who had been declared the supervisors and conservators of the two institutions through the foundation Ordinances compiled in December 1424. Most importantly, it was the Mercers who ran the landed estate, identified tenants, collected rents and paid over the funds. By the time the Mercers were in full possession of all the property, the rents amounted to just over £250, which put them well ahead of all other London Companies. 'The Mercers had suddenly become a major landlord in the city,' notes Anne F. Sutton, 'with greater "lordship" and patronage than any ambitious dream could have envisaged.'[117]

John Carpenter proved himself to be a most loyal and trusted friend who worked diligently on behalf of Whittington long after his demise. One of his last acts was to secure the endowment of the College and Almshouse, which was finally completed by letters patent on 12 May 1432.[118] That same day, as a final mark of approval for the foundation, the actions of the joint executors were ratified by Act of Parliament.[119] And so the last surviving executor was able to obtain royal and parliamentary recognition of Whittington's charity, part of which endures and flourishes to the present day.[120]

Ordinances

The rules and regulations for Whittington's College and Almshouse were drawn up in a set of Ordinances, originally drafted in Latin but translated into English, sealed by his executors in December 1424. Although separate Ordinances were approved for the two institutions, they had much in common, which meant that the daily lives of the residents cannot have been so very different. Both were placed under the jurisdiction of the Master of the Mercers' Company and, ultimately, the Mayor of London.

The College was under the immediate supervision of its own Master who was elected by the five chaplains from among their number at a meeting of their chapter. Stow states that Whittington's executors arranged for 'diuinitie lectures to bee there for read for euer', which indicates that the Master appointed was a highly educated cleric. Masters, who were invariably university academics, were charged with a dual role being also appointed Rector of St Michael's Church.

Chaplains of the College were commanded especially to pray for the souls of their founder, Richard, and Alice Whittington, Richard's parents, Sir William and Lady Joan Whittington, Richard II and Queen Anne, Thomas Woodstock and Eleanor, Duke and Duchess of Gloucester, who were 'speciall lordes and promoters of the seid Richard Whitington'. The instruction for the inmates to pray for the souls of Richard II and Thomas, Duke of Gloucester is quite striking. It is noteworthy that there is no direction to pray for the souls of either of the first two Lancastrian kings. Whittington, as Mayor, must have been aware of Richard II's plan to arrest Gloucester at Pleshey, tacitly accepted it but was later troubled in his conscience, which caused him to order prayers for his soul.[121] There was little he could do at the time to prevent his arrest or subsequent murder. Both the King and the Duke were known personally to him and he was placed in the unenviable position of divided loyalties.

Annually, there was to be an obit said for Richard Whittington (23 or 24 March) and for Alice Whittington (30 or 31 July). Attendance was compulsory for all the members of the College even if they were not actually officiating. Here is revealed, Clay asserts astutely, Richard Whittington's concern for 'the prayers of generations yet unborn', which was the principal motive for founders of Medieval hospitals.[122]

The religious duties of the almsfolk were similarly exacting, since they were required to attend the church daily for matins, mass, evensong and compline. Once a day they were to gather round the tomb of their founder and say psalms and offer prayers in memory of Richard and Alice Whittington. Further, they were required to march wearing their gowns and caps and carrying a banner, immediately behind the Master, Wardens and Liverymen of the Mercers' Company at official processions through the City.[123]

At mealtimes, the priests and the almsfolk ate together in total silence whilst listening to readings of the scriptures. The twelve almsfolk were each to receive 14 pence a week for their keep and the Tutor 16 pence. Gowns were provided. This ensured the priests refrained from wearing bright colours and presented a sober appearance. Almsfolk wore dark brown material, 'not staring, nor blazing and of easy priced cloth'.[124] They were forbidden to enter taverns and were warned against drunkenness, quarrelling and gluttony. They were compelled to occupy their free time in reading, praying or working. Breaches of these rules carried the ultimate penalty of expulsion.

Spoons

According to an inventory reluctantly drawn up by a later Tutor, Thomas Popplewell, in 1582, Whittington had presented to the College of Priests certain items of plate which were subsequently inherited by the Almshouse. Apparently these included twelve silver spoons with gilt knops: 'Plate – item v massers, iiij the founder gave & bossed & bound wth silver and gilt and thother of a nother mans gift... Item xij silver spoons wth. gilte knobbes.' Possibly, they were among Whittington's personal possessions; alternatively, they might have been commissioned to celebrate the conception of his charity. Perhaps they relate to the ceremonial dining of visitors[125] at either his mansion or his Almshouse?

There is no indication whether they were made by provincial or London silversmiths. Perhaps they were purchased from Goldsmiths Row, between Bread Street and Friday Street, Cheapside, where the inventory from an audacious burglary included six silver spoons valued at 14 shillings in 1382.[126] Certainly, they were donated by his executors for secure deposit in a strong box with three locks[127] as a future investment.

Four magnificent silver spoons, apparently part of the original set of one dozen, are in the possession of the Mercers' Company. The hammered bowls of these exquisite spoons, approximately eight inches long, would wonderfully reflect a kaleidoscope of colours by candlelight. They were examined by antique silver expert, Commander George Howe, in his authoritative *English and Scottish Silver Spoons*, where he carefully notes their distinctive Medieval characteristics: the tapering stems, hexagonal knops, fig-shaped bowls, deep drop from the stem to the bowl and absence of a date or maker's mark. He ascribes a date of between 1400 and 1420, which relates perfectly to the foundation of the College.

The backs of the bowls are engraved with a shield displaying the distinctive Whittington coat-of-arms.[128] (It was not until the mid-18th century, when table spoons were introduced, that spoons were placed on their backs, which means that the family crest would have always been visible when these splendid spoons were displayed on the sideboard.) These four spoons are all that remain of Whittington's impressive collection of silverware and jewellery. Certainly, they indicate that Whittington was an admirer of beautiful artefacts and was a connoisseur of fine craftmanship.

Whittington College

Whittington College endured for just over a century. At the Dissolution of the Monasteries, it was inevitably swept away and the property confiscated by the Crown. Remnants of the ecclesiastical buildings – 'le beadehowse alias le Almeshowse alias Goddeshowse' – were acquired by Armigale Wade, a civil servant, for £92 2s 7d by letters patent (4 June 1548).[129] The conveyance contract described the property as 'the capital house and site of Whittington College by St Michael Paternoster in Vintry Ward with a porch and entry leading from the highway called the Royal to the said house, and two chambers above the porch, a small garden abutting north on the east end of the entry, and a hall, a parlour, and a small garden adjacent to the said hall'.

In 1606, a later owner, Sir John Norris, sold it to the Skinners Company for £500. After the Great Fire the site became part of Skinners' Hall.[130] All traces of Whittington College were obliterated except the name 'College Hill'. After the Reformation, the Almshouse itself assumed the name of 'Whittington College' and this is the name for the charitable institution that endures.

Fresh ordinances were delivered to the Tutor on the orders of the Mercers' Company on 30 March 1560. These ordinances – amended when Protestant Queen Elizabeth I succeeded her sister, Catholic Queen Mary – were revised to accommodate the new religion. They emphasised loyalty to the Crown and the reformed Church of England. Prayers for the departed founders were swept away in favour of readings from the Bible. New inmates were in future to be examined with regard to the articles of faith: 'The Lord's Prayer and the Ten

Commandments in English and such other doctrine as is most necessary for every Christian man.'

Whittington College was visualised as a predominantly male institution but from the end of the 17th century onwards it became increasingly common to admit the widows of members of the Mercers' Company. In 1771, the Masters and Wardens noted with some trepidation that only the Tutor was male! Clearly, this was not the original intention of the founder and therefore it was ruled that a man should replace a woman upon her demise until there were at least six male inmates, thus achieving a parity between the sexes!

Highgate Hill

Early in the 19th century the buildings were recognised as being unserviceable and the site eminently unsuitable because of the rapid development of commercialism in the City. The Mercers' Company made the decision in 1818 to replace the antiquated College with a more commodious almshouse. To fund the project, they proposed investing three thousand pounds of the surplus from the Whittington estate in Southsea stock. They then formed a committee instructed to purchase land in the immediate vicinity of the Whittington stone on Highgate Hill. This eminently suitable site belonged, initially, to the Highgate Archway Company but it was eventually purchased outright by the Mercers' Company.

George Smith, the Mercers' own surveyor, was commissioned to prepare plans for a modern almshouse providing sheltered accommodation for thirty women. Approved contractors were Philip and Ward of Blackfriars who were legally appointed on 29 August 1822. Modifications to their original plans included the substitution of iron stoves for kitchen coppers, which were thought less likely to tempt thieves. Houses were to be provided with bath stoves in the upper rooms – a welcome innovation – and fresh water was available by means of submerged tanks and exterior pumps. At an additional cost, each front door was affixed with its own ornate knocker.

Later improvements were the addition of a chiming turret clock and laying on a permanent water supply to every house which was also enlarged with a second bedroom. Gardens were landscaped and a cottage was provided exclusively for the head gardener. A statue of Dick Whittington harkening to Bow Bells by Joseph Carew was positioned before the new Highgate Almshouses. Early engravings reveal Whittington College to have been a symmetrical building, with a central chapel and a profusion of doors, windows and chimneys, set at right angles to the start of the steep hill, approached by a grand sweep.

Felbridge, Sussex

Whittington College remained a feature of Highgate Hill until the postwar period when a proposal was put forward by the Ministry of Transport for road widening at Archway. This scheme necessitated the Mercers' Company seeking an alternative site for their ancient almshouses.

The College was sold for £250,000 and building commenced on the site of the demolished Felbridge Place, an 18th-century Italianate mansion, near East Grinstead, Sussex, in 1965. One year later, the College, which is still administered by the Mercers' Company in their capacity as Trustees of the Almshouse Charity founded under the will of Richard Whittington, was opened to residents, single women in reduced financial circumstances.[131] Described as 'a village within a village', the modern estate initially comprised twenty-eight two-bedroomed self-contained bungalows with separate homes for the Tutor, Matron, Assistant Matron and a gardener.

In 1978, the residential accommodation was enlarged by the addition of seven bungalows, specially designed for married couples, together with a dozen one-bedroom flats and bedsits contained in a single-storey building. Four years later the 'sheltered' accommodation was extended and the number of flats and bedsits doubled. In 2017, fourteen more one-bedroom apartments were completed. Today the estate comprises sixty-five homes, mainly two-bedroom bungalows, but including several one-bedroom apartments and studios. All these flats are grouped around patchwork lawns and gardens with statuary, sundials, fountains and gazebos.[132]

There is a raised woodland walk, a lake with waterlilies and a rhododendron dell. The level of care and comfort continues with the provision of central heating, telephone and television in each residence and there is also conveniently on site a visiting doctor's surgery. A minibus service is available to take residents out for shopping and occasional excursions.

Focal point of the community is the Chapel. This is dedicated to the Holy Ghost and the Virgin Mary. The white ash pews are tinted with sunlight spilling in from the slender stained-glass windows with pleasing modern impressions of countryside themes.[133] A pair of antique chairs flanking the altar bear Whittington's coat-of-arms while a carved coat-of-arms of the City of London on the west wall is from the Mercers' Chapel. The Anglican Chaplain, who is no longer referred to as 'Tutor', is now responsible solely for the spiritual welfare of the residents.

Whittington College encompasses twenty-five acres of manicured grounds planted with rare trees[134] and cultivated woodland carpeted with daffodils and bluebells in spring. A team of gardeners tend the espaliered fruit trees clinging to the mellow brick walls and maintain the trim lawns to create a tranquil haven of peace and beauty for those residents in their twilight years. Today, they might range from a former missionary to a retired nurse. Only a few residents have claimed a family connection with a member of the Mercers. In a corner of the secluded courtyard stands Carew's relocated statue of Dick Whittington harkening to the City bells, a charming reminder of their generous founder and benefactor.

Today, the College is administered by a Manager, at the time of writing Steve Brown. He is assisted by two estate workers and two welfare officers. Application for the Almshouses is open to retired professional people worldwide – spinsters, widows or married couples – although it is expected that they are communicant members of the Church of England. A new resident is welcomed into the community and will be completely cared for by the Mercers' Company.

Each resident will only be required to meet the cost of food, clothing, telephone, outings, holidays and personal expenses. Everything else is free. Medical care, which includes the services of the college doctor, surgery nurse and a visiting physiotherapist, is provided. Additionally, over three hundred pensions and allowances are paid out annually from the Whittington Trust.

Whittington College, which was envisaged during his lifetime, created by his executors and administered for almost six hundred years by his loyal Company of Mercers, remains an enduring testament to the generosity of, and an important memorial to, the historical figure of Dick Whittington.

Notes

Section 1

Chapter One

1. Sylvia Thrupp 'The Merchant Class of Medieval London' University of Chicago 1948
2. Ian Mortimer 'The Perfect King: The Life of Edward III' Jonathan Cape 2006
3. The name 'Plantagenet' is derived from one of their ancestors, Geoffrey, Count of Anjou, who wore in his hat as a good luck charm a sprig of broom. (Latin 'planta genesta'.) This emblem was thought to have been adopted as a gesture of humility during a pilgrimage to the Holy Land. Later it was adopted as the crest of the Angevins.
4. Piers Gaveston was a handsome, young, arrogant knight from Gascony.
5. Hugh le Despenser was known as 'the Younger' to distinguish him from his father, Lord Despenser.
6. Henry II was allowed to retain his duchy providing that he and his successors performed an oath of liege homage every time there was a change of monarchy in France. Successive English kings resented this humiliating ceremony because it allowed the French to make demands for military service and this effectively eroded English liberties.
7. Isabella was the sister of King Charles IV.
8. Philippa was the youngest daughter of Count William of Hainault.
9. Edward II, dressed for head to toe in black, abdicated on 12 January 1327 at Kenilworth Castle.
10. Storming of Nottingham Castle took place on 19 October 1330.
11. Nine knights from Gloucestershire, on average, attended Edward III on his successive French campaigns.

12. Nigel Saul 'Knights and Esquires of Gloucestershire' Clarendon Press 1981

13. Sheriffs were appointed by the Crown on the advice of the Chancellor, Judges and Bishops (who would be able to recommend suitable candidates in their dioceses). He was charged with the duty, assisted by officers, of seeing that the law, civil and criminal, was enforced and the King's peace kept. In the absence of an electoral system the sheriff was also responsible for selecting representatives from their county to serve in Parliament. Many sought to avoid this duty, especially in the towns, since it involved time, trouble and expense. The fact that a man often served two or three terms in his lifetime demonstrates that suitable people were not easily found.

14. Ian Mortimer 'The Perfect King: The Life of Edward III' Jonathan Cape 2006

15. Edward II's army was large and well equipped and therefore his defeat was all the more unexpected and dramatic.

16. Popularly known as Robert the Bruce (1274-1329).

17. The Scottish War of Independence was brought to an abrupt halt with the capture of David II (1324-1371) at the Battle of Neville's Cross in 1346.

18. Edward III's mother, Isabella, was sister of the late Capetian King, Charles IV, who died in 1328. The throne of France was then claimed by his cousin, Philip IV.

19. Edward demonstrated his acute awareness of the effect of the position of the sun on his archers and also the state of wind and tide would have upon this naval engagement.

20. It has been described a 'perhaps the most important war in European history'.
(Clifford J. Rogers 'War Cruel and Sharp: English Strategy under Edward III: 1327-1369' Woodbridge 2000.)

21. Early cannon were shaped like a tall bronze vase, lying on its side. They had a range in excess of about three-quarters of a mile. Edward III probably employed these 'crakkis of wer' during his Scottish campaigns and decided to use them elsewhere in his military engagements, observes Ian Mortimer.

22. Derek Wilson 'The Plantagenets: The Kings That Made Britain' Quercus 2011

23. Mortimer

24. 'Great Kings do not lose important battles.' (Mortimer)

25. The French losses were horrendous: almost a dozen princes (including the blind King John of Bohemia), one archbishop, one bishop, eight secular lords, eighty bannerets (principal knights), 1,500 knights and esquires plus thousands of infantrymen, men-at-arms and genoese crossbowmen. The English losses, by contrast, were minimal.

26. Philip VI would have encouraged the Scots King to invade in order to create a distraction for Edward from his invasion of Northern France.

27. In the conflict an arrow had sliced through David's nose.

28. Rodin's sculpture of the 'Burghers of Calais' placed prominently in that French port is intended as a symbol of French heroism during the Franco-Prussian War. The duplicate sculpture positioned outside the Houses of Parliament in Westminster Square proclaims an entirely different ideal: the benevolence of a powerful Medieval monarch.

29. 'It was conventional in the later Middle Ages for the King's consort to be cast in the role of an intercessor (Saul).

30. After the siege, 'Caleys' was marked as English territory on the 14th-century Gough Map of England. A sketch indicates two buildings, a spired church, a castle with walls and five gates. Calais remained an English possession until the reign of Mary Tudor.

31. George Wrottesely 'Crecy and Calais' Harrison and Son

32. The late Diana, Princess of Wales (1961-1997) was a direct descendant.

33. His mother was Eleanor, eldest sister and coheir of Gilbert de Clair, Earl of Gloucester, whence his father had been styled in documents 'Earl of Gloucester'.

34. Men impressed to serve the King were selected for their military capabilities. Towns and cities vied with one another to turn out well appointed men which meant that a most efficient force could be raised in this manner. The localities paid the men until they joined the King's standard, after which they were paid by the Treasurer of the Household. This regular payment added to the system that had been introduced by Edward III. The localities clothed the men in something approaching uniforms. This was calculated to introduce a spirit of discipline and increase control over the men.

35. Wrottesley

36. Aristocrats were shielded from this first wave of the plague. Hugh le Despenser was a rare exception. Perhaps he caught the disease in London. (Benedict Gummer 'The Scourging Angel'.)

37. These muster rolls are reproduced from the account of Water de Wetewang, Treasurer of the King's Household.

38. Sir Robert Atkyns, antiquarian and genealogist, states that the original name for the family was 'de Vyteinton'.

39. Michael Whittington 'The Whittington Story' Parchment, Oxford 1988

40. An Escheator was a royal official who presided over 'escheats', which were properties taken into state custody either by forfeiture or debt or through lack of an heir.

41. A vill is a small nucleated Medieval settlement.

42. Nigel Saul 'Knights and Esquires of Gloucestershire' Clarendon Press 1981. (He cites K.B. 27/290 Rex m 37.) According to the author, most of the offences of which the gentry were indicted were pleas of trespass.

43. Michael Whittington 'The Whittington Story'

44. Edward Phillips Stratham 'History of the Maunsell Family' Vol 1 Kegan Paul, Trench 1920

45. Froissart 'Chronicles'

46. Ian Mortimer 'Edward III'

47. 'Children were expected to work from a young age, achieve self-sufficiency in their mid-teens and, if they reached adulthood, would be fortunate to live beyond their mid-forties,' according to Benedict Gummer in 'The Scourging Angel'. Whittington, the son of a lesser gentleman, led a more sheltered life and doubled this life expectancy of peasants.

48. Also 'Qwytyngton', but this may have been a clerical error in the Calendar of Pleas and Memoranda of the City of London (14 October 1394).

49. This first 'Book of English Common Law' was complied in 1419 by John Carpenter (*c.*1372-1442), Town Clerk to the City of London during the reigns of Henry IV and Henry V. It is believed to have been drafted upon the instigation of Whittington when Mayor.

50. The Register of Pauntley Church is one of the oldest in the county, reaching back to 1538. Parish registers were made compulsory that year on the orders of Lord Chancellor Thomas Cromwell.

51. A member of this family, Elinor Poole, compiled a recipe book (dated 1604) which offers a glimpse into life at Pauntley Court at the start of the 17th century. A relative of Elinor married George Horner whose grandson is immortalised in nursery rhyme as 'Little Jack Horner'.

52. Pauntley Court has been extensively researched by Bernadette Fallon and Mark Jonson from 'All About Your House', an architectural team based in Cornwall. They produced an informative illustrated document which was privately printed after being commissioned by the family presently living at Pauntley Court.

53. Pevsner, 'Gloucestershire 2: The Vale and the Forest of Dean'

54. In the Middle Ages land that was not farmed was reserved for sport and leisure by lords of the manor. One humbler pursuit was breeding and hunting rabbits, which was a fiercely guarded privilege. Their meat was regarded as a delicacy and their fur a luxury. Rabbits were kept in special enclosures and supervised by a warrener who often lived in his own fortified lodge to protect himself from marauding poachers.

55. Peter and Jean Hansell 'Doves and Dovecotes' Millstream 1988

56. The present font is Victorian.

57. Pevsner 'Gloucestershire 2: The Vale and the Forest of Dean'. There are two magnificent examples of tympanums at St Swithin's Church, Quenington, Gloucestershire.

58. Besant and Rice identify the other remains of stained glass in the same window as those of the Linets, Stauntons and Peresford. All these families were intermarried with the Whittingtons.

59. The dish is inscribed: 'Presented by the Corporation of London to the Vicar and Churchwardens on the occasion of the visit to Pauntley Church of the Right Honourable the Lord Mayor of London, Alderman Sir Harold Gillett to mark the 600th anniversary of the birth of Richard Whittington 11th July 1959.' Another illustrious visitor was Queen Mary who was escorted around Pauntley Church by the Duke of Beaufort in 1941.

60. Mortimer 'The Perfect King: The Life of Edward III'

61. Nigel Saul 'Knights and Esquires'

62. George Marchant 'Edward II in Gloucestershire: A King in Our Midst'

63. David Verey and Alan Brooks 'Pebsner's Architectural Guilds: Gloucestershire 2: The Vale and Forest of Dean'

64. A perplexing mystery surrounds Edward II's tomb. Scholars have deliberated whether it is actually the king's body that was originally buried there. It may, after all, have been part of a brilliant deception. There is a suggestion that Edward's death was fabricated and that he escaped from Berkeley Castle, the seat of Thomas Berkeley, Roger Mortimer's son-in-law, to wander throughout Europe for over a decade before dying after being reconciled with his son, Edward III, in Italy. A convincing conspiracy theory involving substitution of the King's body features in Ian Mortimer's 'Edward III: The Perfect King'.

65. The Cathedral window measures 72 ft (22 metres) x 38 ft (12 metres). It is as large as a tennis court.

66. A curious anomaly is a roundel which appears to show a Medieval man playing golf! Dressed in peasant costume, the 'Gloucester Golfer' is hitting a ball with a curved stick. The roundel is contemporary with the window, extraordinary since golf was then unknown in either England or Scotland. Earliest written reference to golf is in a document dated 1457. Most likely the window depicts a forgotten Medieval game, perhaps 'cambruc', widely played in England in the reign of Edward III. This involved hitting a ball made of leather and filled with feathers. All the same, this does not explain why a sport should be included in this early religious window.

67. A further revelation of the images of host and chalice (representing the bread and wine served at the Eucharist) that appear above the angel on the far right of the window could only be photographed during major renovations at the end of the 20th century.

68. Corporation of London Records Office, Hustings, Pleas of Land, Roll 80 (cited in Caroline Barron 'Richard Whittington: The Man Behind the Myth').

69. Michael Whittington

70. Michael Whittington

71. Inquisition Post Mortem Vol X Edward III No 464, page 370

72. Biographers have embroidered on the circumstances of Sir William's outlawry which hastened his demise. Lysons, preposterously, surmises that it might have been in consequence of a rebellion or that, in turbulent times,

he may have slain an opponent who held high favour at Court. There is yet another suggestion that Dame Joan died giving birth to her third son, Richard, leaving Sir William to remarry. He chose as his second wife Joan, widow of Sir Thomas Berkeley of Coberley. Sir William failed to seek royal permission for this marriage to a noblewoman, which incurred the wrath of the King. John Attwood and Arthur Mee are among the authors who have speculated that Sir William's outlawry was imposed because of his presumption in marrying a Berkeley widow.

Chapter Two

73. The Black Death' was a later coinage since contemporaries did not name the illness but referred to it as 'a mortality' or an 'epidemic'. Colloquially, it was called 'the botch'.
74. Rosemary Horrox (ed) 'The Black Death'
75. The mummified carcass of a rat was found in the Norman Church of St Peter at Sandwich, Kent. It was discovered under heavy masonry in the central aisle by workmen who assumed the rat had been crushed by the fall of the tower with its bells in 1661. The Natural History Museum certified it as 'Rattus rattus' more commonly known as the black (ship or plague) rat. This is now rare in England although still evident in international ports such as Liverpool and London. Sandwich was an important Cinque Port enjoying a brisk trade with the Continent. The black rat is smaller and lighter than the brown rat ('Rattus norvegicus'), the tail is longer, the ears are larger and the skull is more slender and pointed. The brown or Hanoverian rat did not arrive in England until about 1730 and it has since then practically exterminated the black rat. Certainly, black rats have not been found within living memory at Sandwich. Although the colour has faded it should be noted that black rats are sometimes brown and vice versa. The body of the black rat is possibly the oldest existing remains of a rat of which the date of death is certain. It is over 300 years old! It is displayed at Sandwich Museum attached to the Guildhall.
76. Patricia Doyle PhD casts doubt on the Black Death being the result of a flea-born infection but proposes it was a viral infection, perhaps a form of Avian Flu similar to the outbreak of Spanish Flu. She cites a recently discovered archive of Dorset court records from the 14th century that showed about 50% of the people living in the area died of the Black Death, or bubonic plague, in the winter of 1348. 'Because rat fleas are dormant during cold weather, it's unlikely that they could have spread the disease.' (The Wellcome Library) This modern analysis is touched upon briefly by Benedict Gummer in his definitive work, 'The Scourging Angel'. While conceding that the traditional view of the cause of the plague being 'great hordes of rats and their ravenous fleas' may no longer be tenable,

he is reluctant to offer an alternative theory. 'While the arguments against this diagnosis are persuasive, no serious alternative has emerged, other than the suggestion that the pestilence bore a likeness to one of the more virulent haemorrhagic fevers currently found in central Africa.'

77. Charles Creighton 'A History of Epidemics in Britain' Vol 1

78. Benedict Gummer 'The Scourging Angel' Bodley Head 2009

79. The Malmsebury Monk later asserted that the plague 'travelled northwards (from Bristol), leaving not a city, a town, a village, or even, except rarely, a house, without killing most or all of the people there.'

80. Pope Clement VI dismissed this notion pointing out that Jews were as much victims of the plague as Christians.

81. Robert Sullivan 'Rats: A Year with New York's Unwanted Inhabitants'

82. Gummer 'The Scourging Angel'

83. Gummer

84. Capital punishment was carried out without interruption in the country during the plague. Geoffrey Cockerel of Oakham was convicted of larceny and hanged on the gallows. When his body was cut down he was found to be still breathing. As a consequence the King pardoned the knave, perhaps recognising that a higher judge had sought to reprieve him.

85. The ports were reluctantly closed, Sandwich was the first, by royal proclamation, to everyone except 'merchants, notaries and the king's envoys' to prevent gold being shipped abroad and thus weakening the economy still further. (1 December 1349.)

86. Prince William of Windsor, however, may had died of natural causes.

87. It was estimated that the City's makeshift cemeteries received 20,000 corpses. This represented half the population of London. There have been far higher estimates: 30,000, 50,000, 100,000! Ralph Stratford, Bishop of London, acquired three acres of wasteland, 'Nomannesland',outside the city walls in an area now known as Clerkenwell in 1349. He consecrated it specifically for the respectable burial of victims of the Black Death. Later, this acquired the quaint name 'Pardon Churchyard'.

88. The Franciscans or 'Greyfriars' – the first and largest of the mendicant friars – were bequeathed so much land during the Black Death that they became one of the richest landlords in the City.

89. There was a second wave of the Black Death transferred from Calais in 1361. This became known as the 'Children's Plague' because young people, who had not developed a resistance to the infection, were the most vulnerable. Great personages did not escape later bouts of the infection and among the high-born victims was Henry IV's mother, Blanche Duchess of Lancaster, who died in 1369. Bubonic Plague for the next three centuries was never absent from one part or other of Britain. It has often been claimed that it was destroyed in London by the conflagration of the Great Fire of 1666 but there is no scientific basis for this. The last outbreak of

plague reported in this country was in 1906-8 when rats carried by grain ships arriving from Russia killed a dozen cottagers at Ipswich, Suffolk.

90. This shortage included trained labourers and master craftsmen. Numerous churches remained uncompleted though lack of skilled workmen.

91. Cattle and sheep were valued more for leather, wool and dairy products than for meat. Pork was more popular than beef or mutton since swine could fend for themselves in the forests and were available all the year round.

92. During the three centuries before the Norman Conquest England's population had doubled. The generation born in the middle of Edward III's reign witnessed it halve through wars and pestilence.

93. The Statute of Labourers was the first piece of national legislation ever introduced by an English government. A labourer was not necessarily better off having secured a higher wage because food prices escalated after a burning summer, an abysmal harvest and a lengthy drought in the years immediately following the plague. Lords offered food and clothing allowances in order to retain a viable workforce on their estates.

94. Susan Hill 'The Spirit of the Cotswolds'

95. Riley (ed) 'Memorials of London and London Life'

96. Anne F. Sutton 'The Mercery of London'

97. Alternatively, the second pandemic in 1361 may have acted as the spur for Whittington's departure from the country to the city.

98. Benedict Gummer 'The Scourging Angel'

99. The 13th-century map of England, probably based on lost drawings by Roman surveyors, was executed by Matthew Paris, a monk of St Albans. It is held at the British Library. The anonymous map, now thought to date from a decade later, is named after one of its antiquarian owners, Richard Gough. It is held at the Bodleian Library, Oxford.

100. Ben Weinreb and Christopher Hibbert (eds) 'London Encyclopaedia'

101. Mayor FitzAilwyn had twice enacted (1189 and 1212) that thatch was forbidden for roofing although there were still a small number of houses with thatched roofs in 1302. Orders were issued for their owners to reroof with tiles and this date appears to mark the end of thatched houses in London. (Gordon Home, 'Medieval London'.)

102. Wylie 'Henry IV' Vol 3

103. The Palace of Westminster is now known as The Houses of Parliament.

104. A cockerel is the symbol of Saint Peter, patron of the church, who thrice denied Christ before the morning cock crowed.

105. The exceptions are Edward VI and Edward VIII.

106. A.R. Myers 'Chaucer's London'

107. Myers

108. St Paul's is shown in the Agas 'View of London' (*c.*1633) with a tower but lacking a steeple.

109. Myers

110. Calendar of the Patent Rolls Edward III Vol VIII 1348-50 p.459
111. Benedict Gummer 'The Scourging Angel'
112. Sutton
113. A prime example of an Elizabethan travelling salesman is Autolycus in Shakespeare's 'The Winter's Tale'. This rascally pedlar is a self-confessed thief and a 'snapper up of unconsidered trifles'. (Act IV Scene 3)
114. Interestingly, there is still a Mercery Lane leading to the precincts of Canterbury Cathedral. This is a short, narrow Medieval thoroughfare that was once alive with pilgrims who would be tempted by the trinkets for sale in the rows of Mercers' shops.
115. Wylie 'Henry IV' Vol 3
116. An Act of 1388 stipulated that 'he or she which used to labour at the plough and cart or other labour or service of husbandry till they be of the age of twelve years, shall abide at that labour without being put to any mystery or handicraft' (Sullivan). The inference is that rival trades and crafts accepted apprentices from the age of twelve.
117. An Act of 1406 barred families below a certain level of income from placing their children as apprentices. The Mayor and Aldermen, sympathetically, sidestepped this sweeping statute by allowing all freemen, irrespective of their wealth, to be accepted. There was a custom that a man was regarded as of free condition if he had lived undisturbed in the City 'for a year and a day.' (Thrupp).
118. Besant and Rice
119. Besant and Rice
120. Wyle 'Henry IV' Vol 2. At some time before 1437 the Mercers increased the term of apprenticeship to ten years. By 1501 they were refusing to enroll an apprenticeship under the age of sixteen.
121. Thrupp
122. Myers relates an incident whereby an apprentice to a master, appropriately named Batter, enrolled him in a private school run by a priest who 'set him in his kitchen to wash pots, pans, dishes and dress meat' even though his indenture stipulated that he should not be involved in 'defying labour'. This abuse of trust for his education resulted in the apprentice – like the legendary Dick – absconding.
123. 'Umple' was used for kerchiefs.
124. 'References to sleeping places of apprentices, journeymen or servants are meagre.' John Schofield 'Medieval London Houses'.
125. Myers 'Chaucer's London'
126. Peter Ackroyd describes their clothing in Tudor times in 'Shakespeare – The Biography'. Apprentices wore blue gowns in winter and blue cloaks in summer; they were also obliged to wear blue breeches, stockings of white cloth and flat caps.
127. Besant and Rice list these popular taverns frequented by city apprentices.
128. Besant and Rice record the seasonal sports indulged in by the apprentices.

129. Myers 'Chaucer's London'. Lorimers specialised in making spurs, bits and other metal pieces for tack.
130. A failed apprentice could not be offered professional work in the City.
131. Thrupp
132. The Treaty of Bretigny called for Edward III to renounce his claims to the French throne and to the overlordship of Normandy, Maine, Touraine, Brittany and Flanders in return for suzerainty of Calais, Ponthieu and the whole of Aquitaine which amounted to nearly a quarter of France. This treaty, however, remained unratified.
133. Mortimer
134. Saul
135. Edward paid an Italian clockmaker to build this innovative device that would regularly chime the hours in the great tower of Windsor Castle. He commissioned further clocks to be installed at Westminster and Queenborough. Incidentally, the word 'clokke' derives from the French 'cloche', meaning bell, since there was no face in early Medieval clocks. Time was 'told' alone by sound. Medieval folk tended to divide the day into twelve equal hours of day and night. Obviously, this was an inaccurate measurement since the length of daylight varied according to the season. Edward, by introducing timepieces, was attempting to standardise time in a way which was an entirely new concept for Europeans.
136. Mortimer
137. Mortimer
138. The House of Commons appointed Peter de la Mare as its first Speaker at the 'Good Parliament' of 1376.
139. Edward also appointed Justices of the Peace for each county who were given the power to arrest, try and punish minor miscreants at Quarterly Sessions. He thereby laid the foundations of local government, which continues to this day. Richard's brother, Robert served in this capacity on several occasions in Gloucestershire.
140. Sutton
141. Saul
142. Froissart
143. Thomas Walsingham 'Historian Anglicana'
144. Edward III remains one of six monarchs to have ruled England for more than fifty years.

Chapter Three

145. Atkyns asserts 'John Walding held the Manor of Staunton 13 Edward 3. He is soon after called John de Staunton and held the Manor of Baylinwick of Staunton in the Forest of Dean 16 Edward 3 and dyed seized thereof 22 Edward 3.'

146. Staunton is three miles east from Monmouth, fifteen miles south-west of Gloucester.
147. Calendar Inquisition Post Mortem 22 Richard II. Vol 17 No 1215
148. Victoria County History Worcester Vol III
149. Robert's name appears on the receipt Roll of the Exchequer for 1386.
150. Nigel Saul 'Knights and Esquires: 'The Gloucestershire Gentry in the Fourteenth Century' Clarendon Press 1981
151. Saul 'Knights and Esquires'
152. 'Hope' denotes a settlement in a valley.
153. Country churches in Gloucestershire and Herefordshire are, perhaps, the most durable reminders of the Whittingtons.
154. The churchyard cross has a niche in the wide stone base for a statue of the Virgin and Child. This indicates that worshippers did not gather around the cross for their services but faced eastwards towards the cross, which acted as an outdoor altar.
155. Another suggestion is that it is a single elliptical camp built by the Romans to repel the Saxons.
156. National Archives Gloucester 13 February 1423 PROB 11/3. An abstract of Robert Whittington's will translated from the Latin, was made by Frank Hockaday, a former court registrar, and this is now held at Gloucester Archives.
157. Woven tapestries were expensive. They were never decorated with arms unless they were made entirely of wool. Cheaper versions were painted cloths enlivened with stencilled patterns. Popular subjects for these wall hangings – whether woven or stained – were chivalric, heraldic, biblical or legendary. (John Schofield 'Medieval London Houses' Yale University Press 1995.)
158. This is the only mention of seating. Interestingly, 'a long table and two benches' valued at 15s 6d were among the contents of a furniture sale from Pauntley Court in February 1811. They may have been remnants of the Medieval house retrieved from the kitchen after centuries of occupation.
159. Beds were were extraordinary expensive. Private business meetings might be conducted around them. This was why their elaborate carvings and curtains might present the family coat-of-arms. Richard Whittington's sumptuous bed is depicted on his 'College Ordinances'. Whittington's close friend and chief executor, John Carpenter, favoured a religious theme for his bedroom since he bequeathed 'a coverlet and testour of tapestry work with a white bordour powdered with the name of I.H.S. and roses' and 'a litill cloth with an image of Our Lady and Seynt John Baptist over the chamber door'. Edward III possessed a magnificent bed of black worsted decorated with clouds of white worsted and angels of red worsted embroidered with gold and silk playing diverse instruments.

Henry IV's bed travelled ahead of him on tour and was even stowed aboard his ship in preparation for his visit to Calais. Richard II's uncle, the Duke of Gloucester, possessed a bed decorated with images of countryfolk jousting. Richard's tutor, Simon Burley, owned a bed whose curtains were embroidered with sailing ships. This last desirable bed was inherited by Richard II. Prince John of Gaunt bequeathed his son, who became Henry IV, his 'great bed of red and white check camaca (camel hair and silk fabric) embroidered with a gold tree and a turturelle (turtle dove) sitting below ... and the great bed of cloth-of-gold'. Henry V owned a large feather 'bed of cherries', enclosed by a canopy embroidered with shepherds, and a black satin bed, enclosed within three curtains of black tartarin, stamped with gold and silver lions at Westminster Palace. On tour, he placed a throne in front of his portable bed to conduct official business in his chamber. He even appointed a servant, John Green. 'keeper of the king's beds'. (Ian Mortimer '1415: Henry V's Year of Glory'.) Edward, Duke of York, bequeathed his wife, Philippa, 'my bed of feathers and leopard' and also 'my green bed, embroidered with a compass', prior to the Battle of Agincourt. Sir John Pultenay, the London magnate, aping royalty, ordered bedcovers and drapes patterned with fleur-de-lis, eagles, lions, popinjays and apple blossom embroidered in silks. One wonders with all that colour and movement how he manage ever to sleep.

160. The name derives from the village of Worsted in North East Norfolk. This was the centre of the trade where long wool was spun into harder yarn that was used to make the fine, light, rich cloth called 'worsted'. Skilled Flemish weavers who came over to England in the 14th century at the invitation of Edward III helped to develop this industry. Today, only the name of the village and the beautiful Medieval church commemorate this once flourishing trade.

161. The names of the horses are difficult to decipher.

162. An exorbitant 'hearth tax' – notoriously difficult to collect in remote regions – was introduced in 1364. (Ian Mortimer 'Edward III'.)

163. See Mark Johnson and Bernadette Fallon's document about Pauntley Court, privately printed.

164. Michael Whittington says that Guy inherited the Manor of Lypiatt and property in Gloucester in a verbal deathbed request by his uncle, Richard. This is confirmed by Anne F. Sutton in her entry for Richard Whittington in the *Dictionary of National Biography*.

165. John Duncomb 'History and Antiquities of the County of Hereford' Vol. III John Murray 1882

166. Pevsner 'The Buildings of England Gloucestershire 2 The Vale and the Forest of Dean'

167. Michael Whittington 'The Whittington Story' Parchment Press 1988

168. National Archives Gloucester 12 June 1440 PROB 11/3. This translation is a composite from two scholars: Dr. David Wright and Ralph Moffat, Curator of European Arms and Armour, Kelvingrove Art Gallery and Museum, Glasgow.

169. Silverware was a universal form of indoor display among merchants and noblemen. Wealthy folk possessed magnificent collections – cups, spoons, boxes, dishes, ewers, basins – sometimes worth hundreds of pounds. They were cherished for their beauty, especially sculptured and enamelled examples, but they were also a wise investment. Silver, then as now, was readily convertible into cash and accepted as security on loans. Naturally, as here, they formed a major part of any bequest.

170. There are several more bequests that seem to relate to swords but, alas, they are indecipherable: 'I leave my son Thomas a silver ... the pommel covered with feathers. I leave my son Guy a silver ... with a pommel ... with wings.'

171. There are many bequests of armour. A prime example is the will of Edward, Duke of York, in 1415: 'Item je deise a Diprant ma petite cote de maille, le piece de plate qu monseignur le prince ma donna apelle brestplate, le pance (mail skirt) qu fuist a monseigneur mon pere.' Henry V who made his will prior to his French campaign that same year bequeathed his armour to his warlike brother and heir, Thomas, Duke of Clarence. Richard II had given his gift of a valuable breastplate to Henry, Earl of Derby, as an indication of his increasing warm regard at that time of his cousin, who later supplanted him.

172. 'Journal of the Regional Furniture Society' No 20 Summer, 1994. The will of John Whittington (1525) has only two further additions to the furniture at Pauntley: 'A feather bed and the hangings of my rede chamber and also the hangings of the hall and parlour; two great standying coffres, one in the rede chamber, the other in the great chamber'.

173. Gloucester Cathedral Library Deeds VI 9

174. Richard Ashwell, the landlord, was Bailiff of Gloucester

175. 'Gloucester Journal' (13/8/1862). The plaque measures 24 inches high by 8 inches wide.

176. He likened the discovery to the excavations at Ninevah!

177. 'Westmacott, the sculptor, Franks, the Director of the Society of Antiquities and Mr. Albert Wray F.S.A. unanimously decided that it was a work of the fifteenth century ... almost certainly set up by Whittington's great-nephew.' (H.R. Fox Bourne, 'Famous London Merchants'.)

179. The sculpture was discovered in the basement of 146 (now 34) Westgate Street. Richard Compton is listed under 'cabinet makers and upholsterers' at this address in Slater's 'Directory of Gloucestershire' (1858-9). an 18th or 19th century building is shown in 'Byant's Street Views of Gloucester' (1841). All the houses in the street have been renumbered and this particular property has long since been swallowed up in modern stores.

Section 2

Chapter Four

1. Nigel Saul 'Richard II'
2. Wylie 'Henry IV'
3. Saul
4. Quoted in Caroline Barron 'The Reign of Richard II' in Cambridge Medieval History Vol VI
5. Incredibly, the Victorians painted the effigy black! The achievements displayed above the Black Prince's tomb are replicas. The Black Prince's emblem-three ostrich feathers picked up from the field after the Battle of Crecy-and his personal motto, 'Ich Dien' ('I serve') are carved on his tomb. His epitaph expresses his recriminations and regrets: 'I thought little on th'our of Death/So long as I enjoyed breath'. According to Benedict Gummer the Black Prince's tomb is 'among the finest ever created for the English crown'.
6. This custom continued for almost three centuries but terminated at the coronation of Charles II.
7. King Richard II later presented Westminster Abbey with a replacement pair, embroidered with fleur-de-lis, blessed by Pope Urban VI.
8. Sylvia Thrupp 'The Merchant Class of Medieval London'
9. Pepperers and spicers increasingly became known as 'grocers'. They dealt in a variety of commodities: pepper, cloves, mace, ginger, saffron, drugs, dyes, currants, almonds, rice, soap, cotton, silver, tin and lead. All their wares were to be sold strictly by weight on the 'gross balance' and only by wholesale.
10. Thrupp
11. Nigel Saul informs that 'court' and 'household' were not then synonymous. A court did not necessarily imply the presence of the King but indicated the principal administrative headquarters presided over by the King, cleric or magnate. The household consisted of officers appointed to serve the King personally in various capacities.
12. Highest assessments were John Philpott, Mayor (£10); William Walworth and Nicholas Brembre (£5 each).
13. Ruth Bird 'Turbulent London in the Reign of Richard II'
14. 'Serf' derives from the Latin 'servus' meaning slave.
15. Nigel Saul 'Richard II'
16. Barron
17. Saul
18. Chancellor Sudbury was also Archbishop of Canterbury. He responded to the threat of rebellion by building a strong wall around his Cathedral city. Insensitively, he apportioned half the cost to its law-abiding citizens.

19. Richard II was fourteen and so was considered to have left behind his childhood.

20. Sudbury's head with his episcopal cap nailed to it was raised on a pike on London Bridge. Later, it was removed and placed in the Church of St Gregory, Sudbury, Suffolk. During restoration in 2011, this grisly relic was removed from its grille and the Archbishop's face was reconstructed by an expert at Dundee University. Sudbury was revealed to have been a bald, chubby, elderly man. The marks of the axe that decapitated him are clearly visible. ('Country Life' 4 July 2012.)

21. The first Fishmongers' Hall dated from 1310. The second hall was bequeathed to the Company in 1434 but was destroyed by the Great Fire. Its replacement, designed by Edward Jarman, was built in 1671 but this was demolished to make way for the new London Bridge. The present building, designed by Henry Roberts, opened in 1834.

22. Information supplied by Ralph Moffat, Curator of European Arms and Armour, Glasgow Museums.

23. The lack of reprisals may have been because of the number of figures of civic authority who had encouraged the rebellion.

24. The last attempt to institute a community charge in order to fund local government was by Conservative Prime Minister, Baroness Thatcher in 1989, which ultimately led to her political downfall.

25. In 1388, an act was again promulgated that no serf should any circumstance be admitted to the Freedom of the City.

26. Customers were also protected by the regulation of the goods offered for sale and restrictions in the method they might be purchased. It was forbidden, for example, to trade by candlelight when wares might not be properly inspected.

27. Thrupp

28. Saul

29. Sir Simon Burley owned an extensive library including nine French romances, a 'Brut Chronicle', the 'Prophecies of Merlin' and Giles of Rome's 'De Regime Principum'. Richard's uncle, Thomas, Duke of Gloucester, also owned a valuable library comprising eighty-three manuscripts and a great vellum Bible illuminated with his coat-of-arms at Pleshey Castle, Essex.

30. Wylie

31. Marie Louise Bruce 'The Usurper King'

32. Gordon Home 'Medieval London'

33. A.R. Myers 'Chaucer's London'

34. Bruce

35. The anonymous author of the contemporary poem, 'Richard the Redless', adds the amusing detail that 'the slevis slide on the earthe'.

36. Benedict Gummer 'The Scourging Angel'

37. Sylvia Thrupp 'The Merchant Class of Medieval London'

38. Nigel Saul 'Richard II'

39. His enormous height was confirmed when his tomb was opened and his skeleton examined in 1871.

40. Saul quotes the Monk of Evesham who left a rare contemporary description of the King.

41. His first wife, Ann of Bohemia, was an elegant horsewoman who is credited with introducing the elegant style of side saddle for processions.

42. This is the first known English cookery book to survive.

43. Mortar and pestle were in constant demand. The royal chef directed that meat, game, poultry and fish were to be prepared with the instruction: 'smite him to pecys'. 'The aim of cooking was to hash and chop and pound and spice', Molly Harrison, 'The Kitchen in History'.

44. Kay Stanniland 'Extravagance or Regal Necessity? The Clothing of Richard II' in 'The Regal Image of Richard II and the Wilton Diptych'.

45. Splendid garments with their elaborate ornamentation such as these were too valuable to be washed and so it was only the undergarments that were regularly changed.

46. Gervase Matthew 'The Court of Richard II'

47. Stanniland

48. Barron

49. Myers

50. Bevan

51. The Chamberlain was a most important figure. He was often a senior knight and always a friend of the King. Above him, however, was the Steward who had total responsibility for the management of the Royal Household.

52. Saul

53. This was the first Marquisite in English history.

54. Barron

55. Sutton (DNB)

56. Barron

57. Wylie

58. Barron

59. Bevan

60. Marie Louise Bruce 'The Usurper King'

61. Sutton

62. Thrupp

63. 'In reality, there was little democracy in City government because the only time the "people" of London were able to express there voice was when mob rule or riots occurred, which was frequent.' (Nick Bateman.)

64. It is interesting to note the diversity of these councillors: barbers, bellmakers, bowyers, carters, cappers (hatters), coopers, gloves, jewellers, lorimers (makers of bits, bridles and spurs), potters, saddlers and woolmongers.

65. 'Althing' is still the name of the Icelandic Parliament.
66. At that time Cordwayne Street was assessed at £2,195 3s 4d; Coleman Street £1,050 and Aldgate just £30.
67. B. Lambert 'The History and Survey of London'
68. Geoffrey Chaucer, the court poet, lost his lucrative post as Controller of the London Wool Customs, although he was later reinstated on the court payroll as Clerk of the King's Works.
69. From £17,000 to £12,000.

Chapter Five

70. Bruce
71. Saul
72. Saul
73. Barron
74. Santina Levey: 'An Elizabethan Inheritance – The Hardwick Hall Textiles' National Trust 1998
75. The portrait was more sensitively restored to feature in the Shakespeare Exhibition at the British Museum in 2012. The portrait is painted on five oak panels and is 7 feet high by 3 feet 7 inches wide. Throughout history it has been displayed in various parts of the Abbey, including the nave, the building of which King Richard refunded. (Information supplied by the Muniment Room and Library, Westminster Abbey.)
76. More likenesses survive of Richard II than of any other English ruler before Henry VIII.
77. The Diptych was once owned by King Charles I. After his death it was acquired by Thomas, Earl of Pembroke, who displayed it at his ancestral home, Wilton House. It is now exhibited in the Sainsbury Wing of the National Gallery.
78. Lisa Monnas 'Fit For a King: Figured Silks shown in the Wilton Diptych' in 'The Regal Image of Richard II and the Wilton Diptych'
79. Samite was a patterned twill silk imported from Spain.
80. Richard II may have adopted his personal emblem of the white hart because it was an implicit pun on his name, most evident in the French spelling: 'Richart'.
81. Pods of broom – 'cosse de genet' – were initially the emblem of the French King, Charles VI, late adopted by the House of Plantagenet ('Planta Genista').
82. Edmund's blue robe with its buttoned sleeves has a design of paired birds, their necks linked by crowns, separated by a pendant sun. The birds are identified as demoiselle cranes that inhabit the fens of East Anglia, which was Edmund's own territory.
83. The Anglo-Saxon King, Edward the Confessor (c1004-1066), was an alternative patron saint of England.

84. These roses must have been white since yellow roses were not known at that time in England.

85. John of Gaunt in Shakespeare's 'Richard II' (1595) delivers a speech in which he refers to England as 'this little world ... set in a silver sea'. (Act II Scene I) The play was conceived as the first episode in an historical sequence – Richard II', 'Henry IV' Parts One and Two and 'Henry V' – all set within Whittington's lifetime.

86. 'The idea of England as the Virgin's dowry enjoyed a wide currency at the end of the fourteenth century.' (Nigel Saul 'Richard II'.)

87. Richard II's birthday was on the Feast of Epiphany (6 January) which may be reflected in this painting of three Kings – Richard, Edward and Edmund – kneeling before the Virgin and Child.

88. Monnas

89. Saul 'Richard II'

90. Traditionally, the Prior of Christchurch is the first Alderman of the City.

91. Riley 'Memorials'

92. Today, City Beadles are ceremonial attendants of the Aldermen.

93. Ruth Bird 'The Turbulent London of Richard II'

94. Riley 'Memorials'

95. In 1550, the Ward of Bridge Without was created as a sinecure for the Senior Alderman upon his retirement as Lord Mayor. This was abolished in 1978 when the number of Wards returned to twenty-five. Today, the number of Wards remains the same although their boundaries were changed in 2003.

96. A.R. Myers 'Chaucer's London'

97. Mortimer 'The Fears of Henry IV'

98. Henry Knighton's 'Chronicle'

99. Sir Edward Dalyngridge was the builder of Bodiam Castle, Sussex.

100. The replacement of a Mayor with a Warden had been resorted to previously by Henry III who wished to punish the Londoners after they had given their support to the rebel Simon de Montfort in 1265.

101. The loan of 10,000 marks (£6,670) was received by the Exchequer on 22 August 1397. (Patent Rolls 20 Richard II.)

102. 29 August 1392

103. St John the Baptist was Richard II's personal saint. This implies an extended allusion to King Richard in the role of 'Lamb of God'.

104. Barron 'The Reign of Richard II'

105. London Bridge had been rebuilt by Henry Yvele in 1388. The towers of its Drawbridge Gate were then adorned with statues of King Richard and Queen Anne.

106. Fabyan's 'Chronicle' p.538

107. King Richard spent Christmas at Eltham Palace in 1392. Londoners made an extra effort to court King Richard by providing entertainment involving

mummers and minstrels. They made surprising gifts – a dromedary for Richard, a pelican for Anne – on Twelfth Night.

108. Bryan Bevin 'Richard II'. Marie Louise Bruce says the sum was adjusted from £100,000 to £10,000 ('The Usurper King'). Caroline Barron argues it was actually £30,000, 'no mean sum albeit lower than originally proposed'. ('Cambridge Medieval History VI'.)

109. Sutton

110. Kay Staniland 'Richard Whittington and His Sales to the Great Wardrobe in the Years 1392 to 1394' in 'The Journal of the Costume Society' Vol 44.

111. Richard Clifford was 'a sublime and literate' courtier to Richard II. He was appointed Keeper of the Wardrobe in 1390. Later, he was promoted to Keeper of the Privy Seal. An able minister, he was a member of the Council left in charge of England when King Richard went over to Ireland in the summer of 1399. He was replaced as Keeper of the Wardrobe by Sir John Stanley in 1396.

112. PRO E101/402/13. A single, severely damaged membrane also survives from a roll of liveries of 1394. Tantalisingly, there are only a few discernible entries relating to textiles and fur drawn from the stores by the royal tailor, Walter Rauf. (TNA PRO E101/403/6)

113. First surviving account of purchases for the Royal Wardrobe that includes a section described as 'mercery' mentions cloths-of-gold, silks, linen, worsted, tapets, buttons and orphreys dates from 1344-5. (PRO1/390/9 ms 3-6.)

114. Raw silk and silk thread were turned into laces or braids and employed for embroidery by the skilled craftswomen of London.

115. Among the materials supplied by Whittington for the King are two samples described as 'mottele' (multi coloured) and 'radiat' (striped).

116. Sutton 'The Mercery of London'

117. Richard Barber 'Living Legends' BBC Publications 1980

118. Barron

119. This was an important step up the ladder for Whittington. Mayors could only be selected from the Sheriffs of London.

120. Riley 'Liber Albus'

121. Liber Albus

122. Galoshes were shoes either made entirely of leather or with a wooden sole.

123. Barron 'Richard Whittington: The Man behind the Myth'

124. Marie Louise Bruce 'The Usurper King'

125. Henry VII later built his Tudor palace on this same site which he confusingly named 'Richmond' after the castle in Yorkshire from which he obtained his former title, 'Earl of Richmond'.

126. Fabyan's 'Chronicle'

127. Barron 'The Reign of Richard II'

128. There was intense rivalry between the Livery Companies. Often this led to heated disputes and public skirmishes. These came to the fore when processions were being organised through the City. The problem was partly resolved when an order of precedence was laid down by the Lord Mayor and Aldermen in 1515. This still remains today. The first five Companies are the Mercers, Grocers, Drapers, Fishmongers and Goldsmiths. The Merchant Taylors and Skinners were given an equal placing and they agreed to be placed sixth or seventh in alternative years. This gave rise to the phrase: 'to be at sixes or sevens'. Remaining places were occupied by the Haberdashers, Salters, Ironmongers, Vintners and Clothworkers.

129. Today, the Mercers' Company, in common with the City Livery Companies, is still governed by a Master and Wardens, elected annually in July, and a Court of Assistants, consisting of the Master and Wardens, four 'members in waiting' and all past members. Membership currently stands at 250 and while admission to the Freedom is normally by patrimony, it is bestowed, from time to time, by redemption. A General Court of all members is held quarterly.

130. Anne F. Sutton 'The Mercery of London'

131. Riley 'Liber Albus'

132. Besant and Rice

133. Wylie 'Henry IV' Vol 3

134. Sylvia Thrupp 'The Merchant Class of Medieval London'

135. Thrupp

136. Myers 'Chaucer's London'

137. Schofield 'London's Medieval Houses'

138. Information supplied by Canterbury Cathedral Archivists.

139. Later, the Mercers also assumed responsibility for the school originally founded by the Friars of the Hospital of St Thomas of Acon in Cheapside. In 1542, Henry VIII allowed the Company to refound it as 'a free grammar school within the City of London perpetually' with a master and twenty-five children. For a time, children were taught at nearby St Mary Colechurch, approached precariously via a flight of steps over a raised vault. After the Great Fire, the school was rebuilt at Old Jewry. Greek and Latin classics were the predominant subjects but reading, writing, arithmetic, geography, history and merchants' accounts were also taught. At the start of the 19th century, The Mercers' School was moved, appropriately, to College Hill on the site of Whittington's Almshouses. Sadly, this school, one of the oldest in London, closed shortly after the Second World War. The Company is still concerned with other schools founded by eminent Mercers in the 16th century: Collyer's School – now Collyer's Sixth Form College – Horsham, West Sussex (1532), Dauntsey's School, West Lavington, Wiltshire (1543) and Abingdon School, Oxfordshire (1563).

140. Besant and Rice Prior to the office of Mayor, the Portreeve was the principal officer of the City of London. 'Port' was the Old English word for 'market town'.
141. Myers
142. William Herbert 'The History of the Twelve Great Livery Companies' Vol 1
143. Strype
144. Thrupp
145. Herbert
146. Besant and Rice
147. The Mercers are unique among the livery companies in retaining their own private chapel. This postwar building provides a hidden haven in the commercial city. It comprises a square, tranquil room with a domed ceiling. It is beautifully decorated and furnished with white oak pews. The canopy over the altar is crowned with carvings of the Company's arms and the maiden's head. In one corner is a remarkable survival from the original Hospital of St Thomas a Becket over which the present chapel is built, an exquisite carving of the crucified Christ. The tortured figure retains only one discernible of the traditional 'five wounds' – the seeping scar where the soldier's sword pierced his side. Centrepiece of an Easter Sepulchre, this has defied destruction from the Great Fire, the English Reformation and the London Blitz.
148. Schofield
149. Herbert
150. A host of institutions were founded or held their inaugural meetings at Mercers' Hall. They included The Merchant Adventurers, the East India Company, the Bank of England, the Board of Trade, the City and Guilds Institute and the Royal Exchange Assurance (originally known as 'The Mercers' Hall Marine Company').
151. Mercers' Hall in Ironmonger Lane was restored in 1956. The modern Livery Hall is also a long, elegant room, panelled throughout in English oak and illuminated by a trio of antique crystal chandeliers. This stately room with its central table and side buffet intended to display the Company plate, is the scene of annual livery dinners presided over by the Master Mercer.
152. Information supplied by Buckingham Palace. Citizen of London in the 15th Century'.

Chapter Six

153. Adam Bamme's origins are obscure with nothing known about him until 1369. This prominent member of the Goldsmith's Company swiftly gained a reputation for his skilful craftsmanship earning him a place as chief supplier to John of Gaunt.

154. Gregory's 'Chronicle' contained in James Gairdner (ed) 'Historical Collections of a

155. Nicholas Brembre was Mayor 1377-8, 1383-4, 1384-5, 1385-6. John Northampton was Mayor 1381-2, 1382-3.

156. Bevan

157. Riley

158. No 1 Lime Street is famously the address of Lloyds of London.

159. Low Sunday is the first Sunday after Easter, regarded by church authorities as a comparative anticlimax to the celebration of the Resurrection.

160. BL Add ch. 6046

161. BL seals xxxv 41

162. This second Mayoral seal lasted until 1912.

163. This bridge is unique in Britain. A reference is made to its 'olde arche bryckworke' in a survey dating from Tudor times, indicating its antiquity. It appears that it may not have built, however, until the occupancy of Queen Margaret in the period 1450-60. In Whittington's time it could actually have been a sloping timber bridge carried on piles across this deep inner moat.

164. M.V. Clarke and N. Denholm-Young 'Kirkstall Chronicle' Bulletin of the John Rylands Library XV (1931) pp 129-30

165. 'custodiam civitat maiori'

166. Sir John Froissart 'Chronicles of England, France and Spain' Vol 2 Henry G. Bohn 1862

167. Calendar of Close Rolls 1396-1398 Part One pp 190-191

168. Calendar Inquisitions Miscellaneous 1392-9, 223-5

169. Michael A Hicks (ed) 'Revolution and Consumption in Late Medieval England'

170. Shakespeare makes Gloucester's murder the catalyst for Richard II's deposition in the play.

171. Eleanor de Bohun was both Henry's aunt and sister-in-law.

172. John Silvester Davies 'An English Chronicle in the Reign of Richard II'

173. Sutton (DNB)

174. Nick Bateman 'From Rags to Riches: Blackwell Hall and the Wool Cloth Trade c1450-1790', Post Medieval Archaeology Vol 38 No 1 2004

175. Hustings Roll 124 (57)

176. A.H. Johnson 'History of the Guild of Drapers' Vol 1 Clarendon Press 1914

177. Reginald Sharpe (ed) 'Calendar of Letter Books of the City of London' Vol H London 1907. 'Ordinance made by Richard Whityngtone, the Mayor and the Aldermen, with the assent of the Commons of the City, restricting the sale of cloth of Bakewellhalle.' pp.449-50

178. Riley

179. Caroline Barron 'London in the Later Middle Ages' Oxford University Press 2004

180. Lambert
181. Lambert
182. Besant and Rice
183. Wylie
184. Barron points out that Whittington's loans were repaid in cash rather than assignment, which is another indication of royal favour.
185. Besant and Rice
186. Riley
187. Richard II, who was styled 'Lord of Ireland', had been the first English monarch for nearly two hundred years to visit that country when he made a tour in 1394.
188. Matthew
189. Calendar of Papal Registers, 1396-1404. The preamble for Register 58 states that the persons named in the list of applicants are granted a confessor of their choice who may attend them, either upon the hour of their death or, in other cases (ie Whittington) as often as they please. All are dated at St Peter's Rome.
190. Bevan
191. Wylie/Saul
192. Mortimer
193. Thomas Mowbray, Duke of Norfolk, within the first year of his exile died of the plague in Venice.
194. Henry Bolingbroke was exiled for ten years.
195. Henry V demonstrated his veneration for Richard II by transferring his body from the Priory of Kings Langley, Hertfordshire, where it had been hastily interred, to Westminster Abbey. King Richard was finally laid to rest beside his devoted first wife, Anne of Bohemia. Their paired effigies present the royal couple lying peacefully with hands linked in love in St Edmund's Chapel.
196. Calendar to the Patent Rolls: Volume 6 Richard II 1396-1399 (Westminster 17 April 1399) The second person to be nominated was John Cole.
197. Marie Louise Bruce 'The Usurper King'
198. Now Spurn Head.
199. Barron
200. Chronicle de la Traison et Mort de Richart Deux, Roy
201. Henry claimed the throne through a direct male line from Henry III; Edmund Mortimer's claim was through the female line. Edward III had willed his throne to pass solely through male descendants, which recognised his son, John of Gaunt, as next in line after his grandson, Richard, and nullified the claims of the Mortimer family. John's son, Henry, was therefore third in line of accession until Richard altered the line of succession in favour of Edmund Mortimer. Henry sidestepped the thorny issue of his succession by claiming descent from Henry III's second son, Edmund Crouchback, which totally obscured the descent of the first three King Edwards.

202. Bryan Bevin 'Richard II'
203. Richard II was eventually laid to rest in Westminster Abbey. The striking effigy above his tomb portrays the deposed King with feminine features. He has high cheekbones, a long straight nose and heavy-lidded eyes. There are traces of a goatee beard and a small moustache. His hair is short and slightly wavy and held in place by a gold circlet. Apparently the contract for the effigy, made by Nicholas Broker and Godfrey Prest, specified that the images of both Richard and Anne should be actual portraits.
204. Shakespeare 'Richard II' (Act IV Scene 1)
205. Nigel Saul 'Richard II' London 1997

Section 3

Chapter Seven

1. The Feast of St Edward the Confessor had special significance for the Lancastrian dynasty. Henry IV had been sent into exile on this day in 1398 by Richard II, which is why he chose it deliberately, one year to the day, to be crowned in his cousin's place. Henry, in homage to this principal English royal saint, commissioned a chapel in Canterbury Cathedral dedicated to Saint Edward the Confessor.
2. Twenty-four Mercers, 'goodly horsemen', rode with their Wardens to attend Edward IV's coronation procession in June 1461. (Sutton)
3. Wylie 'Henry IV'
4. Princes Henry, Thomas, John and Humphrey. Henry of Monmouth, Prince of Wales, was also Duke of Cornwall and Earl of Chester. He inherited his father's throne as Henry V. Thomas, Duke of Clarence, was next in line to the throne. He developed into a military commander of remarkable courage and ferocity. He was his father's favourite and this led to rivalry between the two eldest brothers. Further, he was suspected of supporting Lollardy. John, Duke of Bedford, was solemn, religious and scholarly. He could read and write in English, French and Latin. Nevertheless, he was also a strong and powerful warrior. Henry V valued him greatly and trusted him implicitly. Humphrey, Duke of Gloucester, was also intellectual but lacked military prowess. Latterly, he amassed a collection of classical texts. The oldest part of the Bodleian Library, Oxford, is named 'Duke Humfrey's Library' in his honour. His patronage was extensive and his exclusive court numbered poets, musicians, doctors and astrologers. 'Never before or since has so much brilliance, energy, courage and intellectual understanding been packed into one generation of the royal family.' (Ian Mortimer '1415: Henry V's Year of Glory'.)

5. This was an artful ploy. By making Prince Henry Earl of Chester, the King secured his own influence and authority over the most turbulent and lawless corner of England. Cheshire archers had formed Richard II's bodyguard. The Prince's leadership proved totally successful. In his own reign the formidable Chester archers won the day at Agincourt.

6. Marie Louise Bruce 'The Usurper King'

7. Edward III had set the precedent for the opening of Parliament in English – French by that time had become too little known – in October 1362.

8. Henry claimed the throne, not as the heir of his grandfather, Edward III, but from his great-great-great grandfather, Henry III. Edward III, sensing his demise, drew up a settlement whereby he made his grandson, Richard II, heir to the throne. A proviso ensured that if Richard died without an heir, then the crown should pass first to John of Gaunt and thereafter his eldest son, Henry of Lancaster. Henry had been brought up believing that he had an inherent right to the throne, although strictly speaking he succeeded not through inheritance but deposition.

9. The Black Death had resulted in great social mobility and this has been postulated as the probable cause of the 'Great Vowel Shift'. Scholars propose that this is the reason why English spelling – always perplexing – no longer reflects its modern pronunciation.

10. Besant and Rice

11. Mortimer

12. Wylie explains the structure of early Medieval Court Parliaments. They were comprised of six degrees or ranks: The King, the Archbishops, Bishops, Abbots and Priors; Lower Clergy; Barons and Knights representing the Shires, two from each, elected through or by the Mayors and Sheriffs in cities and the Bailiffs in boroughs. The Lower Clergy, the Knights, the Burgesses and citizens were collectively styled the 'Commons'. They were paid for their services while attending Parliament. The Knights of the Shires – they numbered seventy-four in Henry's first Parliament – were entitled to speak freely in the name of the county that they represented. The Commons were merely petitioners who entered into consultation with their sovereign but it was the prerogative of the King and his Lords to make the final decision over statutes, grants and subsidies. Attendance, when summoned, was compulsory and absence incurred a heavy fine. The King was always present, unless unwell, and he was entitled to name the place where his Parliament would convene. This might shift rapidly. The 'Long Parliament' (1 March-22 December 1406) was moved from Coventry to Gloucester before settling on Westminster. The business with which Parliament was concerned was threefold: war and matters relating to the King and his family; consideration of laws and amendments of existing acts; and private business contained in petitions by individual orders, districts, boroughs or persons.

13. Henry revoked the despised 'Blankchartres' because they had been sealed under compulsion. They were collected and publicly burned at 'the Standard in the Cheape'.

14. Henry also declared of his own accord that no act should be considered as treasonable apart from those specified in the Great Statute of 1351. Moreover, those iniquitous acts declared to be treasonable in 1397 were to be annulled.

15. Henry was erratic in the manner he bestowed his mercy. A Scottish herald, Brice or Bruce, was found guilty of slandering Henry in France. He was condemned to ride through the streets of London with his face turned towards his horse's tail and then to have his tongue cut out. Henry intervened and sent him back unmutilated to Scotland. William Clark, a native of Chester living in Canterbury, was found guilty of libel and condemned by a military court. He was condemned to have his tongue cut out, his right hand cut off and finally to be beheaded on Tower Hill. This sentence was duly carried out. Henry did not baulk at hanging a Franciscan friar in his frock at Tyburn when he publicly expressed his contempt for his assumption of the throne. One incident revealing the passionate fierceness of his nature was when the French envoy refused to kneel to him as King at Windsor in 1400. Henry's rage was quickly spent, however, because when the Frenchman stood his ground the King himself relented and invited him to dinner!

16. Fells referred to wool plucked from slaughtered sheep. This wool was inferior to the clip and was reserved for poorer cloth.

17. Patent Rolls, 1 Henry IV (24 May 1400) Westminster

18. Wylie explains the difference between Council and Parliament. According to a statute of 1357, a 'council' was composed of 'councillors, prelates, magnates and certain of the most discrete men of the parts adjoining the place where the meeting is held' while a 'Parliament' consisted of'councillors, prelates, nobles and others in the land as the custom requireth'. But in Henry IV's reign there was very little difference between the two.

19. Sutton 'The Mercery of London'

20. Richard's brother, Robert, remained in the military service of Henry IV.

21. One possible explanation of Whittington's survival into the new reign was that his elder brother, Robert, had served the young Henry Bolingbroke in 1375. (Cal. Pat. Rolls 1399-1401 page 183), Nigel Saul 'Knights and Esquires'.

22. Mortimer

23. It amounted to 800,000 crowns.

24. Queen Isabella was later married to the Duke of Orleans' eldest son, Charles, Count of Angouleme, then eleven years of age. Throughout the marriage festivities she remained tearful. Isabella died in childbirth at Blois on 13 September 1409.

25. Patent Rolls, 1 Henry IV (30 January 1400) Westminster
26. Patent Rolls, 1 Henry IV (17 February 1400) Westminster
27. King Henry's features, as carved on the monument, portray a heavy face with broad brow and full cheeks. The coarse, brutish chin is fringed with a forked beard split in the centre and curled in two wisps and there is a stylish, long, curling moustache. The hair is parted in the middle and cropped close around the head on which rests the Lancaster Crown.
28. Ian Mortimer 'The Fears of Henry IV'
29. English was gradually phasing out French as the preferred language of the gentility.
30. Wylie 'Henry IV'
31. Henry purchased his recorder for 3s 4d.
32. Issue Rolls record regular payments to his tooth drawer.
33. Her elder sister, Eleanor, who had married Thomas, Duke of Gloucester, was the richest.
34. Mary, Countess of Derby, died the same month as Queen Anne of Bohemia.
35. The supposed tomb in which the body of Jesus Christ was laid after his crucifixion.
36. Mortimer
37. 'De Heretico Comburendo'
38. It had been noted that Londoners – including royal servants – failed to bow their heads in the streets when a priest passed by on his way to minister to dying parishioners, carrying the Host.
39. Ian Mortimer reveals that Henry used expensive cotton as toilet paper! This is suggested in the 'Boke of Nurture' written by John Russell, who states that the chamber attendant must make sure that 'there be blanket, cotyn or lynen to wipe the nether ende' for his lord in the privy. Another interesting fact is that Henry owned the earliest known portable iron, a padded close stool with a brass bowl. 'The Fears of Henry IV'.
40. Sutton 'The Mercery of London'
41. Bruce 'The Usurper King'
42. One prime example of Henry IV's lavish use of gold cloth is in hangings for his portable beds. They were transported to Gloucester Castle ready for the Parliament of 1407. A detailed description appears in Wylie. King Henry's beds were draped with 'velvet or cloth-of-gold, with their testers, broidered with helms, their celers of blue and green silk and their costers of white worsted worked with the initial 'M' ('Maria?') or the word 'Reposez', each with its cadas (worsted stuff) mattress, sheets, blankets, canvasses, quilts, cushions and coverlets, together with all necessary rings, crotchets (hooks), cords, thread, and so forth, had been already sent beforehand on sumpters from Windsor and the Tower'.
43. Stanisland 'Extravagance or Regal Necessity? The Clothing of Richard II'

44. One of Henry's last orders was for a suite of clothes for his minstrel, William Bingley. (23 November 1412.)

45. Wylie 'Henry IV'. (ROT. PARL., iii, 506)

46. Originally, the Guild of Merchant Taylors was a religious and social fraternity founded prior to the 14th century by an association of citizens who were 'Taylors and Linen Armourers'. Linen Armourers, an allied craft to the Taylors, made the padded tunics ('gambesons') worn under suits of armour. By virtue of successive Royal Charters, commencing with that of Edward III in 1327, the functions of the Guild were extended and by about the 15th century they controlled the trade. Today, the Merchant Taylors' Company, which is an association primarily of philanthropic and social character, concentrates on educational and charitable activities. The Merchant Taylors' earliest Account Book is held at Guildhall Library (MS34048/1). It is accompanied by a transcript complied for the Company in the 1920s (MS 34049/1). The original manuscript is fragile, faded and water stained. After all, it is contemporary with Whittington. The entries are in French and written in a hand difficult to read. The text is heavily abbreviated.

47. A 'garderobe' was a Medieval toilet. It was also the place to store clothes since the noxious vapours were thought to deter moths. The 'garderobier' had the dual task of caring for clothes and cleaning the toilets. The modern equivalent is a wardrobe.

48. Barron 'London in the Later Middle Ages'

49. Constantinople, now Istanbul.

50. Le Brut: 'And yn the iij yere of King Harreys regne, ther was a sterre seyne in ye firmament, yat schewed hym-self yrouz alle ye worlde, for dyuers tokenns yat schulde befalle some after; ye which sterre was named & called be clergie "Stella comota".'

51. Wylie

52. Wylie 'Henry IV'

53. Wylie. Despite the offer of huge rewards, he was never captured and his final years remain a mystery.

54. Sir Henry Percy (*c.*1364-1403) was the eldest son of Henry, First Earl of Northumberland, Fourth Lord Percy of Alnwick. He had earned his reputation as a warrior when fighting against the French and Scots. And he had been awarded high offices in Wales after completing several successful campaigns against Glendower. Shakespeare immortalised him in 'Henry IV; Part One', although he altered facts to heighten the drama. For instance, he portrays Hotspur as the same age as Prince Henry (although, in fact, he was considerably older) who slays him in hand-to-hand combat.

55. Sir Edmund was a younger brother of the deceased Earl of March, named as heir to the throne by Richard II. He was therefore uncle of Edmund Mortimer, Fifth Earl of March, still a minor yet with a stronger dynastic

claim to the English throne than Henry IV. Edmund Mortimer was the great-great-grandson of Edward III. He could trace a direct line through Philippa, only daughter of Lionel, the third son of Edward III.

56. Mortimer

57. It was a maxim of strategists of that age never to engage in an aggressive campaign in winter when the fields were bare and the roads were impassable.

58. Wylie

59. Wylie

60. Plate armour drastically restricted air circulation.

61. Gregory's 'Chronicle' contained in 'The Historical Collections of a Citizen of London' edited by James Gairdner.

62. A bronze statue of Hotspur was unveiled at Alnwick, Northumberland, in 2010.

63. Wylie

64. 26 March/15 October 1403 but also £666 13s 4d (12 June), £200 (17 July) and £100 (16 December) repaid by assignment in 1403.

65. Wylie, writing in Victorian times, makes the gruesome observation: 'Of the college buildings not a vestige now remains; but even yet the delver's spade digs through a mass of human bones below the turf.'

66. Characteristically, Henry showed them mercy. Pontefract and Knaresborough Castles were crammed with prisoners. Yet the number of prisoners who were executed was remarkably few and there was a long list of pardons.

67. Wylie

68. War Treasurers were abolished in the 'Long Parliament' of 1406.

69. Edward III had introduced the wool subsidy as an ingenious method of raising ready cash for funding the war with France in 1340. From time immemorial the sovereign had claimed, as his customary due, payment of half a mark (6s 8d) upon every sack of wool exported from his shores and this claim was never disputed. The King might also raise additional funds for his revenue by acting as the 'middleman' on the purchase of wool before its export, a device to which nobody objected because the only losers were consumers abroad. Wylie explains how the scheme operated. A fair price was fixed for the farmers' wool. Naturally, the value fluctuated, but only within narrow limits, and the average was £5 per sack in the home markets in the later Medieval period. It was then purchased at that precise price by the King's officials who immediately resold it to the wool merchants for exportation. They paid a reduced price per sack (say £4) but promised to pay the larger custom to the King once their goods were exported. This additional sum, around £2, was called the 'wool subsidy'. The merchants recovered the cost by raising the price of exported wool sold to foreign dealers. The clever financial scheme made a tidy profit of

at least an extra pound per sack for the King which, in addition to his 'ancient customs' of half a mark, swelled the royal coffers.

Chapter Eight

70. This is the first recorded incidence of that phrase being used in a marriage ceremony.
71. Wylie 'Henry IV'
72. Wylie 'Henry IV' Pells Issue Roll 5 Henry IV., MICH (19 February 1404.)
73. Among Henry's favourites to receive the coveted collar was the poet, John Gower, after he dedicated his greatest work, 'Confession Amantis' (1390) to Henry instead of Richard.
74. As King, Henry adopted a variety of emblems: an antelope, a white swan, a fox's brush, a greyhound and as an alternative flower, a speedwell.
75. Freiderich W.D. Brie (ed) the 'Brut'
76. Mortimer 'The Fears of Henry IV'
77. Mortimer 'The Fears of Henry IV'. The author calculates that Joan, from the day of her marriage, cost the public purse an extra ten thousand marks (£6,670) annually.
78. Issue Rolls: 3 Henry IV (19 April 1401)
79. Barron
80. Wylle 'Henry IV'
81. Known as the 'Bohemian' or 'Palatine' crown, it is recorded in a list of jewels and plate drawn up after Richard II's deposition in 1399.
82. The formal betrothal took place at Lambeth on 26 December 1405.
83. Issue Rolls: Easter, 7 Henry IV (28 July 1405) (E403/587 m 10). The abbreviated Latin word is almost certainly to be expanded as 'perlis' meaning 'pearls'. The confusion results from the fact that the first letter is not a single 'p' but a contracted 'per' which is followed by an 'l' with 'is' reduced to a mark of abbreviation. It is, however, possible that the abbreviation could be expanded in an alternative way. The word 'pearlin' would mean silk or thread lace or, in the plural, edgings of material or clothes trimmed with it. (Dr. David Wright.) Wylie seems wide of the mark preferring 'pellibus' meaning skins or 'wildware'.
84. Calendar of Select Pleas and Memoranda of the City of London (17 May 1382). The pearls, which were produced in court, were valued at 424 pearls at 1½d each (53s); 294 at 2½d each (£3 1s 3s); 180 at 1¼d each (18s 9d); 1½ oz 3¾ dwt. at 16s 8d the ounce, (28s 1d); 1 1/8 oz at 10s the ounce (11s 3d): Total £8 12s 4d.
85. Barron. Thomas Pynchoun acknowledged receipt of his property on 31 July 1406. Thereafter, Pyncheon and Whittington became business partners. They acted together in a property transaction involving shops in the Parish of St Michael Cornhill.

86. Barron. This money was repaid by assignment on 28 July. P.R.O. E403/587. There is another loan, for £666 13s 4d recorded as paid on that same date and repaid by assignment on 6 August 1406.
87. Wylie 'Henry IV'
88. Wylie 'Henry IV'
89. Miniver is unspotted white fur derived from the stoat. (Lockett, however, says that miniver was derived from the red squirrel.)
90. Ann Monsarret 'And the Bride wore... The Story of the White Wedding'. White was not yet thought of as a bridal colour. Monsarrat does not refer to any earlier royal brides wearing white as part of their wedding outfit but her research was based on secondary sources.
91. Alison Weir, 'The Six Wives of Henry VIII'. Edward IV broke with tradition by marrying a commoner, Elizabeth Woodville, in 1464. The couple provoked the nation's condemnation for their folly in marrying for love.
92. The marriage age was fixed in England at fourteen for girls and seventeen for boys.
93. Afterwards there is a marked decline in Whittington's trade in mercery to the royal household. Rival merchants in London and Italian dealers abroad soon overtook him in commissions. Admittedly, little is known of Whittington's sales, apart from special occasions, at the start of the Lancastrian dynasty. There are no surviving rolls nor account books for the Great Wardrobe between the extravagant spending of Richard II in 1392-4 and the modest expenditure of Henry IV recorded in the account book for 1407-9. William Lovenay was then succeeded by Richard Clifford, by which time Whittington's supplies of materials to the crown had practically ceased. In that latter period Whittington sold materials worth only £126 15s 4d to the Great Wardrobe. Indeed, the total expenditure of the crown in these years was comparatively moderate. Obviously, this was the effect of the general policy imposed upon the royal household to tighten its belt!
94. Mortimer
95. Wylie
96. Thrupp 'The Merchant Class of Medieval London'
97. Harleian Charter 57 G 36
98. Barron 'The Reign of Richard II'
99. Besant and Rice
100. Wedding customs are from Alison Weir's introduction to 'The Six Wives of Henry VIII'. Details related there refer to the Tudor period but also apply to the Medieval Age.
101. Calendar Inquisitions Post Mortem TNA: C 138/9 No 38 (Swindon 23 September 1414.)
102. Jean Imray 'The Charity of Richard Whittington'
103. Calendar Inquisitions Post Mortem Vol 20 No 216 (Crewkerne 23 September 1414.)

104. The law of inheritance was perfectly simple. Sons inherited their father's property in order of seniority. A daughter could inherit if there was no male heir but if she married the property passed absolutely to her husband. If there was more than one daughter then the property was divided into equal shares. This often resulted in a great estate becoming a series of extremely small holdings.

105. Barron points out that it was John and Eleanor's son, John, who finally inherited the Fitzwaryn estates.

106. Barron considers that Whittington, at one time, also part owned Fitzwaryn's manor of Poorstock in Dorset. Whittington is recorded as holding lands at Melbury Osmond, Fifehead Neville, Blackland, Ramsbury and Mappowder in Dorset. Perhaps these formed part of the Poorstock estates held as security on money loaned to his father-in-law for a short time until the debt was repaid.

107. First Mayor, Henry FitzAlwin, had insisted new builds were to be constructed of these materials after a series of disastrous fires in the 11th century.

108. Sutton 'The Mercery of London'

109. Thrupp

110. London Mayors seem to have adopted a freewheeling attitude towards their coats-of-arms. They assumed emblems that they thought adequately expressed their personal interests or achievements. In the fifteenth century, Heralds began to take control over such matters and, thereafter, the Mayor's arms were formalised. The College of Arms in England is directly overseen by the Earl Marshal, the Duke of Norfolk, on behalf of his sovereign. Under the Duke appear three Kings of Arms: Garter (who presides), Clarenceux (whose jurisdiction is south of the Trent), and Norroy (whose jurisdiction is north of the Trent). Under the Kings are six Heralds – Somerset, Chester, Windsor, Richmond, Lancaster and York – and four Pursuivants – Rouge Croix, Rouge Dragon, Porcullis and Bluemantle. The first King of Arms, William Bruges, was appointed at the time of Agincourt.

111. Today an annulet is a small circle in heraldry employed as a mark of cadency. It is added by a fifth son to differentiate his inherited family shield. First son employs a label (similar to a triple toothed comb). Second son employs a crescent. Third son employs a mullet (a star). Fourth son employs a martlet (a bird). Fifth son employs an annulet (gold ring).

112. Though according to Sir Anthony Wagner, Garter King of Arms, 'The annulet is not, as Lysons thought, a mark of cadency (this would be an anachronism), but an integral part of the coat, perhaps an old difference,' 'Historic Heraldry of Britain'.

113. His crest, described as 'a Lion's Head, erased Sable, langued Gules', is a black lion's head shown as though torn from the body with a ragged neck (erased) and a black tongue.

114. Information supplied by the College of Arms.

115. London Metropolitan Archives CLC/521/MSS 02903 (7 May 1402). This is a receipt from 'Thomas Gerberge, knight, Richard Whytynton, citizen and Mercer of London, and William Gylot, clerk, Receivers General in England' acting for Edward Plantagent, Earl of Rutland and Corke, for two hundred and thirty-three pounds six shillings and eight pence paid in gold by 'Hugh de Holes, Chivaler' as the purchase price of 'the Manor of Oxeye Richard with its appurtenances in the County of Hertford'.

116. London Metropolitan Archives CLC/521/MSS 03457 (13 May 1410) Whittington's seal is the second from the left in a string of five hanging seals attached to an impressive parchment that appears to concern the purchase of a tenement in London.

117. British Museum Add MS 14820 (H). The letter is printed in 'Royal Letters, Henry IV' (ed) F.C. Hingeston-Randolph, ii (pages 271-4)

118. Skinners' Hall Deed No 59 (1 December 1418). The deed is held at Guildhall Library.

119. National Archives E 40/2006 (9 March 1422)

120. In English law, 'mainpernor' offers surety for a man's appearance at court on a stipulated day.

121. Thomas Wandesford, Master of the Mercers in 1437, owned Whittington's mansion and hosted a feast there for the brethren.

122. Sutton

123. A.R. Myers 'Chaucer's London'

124. Besant and Rice

125. It appears to have been the practice for the livery cloth to be bought communally. This made it cheaper when each member paid his fair share. He then ordered his tailor to cut the cloth to fit according to his means.

126. Myers

127. Sutton

128. Myers

129. Herbert 'The Twelve Great Livery Companies'

130. Anne F. Sutton 'I Sing of a Maiden', The Mercers' Company 1998

131. Vanessa Harding and Laura Wright (eds) 'London Bridge Accounts: 1381-1358' London Record Society 1995

132. Patricia Pierce 'Old London Bridge'

133. Incredibly, this narrow thoroughfare was the scene of a tournament on St George's Day 1390. The contest arose from a dispute between a Scottish Lord, David de Lindsay, and an English nobleman, John de Welles, over which of these two nations was the most valiant. King Richard II presided, seated prominently on a dais under a panoply of cloth-of-gold, had a grandstand view as the two contestants jousted 'with speares sharpe ground for life and death'. (Another account insists the spears were blunt.)

The romantic tale is rehearsed in Gordon Home's 'Old London Bridge' (John Lane/Bodley Head 1931)

134. A superbly detailed model of Old London Bridge is displayed inside St Magnus the Martyr in Lower Thames Street. The church marks the northern approach to the original bridge and Medieval stonework is piled up opposite its porch at the Bottom of Fish Street Hill. The model, which gives a marvellous impression of the clutter and chaos of the narrow passageway, was made by David Aggett, a liveryman of the Worshipful Company of Plumbers, in 1987.

135. Sheriffs were elected on St Matthew's Day (21 September) and were presented at the Exchequer on Old Michaelmas Day (11 October). Today, they are elected annually from among the Aldermen on Midsummer Day.

136. Bowsher

137. Besant and Rice

138. Whittington was never addressed as 'Lord Mayor' because that title only came into being at the end of the 15th century.

139. Ruth Bird 'Turbulent London'

140. The Recorder was a professional lawyer, qualified to advise the Mayor and Aldermen on legal matters after training at one of the Inns of Court.

141. Riley 'Liber Albus'

142. From 1384, the new Sheriffs, at the King's insistence, also had to be sworn in before the Barons of the Exchequer instead of before the Mayor and Aldermen. 'The Mayor protested but the Crown prevailed.' (Thrupp)

143. The Mayor's wonderful attire is described at a late pageant when Henry VI rode into the City of London in 1432: 'The mayor's robes outshone all ... In rede Crymson velwett, and a grete velwett hatte furred royally, and a girdell of gold aboute his mydell, and a bawdricke of gold aboute his neck, trillying down behynde hym.' (The 'Brut' No 136 p.462.)

144. The Mayor's Swordbearer was a coveted role. John Medford esquire was the City's Swordbearer from 1467 to 1485. He received an annual salary of twenty shillings and an apartment over the Guildhall gateway. The Mayor and his Swordbearer took precedence even over the Dukes in formal processions.

145. Riley 'Liber Albus'

146. William Cooke Taylor 'Chapters on Coronations'

147. John James Baddeley 'The Guildhall of the City of London' Simpkin, Marshall, Hamilton, Kent and Co 1898

148. Martha Carlin 'Medieval Southwark'

149. A. R. Myers 'Chaucer's London' Amberley 2009

150. Thrupp

151. Valerie Hope 'My Lord Mayor: Eight Hundred Years of London's Mayoralty'. Weidenfeld and Nicolson 1989. According to Whittaker's

'Almanac' (2012) 'In England and Wales the chair of a borough council may be called a mayor and the chair of a city council may be called lord mayor (if lord mayoralty has been conferred on that city).' In 2012 there were 23 Lord Mayors.

152. Thrupp

153. Patricia Pierce 'Old London Bridge'

154. Wylie

155. Presumably, the Giant referred to one of either the legendary figures originally known as 'Gogmagog' and 'Corineus', later transformed into the more familiar 'Gog' and 'Magog'. Outsize statues of these legendary creatures were a feature of pageants and parades from at least the beginning of the 15th century. Supposedly, these mythical giants were the warriors involved in a pre-Christian conflict that resulted in the founding of New Troy, the capital city of Albion (England). Modern representatives of Gog, an Ancient Briton, and Magog, a Trojan invader, stand in the Great Hall at Guildhall and occasionally they will make an appearance in the Lord Mayor's Show.

156. Myers

157. Myers

158. Wylie 'Henry IV'

159. Gregory's 'Chronicle' contained in 'Historical Collections of a Citizen of London in the 15th Century', ed James Gairdner Camden Society 1876

160. Barron

161. 'Liber Albus' translated by Henry Thomas Riley Richard Griffin and Company 1861

162. Record Book of the Brewers' Company

163. Informative displays concerning the history of eel fishing can be found at both the Gloucester Folk Museum and the Museum of London.

164. '(Chipstead) and his companions endeavoured to stay the Wardens at their Hall in Fastres Lane for having treated with the Mystery of the Pelters.' W.S. Prideaux, 'Memorials of the Goldsmiths' Company' Eyre and Spottiswood 1896.

165. Goldsmiths' Company Hall in Foster Lane had recently been rebuilt by Drew Barentyne. It was a splendid building that encompassed a courtyard, an essay office, vaults, an armoury and a granary. ('The London Encyclopaedia'.)

166. Lisa Jefferson, 'Wardens' Accounts and Court Minute Book of the Goldsmiths' Mistery of London: 1334-1416.' Woodbridge, Boydell and Brewer. 2003

167. Jefferson

168. Myers

169. H.T. Riley (ed) 'Memorials of London Life'

170. According to Myers, 'A priest who was caught with a woman was to be brought to the Tun prison in Cornhill, attended by minstrels, but after the third offence to be driven out of the city.'

Chapter Nine

171. Barron provides a detailed record of fifty-eight loans.
172. These loans need to be put into context, however, because in the middle of the previous century the loans to the Crown by prominent noblemen, merchants and landlords – Bishop Henry Beaufort, Henry Picard, William and Richard de la Pole – reached five figures.
173. Grafton's 'Chronicle or History of England: 1569' Vol I pp.499-500 reprinted 1809
174. Whittington's loan even then was not always the largest at any one time. In 1406, John Norbury and John Hende both doubled Whittington's loan of £1,000.
175. Imray
176. Mortimer
177. Wylie
178. Barron
179. Barron
180. The total amounted to £21,562. The Medieval accounting system, however, means that it cannot be ascertained whether or not several of these loans were in fact replacements of previous ones. Obviously, this would exaggerate the total.
181. Sutton
182. Deuteronomy 23 v 19: 'You shall not lend upon interest to your brother.'
183. Richard Barber 'Living Legends' BBC Publications 1980
184. Imray
185. Barron
186. Excavations uncovered a Roman quay but there was no evidence of a Roman 'portoria' (Custom House).
187. After the Norman Conquest there was a large increase in the import of wine, particularly from Gascony. A levy on wine, 'prisage', was introduced for the benefit of the king and his court. The royal butler was charged with the selection of imported wines but was limited to one tun in twenty-one from before the mast, one from behind – and he was certain to pick the best barrels. At ports beyond the reach of him or his agents the allocation of wine was commuted to payment of money, known as 'butlerage'.
188. Graham Smith 'Something to Declare'. Stow lists Edward III's 'auncient customes' on ships landing at Billingsgate: 'of two quarters of corne measured, the king was to have one farthing. Of two quarters of sea coale measured a farthing, of every thousand Herring a farthing etc.'

189. The title 'comptroller' died out in the United Kingdom when Custom and excise were merged just after the First World War, although it remained in use throughout the Commonwealth. Collectors in charge of geographical regions called 'collections' remained until the last decade. In London, in addition to the London Port Collection, there was London North, London South, London Central and London Airports. Around the coast of Britain these collections were named after the principal port of the region, i.e. Southampton Collection, Plymouth Collection, Portsmouth Collection, Dover Collection etc.

190. Gordon Home 'Medieval London'

191. Chaucer's term of office lasted from 1374 until 1376. He was following in the footsteps of his grandfather and father who had both held positions in the customs service.

192. Graham Smith 'Something to Declare'

193. Wylie

194. The King and his Council levied a duty known as 'small custom' (amounting to three pence in the pound) on articles imported or exported through all the ports. Goods arriving be sea at Boston during October and November 1400 – olive oil, onions, garlic, fish, copper, ermine, linen thread and fustian – valued at £3,923 were charged a 'small custom' of £48 7s. A worthwhile sum to swell the country's coffers.

195. 'Tonnage' referred to a tax on every tun (cask) of imported wine; 'poundage' to a tax on every pound weight of exported and imported merchandise.

196. London Encyclopaedia

197. London Encyclopaedia

198. The Custom House was one of the unluckiest buildings in the City of London. Churchman's building was destroyed by fire in 1559. It was rebuilt almost immediately by William Paulet. This building suffered the same fate in the Great Fire. It was replaced by a grand two-storey building with wings, designed by Sir Christopher Wren. But then this building was destroyed by a nearby gunpowder explosion. Again, it was rebuilt by Thomas Ripley between 1715 and 1727. Ripley's building featured the famous 'Long Room' where official documents were consulted regarding duties payable on cargoes. The huge growth in seaborne trade resulted in the necessity for an even larger building almost a century later. David Laing, official surveyor for the Customs Board, completed a new Custom House between 1813 and 1817. Soon after Laing began his construction, Ripley's building was destroyed by fire. Laing's building, too, suffered a miserable fate. In 1825, a section of the upstairs 'Long Room' collapsed into the warehouse below. The reason was that the beech piles on which the building rested had rotted because of their close proximity to the River Thames. The facade and the first floor 'Long Room' were then rebuilt

by Robert Smirke. Although the east wing suffered bomb damage in the Second World War Blitz, Smirke's impressive Custom House survives along the Embankment.

199. The Stocks Market also occupied this same site.
200. Barron
201. This phrase which introduced the Ordinance of the Staple is quoted in Eileen Power's 'The Wool Trade in Medieval History'
202. David Buirski 'The Woolmen's Tale'
203. Quoted in Power
204. Alison Lockett 'The Wool Trade'
205. The name is said to derive from the sheep cotes in which the sheep were kept at night.
206. Information supplied by Thomas Jackson, 'Oxstalls Farm', Frampton Mansell, Gloucestershire.
207. Centre of the Cotswold wool trade was Northleach. The beautiful church proclaims the piety and gratitude of farmers, dealers and merchants to God. Brasses depict successful wool merchants, including John Fortey whose feet are planted squarely on a sheep and woolsack, and William Greville is described as 'the flower of wool merchants in all England'.
208. Flanders referred to the area now covered by Belgium, parts of Holland and Northern France.
209. Lombardy was part of Northern Italy.
210. 'Carding' meant straightening out and blending wool fibres ready for spinning while 'combing' meant removing short fibres and arranging long fibres parallel ready for worsted spinning.
211. Power
212. Barron
213. Sutton estimates that Mercers may have accounted for one third of the annual shipments of wool exports by the beginning of the 15th century.
214. Whittington and London acknowledged a debt of £187 16s 10d owed to the Crown for Customs and subsidies for wool they exported jointly prior to Easter 1407.
215. Gummer 'The Scourging Angel'
216. Robert Gardiner (ed) 'Cogs, Caravels and Galleons'
217. A 13th-century seal from Danzig (Gdansk), Poland, features the North or Pole Star to symbolise the helmsman's reliance upon primitive astro-navigation.
218. Alison Lockett 'The Wool Trade'
219. Chaucer, 'Prologue to the Canterbury Tales' (lines 276/7)
220. Stow
221. Power
222. Smith 'Something to Declare'
223. Eileen Power 'The Wool Trade in English Medieval History'

224. Power

225. Originally, the London Staple was situated at the western boundary of the City, marked by Staple Inn, High Holborn. Later, it was moved to Westminster on the site now occupied by New Palace Yard beside the Houses of Parliament.

226. The location of the Staple varied and for a time it was Middleburgh (1383-8 and 1392). This meant that the focus of all English trade was moved temporarily to that town. The Middleburgh Staple was provided with its own Mayor and it is likely, too, that the English Chapel of St Thomas was established at this period. The town was second in importance only to Bruges until Antwerp rose to dominate the concerns of English traders.

227. John Olney, a Mercer with family connections in London and Coventry, claimed to be the first Englishman born at Calais.

228. Alison Lockett 'The Wool Trade' Methuen 1974

229. Wares that came under the compulsory control of the staple were mainly raw materials for manufacture and comprised wool and skins, sheepskin and leather.

230. Wylie

231. Close Rolls, 9 Henry IV, membrane 4d (13 August 1408, Westminster)

232. Barron

233. Edward III experienced the terror of French invaders when they captured his wool fleet berthed at Southampton in 1338. Five ships, including his prestigious *St George*, and one of his largest, *Christophe*, plus his flagship. *Edward*, were targetted. These ships, the pride of his navy, presumably were acting as escorts to the cogs carrying wool. The King suffered the indignity of watching them turned against him at the Battle of Sluys in 1340. They were swiftly regained.

234. National Archives E 122/34/3

235. C.P.R. 1403-9, 178

236. Issue Roll 1 Henry V Michaelmas (10 October 1413)

237. Michael Wood 'In Search of Shakespeare'

238. Register of the Guild of Holy Trinity, St Mary, St John the Baptist and St Katherine of Coventry' (ed) Mary Dormer Harris Dugdale Society 1935

239. Fortunately, St Mary's Hall survived the 'Baedeker Raids' of the Second World War. It still stands just south of the Cathedral ruins, in Bayley Lane. Although 'Trinity Guild' no longer exists, St Mary's Guildhall is constantly employed for private and civil functions.

240. These 14th-century windows were already in a decayed condition by the 18th century. Both windows were replaced by the early 19th century, but the restorers failed to retain any of the historic glass. What became of the remainder of the removed glass is not known and the later versions did not reproduce every detail of the originals.

241. In 1409, Richard Whittington, John Shadworth and Thomas Fauconer shared a joint interest in an estate in Coventry.
242. Sutton (DNB)
243. Barron
244. The 'alnager' was the official supervisor of the measure and quality of manufactured woollen cloth.
245. Calendar of Pleas and Memoranda Rolls of the City of London: 1413-1437. Ed A.H. Thomas Cambridge University Press 1943
246. Sutton
247. Barron
248. Sutton
249. Barron
250. Barron
251. Sutton
252. Barron
253. Barron
254. Ian Mortimer Edward III
255. Saul
256. Wylie 'Henry IV'
257. Elizabeth Woodville.
258. Barron observes: 'As the heroic deeds of English knighthood moved further away from the battlefield onto the printed page, so it became increasingly possible for the merchants of London to become knights themselves.'
259. Leprosy, for over two centuries, had been a dreadful scourge all over Europe, where it was known as the 'Great Malady'. Symptoms recorded seem similar to those of which Henry complained: 'ponderous and grievous dreams with sharpness, burning and pricking in the flesh'. There was then no known remedy and isolation was inevitable to avoid it spreading. Lepers were banned from towns and cities. They were branded on the cheek, their clothes were burned and they were turned away naked. They might beg outside the gates but were compelled to sound clappers to warn passers-by to shun them. They were forbidden to wash in the common stream or draw water from the common bucket. If they spoke to travellers they must stand where the wind would carry away their tainted breath. If a leper consented to give up his liberty, the burial service would be read over him and he was treated as if he were literally dead. Thereafter, he became an inmate of the tiny shacks – 'measlecotes' – located in fields far from the walls of the city. He then relied upon scraps of food donated by Christian charity.
260. Wylie explains this 'strange infernal machine' called 'a caltrappe' or 'a hirun with thre braunchis'. This deadly device was equipped with poisoned spikes, so arranged that they would pierce the body of whoever lay down upon it. Luckily, it was discovered in advance hidden in the royal bed.
261. Mortimer

262. Joseph Shatzmiller 'Jews, Medicine, and Medieval Society'

263. Prince Henry retired amicably as regent on 30 November 1411.

264. Wylie

265. Although the 'Chronicles' refer to the winter of 1410, it is far more likely to have been that of 1408. Ian Currie 'Frosts, Freezes and Fairs, Chronicles of the Frozen Thames and Harsh Winters in Britain Since 1000 A.D.'

266. Wylie

267. Stow

268. Lady Alice could not have died from either of these infections. The Plague was so contagious and spread with such enormous momentum that the victim would have been dead long before a doctor could arrive from abroad. Influenza did not sweep through the country until towards the end of the fifteenth century. Creighton, the expert on epidemics, asserts: 'This strange disease, which came to be known all over Europe as "The English Sweat", was a new type of infection first seen in the autumn of 1485.' (Charles Creighton 'A History of Epidemics in Britain' Vol. 1.)

269. Chaucer, in his Prologue to 'The Canterbury Tales', presents his Doctor of Physic as diffident to all but paying customers and viewing the plague as a welcome source of income: 'And yet he was but esy of dispence;/He kepte that he wan in pestilence.' Lines 441-2.

270. Fr. Roll II Henry IV 20

271. Joseph Shatzmiller 'Jews, Medicine and Medieval Society', University of California Press 1995. Myers points out that physicians and surgeons were kept busy by the violence of everyday life in the City.

272. Caroline Barron 'Richard II, Image and Reality, Making and Meaning, The Wilton Diptych'

273. Rosemary Horrox (ed) 'The Black Death'

274. Unnoticed by the chroniclers, their line can be difficult to trace. Indeed, researchers have made unconvincing attempts to connect them with the Seymour family, a prominent member of whom was Queen Jane, third consort of Henry VIII.

275. Calendar Inquisitions Post Mortem Vol 22 No 368. TNA C139/13/59mm 1-2 (21 February 1424.) Traditionally, a girl would have two female godparents and one male; a boy vice versa.

276. Richard Harold St Maur, 'Annals of the Seymours' Trubner, Trench, Kegan and Paul 1902

277. Calendar of the Pleas and Memoranda of the City of London (18 March 1409)

278. 'Liber Albus'

279. Barron

280. Mortimer

281. Shakespeare makes much of these two incidents – Prince Henry's removal of the crown and King Henry dying in Jerusalem – in 'Henry IV, Part Two'.
282. Prince Thomas was absent in France but he arrived home in time for his father's funeral.
283. Wylie 'Henry IV'. The short, stout, bald figure depicts Henry IV crowned and caped. His clenched fists are due to the fact that Cromwellian soldiers lopped off his fingers!
284. Wylie points out that it may be a mistake to assume that Henry's 'thick bifid beard' was actually red during his life 'for it is said to be an observed fact that human hair often turns red after long interment'.
285. Wylie
286. Wylie 'Henry IV'
287. Mortimer 'The Fears of Henry IV'
288. Bevan 'Richard II'

Section 4

Chapter Ten

1. Anne F. Sutton, Richard Whittington 'Dictionary of National Biography'
2. Custom decreed that kings should be crowned on Sundays.
3. Etiquette forbade guests to scramble for the best platters, lick plates with their tongue, drip sauce on their breast, spread butter with their thumb or clean their teeth with the tablecloth.
4. Apparently, the King not only refused food but fasted for three days afterwards.
5. Wylie, 'The Reign of Henry V'
6. Legend asserts that the monastic church dedicated to St Peter was built by King Sebert of the East Saxons in the 7th century on Thorney Island. This was a prime site for an ecclesiastical foundation because of the availability of fresh water from the numerous springs and plentiful supply of fish in the nearby River Thames. A Charter purporting to be issued by King Offa of Mercia granted land to St Peter and needy parishioners 'in that terrible place which is called Westminster'. Certainly, a thriving monastery existed there by the time that Edward the Confessor became King in 1040.
7. Pope Leo IX released King Edward from his vow to make a pilgrimage to the tomb of the Apostle Peter in Rome on condition that he founded or restored a monastery dedicated to that saint. Edward moved his palace to Westminster and began constructing a new church on the site of the previous building on Thorney Island. Nothing now exists of Edward's solid cruciform church, although the Norman undercroft and Chapel of the Pyx in the cloisters remain.
8. The present nave is far higher than any other English church: 103 feet.

9. 'The old church was pulled down as far west as the nave, the new building being started from the east, as was the custom with medieval builders.' ('The London Encyclopaedia' edited by Ben Weinreb and Christoper Hibbert.)

10. Westminster Abbey features on the Bayeux Tapestry. This was actually an embroidery, probably worked at the Canterbury School of Needlework, which dates from just after the Norman Conquest. The Saxon Church of St Peter, which became known as Westminster Abbey, is presented in a state of near completion with a central tower and transepts. A builder is precariously fixing a weathercock to the lead roof. Westminster Abbey is depicted with the hand of God appearing through the clouds to bestow his blessing on the already consecrated building.

11. Officially, there is no such place as 'Westminster Abbey'. It ceased to be an abbey when the monks left in January 1540. It ought correctly to be styled 'The Collegiate Church of St Peter, Westminster'. St Paul's, of course, was East Minster.

12. An entry in the account roll for 1401/2 – 'de Ricardo Whytington ad opus nove ecclesie' – occurs alongside the amount £6 13s 4d. (Proceedings of the British Academy' Vol IV.)

13. There are extant three account rolls of the two Richards-from 7 July 1413 to Christmas 1416; from Christmas 1417 to Christmas 1418 and from Christmas 1420 to Christmas 1421. In addition, there is an account of all monies received from Henry Kays, warden of the Hanaper, from 21 March 1413 to 31 August 1422. The Hanaper was originally a wicker basket for holding a drinking vessel with a stem called a 'hanap'. It was also used in the Chancery for a wicker basket containing documents. It then became the name of a department of Chancery-under a clerk or warden, into which were paid fees for the sealing of writs, patents and charters.

14. 'Historical Memorials of Westminster Abbey' by Dean Arthur Penrhyn Stanley

15. Wylie 'Henry V'

16. One suggested derivation of this derogatory name is the Dutch word, 'lollaerd', meaning 'a mumbler'. A simple translation suggested by Gwynedd Sudworth is 'wagging tongues'. It must be remembered that neither Edward III nor Richard II burned heretics and Henry IV executed only two fanatics.

17. Shakespeare caricatured Oldcastle by transforming him from a valiant soldier and virtuous martyr into an obese, drunken, cowardly, rascally, braggart in his history plays, 'Henry IV' (Parts 1 and 2), 'Henry V' and the comedy, 'The Merry Wives of Windsor'. He was forced by an irate descendant, William Brooke, Lord Cobham, to change the name of his comical character from 'Oldcastle' to 'Falstaff'. Lord Cobham

happened to be the Lord Chamberlain responsible for licensing plays. Perhaps he was alerted to the supposed insult after watching the play in the presence of Queen Elizabeth I? The result was that the Master of the Revels caused the playwright to make a humiliating public apology: 'Oldecastle died a Martyre, and this is not the man ...' Michael Wood in his 'In Search of Shakespeare' (BBC Publications 2003) suggests that Shakespeare, a secret Catholic, deliberately insulted the Protestant martyr by presenting him as a 'pampered glutton'. For a discussion of Falstaff's theatrical character consult the scholarly introduction to the Arden Shakespeare edition of 'King Henry V' by A. R. Humphreys. For details of his historical life see 'Shakespeare: the Biography by Peter Ackroyd.

18. Holinshed Vol. III page 62

19. The bridge would have been the ideal site for an ambush. 'If the kidnappers closed both ends of the bridge while Robert and Guy were in the middle, there would be no chance of escape.' Michael Whittington, 'The Whittington Story'.

20. The King's peace did not then extend into mid-Wales, which means that they were far beyond rescue.

21. Grant of Application of Robert Whittington to the Parliament for Redress, Parliamentary Rolls A.D. 1416 4 Hen. V

22. Caroline Barron 'Richard Whittington: the Man and the Myth'.

23. Caroline Barron 'Richard Whittington: the Man and the Myth'.

24. Whittington's brother, Robert, represented Gloucestershire in the Leicester Parliament. Presumably, he took this opportunity to denounce supporters of Lollardy after his own traumatic ordeal.

25. H.T. Riley (ed) 'Memorials of London'

26. John A.F. Thomson 'The Later Lollards'

27. Cal. Papal Registers, 1396-1404, 130. (Barron page 232.)

28. Wylie 'The Reign of Henry V'

29. Nigel Saul 'Richard II'

30. Edward III claimed the throne of France by right of inheritance from his grandfather, Philippe IV. This became the principal cause of conflict when the French throne fell vacant in 1328. He assumed the arms and title of King of France and adopted the motto, 'Dieu et mon droit' ('For God and my right'. The 'right' referred to his claim to the throne of France. King Edward's attempts to regain the French throne led to the start of the Hundred Years War, which lasted five generations (1337-1453).

31. The dauphin was exceedingly indolent. He slept all morning and dined at midnight. He then spent the early hours dancing to music and dallying with his mistress. 'He had never resisted anything,' comments Ian Mortimer, 'let alone an invasion.'

32. Catherine's precocious older sister, Isabella, was the second wife of Richard II. Yet another child bride, she was Queen Consort of England 1396-1400. Negotiations had also taken place for Henry to marry Catherine but these ceased upon the death of Henry IV. The French King, Charles V, did not object to the marriage but to the preposterous dowry and Henry's claim to the throne of France. When Henry finally met Catherine at Meulan, he was enamoured of her great beauty.

33. Wylie 'Henry V'

34. Henry, in fact, pawned all his jewels and most of his crowns. His treasure chest included gold and silver coronets, brooches, rings, goblets, bowls, candlesticks, swords, spurs, belts, even dog collars... He also proffered the vestments and reliquaries from his private chapel as security.

35. Prior to Henry's second campaign in France Sheriffs were ordered to have six of the wing feathers plucked from every goose, except breeders, and to have them packed and forwarded to London for winging arrows. (10 February 1417.)

36. This curious fusion of worship and warfare is exemplified in the construction of Medieval churches. Almost invariably, they consisted of a tranquil nave affixed to an embattled watchtower.

37. Sir William Laird Clowes, 'The Royal Navy: A History from the Earliest Times to the Present' (1899)

38. Warhorses were professionally trained and highly prized. Types of horses that accompanied the English army would have included coursers, palfreys, rouncies, amblers, trotters and packhorses.

39. Henry V has been hailed as the originator of the passport. Known as 'Safe Conducts', they were formalised by Act of Parliament in 1414. Shakespeare in 'Henry V' has the King in his 'band of brothers' speech prior to Agincourt declare: 'Let him depart: his passport shall be made' (Act IV Scene III). Martin Lloyd, author of 'The Passport, The History of Man's Most Travelled Document', points out that the word 'passport' does not appear in English law until 1548 and that the 'safe conduct' was in existence at least five centuries earlier. Its main purpose was to allow free passage between walled towns and cities in England. The 'Anglo Saxon Chronicle', however, describes how King Edward the Confessor awarded a 'safe conduct' for Earl Godwin in 1051 to encourage him to leave the kingdom. Interestingly, Martin Lloyd in his book suggests that one of the reasons that Henry V would not have allowed unhindered passage between England and France was that he did not want the French to have details concerning his secret weapon, the longbow.

40. One of Henry's chaplains penned a vivid account of the French campaign that culminated in the Battle of Agincourt. He scribbled notes as he sat in the baggage train, quaking with fear and praying for victory. Wylie

confidently identified the author as Thomas Elmham, a Cluniac monk, Treasurer of St Augustine's Abbey, Canterbury.

41. A warship, as a rule, was little more than a merchant vessel employed for the purpose of fighting. When transporting armed troops she would be equipped with fore and aft castles that might be fixed or removed as necessary. A few historians have termed Henry V 'Founder of the English Navy' but this appellation is undeserved since he sold all his warships towards the end of his reign. A comprehensive discussion of the Medieval world of shipping appears in Wylie's 'The Reign of Henry V'. The list of ships is taken from 'Rotuli Normanniae' 5 Henry V (1417) quoted in Lysons.

42. Calendar of the Close Rolls, Westminster, 15 June 1415 (3 Henry V) membrane 19

43. Calendar of the Close Rolls, Westminster, 16 June 1415 (3 Henry V) membrane 18

44. Sir Thomas Gray, as a convicted traitor, was hanged, drawn and quartered. Richard, Earl of Cambridge, and Henry, Lord Scrope (who may have been perfectly innocent but misguided in consorting with the plotters) were beheaded. Their rotting heads were ordered to be publicly displayed in remote quarters across England. The accompanying paperwork involved was astronomical.

45. Wylie 'Henry V' Vol 1

Chapter Eleven

46. A contemporary chronicler, the monk of St Denis, hailed Harfleur as 'the most admirable port in Normandy, sending out ships to all corners of the world and bringing back every type of foreign merchandise to provision and enrich the whole kingdom'.

47. Artillery employing gunpowder had not yet superseded the older methods of battery. Gun technology was then in its infancy and the deployment of cannon, owing to their immense weight, shortness of range and difficulty of handling, was strictly limited. Early cannon were cast in church bell foundries and their stumpy bronze, brass or iron barrels were invariably bell-shaped. They were fired intermittently in battle because the whole process of loading them and firing them was tortuous. Indeed, a gun might be fired only once in battle! Although clumsier versions of these 'grete gunnys' – single or double barrelled – that 'blew forth stones by the force of ignited powders' had been in use for almost one hundred years, they were still regarded as an aside to the real action. Larger cannon commonly acquired individual names – 'London', 'Goodgrace', 'Thomas with the Beard'. Richard II had access to seventy-three cannon cast by Wiliam Woodward with a stock of 4,000 lb of gunpowder. One weighed seven hundredweight, had eleven

barrels and could fire ten lead bullets at the same time as its stone ball. (Gervase Matthew 'The Court of Richard II') Henry IV had been at the cutting edge of gunnery technology, according to Ian Mortimer, 'designing cannon himself, and deploying them with great effectiveness in sieges'. ('1415: Henry V's Year of Glory.') His 'great cannon' (presumed to be the two-ton giant known as 'The Messenger') blew up (or burst) at the Siege of Aberystwyth, although it is assumed that his own design proved far more durable and was capable of shooting boulders at high velocity into castle walls. Wylie believes that the first time cannon were employed effectively in battle on English soil was at the Siege of Berwick in 1405.

48. Dauphin Louis, as Governor General of France, had reached Vernon, a mere seventy miles upriver from Harfleur.

49. The Warden of the Cinque Ports had sent Kent fishermen over with their boats to ensure a further supply of fresh fish.

50. Ian Mortimer greatly reduces this estimated number by contemporary chroniclers in an appendix to his authoritative '1415: Henry V's Year of Glory'.

51. The bodies of noblemen who died were boiled in a huge cauldron so that their skin peeled away leaving their skull and bones, which were shipped home. The heart was previously removed.

52. Foedera edited by Thomas Rymer

53. Most of these valuables were stolen from the lightly guarded baggage train during the heat of the battle of Agincourt.

54. Calais was English territory from the reign of Edward III to that of Mary I. The surrounding area known as the 'Pale of Calais' was held by the English as a bridgehead on the mainland of Europe.

55. 'The Bataille of Agincourt' by John Lydgate

56. Ominously, Christine de Pizan, a contemporary authority on warfare, asserted in her treatise, 'The Book of Deeds of Arms and Chivalry' (1410): 'For it had often been noted that a small number of desperate men will conquer a large and powerful army'. A discussion of the actual numbers of the opposing army appears in an appendix to Ian Mortimer's '1415: Henry V's Year of Glory'. The author comes to the persuasive conclusion that the English army comprised 8,000 to 9,000 men and that the French army was no more than 12,000 to 15,000. So the English were outnumbered by slightly less than two to one.

57. Shakespeare's 'Henry V' Act IV Chorus

58. Agincourt changed its name from Azincourt. In the village an Information Centre presents through modern media all the stages of the decisive battle. The commentary is surprisingly generous towards the English aggressors.

59. The French battle plans survive.

60. The Duke of York died on the field. His mauled body were boiled in a cauldron and his bones shipped back to England for burial at Fotheringay.

The Earl of Suffolk, who also died on this campaign, was returned onboard the same ship to be buried at Wingfield, Suffolk.

61. Thomas, Lord Camoys, had married Hotspur's widow, Elizabeth Mortimer, aunt to the Earl of March.

62. A recent project by two eminent academics-Dr. Adrian Bell of Reading University and Professor Anne Curry of Southampton University-has resulted in a Medieval Soldier Database that records the names of 250,000 soldiers who fought throughout the Hundred Years War. They have compiled a comprehensive list of men-at-arms and archers whose names appear in the muster roles held at the National Archives. Guy's name appears (corrected from 'Ivo') as 'Whytyngton'. National Archives (TNA) E101/ 45 / 13 m. 4d. There are several more entries for soldiers with a similar surname and there is a possibility that these men may be distant relatives of Richard Whittington: John Whytyngton, (archer) Reginald Wittyngton (man-at-arms) William Whityngton (archer) and Richard Whityngton (archer).

63. Sir Thomas Erpingham was an undisputed hero at Agincourt yet he had showed himself to be cruel and sadistic in the deposition of Richard II.

64. The Lord Mayor of London in 2012, Alderman David Wootton, was a Liveryman of both the Fletchers and the Bowyers Companies.

65. Prior to Henry's second French campaign (1417-1421) county Sheriffs were ordered to have six of the wing feathers from every goose, except breeders, plucked, packed and forwarded to London. (10 February 1417.)

66. There is a persistent story that before the battle Henry warned his archers that, if captured, the French would cut off the middle two fingers from their right hand to prevent them from ever firing a bow again. Before battle, it became the practice for archers to wave these two fingers in defiance and their V sign persists today as an insulting derisive gesture.

67. Ironically, the bearer of this cleft crimson silk banner was killed in battle.

68. This incident is attested by an examination of his dented helmet displayed above his tomb at Westminster Abbey.

69. French chroniclers were reluctant to condemn Henry's barbarous cruelty since they admitted that their own leaders would have taken the same necessary precaution of massacring prisoners while under renewed attack. Curiously, they tended to condemn Brabant's bravado although they sometimes referred to King Henry V as 'cut-throat'. Allmand, in his biography of Henry V, contends that Henry's orders were not actually carried out. On the 593rd anniversary of Agincourt, however, a revisionist conference was held on the site of the battle. Academics at that time suggested that the number of Frenchmen was grossly exaggerated and they accused Henry of war crimes, thus applying modern morality to Medieval tactics. (*Daily Telegraph* 25 October 2008.)

70. According to Boris Johnson in his flippant 'Johnson's Life of London' the French lost 'three dukes, eight counts, a viscount and archbishop'.

71. Shakespeare includes this scene in 'Henry V'. The king enquires the name of the nearby castle and calls the battle after it. (Act IV Scene VII) If it was indeed true that Henry remained unfamiliar with the one prominent landmark adjacent to the battlefield then it would hardly have inspired his commanders with confidence. The site of Agincourt Castle is now occupied by a sprawling farm.

72. Ian Mortimer '1415: Henry V's year of Glory'

73. During World War Two, Prime Minister Winston Churchill asked Laurence Olivier to film Shakespeare's 'Henry V'. His intention was to prepare England psychologically for the D-Day landings in Normandy that were to liberate Europe from Nazi occupation. Olivier as the King delivered the stirring speeches in truly patriotic style to convince English and American cinema audiences of their rightful role in resisting oppression. In the film, the Cambridge Plot was omitted since it suggested that, in Henry's invasion, there had been dissent.

74. H.T. Riley (ed) 'Memorials of London'

75. The number of mounted craftsmen in the procession was estimated to have been between 15,000 and 20,000. This impressive figure demonstrates the strength of the reserve left behind to guard the country during the King's absence.

76. It had taken a month of feverish preparations to welcome home England's hero. Mercers, Haberdashers, Glovers, and Tailors had worked frantically preparing fine garments and accessories. Bakers baked bread; Brewers brewed beer.

77. It also had associations with religion and Roman emperors.

78. One distinguished French prisoner was Charles, Duke of Orleans, who languished in the Tower of London for a quarter of a century before his ransom was paid in full. He spent his time composing poems and ballads. One manuscript containing a romantic ballad was illustrated by a composite view of the Tower. In the far corner, a portion of London Bridge is shown with a view of the Chapel of St Thomas Becket. This is the earliest contemporary illustration of Old London Bridge.

79. Barron 'Richard Whittington: the Man and the Myth'

80. 'Calendar of Plea and Memoranda Rolls of the City of London: 1413-1437' ed A.H. Thomas, Cambridge 1943

81. St Erkenwald was a late 7th-century Bishop of London. The spiritual leader of the East Saxons, many miracles were attributed to him upon his demise. His remains were sealed within a leaden casket fashioned 'in the form of a gabled house or church' supposed to represent the fact that he was patron saint of London. Early in the 16th century his tomb became the site of pilgrimage of lawyers. His cult survived for over 800 years

before dwindling for the last four centuries. Erconwald St, East Acton, is an obscure reminder of his once great name.

82. A carol is generally, though not exclusively, religious. The word originates from Old French and simply means a circle dance. The song is contained in Maitland's 'English Carols of the Fifteenth Century'. The chorus translates: 'England give thanks to God for the victory.'

Chapter Twelve

83. Barron

84. Riley's 'Memorials'. 'Rude or damaging remarks made to the Mayor or Aldermen were always held to involve disrespect to the King and were clearly thought of as a sin rather than a misdemeanour' (Thrupp). She cites a woman who called an Aldermen a thief when he complained of untidiness outside her house and was imprisoned; another found guilty of slandering William Walworth was sentenced to pay him £40 fine in damages and to stand in the pillory, although on her promise of good behaviour the sentence was remitted.

85. London's first Mayor, Henry FitzAylwin, had served a phenomenal period of twenty years in the 12th century. And in the 14th century there had been several occasions on which a Mayor had served two or more years in succession, including Whittington.

86. H.T. Riley 'Memorials of London and London Life in the XIIIth, XIV and XV Centuries'

87. Fishmongers, who had acquired extraordinary privileges by the middle of the 14th century, found their powers curtailed by the beginning of the 15th century. Indeed, they were almost entirely ousted from serving as Mayor. In the quarter of a century prior to 1388, there were seven Mayors who were fishmongers. After that date there was only one: William Askham in 1403.

88. A naker was a small kettle drum imported from Europe in the thirteenth century. It was played in pairs to accompany chamber music, dancing and military parades.

89. Rev. Samuel Lysons 'The Model Merchant of the Middle Ages'

90. Sutton

91. Barron

92. In the minute books there is a rare reference to the crystal sceptre (28 October 1524): 'the best Mace which ys used to be borne by the mayer for the tyme being before the King's grace within the Citie'. This seems to imply that at that time it was never used except when borne before the sovereign and that it was always carried personally by the Mayor, and not borne before him.

93. Riley 'Memorials'. Stow asserts that the Mayor, Henry Barton, first ordained that 'Lanthornes with light to bee hanged out on the Winter evening betwixt Hallowtide and Candlemass' in 1416.

94. Peter Ackroyd 'London: The Biography' Chatto and Windus 2000

95. Wylie 'Henry IV'. Edward III enjoyed mummings and disguises and placed an order for 'ten dozen false faces complete with beards' for competitors in one of his tournaments. According to Ian Mortimer, fancy dress-merchants, friars, devils, dragons, angels and even drag-were part of the entertainment at his court.

96. Ian Mortimer '1415: Henry V's Year of Glory'

97. 'Calendar of Plea and Memoranda Rolls of the City of London: 1413-1437' ed A.H. Thomas, Cambridge University Press 1941

98. Riley 'Memorials of London'

99. Myer's 'Chaucer's London'. Taverns such as 'Saracen's Head', 'The Swan', Boar's Head' and 'Cross Keys' in Smithfield were notorious as brothels. But respectable taverns could be found even in the dubious district of Southwark: 'The Walnut Tree', where leading guildsmen met, and 'The Tabard' where pilgrims assembled. Famous innkeepers in literature are Harry Bailey in Chaucer and Mistress Nell Quickly in Shakespeare. The ale drawer in Ben Jonson's 'Every Man in His Humour' was based upon a true character, George of 'The Myter in Cheape'.

100. William Porland was the Clerk to the Company for the period of 1418-1440. He used three languages in his writings – Latin, Norman French and Middle English – apparently indiscriminately. The Latin, however, was not transcribed into English. His book is not in chronological order and, confusingly, he appears to return to fill up blank spaces at a later date.

101. The Dyers and the Vintners are the two companies who were noted for their 'swan dinners'. They still share their monopoly with the sovereign and with St John's College Cambridge over these Royal birds. In the fifteenth century swan was a great luxury which only the wealthy could afford to serve at their banquets. The Brewers' Company spent £38 on poultry, including twenty-one swans, for their election day feast in 1425. Swan was generally stuffed with herbs and roasted like chicken, turkey or goose, for several hours until tender. Slow cooking was recommended because its legs and wings are inclined to be tough owing to its powerful swimming. 'It does not in fact taste as delicious as it sounds,' Jennifer Lang assures us. And so it is difficult to understand its Medieval reputation as an appetising dish – Jennifer Lang 'Pride without Prejudice'. (As a protected species, today swans are not eaten by anyone.)

102. 'Abstract of the Contents of the Records of the Brewers' Company: 1418-1440' (MS5441) Guildhall Library

103. The City Corporation appointed Ale Connors – two to four in each ward – who were required to taste each fresh brewing offered for sale and assign it to one of the grades fairly priced by the Mayor. Supposedly, the Conner wore leather breeches to assist him in testing the quality of the brew. He was provided with two pints of ale: one pint he poured onto a wooden

bench and then sat in the spillage, the second he consumed. If when he had quaffed this second pint his breeches stuck to the bench then the ale was considered to be of a suitable standard for retail. 'The brew-wife's ale must not be red or ropy, but well sold and scummed and certified on the ale-konner's assay as good, able, and sety for man's body,' Wylie explains, unhelpfully. Surprisingly, there are official ale conners today. Four freemen of the City have this enviable job, which pays precisely £10 per annum. Elected on Midsummer's Day (21 June) their duty is to taste the ale in new pubs. Their role is purely ritualistic and has no legal bearing.

104. Besant and Rice

105. Traditionally, ale was brewed by the innkeeper's wife before local breweries began their delivery rounds to inns and taverns. When the ale was brewed and ready to be sold, she propped her ale stick or bush above the front door as a sign to entice in her regular customers.

106. Brewers' Company Records

107. Brewers' Company Records

108. Robert was the brother of Henry Chichele, Archbishop of Canterbury.

109. 'A Book of English: 1384-1425' (eds) E.W. Chambers and Marjorie Daunt

110. Barron

111. Mia Ball 'The Worshipful Company of Brewers: A Short History'

112. Sutton

113. Freidrich Brie (ed) 'Le Brut'

114. Wylie 'Henry V'

115. Freiderich Brie (ed), 'Le Brut.'

116. A chapbook written by 'T.H.' (presumed to be Thomas Heywood) confidently asserts that Whittington was an honoured guest: 'and upon the left hand next to the cupboard sat Sir Richard Whittington (now the third time Lord Mayor ... and his brethren the Aldermen of London.' The event takes place on St Matthew's Day (29 November). This is inaccurate embellishment! Accurate details of Queen Catherine's Coronation banquet are gleaned from two almost identical sources: 'The Historical Collections of A Citizen of London in the Fifteenth Century' edited by James Gairdner (which is derived from British Museum MS Egerton 1995 ff 113-222) and 'The Brut' or 'The Chronicles of England' (edited from MS Rawl. B 171 at the Bodleian Library). These texts merely make reference to the 'mayre of London' at the banquet. Clearly, Heywood mistook Whittington's mayoral years or, more likely, conflated matters to colour his text. Nevertheless, it is inconceivable that such a prominent citizen as Richard Whittington would not figure among the honoured guests.

117. According to 15th-century etiquette books, at formal feasts merchants should be seated at the same table as esquires though the Mayor of London should be seated with chief judges, barons and mitrered abbots. A R Myers, 'Chaucer's London'

118. Rev. Samuel Lysons, 'The Model Merchant of the Middle Ages'. The original source for the story is Fabyan's Chronicle.

119. Sir Henry Picard, Mayor in 1356, was a leading wine merchant who once entertained four monarchs – Edward III, John II, David II and Pierre de Lusignan, King of Cyprus – at his London home. (Gordon Home 'Medieval London'.)

120. Besant and Rice 'Sir Richard Whittington'

121. Imray 'The Charity of Richard Whittington'

122. Juliet Barker rehearses but ultimately dismisses persistent negative comments concerning Henry's three French campaigns: 'By reigniting the war with France, Henry V committed his country to decades of warfare and heavy taxation to pay for it; he has been blamed for sowing the seeds that would lead to England itself being torn apart by civil strife in the Wars of the Roses.'

123. Henry's remains were laid in a hallowed place between the shrine of Edward the Confessor and the Chapel of the Virgin. His elaborate tomb was formed of Caen stone and Purbeck marble. Queen Catherine caused an effigy of her husband to be placed above it. The head was formed of solid silver, the body of oak covered with silver gilt. Originally, these relics were displayed on a tie-beam above Henry V's Chantry Chapel but they have now been removed for preservation to the Abbey Museum. Although these trophies were long considered to have been actually used in battle, this type of helm and shield were no longer evident in the field in Henry V's lifetime. More likely, they were part of the King's insignia, which would also have comprised a tabard, pair of gauntlets and spurs (all no longer extant) carried by the heralds at his funeral. King Henry V's tomb remains one of the most significant monuments of Westminster Abbey. Information supplied by Dr. Dora Thornton, British Museum, and Christine Reynolds, Westminster Abbey.

124. Wylie and Waugh, 'The Reign of Henry V'. Charles VI died only a few weeks after Henry V on 20 October 1422. Dauphin Louis had died on 18 December 1415. His young brother, Dauphin Charles, then ruled, in part through the military support of Joan of Arc, as Charles VII.

Section 5

Chapter Thirteen

1. Ian Mortimer 'Henry V: 1415'

2. The Lancastrian dynasty, composed of three successive sovereigns and founded by Henry IV, died out in 1471 when Henry VI was murdered on the orders of Edward IV, the grandson and heir of Richard of

Conisborough, Earl of Cambridge, and the great-nephew of Edmund Mortimer, Earl of March.

3. Thrupp, 'The Merchant Class of Medieval London'
4. The Fitzwaryns were loyal companions to Duke William who came over to England at the Norman Conquest. They were descendants from a Norman knight, Guarine de Meez, and therefore referred to as 'Sons of Guarine'. Anglicised, this became 'Fitz' (meaning 'son of') and 'Waryn' ('Gu' in Norman French equates to 'W').
5. TNAC 76/64 m.7; C 76/64 m. 26
6. Michael Whittington 'The Whittington Story'
7. Thrupp 'The Merchant Class of Medieval London'
8. The busy town of Wantage, which lies on the southern side of the Vale of the White Horse, was formerly in Berkshire but after local reorganisation in 1974 was moved into Oxfordshire.
9. Calendar of Inquisitions Post Mortem Vol 20 No. 214 (Swindon 29 October 1414) TNA C 138/9 No 38
10. According to an essay, 'Bold As Brass' by Nigel Saul, brass effigies were beginning to become an attractive alternative to sculptured funerary monuments in churches from the mid-13th century onwards. ('Heraldry, Pageantry and Social Display in England'.)
11. Information supplied by Ralph Moffat, Curator of European Arms and Armour, Glasgow Museums.
12. E 329/30
13. Sir Ivo's will is held at Lambeth Palace Library. (Register Chichele ff 270-1.) Translation from the Latin by Dr. David Wright.
14. Calendar of Inquisitions Post Mortem Vol 20 No 216 (Crewkerne 23 September 1414). After Alice's early demise, Eleanor became the sole heir to the remainder of their father's estates.
15. The Westminster Council decreed on May 1127 that abbesses and nuns were forbidden to wear expensive furs although cheaper ones such as cat were allowed. It is unpleasant to record that pelts of cats were highly prized because they frequently formed the pelisses of abbesses.
16. Sir John Chidiok or Chideok, Lord Fitzpayn, succumbed to dysentery at Harfleur and died in 1415.
17. Lysons
18. Imray 'The Charity of Richard Whittington'
19. London Metropolitan Archives CLC/521/MS03458 (II Henry IV (1410)
20. Barron 'Richard Whittington: The Man and the Myth'. Barron lists several complicated transactions of properties in London parishes with which Whittington and his fellow Mercers were associated: St Alban Wood Street, St Antholin, St Mary Aldermanbury, St Mildred Bread Street and St Swithin.
21. Cal. Inq. Post. Mort Vol 17 No 1048, Hertford, St Clement's Day, 21 Richard II (1398)

22. Besant and Rice
23. Sutton 'The Mercery of London'
24. Myers
25. Barron
26. Imray 'The Charity of Richard Whittington'
27. They form the means of access to two houses joined together. The older building is a typical merchant's dwelling of the 18th century. In 1746, it was occupied by Sir Samuel Pennant who kept his mayoralty there in 1749-50. A previous occupier was Sir Robert Goschall, Lord Mayor, 1741-42. Both men died in office.
28. A conjectural map of Whittington's estate based upon a plan of the parish of St Michael Paternoster Royal (dated 1827) appears in Imray's book.
29. Flemish bricks were imported for the curtain wall of the Tower of London in the late 13th century. The reconstructed Sheen Palace by Henry V in 1414 appears to have been the first extensive employment of brick in a royal building programme. Thereafter, it started to become fashionable as a building material. It was a far cheaper alternative to stone mainly because kilns could be erected nearer than the stone quarries were to London. By the late 15th century there were several brickmakers recorded east of the City. All the same, brick was rarely used in quantity for domestic buildings before the mid-15th century. It could be combined with stone and used for exterior walls, chimneys and undercrofts. Crosby Hall, Sir John Crosby's mansion in Billingsgate, was built on a brick undercroft in 1466.
30. Information supplied by John Clark, Senior Curator (Medieval), Department of Early London History and Collections, Museum of London.
31. Barron. (This corrects Imray who lists the three parishes as St Andrew by Baynard Castle, St Michael Bassieshaw and St Botolph-without-Bishopsgate.) Imray, however, gives the dates of all three transactions.
32. Imray compares this date with the date of the deeds conveying the reversion of certain lands in Somerset and Wiltshire by Sir Ivo Fitzwaryn at his demise to Alice and her husband and she conjectures that this just might have formed a marriage settlement. 'If Whittington did not marry Alice Fitzwaryn until 1402 then he must have married comparatively late in life,' she propounds, 'and a wealthy marriage can certainly not have been the basis of his fortune.' This is not an improbable suggestion and indeed, a late marriage might explain why Whittington was childless.
33. Barron
34. 'The Cartulary of St Bartholomew's Hospital'. This also informs us that Whittington's executors acquired a tenement called 'Le George on the Hoop' in 'Temestreet' (Thames Street) 'for the gift of the college of the said Richard'. This, according to Myers, boasted thirty-two beds, extensive stables and spacious cellars.

35. Surprisingly, 'The Tabard', as a sign, is rarely found in London. A tabard is a sleeveless tunic, mantle or surcoat. When it is worn by heralds it is emblazoned with heraldic emblems and devices. Bryant Lillywhite notes a 'Tabard in the Ryalle' in 1467 in his 'London Signs'. He also gives various spellings for 'Royal': Ryalle, Reole, Riole, Ryall, and Ryole. The most famous 'Tabard Inn' was, of course, at Southwark. This early 14th-century hostelry was where pilgrims lodged overnight because, being situated outside the City of London, they would not have to wait for the gates to open before making an early start through Kent for Canterbury Cathedral.

36. According to Imray, Whittington built the church on the land purchased from Weston. Whittington's executors built the College on the residue of land acquired for the church and the Almshouse on part of the tenement called 'The Tabbard on the Hoop'. Attwood says that the College was built on land donated by Mayor Knoles and the Commonalty of London.

37. Inquisitions made on the death of Sir Ivo Fitzwaryn in September 1414 indicate that Alice was alive in August 1402. At that time, she and her husband were parties to some deeds by which her father granted them the reversion of certain manors in Somerset and of land in Wiltshire at his demise. The Inquisitions also state that Alice predeceased her father, leaving no heirs, and that all his property in Somerset, Wiltshire, Dorset and elsewhere descended to his eldest daughter, Eleanor, wife of John Chydock. The inference is that Alice died sometime between 1402 and 1414.

38. Thrupp 'The Merchant Class of Medieval London'

39. From the 12th and 13th centuries London was a leading centre of the wine trade. Merchants from Bordeaux and Rouen hired stone cellars to store their wine near wharves on the quayside. A part of Upper Thames Street is still called Vintry. The Vintners dealt in a variety of imported wines. Most were dry wines from Gascony, south-west France, and the Rhineland, western Germany, but more expensive sweet wines were from the Levant, Germany, Italy, Portugal, Spain and Cyprus. Generally, the cheaper wines tasted harsh and sour and it became a common practice to blend them with honey, herbs and spices. Interestingly, the imports of wine were so great that the capacity of ships was measured by 'tonnage' – the number of tuns – that they could transport in their holds.

40. An alternative suggestion is that it derives from 'Tower Royal'. The substantial building was owned by Edward II's consort, Queen Philippa, in 1331 to store her substantial wardrobe. Later, the 'Queen's Wardrobe' was acquired for ecclesiastical purposes by the Dean and Chapter of Westminster. In the reign of Richard II, the Crown recovered it first for Richard's mother, Joan, Princess of Wales, who took up residence in grand style, and secondly for his consort, Anne of Bohemia. Subsequently, this imposing building was converted into stables but by the time of Elizabeth I it had been divided into tenements. It was consumed by the Great Fire.

41. Imray: 'Almost certainly he regarded it as a work of piety for the welfare of his own soul.'

42. His appointment would have been influenced by John Carpenter who, as chief executor, ran the College until his own demise in 1442. Pecock was also an acquaintance of John Coventry, another of Whittington's executors, who had died in 1429.

43. Imray 'The Charity of Richard Whittington'

44. Ann Saunders and John Schofield (eds) 'Tudor London – A Map and A View'

45. The reverse of these two plates has an image of the Tower of Babel (Genesis 11 vv 1-9). The connection between the mythical tower and the copper plates poses a puzzle. The compiler of this Tudor map would have needed to climb church towers, including St Paul's, to make his preliminary sketches. The builders of the Biblical tower had the same purpose to reach the skies to gain a vantage point where they might observe the kingdoms of the world. God, according to the Genesis story, was offended by the foolishness of the builders and confounded their language; hence 'Babel' or 'babble'.

46. Peter Ackroyd 'London – The Biography of a City'

47. The incised inscription reads: 'On this site once stood a monument to Richard Whittington 1358-1423, Mercer, Four times Mayor of London'.

48. The association with St Michael Paternoster Royal and the 'Missions to Seafarers' appears to originate from a charter obtained by the Mercers' Company on 13 January 1394. This empowered the Mercers' Company 'to hold land for the benefit of those who by misfortune at sea and other casualties were so poor as to receive alms from other Christian people'. Richard Whittington was elected Master of the Mercers' Company in June 1395-18 months after the date of the charter-and, assuming he already had some standing with that company, it is reasonable to conjecture he had a hand in forming the Charter.

Chapter Fourteen

49. A.H. Thomas (ed) 'Calendar of Plea and Memoranda Rolls of the City of London: 1431-1437' Cambridge University Press 1943

50. Barron

51. Sutton: 'This capacity to avoid all criticism suggests a character of austere correctness coupled with an ability to inspire trust.'

52. Thrupp 'The Merchant Class of Medieval London'

53. Sutton 'Dictionary of National Biography'

54. Richard Whittington's will is held at Lambeth Palace Library. It is located in the Register of Henry Chichele Vol II (1414-1443) ff 354-356. This translation is by Dr. David Wright. 'In the fourteenth century, wills were

normally only made when the sufferer genuinely feared death was close.' (Ian Mortimer 'Edward III'.) Peter Ackroyd states that in Elizabethan times the period between a person drawing up a will and his demise was only a matter of a fortnight. ('Shakespeare: The Biography')

55. Thrupp asserts that the highest sum named in a surviving 14th-century will was £80. This was by William Thorneye, Alderman, who died in the year of the Black Death. His is compared with three other Aldermen who left £20, £30 and £40 respectively. A few wealthy citizens set the sum at around £4, preferring their money to be distributed among the poor.

56. Thrupp 'The Merchant Class of Medieval London'

57. The executors were handsomely rewarded for their services: John Carpenter received £40; John Coventre £20; William Grove £10 and John White 20 marks. William Babyngton as supervisor was to receive £20 for his labours. Babyngton's role, however, is difficult to understand since there is no record of his participation in the executorship apart from the building of St Bartholomew's Hospital.

58. Stow. His preferred title, 'Secretary to the City', seems to have been a title invented by himself.

59. St Peter upon Cornhill is reputed to occupy the oldest Christian site in London. Located on the corner of Cornhill and Gracechurch St., it covers the foundations of the Roman basilica. Allegedly, it was founded by Lucius, first Christian King of Britain, in 179 AD. Destroyed in the Great Fire, rebuilt by Wren it escaped the Blitz. In 1872, the church was renovated by Wyatt who retained the wooden screen designed by Wren's daughter, Jane, the fine pulpit with its sounding board, the font with its pre-Fire cover and the Father Smith organ on which Mendelssohn twice played. The curious red brick tower is topped with a dome which, in turn, is surmounted by an obelisk and a massive representation of St Peter's key to Heaven. The elevated graveyard is mentioned by Charles Dickens in 'Our Mutual Friend' (1865).

60. 'Liber Albus'

61. Eamon Duffy 'The Stripping of the Altars: Traditional Religion in England: 1400-1580'

62. There are still clues to the sites of these Medieval churches. All Hallows in Honey Lane stood opposite the Standard in Cheapside. A church is known to have existed there since 1200 and it is thought from records that it was a simple, narrow, rectangular building with a belfry and a steeple. Its parish – one acre – was one of the smallest in London. Nevertheless, it was patronised by the Grocers' Company. After the Great Fire the site was cleared and turned into a marketplace. Today's Honey Lane has migrated slightly to the east of its original site. (Michael Byrne and G.R Rush, 'St Mary-le-Bow, A History'.) Three other sites have been turned into 'little gardens for wayfarers'. (Wilberforce Jenkins, 'London Churches Before

the Great Fire') A portion of the churchyard of St Mary Staining is now a pretty rose garden in Oat Lane off Wood Street, while that of St Alphege is bounded by a high section of the Roman Wall alongside London Wall. St Alphage or Aphege was an Archbishop of Canterbury who was stoned to death by the Danes at Greenwich in 1012. The abandoned churchyard of St Pancras in Soper Lane off Queen Street is sadly neglected and overshadowed by modern office blocks. Its parish would have been flooded with Mercers in the Middle Ages.

63. St Mary without Bishopsgate was also called St Mary Spital or Spittle. Founded in 1197 by Walter Brune (or Brown) Sheriff, and his wife, Rose, it provided one hundred and eighty beds for the poor. It was administered by the Austin Canons. St Mary of Bethlehem Hospital for lunatics was commonly called 'Bedlam'. Founded in 1247 by Simon Fitzmary, Sheriff, 'distracted' patients were chained to the wall and, when violent, whipped. When the hospital was removed from Moorfields to Lambeth in 1815, all the patients were transported by hackney carriages. St Thomas in Southwark probably formed part of the Priory of St Mary Overie. Although it was founded by the Prior of Bermondsey in about 1106, it cannot have assumed this name until after the cannonisation of Thomas Becket in 1173.

64. Probably St Giles in the Fields where there was a leper hospital. People afflicted with the disease were banished to colonies beyond the City walls.

65. St Mary without Cripplegate was founded in 1329 by Whittington's predecessor, William Elsing, Mercer and Mayor, to provide care for one hundred poor men and women, particularly blind and disabled priests. It was administered by the Austin Canons and Elsing was elected their first Prior. The site of 'Elsing Spital', as it was popularly known, is marked by an extensive garden alongside London Wall. Prior William had inherited a fortune from his brother, Richard, who owned a Mercer's shop in Soper Lane. He employed three apprentices – Nicholas, William and Hugh – to supervise the sale of his diverse wares, the bulk of which consisted of wool and linen from his home county, Norfolk. Interestingly, Elsing's inventory is the earliest surviving of a London Mercer. (PRO E154/1/18a.) A remarkable number of Mercers came from Norfolk and rose, like Elsing, to become Aldermen, Sheriffs and Mayor and also benefactors of the City of London. Whittington's executor, John Carpenter, also left sizable bequests to all these worthy institutions in his will dated 8 March 1441.

66. A silver SS collar is displayed at the Museum of London. This is formed of 41 links, each in the form of the letter S, joined by pairs of rings. At the front, the ends meet in a pair of simulated buckles and chapes from which a jewelled pendant or a family or political badge could be suspended. Collars of varying degrees of value were presented to subjects the Lancastrian kings wished to honour. The collar exhibited, it is

suggested, was probably made for someone below the rank of knight (like Whittington) because it was an emblem of authority for a government official or ambassador. (Tessa Murdoch, 'Treasures and Trinkets: Jewellery in London from Pre Roman Times to the 1930s'.) Conversely, Ian Mortimer in 'The Fears of Henry IV' demonstrates that the collar was actually worn by high-ranking noblemen, even royalty. Indeed, Henry, while Duke of Lancaster, was himself known as 'the one who wears the S.' Mortimer investigates further the meaning of the Lancastrian livery collar. Many antiquaries, he points out, have accepted that they mean 'soverayne' (sovereign) souveignez (remember) without considering their significance. Henry of Lancaster presented many of these collars to his supporters, but since they were distributed before he was King the act would have been treasonable. Far more probably they represent the vernacular phrase 'souveyne vous de moi' which translates simply as 'Remember me'. And this phrase is often represented as a rebus in the form of the forget-me-not. It appears frequently on jewellery and embroidery on clothing. Yet even this interpretation presents a puzzle because 'vous' is formal. And, who, precisely is to be remembered and why? Curiously, there is no mention of Whittington's SS collar in Robert's own will. Perhaps, if it was a chain of office, then it would not have been Whittington's gift to bestow. The bequest, after all, cannot now be verified.

67. Barron 'Whittington: The Man and the Myth'
68. Grafton's 'Chronicle'
69. This illumination introduces the English translation of the 'Ordinances' for the governance of Whittington's 'Goddeshouse', or almshouse, still held by the Mercers' Company. These ordinances comprise twenty folios of vellum collected together to form a modest book measuring 12 x 8 inches when open, with a plain parchment cover.
70. William Abell was an illuminator who was most prolific between the period 1440-1465. His work is identifiable by facial types, colouring, drapery and landscapes. Another peculiarity, as in the Whittington deathbed scene, is that his figures overlap. He appears to have been the churchwarden of St Nicholas Fleshshambles in the City of London. This church had a connection with St Bartholomew's Hospital whose 'Cartulary' Abell also illuminated. His miniature features John Cok, its compiler, adoring the cross.
71. Richard Marks and Paul Williamson (eds) 'Gothic: Art for England: 1400-1547'. Besant and Rice also note Whittington's strongly marked features and the 'distinct and characteristic' faces of his executors.
72. Throughout the Middle Ages the board behind the bed was known as either the 'testor' or 'dorser' while the canopy was called the 'celour'. Whittington's bed is depicted as having both a testor and a demi-celour with drapes. A full celour would denote even higher status. By the 17th century the meaning

of these terms – testor and celour – had been reversed. Penelope Eames 'Medieval Furniture'.

73. Thrupp points out that a merchant's close circle of friends – the men that he would trust to administer his estate or act as guardians of his children – were almost invariably merchants and frequently members of his own company. Their friendship would have arisen from association in business or in company affairs.

74. Byrne and Rush 'St Mary-le-Bow, A History'

75. Information on costume supplied by Susan North, Curator of Fashion 1550-1800, Victoria and Albert Museum. Experts warn against a too literal reading of the scene. They point out that it was unlikely that the artist actually witnessed Whittington's demise and that the illumination conforms to pictorial conventions for such deathbed scenes in 15th-century manuscripts. This is, in any case, a composite scene: the executors are present at the same time as the future almsmen.

76. The Oxford English Dictionary defines a 'bedesman' or 'beadsman' as 'one paid or endowed to pray for others; a pensioner or almsman charged with the duty of praying for the souls of his benefactors'. The Old English word 'bede' means a prayer. The Catholic Encyclopedia: 'Bedesman was at first the term applied to one whose duty was to pray for others, and thus it sometimes denoted the chaplain of a guild. But in later English a bedesman is simply the recipient of any form of bounty; for example, a poor man who obtains free quarters in an almshouse, and who is supposed to be bound in gratitude to pray for his benefactors.' Henry V employed 24 bedesmen to pray for him at a cost of 2d per day. Wylie 'The Reign of Henry V'

77. Whittington's doctor mirrors the Ellesmere miniature of the 'Doctour of Physik' in Chaucer's 'Canterbury Tales'. There, the doctor is depicted examining a urinal while riding on horseback through the Kent countryside. Evidently, a phial of urine was the emblem of the medical profession since it commonly appears in contemporary illustrations of sickbed scenes. Chaucer's doctor is a worthy representative of his profession since he had studied the ancient scholars widely, although he is censured for not reading his Bible. This 'verrey parfit practisour' has amassed a fortune by sharing his knowledge with fellow medics and his wealth is expressed in the illustration by his expensive taffeta and fur hooded robe. A university graduate might study for about fourteen years to obtain a doctorate in medicine in Medieval times. He would have been required to read authoritative classical texts such as those by Galen and Aristotle. In the absence of anatomical dissection and post mortems, he would have learned a great deal of theory based upon the positions of the planets and the signs of the zodiac. Further, he would have been taught to study the constitution of a patient's body based on

the four humours – melancholy, choler, phlegm and blood – determined by the most prominent pagan gods. This reliance on celestial influences for diagnoses was accepted internationally and even had the sanction of the Church. Wylie in 'The Reign of Henry V' gives some interesting insights into Medieval medicine on the Continent. At Bordeaux, as in most other places in France, doctors were appointed by town officials who paid their fees and required them to appear, together with their apothecaries, in the Church of St Eloi to take an oath at the altar that they would not poison their patients. The ailing Henry IV took the study of urine by physicians so seriously that he commissioned a treatise on uroscopy.

78. Information supplied by Dr. Marc Feeney.

79. This first English copy has a brief dedicatory verse at the end naming the four current Wardens of the Mercers' Company. They include Geoffrey Boleyn, grandfather of Anne, the second wife of Henry VIII.

80. This second English version which dates from a decade later was probably a fair copy made for the Almshouse. The various versions of the ordinances are discussed in an appendix to Imray's 'The Charity of Richard Whittington'.

81. Friedrich W.D. Brie 'The Brut of The Chronicles of England'

82. Mercers' Company records. (Quoted in Lysons.)

83. Wylie

84. Wheatley

85. Marie Louise Bruce 'The Usurper King'

86. Thrupp 'The Merchant Class of Medieval London'

87. Carpenter would have ensured that Whittington's armorial bearings would have been prominently displayed at the funeral. The tomb would have born the impaled arms of Whittington/Fitzwaryn.

88. Thrupp 'The Merchant Class of Medieval London'

89. Lysons proposes that the English translation misses much of the clever play on words in this Latin epitaph. The suggestions he makes, however, are not entirely convincing.

90. John Strype, 'A Survey of the Cities of London and Westminster' (1720):

Ut fragrans Nardus
Fama fuit iste Richardus
Albificans Villam,
Qui juste rexerat illam,
Flos Mercatorum,
Fundator Presbyterorum,
Sic et egenorum,
Testis sit certus eorum.
Omnibus exemplum

barathrum vincendo morosum,
Condidit hoc Templum,
Michaelis quam speciosum?
Regia spes et pres:
divinis res rata turbis.
Pauperibus Pater,
Et Major qui fuit urbis,
Martius hunc vicit,
En annos gens tibi dicit,
Finiit ipse dies,
Sis sibi Christe quies.
Amen

91. Stow's first editor, Sir Anthony Munday, describes Whittington's 'goodly plain tomb in the chancel, with new banners to adorn it, very lately hung up'.
92. 'Finiit ipse dies'.
93. Thrupp 'The Merchant Class of Medieval London'
94. 'En annos gens tibi dicit'
95. John Stow 'A Survey of London' (ed) Charles Lethbridge Kingsford
96. 'Autobiography of Thomas Mountague'. 1553 Camden Society
97. 'The Diary of Henry Machyn' (ed) J.G. Nichols
98. Imray 'The Charity of Richard Whittington'
99. 23 July 1944
100. Richard Whittington was not the only Mayor of London to be buried in this church. Others were Sir John Yonge, grocer (died 1466) and Sir William Bayley, Draper (died 1524). An impressive monument to a later Lord Mayor, Sir Samuel Pennant, sculpted by Rysback, survives from 1750. He died from gaol fever caught from prisoners in the dock.
101. Imray 'The Charity of Richard Whittington'
102. An online conversion system translates Whittington's fortune into modern terms: The 'National Archives Currency Converter' states that in 1420 £6,500 would now be worth £4,180,000 and £7,000 would be worth £4,500,000. Such conversions are notoriously tricky.
103. In theory the gross Whittington rents amounted to approximately £250, a phenomenal amount, while the obligations to the College and almshouse were £103. The surplus remained the Company's with loans to members constituting an additional charity, as directed by Carpenter. (Imray.)
104. Epitaph copied onto a flyleaf of the Mercers' Company Record of benefactor's will. (f123)

Section 6

Chapter Fifteen

1. Barron
2. Boris Johnson, 'Johnson's Life of London'
3. It is probably meaningless to correlate Whittington's estate into today's equivalent but certainly he would be regarded as a multi-millionaire.
4. The value of his property amounted to approximately £1,200 according to Imray.
5. Lysons mentions a collar of SS, three dozen cups with covers, three basins and ewers, three nests of bowls, three flagons and three livery pots that Whittington owned at one time but then presented to his brother, Robert. Sir Ivo FitzWaryn bequeathed Whittington a cup of silver gilt with a cover and a pair of rosaries of pure gold enamelled in red with jewels of gold enamelled with white in the form of the head of St John the Baptist.
6. Sutton 'The Mercery of London'
7. Thrupp 'The Merchant Class of Medieval London'
8. 'The combination of civic works and conspicuous piety, often through private sponsorship, was a strong tradition by the late twelfth century', according to Schofield.
9. St Anthony's Hospital was the only institution allowed to own pigs in London. They wore bells to identify them as they roamed the streets, and this also drew attention to their owners' laudable charity.
10. First-floor accommodation was added to the public latrine attached to Guildhall Chapel Yard in the mid-14th century.
11. London Metropolitan Archives
12. Whittington's toilet became so popular that public conveniences in the City came to be colloquially called 'longhouses'.
13. Formerly, the River Wells, afterwards called the Fleet Ditch, the Walbrook, that ran through the heart of the City, and a bourn that ran through Langbourn Ward, furnished an ample supply of water. When these water courses became polluted within the walls, the citizens still had recourse to the streams outside the town, principal of which was Holbourn (or Oldbourne) stream which fed into the River Wells, where now stands Holborn Viaduct. Principal wells were Holy Well, Clement's Well and Clark's or Clerken Well at the west end of Clerkenwell Church.
14. A peculiarity of elm is that it has a twisted grain which renders it less likely to split when exposed to the elements.
15. The site is now marked by Marble Arch.
16. Thrupp 'The Merchant Class of Medieval London'
17. John Schofield 'Medieval London Houses'. 'The London Encycoplaedia'
18. A.R. Myers 'Chaucer's London'

19. Monasteries, aware that cleanliness was next to godliness, organised their own water supply. They were the pioneers of domestic sanitation in the City.

20. 'Cripplegate' had no connection with cripples. It derived from the Anglo-Saxon word 'crepel', meaning a tunnel. After the curfew was sounded all the City gates were shut for the night and then the only entrance was through a heavily guarded underpass at Cripplegate. This ran from the town gate, which stood at the northern end of Wood Street, to the Barbican, a fortified watchtower outside the walls, built by the Romans. No one could penetrate the postern unless he knew the password. Cripplegate was rebuilt by the brewers in 1244 and in 1336 timbers from Guildhall were employed in its repair. In 1491 it was completely rebuilt through a bequest by Edmund Shaa, goldsmith and former Mayor. Besant informs us that there was a prison for debtors attached to it and also a postern for the convent of Greyfriars. Cripplegate was demolished in order for street widening in 1760.

21. Stow

22. Stow

23. Gregory was Mayor in 1451.

24. Gregory is relying on a contemporary document (BL, Egerton MS 1995 fol 86v) that is the sole surviving reference to Whittington's charity at St Thomas' Hospital. This is contained in 'Historical Collections of a Citizen of London in the 15th Century' (ed) James Gairdner.

25. The Council of Lyons limited the orders of mendicant or begging friars to four: the Dominicans, or preachers, called 'Black Friars'; the Franciscans, or Minorites, called 'Grey Friars'; the Carmelites, or 'White Friars', and the Augustinians or Austins. Nine Franciscans first arrived in England. Five friars remained in Canterbury and four – only one was a priest – travelled to London. Although the Dominicans settled in Holborn in 1221, the Franciscans were the first to have a permanent home in London. The Carmelites founded their house south of Fleet Street in 1241 and the Augustinians built their church in Broad Street in 1253. Undoubtedly, the most influential Friary in London was that of the Dominicans. The Archbishop of Canterbury acquired the sites of the decayed Castle Baynard and Montifochet Tower south-west of St Paul's Cathedral for them to build their house in 1275.

26. Walter Besant 'London'

27. Benedict Gummer 'The Scourging Angel'

28. Among the tombs was that of a descendant of Whittington. Thomas, the grandson of Richard's nephew, Guy, who had inherited the manors of Sollers Hope and Pauntley, died when on a visit to London in the winter of 1470. The Latin inscription: 'Gulielmus Whytyngton armiger Diominus de

Pauntley in Comi: Glouc: obit Novr. 1470' is preserved in John Duncomb's 'History of Herefordshire' Vol. III.

29. A.R. Myers 'Chaucer's London'

30. Remembering, of course, that a library refers foremost to a collection of books rather than the building in which it is housed. Actual cost was £556. The outstanding amount was donated by a friar, Dr. Thomas Winchelsey.

31. Thrupp 'The Merchant Class of Medieval London'. The only merchant known to have invested significantly in collecting books was Sir William Walworth. He bequeathed nine religious books to churches and a law library, worth £100, to his brother. The value of books depended not so much on the content, but the binding, lettering and illumination. In all cases they made munificent gifts.

32. A.R. Myers 'Chaucer's London'. An early commercial lending library was introduced by John Shirley, who died in 1456. He owned a large house and four shops from where he enjoyed a considerable trade from hiring out manuscripts by English authors Chaucer and Lydgate, in addition to books on devotion and sport.

33. Barron 'Richard Whittington: The Man and the Myth'

34. The arms were identical with those that appeared on the Ordinances of his Hospital and those displayed by the Whittingtons of Gloucestershire. 'This representation of Whittington's arms is of interest', notes Barron, 'since there can be no doubt that these were the arms and the crest which he chose to use in his lifetime.'

35. The interior was 'all seeled with Wainscot, having twentie eight desks, and eight double setles of Wainscot'. Kingsford Vol I.

36. William Caxton, inventor of the printing press, was not born until 1422.

37. A.E. Douglas-Smith in his 'City of London School' confidently proposes they were carried away by Protector Somerset. Richard Barbor in 'Living Legends' asserts: 'Half a dozen of the books from Greyfriars survive, scattered in libraries from London to Rome... An enquiry to the Vatican Library, however, brought a negative result.'

38. The name 'Smithfield' is said to derive from 'smooth field'. It was the site of the infamous Bartholomew Fair, held annually from the reign of Henry I to Queen Victoria. It became a place of entertainment that ranged from royal tournaments to public executions. During sewer excavations in 1849, blackened stones, charred remains of posts and dismembered human bones were found as grisly reminders of the burning of Protestants in the reign of Mary I. Ironically, the last English martyr to suffer there was named Bartholomew Legate. Today, Smithfield meat market is in close proximity to St Bartholomew's Church. The Butchers' Company hold their annual service there.

39. Rahere is traditionally referred to as 'the jester' but, in truth, it is not known what role he played at the court of Henry I.

40. In 1381, Wat Tyler, leader of the Peasants' Revolt, after inciting a rebellion and confronting Richard II, was carried there mortally wounded from a wound inflicted by the Mayor, William Walworth. He was pursued by the King's men, dragged from his sickbed and decapitated at Smithfield.

41. St Bartholomew's Fair was held each year for three days beginning on 24 August which was the Feast of St Bartholomew in the church calendar. It was a mixture of trade and fun fair. Initially, it promoted the wares of Clothiers and Drapers. Over the years it gained a dubious reputation and for this reason it was closed in 1855. Cloth Fair, a pretty street alongside the church, recalls the site.

42. Rahere's wooden coffin was opened in Victorian times. The deceased First Prior still wore his leather sandals. By tradition, Priors of the Augustinians were always buried wearing their sandals.

43. High atop a stone column in the south transept is a curious carving of a cat. It is known as the 'Smithfield cat'. No explanation is offered as to why it should be there.

44. 'There are great Romanesque columns north and south at ground level with a triforium gallery above and a clerestory beneath the flat wooden roof. The east end was restored to its original apsidal shape in the nineteenth century and the apse arcade is surrounded by an ambulatory. The quire leads inexorably to the focal point of the whole church - the high altar.' Rev. Dr. Martin Dudley 'Guide to Saint Bartholomew the Great' (1999).

45. Norman Moore 'The History of St Bartholomew's Hospital' Vol II

46. The medical school established by the surgeon, Abernethy, in 1822, became a Constituent College of the University of London in 1900. In 1921, the school's status was radically changed when it was incorporated by Royal Charter under the title, 'The Medical College of St Bartholomew's Hospital in the City of London'. Towards the end of that century, the Medical College moved away from direct connection with the Hospital and in 1995 it was merged with the London Hospital Medical College to become 'St Bartholomew's and the Royal London School of Medicine and Dentistry', now part of Queen Mary (College) University of London.

47. St Bart's is, in fact, the oldest hospital still on its original site in England.

48. Barron 'London in the Later Middle Ages'

49. A deposit of one hundred shillings (£5) was required as guarantee of good behaviour upon removal of a prisoner's irons. H.T. Riley (ed) 'Liber Albus'.

50. Peter Ackroyd says prisoners were known as 'nightingales' in 'London: The Biography'.

51. Lysons says that the keepers of Newgate and Ludgate both died of gaol fever in 1414. Quoting from a contemporary document, he describes Ludgate as 'febel over litel, and so contagious of eyre yat hit caused the deth of many men'.

52. Besant and Rice 'Sr Richard Whittington'. Freemen, they explain, chose rather to live in gaol than to work and pay their debts. Moreover, they were suspected of spending their time in devising further methods of duping honourable citizens.

53. Whittington's order recorded in Norman French is translated in 'Memorials of London and London Life in the 13th-15th Centuries' (ed) H. T. Riley (1868).

54. Stow. 'He did not specify that they should rebuild the prison of Newgate, but they appear to have known his desire.' W. Eden Hooper, 'History of Newgate and the Old Bailey' (1935). Whittington's executor, John Carpenter, was also inspired to leave money for prisoners of Newgate, Ludgate, Marshalsea, the Fleet and King's Bench.

55. 'Also the same yere Newgate was be gon to be made a Newgate by the executourys of that famos marchant and merser, Rycharde Wytyngdone', James Gairdner (ed.) 'Historical Collections of a Citizen of London in the 15th Century'.

56. Barron 'London in the Later Middle Ages'

57. Donald Rumelow, 'The Triple Tree'

58. Peter Ackroyd 'London - The Biography'

59. Inevitably, water from this fountain was contaminated and caused illness among the inmates. About 1435, the Priory and Hospital of St Bartholomew offered their surplus supplies to the prisoners of Newgate and Ludgate (Anthony Babington 'The English Bastille' 1971). Although conduits had been erected in the City streets from 1236, St Bartholomew's Priory and Hospital may have been among the first places in London to have their own water supply. The water was carried through lead pipes and aqueducts from springs in the priory's manor in Canonbury and Islington. There was a covered cistern in the close and the water went from there into the Hospital and then flowed on to Ludgate and Newgate. Rena Gardiner 'The Story of Saint Bartholomew the Great' (2005).

60. Maitland

61. Pennant's 'Tour of London' (1805). A few chapbooks assert that there was a statue of Whittington with a cat in his arms carved in stone over the archway of Newgate Gaol. This seems most unlikely. Wheatley also makes the dubious claim that the executors 'caused the merchant's arms to be graven in stone' upon the facade.

62. The derivation of the name 'Guildhall' is possibly from the Old English 'gildan' (to pay). The Medieval term for a trade guild was a 'mystery', which is derived from the Latin 'misterium' (an occupation). The mystery play cycles, which were open-air Biblical dramas performed on carts placed around city streets, were so named because they were presented by certain trade guilds at Coventry, Chester and York.

63. John Schofield, 'Medieval London Houses'

64. Bowsher, Dyson, Holder and Howell, 'The London Guildhall'

65. Wylie in 'Henry IV' Volume I ascribes the initial rebuilding to Thomas Knolles during his second Mayoralty. Apparently, when he left office, he ceased the building works. Methods were employed to acquire funds including charges for the enrollment of wills and deeds, the use of the Mayor's seal and levying tolls on citizens crossing London Bridge. Freemen and apprentices were taxed alike to complete this iconic building 'that should have been the pride of every London craftsmen'.

66. Bowsher, Dyson, Holder and Howell 'The London Guildhall'

67. Guildhall Yard was the subject of extensive exploration at the end of the 20th century by a team of archaeologists from the Museum of London. A detailed report on its findings was prepared by Nick Bateman, Senior Projects Manager, and published in 'The Archaeology of Reformation 1480-1580' (edited by David Gaimster and Roberta Gilchrist) for The Society for Post Medieval Archaeology. Substantial remains were uncovered of the chapel, college and library but the most important discovery was of a Roman amphitheatre. The story of the chance discovery of this vast amphitheatre is also told by Nick Bateman in 'Gladiators at the Guildhall' published by the Museum of London Archaeological Service in 2000. The amphitheatre, which dates between A.D. 70-300, was the scene of animal fights, public executions, and occasional gladiator combats. The site of the amphitheatre 18 feet below ground level, which held 5,000 spectators, is marked by an oval pattern of black paving stones in Guildhall Yard. The actual remains – the entrance to the arena, two rooms flanking it and a substantial part of the arena itself – can be inspected in a spectacular exhibition in the basement of Guildhall Art Gallery.

68. Chantry chapels commenced in England in the 13th century as sanctified areas within existing cathedrals and (later) chapels where dedicated masses could be offered for the souls of the departed. Normally, chantries were sponsored by close relatives of the deceased or members of a guild, but the wealthiest donors could afford to pay for a number of priests – a 'College' – to celebrate more regular chantry masses. Certainly, a College was the most expensive form of chantry endowment. Chantry chapels increased in popularity after the devastating plagues of the mid-14th century. It is possible that Guildhall Chapel was enlarged as a response to the disaster. The founding of Guildhall College, which may have been a direct reaction to the pestilence, inspired a mayoral fashion. In 1381 William Walworth founded a College at St Michael Crooked Lane, while in 1410 Richard Whittington established a College at St Michael Paternoster Royal.

69. Nick Bateman, 'Gladiators at the Guildhall'

70. Bowsher, Dyson, Holder and Howell. The London Guildhall'

71. This majestic room – intended as a stage for civic display – was also the scene of state trials including those of Lady Jane Grey and Archbishop Thomas Cranmer, both accused of High Treason.

72. The hard, grey-green limestone known as Purbeck came from Dorset and comprised small freshwater mussel and snail shells, which allowed a high polish.

73. John Schofield in 'Medieval London Houses' records that much of the plain window glass and most of the coloured glass for Medieval buildings came from abroad until the development of glass making in London itself in the late 16th century.

74. One survival in the Great Hall is a 15th-century Gothic arched 'wind-eye' or window along the south wall, where the latticed panes are still filled with horn.

75. Neither Whittington nor Bury made a specific provision for a library in their wills. The initiative for this joint enterprise was probably taken by the Common Clerk, John Carpenter, who himself lent books to the new library. Indeed, he may have been consciously developing one of Whittington's passions since during his later life, he had made a donation towards the funding of Greyfriars Library. Interestingly, Whittington's former apprentice, Thomas Roos, bequeathed a copy of 'Piers Plowman' to Guildhall Library. (Sutton 'The Mercery of London'.)

76. Brewer has the interesting note that 'Liber Albus' was the original name for the book but later this applied only to the transcript. It changed its name to 'Liber Niger' ('Black Book'). The first couplet of a late anonymous inscription in Latin on the flyleaf translates as: 'This book, which once was white, has black become/Mark'd through and through by many a greasy thumb'. The precious volume, safely stored in the stone arched cellars deep under Guildhall, survived the Great Fire.

77. Boris Johnson 'Johnson's Life of London'

78. 'Of equal significance is the fact that this was the first library to be founded by a layman as a work of charity, for the benefit of the soul of the testator, and the first to be effectively administered by a civic authority.' Nick Bateman in his article, 'John Carpenter's Library' in 'The Archaeology of Reformation 1480-1580'.

Chapter Sixteen

79. 'Lead as a roof covering is no heavier than thatch ... but it was too expensive for widespread use at the domestic level.' (John Schofield, 'London Medieval Houses'.)

80. Calendar of Pleas and Memoranda of the City of London (24 February 1398.)

81. Stow

82. Calendar Inquisitions 12 Henry IV (1411)

83. Barron 'London in the Later Middle Ages'
84. John Schofield, 'Medieval London Houses'
85. Ben Weinreb and Christopher Hibbert, 'The London Encyclopaedia'
86. Peter Jackson London Bridge – A Visual History
87. It was so well constructed that it lasted for the next six hundred years.
88. A.R. Myers 'Chaucer's London'
89. Patricia Pierce 'Old London Bridge'
90. Old London Bridge stood in the parish of the riverside church, St Magnus the Martyr. A finely detailed model of Old London Bridge is displayed inside the church.
91. A.R. Myers 'Chaucer's London'
92. Gordon Home 'Old London Bridge'
93. Pierce 'Old London Bridge'
94. The head of Sir Thomas More was among those displayed. He was executed on 6 July 1535 for refusing to acknowledge Henry VIII as Supreme Head of the Church in England. Eventually, his daughter, Margaret, paid the bridge keeper to toss it over the side where she caught it in her apron 'lest it should be foode for fishes' as she was rowed alongside in a boat. More's head is kept in a casket and displayed behind a grille in Saint Dunstan's Church, Canterbury.
95. The Bridge House Trust prospers to the present day. The charity built Blackfriars Bridge, purchased Southwark Bridge and just over a century ago constructed Tower Bridge. In 2020, the Trust also took over the ownership of the Millenium 'Wobbly' Bridge over the Thames between St Paul's and Bankside.
96. Seven Mercers or their executors were benefactors of Rochester Bridge between 1409 and 1466.
97. Besant and Rice 'Sir Richard Whittington'
98. A fragment of an elm pile, originally shod with iron, is displayed in a window embrasure in the Bridge Chapel. It was one of ten thousand piles hammered into the riverbed to form the foundations of the Medieval bridge.
99. Maurice Hussey 'Chaucer's World'
100. Pilgrims gathered at The Tabard Inn, Southwark.
100. Benedict Gummer 'The Scourging Angel'
101. There are six surviving bridge chapels. They are Bradford-on-Avon, Derby, Rochester, Rotherham, St Ives (Cambridgeshire) and Wakefield. The latter is the oldest and dates from circa 1342.
102. The word 'pontiff' derives from 'bridge builder' referring to the Pope's role in building a bridge between God and man.
103. Interestingly, London's Millennium Bridge points directly towards St Paul's Cathedral.
104. Today, the equivalent would be an airport chapel.

105. Gordon Home 'Old London Bridge'
106. Bridges and roads were considered suitable recipients of charitable donations or bequests in Medieval times. Both Whittington and Fitzwaryn left funds for the repair of roads in their wills.
107. Entries on the ancient parchment roll relate to the differences between the actual and the nominal value of the monetary gifts by certain benefactors.
108. Brewer 'Carpenter's Life'
109. Schofield 'London Medieval Houses'
110. 'One must not overlook the natural inclination which a man like Whittington must have had to trust to his own kind.' (Imray.)
111. Wylie expounds upon Whittington's laudable purpose for his Almshouse. It was intended 'for such poor persons which grievous penury and cruel fortune hath oppressed and be not of power to get their living by craft or by any other bodily labour'. ('The Reign of Henry V'.)
112. 'Additional Ordinances' (February 1424/5)
113. 16 December 1424
114. 'Whittington's London estate was sufficient and substantial, but it was not outstandingly large,' according to Barron, 'and he does not appear to have been interested in becoming a property magnate.'
115. To these Barron adds a further property in the parish of Kyrounslane (now 'Maiden Lane' acquired in 1415.
116. Imray 'The Charity of Richard Whittington'
117. Anne F. Sutton 'The Mercery of London'
118. Carpenter also purchased a messuage with garden adjoining the house of the College of Priests from Thomas Knolles and his son.
119. 'Rotuli Parliamentorum' 10 Henry VI No 1
120. Although the Mercers' Company no longer controls trade, it plays an extremely busy and productive role, which extends far beyond the confines of the City of London. Traditionally, it has been actively involved in a host of charitable, ecclesiastical and educational institutions but the recently established and endowed Mercers' Charitable Foundation also includes patronage of the arts, science and conservation.
121. Barron
122. Clay 'The Medieval Hospitals of England'
123. Herbert 'The Twelve Great Livery Companies'
124. Imray
125. During the reign of Richard II it became the custom to eat with spoons rather than fingers or bread. Evidence for the employment of spoons at table is found in the court recipe book, 'The Forme of Cury'.
126. Details of the burglary are related in A.R. Myers' 'Chaucer's London'.
127. Also referred to as 'hutch', 'cornchest' or 'almsbox'.
128. The Mercers' Company also holds an oddly shaped tooled leather case, which according to experts at the British Museum, dates from the same

period. This is thought to have been made specially to hold the treasured spoons. Traditionally, it is known as the 'Whittington spoon box'.

129. Imray 'The Charity of Richard Whittington'

130. 'Calendar of the Records of the Skinners' Company' (Section 5, 'Deeds of Title' Ms 31302/322 'Lands in Whittington College') London Metropolitan Archives.

131. The actual move from Highgate to Felbridge took place on 29 September 1966.

132. The estate is divided into three distinct complexes: the original almshouses built by the Mercers' Company; 'Arkendale' (named after a 20th-century house, formerly 'Exton Court', that stood in the grounds of Felbridge Place) and 'Ebbisham', named after a prominent 20th-century Mercer, Lord Ebbisham).

133. Designed by Alfred Fisher.

134. Trees include graceful Wellingtonias, colourful Pseudo Acacias, a spindly 'fossil tree' (*Ginkgo biloba*), a short 'pocket handkerchief tree' (*Davidia*) and an impossibly tall 'monkey puzzle' (*Araucaria araucana*).

Acknowledgements

Additional photographs supplied by Liz Mott and Ian Giles.

I am most grateful for the specialist knowledge of and additional research from Dr David Wright, M.A., Ph. D., F.S.G. Thanks also to

Dr Remy Ambuhl
William Ashworth, University of Liverpool
Brenda Bainbridge
William Bassett, Beadle, The Worshipful Company of Skinners
Nick Bateman, Museum of London
Dr Adrian R. Bell, Senior Lecturer in the History of Finance, University of
   Reading
Ian Betts, B.A., PH.D., Senior Finds Specialist (Building Materials), Archaeological
   Department, Museum of London
Bonham's Auctioneers
The British Library
Steve Brown, Manager, Whittington College
Buckingham Palace Press Office
Steve Butler, UK Border Agency, National Museum Liverpool
Marian Campbell, Senior Curator of Metalwork, Victoria and Albert Museum
Canterbury Cathedral Archives
Justin Cavernelis-Frost, Trust archivist, St Bartholomew's Hospital, Smithfield
David Chamberlain
William Chapman, Private Secretary to the Lord Mayor of the City of London
Christ's Hospital, Horsham
John Clark, Curator Emeritus at Museum of London
Gordon Clarkson
Frederick Clements

The College of Arms
The Cotswold Sheep Society
Coventry History Society
Nigel Cox, Curator, Social History, Gloucester Folk Museum
Murray Craig, Clerk of the Chamberlain's. Court, Guildhall
Dr Martin Dudley, Rector, the Priory Church of St Bartholomew the Great, Cloth Fair, London
M. Bruno Duvernois, Directeur des Fouilles, Archeologiques, Harfleur
Edwin Ehrman, Curator of Textiles and Fashion, Costume Department, Victoria and Albert Museum
Bernadette Fallon and Mark Johnson, 'All About Your House', Cornwall
D Marc Feeney
Steven Freeth, Archivist, The Merchants' Taylor Company
Frances Fyfield
Catherine Gerbrands, Archivist, *The Stage*
Dr James Gibson, Archivist, The Rochester Bridge Trust
Gloucester Archives
Jeremy Goldsmith, Assistant to Rouge Dragon, College of Arms, London
The Guildhall Library
The Imperial War Museum
William Harrison
Rev. Canon Bruce Hawkins
Pat Heath
Terry Heard, M.A., B.A., Archivist, City of London School
Rev Canon John Holder, Priest-in-Charge, St Giles' Church, Coberley
Val Horsler
Mary Horsnell
Rev David Ivorson, Chaplain, Whittington College
Thomas Jackson
Christopher Jeens, Archivist, Gloucester Cathedral
Anne Jones
Jackie Keilly, Curator, Department of Archaeology Collection and Archive, Museum of London
Philip Lankaster, FSA, Honorary Visiting Fellow, Department of History of Art, University of York
Glenda Law
Richard Luckett, Pepys' Librarian, Magdalene College, Cambridge
Marcus Lynch, Manager, St Mary's Guildhall, Coventry
Prue MacGibbon, Archivist, Brewers' Company
Gregor MacGregor
Raya McGeorge, Archivist, Fishmongers' Company
Simon Meyer, Steeple Master, St Mary-le-Bow
Mansion House

Acknowledgements

Alexander Micklem, Pleshey Castle

The Milestone Society

The Missions to Seamen

Dr Rosie Mills, Assistant Curator, Metalwork Collection, Victoria and Albert Museum

Ralph Moffat, Curator of European Arms and Armour, Kelvington Art Gallery and Museum, Glasgow

Rev Dr Peter Mullen, Rector, St Sepulchre-without-Newgate

The National Gallery

National Maritime Museum, Greenwich

National Railway Museum, York

Susan North, Curator of Fashion 1550-1800, Victoria and Albert Museum

Canon David Parrot, Vicar, St Lawrence Jewry

Dood Pearce, Newent History Society

Rev Patricia Philips, Rector, St John the Baptist, Pauntley

Christine Reynolds, Assistant Keeper, The Muniments Rooms and Library, Westminster Abbey

Thom Richardson, FSA Keeper of Armour, The Royal Armouries, Leeds

Kelda Roe, Archives Assistant, Archives and Chapter Library, Windsor Castle

Jane Ruddell, Archivist and Curator, The Mercers' Company

Alec and Mary Russell, The Dick Whittington Inn, Gloucester

Joe Silman – Monerri

Christine Skelding

Rev Canon John Slater, SS Peter and Paul, Wantage

Rev Tristram Rae Smith, Rector, St Michael's Church, North Cadbury

The Society of Antiquities

Paul Symes, Head of Design, Fortnum and Mason, Piccadilly

Victor Thomas

Dr Dora Thornton, British Museum

Trinity College Library, Cambridge

Amelia Walker, Senior Library Assistant, Wellcome Library

Sir George White, Bt, Consultant Keeper, The Clockmakers' Museum, Guildhall

Nick Wickenden, Museums' Manager, Cheltenham

Joseph Wisdom, Librarian, St Paul's Cathedral

Helga Wood

Rev Dick Woodger, Vicar, SS Peter and Paul, Northleach

Worcester City Library

The Worshipful Company of Brewers

The Worshipful Company of Stationers and Newspaper Makers

Bibliography

Peter Ackroyd *London, the Biography* Chatto and Windus 2000

Peter Ackroyd *Shakespeare: The Biography* Chatto and Windus 2005

Diana Alexander *The Story of Coberley, Gloucestershire* privately printed 1980

Jonathan Alexander and Paul Binski (eds) *Age of Chivalry: Art in Plantagenet England, 1200-1400* Weidenfeld and Nicolson 1987

Christopher Allmand *Henry V* Methuen 1992

Harold Arthur, Viscount Dillon 'Inventory of the Goods and Chattels belonging to Thomas, Duke of Gloucester' *Royal Archaeological Journal* 1894

Sir Robert Atkins *The Ancient and Present State of Gloucestershire* E.P. Publishing/Gloucestershire County Library 1712 (reprinted 1974)

John Attwood *Dick Whittington – Fact and Fable* Regency Press 1988

John James Baddeley *The Guildhall of the City of London* Simpkin, Marshall, Hamilton and Kent 1898

Richard Baker *Richard Baker's London: A Theme with Variations* Jarrold 1989

J.J. Bagley *Life in Medieval England* Batsford 1960

Mia Ball *The Worshipful Company of Brewers: A Short History* Hutchinson Benham 1977

Richard Barber *Living Legends* BBC Publications 1988

Juliet Barker *Agincourt* Little, Brown 2005

Sir Henry Barkly 'The Berkeleys of Cobberley' in *Transactions of the Bristol and Gloucestershire Archaeological Society* Vol XVI (1892-3)

Caroline Barron *London in the Later Middle Ages* Oxford University Press 2004

Caroline Barron 'Richard Whittington: The Man Behind The Myth' *Studies in London History* Cambridge University Press 1969

Caroline Barron *The Reign of Richard II* Cambridge Medieval History Vol VI

Nick Bateman 'From Rags to Riches: Blackwell Hall and the Wool Cloth Trade c.1450-1790' *Post Medieval Archaeology* Vol 38 No 1 2004

Nick Bateman *Gladiators at the Guildhall* Museum of London Archaeological Services 2000

Patrick Beaver *The Spice of Life* Elm Tree/Hamish Hamilton 1979

George Frederick Beltz *Memorials of the Most Noble Order of the Garter* Pickering 1841

Mervyn Benford *Milestones* Shire 2002

Walter Besant *London* Chatto and Windus 1894

Walter Besant and James Rice *Sir Richard Whittington, Lord Mayor of London* Chatto and Windus 1902

Bryan Bevan *Richard II* Rubicon Press 1990

Ruth Bird *The Turbulent London of Richard II* Longmans, Green and Company 1949

Maggie Black *Food and Cooking in Medieval Britain* English Heritage 1985

Claude Blair *European Armour c1066 to c1700* Batsford 1958

John Bloxham *Walks Around London* Francis James 1937

E.M. Borrajo *The Guildhall Library: Its History and Present Position* Library Association Record 1907

John Bouchier (ed) *The Ancient Chronicles of Sir John Froissart* Vols 1-4 London 1814

David Bowsher, Tony Dyson, Nick Holder and Isca Howell *The London Guildhall: An Archaeological History of a Neighbourhood from Early Medieval to Modern Times* Museum of London Archaeological Services 2007

Gyles Brandreth *Discovering Pantomime* Shire 1973

Thomas Brewer *Memoir of the Life and Times of John Carpenter* 8 Vols Arthur Taylor 1856

Friedrich W D Brie (ed) *The Brut or The Chronicles of England* Part II Kegan Paul, Trench and Trubner 1908

John Russell Brown *Shakespeare and His Theatre* Kestrel 1982

Marie Louise Bruce *The Usurper King: Henry of Bolingbroke 1366-99* Rubicon Press 1986

Arthur Bryant *Set In A Silver Sea* William Collins 1953

Bill Bryson *Shakespeare: The World As a Stage* Harper Collins 2007

David Buirski *The Woolmen's Tale* The Company of Woolmen Publications 1999

Peter Bushell *London's Secret History* Constable 1983

H.J. Byron *Whittington Junior and His Sensational Cat* (playscript) 1862

Michael Byrne and G.R. Rush *St Mary-le-Bow* Wharncliffe Books 2007

Martha Carlin *Medieval Southwark* Hambledom Press 1996

R.W. Chambers and Marjorie Daunt (eds) *A Book of English: 1384-1425* Clarendon Press 1951

M.V. Clark and N Denholm-Young 'Kirkstall Chronicle' *Bulletin of the John Rylands Library* VV 1931

Rotha Mary Clay *The Medieval Hospitals of England* Methuen 1909

Antony Clayton *The Folklore of London* Historical Publications 2008

Sir William Laird Clowes *The Royal Navy: A History from the Earliest Times to the Present* Sampson Low, Marston and Company 1897

Gerald Cobb *London City Churches: A Brief Guide* Corporation of London, Records Office 1962

Mary Cobb *Bells In Our Time* David and Charles 1973

Arthur Collins, Sir Egerton Brydges *The Complete Peerage of England* F.C. and J Rivington, Otridge and Son 1812

William T. Cook *The Society of College Youths: 1637-2005* privately printed 2005

W.H. Cooke (ed) *Duncomb's Collections Towards the History and Antiquities of the County of Hereford* 1882

Charles Creighton *A History of Epidemics in Britain* Vol 1 Cass and Co 1965

Peter Cross and Maurice Keen (eds) *Heraldry, Pageantry and Social Display in Medieval England* Boydell 2002

Hugh Cunningham *The Life and Times of Dick Whittington – An Historical Romance* Simpkin, Marshall and Co. 1841

Phillis Cunnington and Catherine Lucas *Charity Costumes* A and C Black 1978

Ian Currie *Frosts, Freezes and Fairs, Chronicles of the Frozen Thames and Harsh Winters in Britain Since 1,000 A.D.* Frosted Earth Publications 1996

F.J. Harvey Darton *Children's Books in England* Cambridge University Press 1958

I.C.P. Dear and Peter Kemp (eds) *The Oxford Companion to Ships and the Sea* Oxford University Press 2005

Rev John Silvester Davies *An English Chronicle of the Reigns of Richard II, Henry IV, Henry V and Henry VI* Camden Society 1856

C Deal *Short Account of Pleshy: Its Lords and Antiquity* John Dutton 1903

A E Douglas-Smith *City of London School* Blackwell 1937

Richard Duckworth and Fabian Stedman *Tintinnalogia or The Art of Ringing* Kingsmead 1970

Eamon Duffy *The Stripping of The Altars: Traditional Religion in England 1400-1580* Yale University Press 1992

Kathryn Dun *Beautiful Sheep* Francis Lincoln

John Duncomb *History and Antiquities of the County of Hereford* John Murray 1982

Penelope Eames *Medieval Furniture* The Furniture History Society 1977

Roger H. Ellis *Catalogue of Seals in the Public Record Office: Personal Seals* Vol 1 HMSO 1978

V.I.J. Flint 'The Hereford Map' *Transactions of the Royal Historical Society* 1998

H.R. Fox Bourne *Famous London Merchants* London 1868

Sir John Froissart *Chronicles of England, France and Spain* Vol 2 Henry G Bohn 1862

Bibliography

Bill Fuller *A Visitor's Guide to Wantage, Past and Present* William Walker 1901

James Gairdner (ed) *The Historical Collections of a Citizen of London in the 15th Century* Camden Society 1876

Rena Gardiner *The Story of Saint Bartholomew the Great* privately published 2005

Robert Gardiner (ed) *Cogs, Caravels and Galleons: The Sailing Ship 1000-1650* Conway Maritime Press 1994

Michael Glover *A New Guide to the Battlefields of Northern France* Michael Joseph 1987

G.L. Gomme and H.B. Wheatley (eds) *Chapbooks and Folk Lore Tracts* Villion Society 1885

Neville M Goodman 'Notes on the Body of the Black Rat Found in St Peter's Church, Sandwich' *Kent Archaeological Review* Autumn 1974

Dillian Gordon, Lisa Monnas and Caroline Elam (eds) *The Regal Image of Richard II and the Wilton Diptych* Harvey Miller 1997

Lindsay Granshaw and Roy Porter (eds) *The Hospital in History* Routeledge 1989

Hilary Green *International Trade in the Middle Ages* Amberley Books 2022

Sarah Gristwood *Elizabeth and Leicester* Bantam 2007

Kelly Grovier *The Gaol, the Story of Newgate – London's Most Notorious Prison* John Murray 2008

Warren Grynberg *Images of the City of London: The Square Mile Revealed* Breedon Books 2005

Benedict Gummer *The Scourging Angel: The Black Death in the British Isles* Bodley Head 2009

Carol Haines *Marking The Miles, A History of English Milestones* Carol Haines 2000

Stephen Halliday *Newgate, London's Prototype of Hell* Sutton 2006

Peter and Jean Hansell *Doves and Dovecots* Millstream 1988

Vanessa Harding and Laura Wright (eds) *London Bridge: Selected Accounts and Rentals, 1381-1358* London Records Society 1995

Cynthia Harnett *Ring Out Bow Bells* Methuen 1953

Molly Harrison *The Kitchen in History* Osprey 1972

P.D.A. Harvey *Mappa Mundi – The Hereford World Map* Hereford Cathedral 2002

William Herbert *The Twelve Great Livery Companies* Vol 1 David and Charles 1968

Georgette Heyer *My Lord John* Bodley Head 1975

Thomas Heywood (ed Henry B Wheatley) *The History of Sir Richard Whittington* The Villon Society 1885

Christopher Hibbert *Agincourt* Batsford 1964

Michael A Hicks (ed) *Revolution and Consumption in Late Medieval England* Boydell Press 2001

Susan Hill *The Spirit of the Cotswolds* Michael Joseph 1988

Thomas Hinde *Carpenter's Children* James and James 1995

F.C. Hingeston-Randolph (ed) *Royal Letters, Henry IV* Longman, Green, Longman and Roberts 1860

Anthony Hobson *Grand Libraries* Weidenfeld and Nicolson 1970

Gordon Home *Medieval London* Ernest Benn 1927

Gordon Home *Old London Bridge* John Lane/Bodley Head 1931

William Eden Hooper *History of Newgate and Old Bailey* Underwood 1935

Valeria Hope *My Lord Mayor: Eight Hundred Years of London's Mayoralty* Weidenfeld and Nicolson 1989

Rosemary Horrox (ed) *The Black Death* Manchester University Press 1994

Commander and Mrs E.P. Howe *English and Scottish Silver Spoons, Medieval to Late Stuart* privately printed 1952-7

Isca Howell, David Bowsher, Tony Dyson and Nick Holder *The London Guildhall* Museum of London Archaeological Services 2007

Maurice Hussey *Chaucer's World* Cambridge University Press 1967

Jean Imray *The Charity of Richard Whittington* Athlone Press 1968

Peter Jackson *London Bridge: A Visual History* Historical Publications 2002

Alan Jenkins *The City: London's Square Mile* Viking Kestrel 1988

Wilberforce Jenkinson *London Churches Before the Great Fire* Society for the Promotion of Christian Knowledge 1917

Llewellyn Jewitt *The Corporation Plate and Insignia of Office of the Cities and Towns of England and Wales* Vol 2 Bemrose and Sons 1895

Rev A.H. Johnson *The History of the Worshipful Company of the Drapers of London* Vol I Clarendon Press 1914

Boris Johnson *Johnson's Life of London: The People Who Made the City* Harper Press 2012

P.E. Jones 'Whittington's Longhouse' *London Topographical Record* Vol XXIII 1974

Sydney R Jones *Thames Triumphant* Studio Publications 1943

A.R.J. Jurica (ed) *The Victoria County History of Gloucestershire (Newent)* Vol XII Boydell and Brewer 2010

D. Keane, A. Burns and A. Saint *St Paul's: The Cathedral Church of London 604-2000* Yale University Press

Nellie J.M. Kerling (ed) *Cartulary of St Bartholomew's Hospital* Privately printed 1973

Charles Lethbridge Kingsford *Prejudice and Promise in Fifteenth Century England* Oxford University Press 1925

Charles Lethbridge Kingsford (ed) *John Stow: A Survey of London* 2 Vols Oxford 1908

B. Lambert *The History and Survey of London* Vol 2 Highes 1806

Jennifer Lang *Pride Without Prejudice* Perpetua Press 1975

Bibliography

Robert Latham and William Matthews (eds) *The Diary of Samuel Pepys: A New and Complete Transcription* Volume 9 Bell and Hyman 1970-1983

Santina Levey *An Elizabethan Inheritance: The Hardwick Hall Textiles* National Trust 1998

Val Lewis *Ship's Cats* Nauticalia 2001

Bryant Lillywhite *London Signs* Allen and Unwin 1972

Katherine Lines *Dick Whittington* H.Z. Walk 1970

Martin Lloyd *The Passport, The History of Man's Most Travelled Document* Sutton 2003

Alison Lockett *The Wool Trade* Methuen 1974

C.E. Long (ed) *Richard Symond's Diary of the Marches of the Royal Army* Cambridge University Press 1997

David Long *Spectacular Vernacular: London's Most Extraordinary Buildings* Sutton 2006

Rev Samuel Lysons *The Model Merchant of the Middle Ages* Hamilton, Adams and Co. 1860

Rev Joseph McCulloch, M.A. *St Mary-le-Bow* Pitkin 1970

Barry McKay *Chapbooks* Incline Press 2003

J.A. Fuller Maitland *English Carols of the Fifteenth Century* Leadenhall Press 1891

George Marchant *Edward II in Gloucestershire: A King in Our Midst* privately printed 2007

Richard Marks and Paul Williamson (eds) *Gothic: Art in England, 1400-1547* Victorian and Albert Museum 2003

G.H. Martin (ed) *Knighton's Chronicle: 1337-1396* Oxford Medieval Texts 1995

Gervase Matthew *The Court of Richard II* John Murray 1968

Arthur Mee *Gloucestershire* Hodder and Stoughton 1966

Peter Mills and John Oliver *The Survey of Buildings in the City of London* London Topographical Records 1962

Ann Monsarrat *And The Bride Wore...The Story of the White Wedding* Gentry Books 1973

Norman Moore *The History of St Bartholomew's Hospital* C. Arthur Pearson 1918

Ian Mortimer *1415: Henry V's Year of Glory* Bodley Head 2009

Ian Mortimer *The Fears of Henry IV* Jonathan Cape 2008

Ian Mortimer *The Perfect King – The Life of Edward III* Jonathan Cape 2006

E.V. Morton *In Search of London* Methuen 1951

Teresa Murdock *Treasures and Trinkets: Jewellery in London From Pre Roman Times to the 1930s* BAS Printers, Hampshire 1991

A.R. Myers *Chaucer's London: Everyday Life in London 1342-1400* Amberley Books 2009

J.G. Nicholls (ed) *The Diary of Henry Machyn, Citizen and Merchant Taylor of London 1550 -1563* Camden Society 1848

Alfred Noyes *Tales of the Mermaid Inn* Frederick A. Stokes 1913

Will Owen *Old London Town* Arrowsmith 1921

William Page (ed) *The Victoria History of the Counties of England* Vol IV Berkshire St Catherine Press 1924

Kenneth Nicholls Palmer *Ceremonial Barges on The River Thames* Unicorn Press 1997

E.H. Pearce *Annals of Christ's Hospital* Hugh Rees 1908

Kathleen Philp *Reflected in Wantage* Wessex Press 1992

Patricia Pierce *Old London Bridge* Headline 2001

Eileen Power *The Wool Trade in English Medieval History* Oxford University Press 1941

Adrian Prockter and Robert Taylor (eds) *The A-Z of Elizabethan London* London Topographical Society 1979

Arthur E Rayden *Mercers' Hall* Country Life Ltd 1947

Brigitte Resl *A Cultural History of Animals in the Middle Ages* Berg 2007

John Richardson *Highgate* Historical Publications 1984

H.T. Riley (trans) *Liber Albus: The White Book* Richard Griffin and Company 1861

H.T. Riley (ed) *Memorials of London and London Life in the 13th-15th Centuries* Longmans, Green and Co 1868

Brenda Roen *The Mythical Creatures Bible* Octopus 2008

Nicholas Rogers 'The Original Owner of the Fitzwarin Psalter' *The Antiquities Journal* Vol 69 1989

Ida M. Roper *The Monumental Effigies of Gloucestershire and Bristol* privately printed 1931

J.S. Roskell, L. Clark and C. Rawcliffe (eds) *The History of Parliament: The House of Commons (1386-1421)* Boydell and Brewer 1993

Donald Rumbelow *The Triple Tree – Newgate, Tyburn and Old Bailey* Harrap 1982

Thomas Rymer (ed) *Foedora* Apud Joannem Neulme 1739-1745

Joyce E. Salisbury *The Beast Within: Animals in the Middle Ages* Routledge 2001

Nigel Saul *Knights and Esquires: The Gloucestershire Gentry in the Fourteenth Century* Clarendon Press 1981

Nigel Saul *Richard II* London 1997

Ann Saunders and John Schofield (eds) with an introduction by John Fisher *Tudor London: A Map and A View* London Topographical Society Publication No 159 2001

Ernest A. Savage *Old English Libraries* London 1911

John Schofield *London's Medieval Houses* Yale University Press 2003

John Schofield *The Building of London* British Museum Publications 1984

John Schofield *The Building of Britain* Sutton 1999

Andrew McConnell Scott *The Pantomime Life of Joseph Grimaldi* Canongate 2009

Joseph Shatzmiller *Jews, Medicine and Medieval Society* University of California Press 1995

W.S. Simpson *St Paul's Cathedral and Old City Life* Elliot Stock 1894

Osbert Sitwell *The True Story of Dick Whittington – A Christmas Story for Cat Lovers* Home and Van Thal 1945

Graham Smith *Something to Declare* George Harrap and Co. 1980

George Speaight *The History of The English Puppet Theatre* Robert Hale 1955

Richard Harold *St Muir Annals of the Seymours* K. Paul, Trench, Trubner and Company 1902

Kay Staniland 'Richard Whittington and His Sales to the Great Wardrobe in the Years 1392-1394' *Journal of the Costume Society* Vol 44

Arthur Penrhyn Stanley, D.D. *Historical Memorials of Westminster Abbey* John Murray 1882

Edward Philips Statham *History of the Maunsell Family* Vol I Kegan Paul, Trench and Co. 1917

Gwynedd Sudworth *Richard Whittington, London's Mayor* Robert Hale 1975

Robert Sullivan *Rats: A Year With New York's Most Unwanted Inhabitants* Granta 2005

Anne F. Sutton *I Sing of A Maiden* The Mercers' Company 1988

Anne F. Sutton 'Richard Whittington' *Dictionary of National Biography* Oxford University Press 2004

Anne F. Sutton *The Mercery of London* Ashgate 2005

Richard Tames *City of London Past* Historical Publications 1995

William Cook Taylor *Chapters on Coronations* John W Parker 1858

A.H. Thomas (ed) *Calendar of Plea and Memoranda of the City of London* Vol 2 (1364-1381) 3 (1381-1412 and 4 (1413-1437 Cambridge University Press 1932

John A.F. Thomson *The Later Lollards* Oxford University Press 1965

Walter Thornbury *Old and New London* Cassell, Peter and Gilpin 1881

Sylvia Thrupp *The Merchant Class of Medieval London: 1300-1500* University of Chicago Press 1948

John Timpson *Timpson's England* Jarrold 1987

M.W. Tisdall *God's Beasts* Charlesfort Press 1998

W. Outram Tristram *Coaching Days and Coaching Ways* Macmillan 1888

Sir Travers Twiss QC *The Black Book of the Admiralty* (4 Vols) 1871-1876

Jenny Uglo *Hogarth, A Life and a World* Faber and Faber 1997

David Verey and Alan Brooks *The Buildings of England: Gloucestershire Vol 2 The Vale and Forest of Dean* Penguin 1970

Alex Vincent *The Lost Churches and Chapels of Kent* S.B. Publications 2005

Sir Anthony R. Wagner *Historic Heraldry of Britain* Oxford University Press 1939

Kathleen Walker-Meikle *Medieval Cats* British Library 2001

Kathleen Walker-Meikle *Medieval Pets* Boydell 2012

Ben Weinreb and Christopher Hibbert (eds) *The London Encyclopaedia* Macmillan 1983

Alison Weir *The Six Wives of Henry VIII* Bodley Head 1991

D. Welendar *The History, Art and Architecture of Gloucester Cathedral* Alan Sutton 1991

Jennifer Westwood *Albion – A Guide to Legendary Britain* Grafton Books 1985

Michael Whittington *The Whittington Story* Parchment (Oxford) Ltd 1988

Benjamin Williams (ed) *Chronique de la Traison et Mort de Richard II* English Historical Society 12 1846

J.W. Willis Bund (ed) *The Victoria County History* Vol 3 Constable 1913

C. Willet and Phillis Cunnington *Handbook of Medieval Costume* Faber and Faber 1952

Derek Wilson *The Plantagenets, the Kings that Made Britain* Quercus 2011

John Wittich *London Villages* Shire 1976

George Wrottesley *Crecy and Calais* Harrison and Sons

James Hamilton Wylie *History of England Under Henry IV* Vols 1-4 Longmans, Green and Co. 1884

James Hamilton Wylie and William Templeton Waugh *The Reign of Henry V (3 Vols)* Cambridge University Press 1914-1929

Newspapers and Magazines

The Daily Mail (23 July 2006)

The Daily Telegraph (25 October 2008)

The Guardian (31 October 2009)

Illustrated London News (Christmas Issue 1996)

The Lady (6 January 1983)

The Telegraph Magazine (8 December 2012)

Index

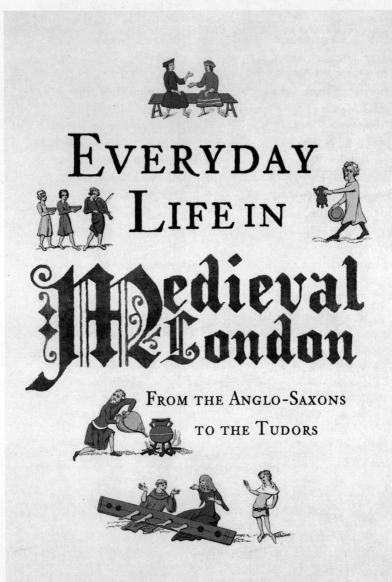

EVERYDAY
LIFE IN
Medieval London

FROM THE ANGLO-SAXONS
TO THE TUDORS

TONI MOUNT

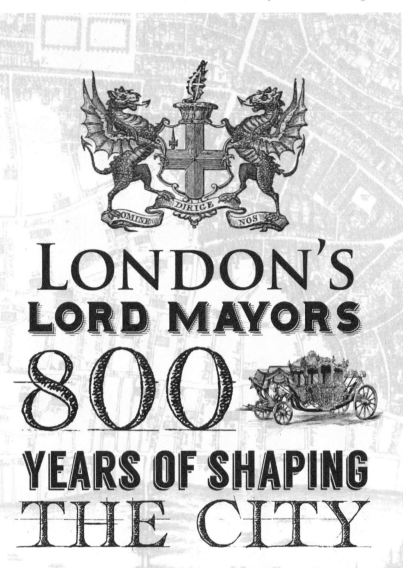

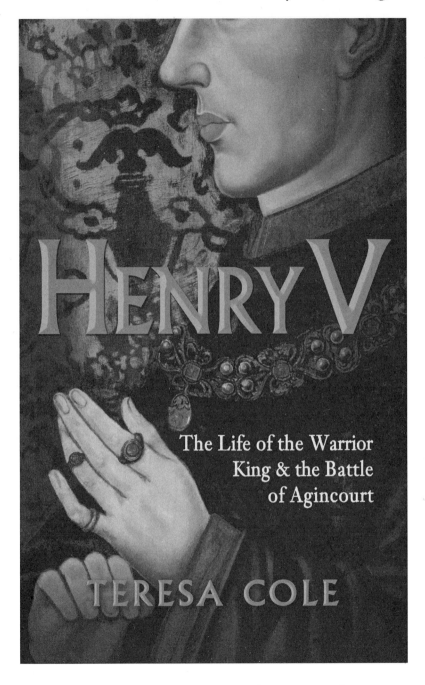